# Service Level Agreements for Cloud Computing

Philipp Wieder • Joe M. Butler
Wolfgang Theilmann • Ramin Yahyapour
Editors

# Service Level Agreements for Cloud Computing

Foreword by Jessica McCarthy

Springer

*Editors*

Philipp Wieder
IT & Media Center
Service Computing Group
TU Dortmund University
Dortmund
Germany
philipp.wieder@udo.edu

Joe M. Butler
Intel Ireland Limited
Leixlip, Kildare
Ireland

Wolfgang Theilmann
SAP Research
Karlsruhe
Germany

Ramin Yahyapour
IT & Media Center
Service Computing Group
TU Dortmund University
Dortmund
Germany

ISBN 978-1-4899-8775-4      ISBN 978-1-4614-1614-2  (eBook)
DOI 10.1007/978-1-4614-1614-2
Springer New York Dordrecht Heidelberg London

Springer is part of Springer Science+Business Media (www.springer.com)

*The SLA@SOI project is dedicated to provide a business-ready service-oriented infrastructure empowering the service economy in a flexible and dependable way.*

# Foreword

SLA@SOI is one of the most significant projects funded under the European Union's Seventh Framework Programme. With a budget of over 15 million Euros and a consortium of twelve partners, SLA@SOI is a comprehensive integrated project of broad scope, touching market segments in areas including management of service level agreements (SLAs), service-oriented infrastructures (SOIs), cloud computing, enterprise service buses and XaaS provisioning (including Platform as a Service, Software as a Service, Infrastructure as a Service, etc). Relevant initiatives include global-scale commercial offerings, well-supported open source projects, and large, strategic publicly-funded research initiatives.

SLA@SOI operates within highly dynamic and fast-moving domains, and many world-class players are very active in areas in which SLA@SOI can make most impact, namely cloud computing and service-oriented architectures. We in SLA@SOI believe that SLAs are a key technology for transforming service and cloud offerings into tradeable goods. The project has invested three years of in-depth research and analysis into the SLA domain, developing a comprehensive architecture and reference implementation for SLA management, then evaluating and incorporating these results in four distinct and complementary industrial use cases.

Specifically, the SLA@SOI project aims to enable automatic negotiation of personalised SLAs across multiple providers, such that individual SLAs for thousands of customers can be automatically managed and optimised. Most industrial service providers have not yet come to terms with this notion of providing automated SLAs with their service offerings, which is very promising from SLA@SOI's perspective. Currently, market leaders still rely on highly manual processes for making claims on SLA violations.

Machine-readable SLAs, on the other hand, will allow consumers and providers of online services to precisely specify the services and service levels they require, confirm that SLAs are being met, and automatically deal with any SLA violations. SLA@SOI provides a framework under which automatic SLA negotiation and SLA-aware optimisation become feasible. Machine-readable SLAs allow service levels to be personalised, automatically negotiated, aggregated, and continuously assured.

The book presents a unique insight into the SLA@SOI project, with a focus on reference architectures, open reference case examples, SLA models, service construction meta-models, and approaches to infrastructure monitoring and runtime prediction. The book also recounts the results of four SLA@SOI use cases—in e-government, Telco service aggregation, ERP hosting, and enterprise IT—analysing outcomes from a business and technical research perspective.

As exploitation manager for SLA@SOI, I have observed firsthand the interest this research project has generated from both industry and academia. The project is differentiated from other commercial and research offerings in that it has an SLA-driven approach that considers a range of stakeholders (e.g. service providers, software providers, infrastructure providers and service customers) while explicitly tackling challenges at the business, software and infrastructure levels. SLA@SOI aims to provide an automated and holistic awareness of personalised SLAs alongside a business-ready SOI that empowers the service economy and Future Internet in a flexible and dependable way.

By defining a cohesive research agenda for Europe going forward, the Future Internet initiative will provide important medium- and long-term opportunities for exploitation of SLA@SOI.

Dublin, June 2011                                                *Jessica McCarthy*

# Preface

IT-supported service provisioning is of major relevance for almost all industries and IT domains. And with the evolution of ecosystems where everything can become a service and the actual IT provisioning is virtualized, the importance of service-related infrastructures will further increase. The so-called clouds already have the buy in from industry, resulting in terms like everything-as-a-service, scale out, multi tenancy, and pay-as-you-go become increasingly popular to describe this new approach, showing on the one hand the business model behind the cloud offerings and on the other hand underlining its commercial character. From a research perspective, this somehow young discipline offers a large variety of topics and novel topics will certainly emerge.

The research project SLA@SOI (funded under the Seventh Framework Programme with grant number FP7- 216556) provides a major milestone for the further evolution towards a service-oriented economy, where IT-based services can be flexibly traded as economic good, i.e. under well-defined and dependable conditions and with clearly associated costs. Eventually, this will allow for dynamic value networks that can be flexibly instantiated thus driving innovation and competitiveness. SLA@SOI created a holistic view for the management of service level agreements (SLAs) and provides an SLA management framework that can be easily integrated into a service-oriented infrastructure.

Europe has set high goals in becoming the most active and productive service economy in the world. Especially IT supported services evolved into a common utility which is offered and consumed by many stakeholders. Cloud computing gained significant attention and commercial uptake in many business scenarios. This rapidly growing service oriented economy has highlighted key challenges and opportunities in IT-supported service provisioning. With more companies incorporating cloud-based IT services as part of their own value chain, reliability and dependability become a crucial factor in managing business. Service level agreements are the common means to provide the necessary transparency between service consumers and providers.

SLA@SOI as a major European project addresses the issues surrounding the implementation of automated SLA management solutions for service oriented infrastructures and evaluates their effectiveness. As of today, SLAs are in general either not yet formally defined, or they are defined by a single party, mostly the provider, without further interaction with the consumer. Or SLAs are negotiated in a lengthy process with bilateral human interaction. For a vivid IT service economy, better tools are necessary to support end-to-end SLA management on a holistic scale.

SLAs are particularly relevant to cloud computing, an increasingly important and relevant deployment model for infrastructure, services, or platforms. SLA@SOI allows such services to be described by service providers through formal template SLAs. Once these template SLAs are machine readable, service composition can be established using automatic negotiation of SLAs. Moreover, the management of the service landscape can focus on the existence and state of all necessary SLAs.

A major innovation of SLA@SOI is the multi-layered aspect of the service stack. Typically, a service is dependent on many other services. For example, the offering of a software service requires infrastructure resources, software licenses or other software services. The SLA framework developed by SLA@SOI supports the configuration of complex service hierarchies with arbitrary layers. This allows end-to-end management of resources and services for the business value chain.

This book covers a large number of topics related to Clouds and service oriented infrastructures that are relevant for researchers and practitioners. It is divided into eight parts, as there are 'Introduction to Service Level Agreements in Service Oriented Infrastructures', 'Foundations for Service Level Agreements', 'Scientific Innovations', 'Core Components of the Service Level Agreements Framework', 'Management of the Business Layer', 'Management of the Software Layer', 'Management of the Infrastructure Layer', and 'Selected Business Use Cases'. Comprising 21 chapters in total, this book addresses fundamental topics related to service provisioning and SLAs, it tackles scientific challenges including the modelling of the relationships between SLA properties, and it introduces a generic management framework, as well as its layers and components, that can be applied to a large variety of use cases. Last but not least, the book highlights four such use cases to demonstrate the applicability of the framework and to give users and IT providers hints on how to integrate and provide services governed by guarantees on service-quality.

We hope that readers benefit from the results of three years of research and development conducted by SLA@SOI and, at the same time, enjoy the book.

Dortmund, Karlsruhe, Leixlip                                      *Philipp Wieder*
July 2011                                                            *Joe M. Butler*
                                                              *Wolfgang Theilmann*
                                                                *Ramin Yahyapour*

# Acknowledgements

The outstanding research and development results produced by the SLA@SOI project, and hence also the book at hand, would not have been possible without the dedication of numerous people. Although it is not possible to mention everybody involved in the project, especially since SLA@SOI collaborated with a large number of other projects, standardisation bodies, and industrial fora, the editors would like to express special gratitude to the following people. First and foremost the editors would like to thank all the project partners for three years of great work. Although this book cannot cover all outcomes of the project, it provides a brought yet detailed overview of the various scientific and technical achievements, which comprise contributions from everyone active in the project. The editors gratefully acknowledge the guidance from the European Commission and the project reviewers. Their evaluation of the progress of the project and the assessment of direction and results helped to make SLA@SOI a success. The quality of the book has been confirmed and strengthened with the help of experts who carefully examined the various book chapters and who provided feedback on scientific and technical content. The editors would like to acknowledge the contribution of the following scientists:

- Simon Caton, Karlsruhe Institute of Technology
- Björn Hagemeier, Forschungszentrum Jülich
- Peter Hasselmeyer, NEC Laboratories Europe
- Sebastian Hudert, University of Bayreuth
- Bastian Koller, Universität Stuttgart
- Andreas Metzger, University of Duisburg-Essen
- Ariel Oleksiak, Poznan Supercomputing and Networking Center
- Alexander Papaspyrou, TU Dortmund University
- Alexander Willner, Universität Bonn
- Oliver Wäldrich, Fraunhofer-Institute for Algorithms and Scientific Computing
- Wolfgang Ziegler, Fraunhofer-Institute for Algorithms and Scientific Computing

Last but not least the editors would like to thank Cristy Burns for reviewing the book and the people at Springer for their support and help during the process of publication.

# Contents

**Part I Introduction to Service Level Agreements in Service Oriented Architectures**

**Motivation and Overview** . . . . . . . . . . . . . . . . . . . . . . . . . . . . . . . . . . . . . . . . 3
Joe M. Butler, Ramin Yahyapour, and Wolfgang Theilmann
    1        Socio-economic Context and Motivation . . . . . . . . . . . . . . . . . . . . . 3
            1.1      Towards a Service Economy . . . . . . . . . . . . . . . . . . . . . . . 3
            1.2      Cloud Computing . . . . . . . . . . . . . . . . . . . . . . . . . . . . . . . 4
            1.3      Future Internet . . . . . . . . . . . . . . . . . . . . . . . . . . . . . . . . . 4
            1.4      Business Need for Systematic SLA Management . . . . . . . 5
    2        Vision . . . . . . . . . . . . . . . . . . . . . . . . . . . . . . . . . . . . . . . . . . . . . . 5
    3        Technical Perspective . . . . . . . . . . . . . . . . . . . . . . . . . . . . . . . . . . 7
    4        Related Concepts . . . . . . . . . . . . . . . . . . . . . . . . . . . . . . . . . . . . . 8
            4.1      ITIL . . . . . . . . . . . . . . . . . . . . . . . . . . . . . . . . . . . . . . . . . . 8
            4.2      Autonomic Management . . . . . . . . . . . . . . . . . . . . . . . . . 9
    5        Conclusion and Book Overview . . . . . . . . . . . . . . . . . . . . . . . . . . 10
    References . . . . . . . . . . . . . . . . . . . . . . . . . . . . . . . . . . . . . . . . . . . . . . . 10

**A Reference Architecture for Multi-Level SLA Management** . . . . . . . . . . 13
Jens Happe, Wolfgang Theilmann, Andrew Edmonds, and Keven T. Kearney
    1        Introduction . . . . . . . . . . . . . . . . . . . . . . . . . . . . . . . . . . . . . . . . . 14
    2        Scope and Goals . . . . . . . . . . . . . . . . . . . . . . . . . . . . . . . . . . . . . 14
    3        Foundation Concepts . . . . . . . . . . . . . . . . . . . . . . . . . . . . . . . . . . 15
            3.1      Service Hierarchy . . . . . . . . . . . . . . . . . . . . . . . . . . . . . . 15
            3.2      Management of Services and SLAs . . . . . . . . . . . . . . . . . 17
            3.3      Data Models . . . . . . . . . . . . . . . . . . . . . . . . . . . . . . . . . . 19
    4        Architecture . . . . . . . . . . . . . . . . . . . . . . . . . . . . . . . . . . . . . . . . 20
            4.1      Building Blocks . . . . . . . . . . . . . . . . . . . . . . . . . . . . . . . . 20
            4.2      Top-Level Architecture . . . . . . . . . . . . . . . . . . . . . . . . . . 23
            4.3      Main Components . . . . . . . . . . . . . . . . . . . . . . . . . . . . . . 25
    5        Conclusions . . . . . . . . . . . . . . . . . . . . . . . . . . . . . . . . . . . . . . . . 26
    References . . . . . . . . . . . . . . . . . . . . . . . . . . . . . . . . . . . . . . . . . . . . . . . 26

**The Open Reference Case** . . . . . . . . . . . . . . . . . . . . . . . . . . . . . . . . . . . . . .  27
Christoph Rathfelder, Benjamin Klatt, and Giovanni Falcone
    1        Background . . . . . . . . . . . . . . . . . . . . . . . . . . . . . . . . . . . . . . . . . .  27
    2        Adapted ORC Use Case Scenario . . . . . . . . . . . . . . . . . . . . . . . . . . .  28
             2.1        Stakeholders . . . . . . . . . . . . . . . . . . . . . . . . . . . . . . . . . . .  29
             2.2        Supported Business Process . . . . . . . . . . . . . . . . . . . . . . . .  30
    3        ORC Architecture and Services  . . . . . . . . . . . . . . . . . . . . . . . . . . .  30
             3.1        ORC Services  . . . . . . . . . . . . . . . . . . . . . . . . . . . . . . . . . .  32
    4        ORC Deployment Options . . . . . . . . . . . . . . . . . . . . . . . . . . . . . . . .  35
    5        Interactions with the SLA@SOI Framework . . . . . . . . . . . . . . . . . .  35
             5.1        Discovery Interaction  . . . . . . . . . . . . . . . . . . . . . . . . . . . .  37
             5.2        Provisioning Interaction  . . . . . . . . . . . . . . . . . . . . . . . . . .  38
             5.3        Monitoring Interaction  . . . . . . . . . . . . . . . . . . . . . . . . . . . .  39
    6        Conclusion . . . . . . . . . . . . . . . . . . . . . . . . . . . . . . . . . . . . . . . . . . .  40
    References . . . . . . . . . . . . . . . . . . . . . . . . . . . . . . . . . . . . . . . . . . . . . . . . . .  40

**Part II  Foundations for Service Level Agreements**

**The SLA Model** . . . . . . . . . . . . . . . . . . . . . . . . . . . . . . . . . . . . . . . . . . . . . . .  43
Keven T. Kearney and Francesco Torelli
    1        Introduction . . . . . . . . . . . . . . . . . . . . . . . . . . . . . . . . . . . . . . . . . .  43
    2        Basic Concepts . . . . . . . . . . . . . . . . . . . . . . . . . . . . . . . . . . . . . . . .  45
    3        SLAs and SLA Templates . . . . . . . . . . . . . . . . . . . . . . . . . . . . . . . .  47
             3.1        SLA(T) Parties . . . . . . . . . . . . . . . . . . . . . . . . . . . . . . . . . .  48
             3.2        SLA(T) Interface Declarations . . . . . . . . . . . . . . . . . . . . . .  49
             3.3        SLA(T) Agreement Terms  . . . . . . . . . . . . . . . . . . . . . . . . . .  50
    4        Interface Specifications  . . . . . . . . . . . . . . . . . . . . . . . . . . . . . . . . .  52
    5        Value Types (the abstract constraint language)  . . . . . . . . . . . . . . . . .  54
             5.1        Constraint Expressions . . . . . . . . . . . . . . . . . . . . . . . . . . . .  54
             5.2        Constants and Datatypes . . . . . . . . . . . . . . . . . . . . . . . . . . .  56
             5.3        Parametrics . . . . . . . . . . . . . . . . . . . . . . . . . . . . . . . . . . . . .  57
    6        Domain-Specific Vocabularies  . . . . . . . . . . . . . . . . . . . . . . . . . . . .  58
    7        An Example SLA . . . . . . . . . . . . . . . . . . . . . . . . . . . . . . . . . . . . . . .  60
    8        Conclusion . . . . . . . . . . . . . . . . . . . . . . . . . . . . . . . . . . . . . . . . . . .  66
    References . . . . . . . . . . . . . . . . . . . . . . . . . . . . . . . . . . . . . . . . . . . . . . . . . .  67

**Service Construction Meta-Model**  . . . . . . . . . . . . . . . . . . . . . . . . . . . . . . .  69
Jens Happe, Wolfgang Theilmann, and Alexander Wert
    1        Introduction . . . . . . . . . . . . . . . . . . . . . . . . . . . . . . . . . . . . . . . . . .  69
    2        Service Hierarchy . . . . . . . . . . . . . . . . . . . . . . . . . . . . . . . . . . . . . . .  70
    3        Software Landscape . . . . . . . . . . . . . . . . . . . . . . . . . . . . . . . . . . . . .  71
    4        Core elements of the SCM . . . . . . . . . . . . . . . . . . . . . . . . . . . . . . . . .  72
             4.1        ServiceType . . . . . . . . . . . . . . . . . . . . . . . . . . . . . . . . . . . . .  72
             4.2        Service Implementation  . . . . . . . . . . . . . . . . . . . . . . . . . . .  73
             4.3        ServiceBuilder . . . . . . . . . . . . . . . . . . . . . . . . . . . . . . . . . . .  75
             4.4        Service Instance . . . . . . . . . . . . . . . . . . . . . . . . . . . . . . . . . .  76

5    Example . . . . . . . . . . . . . . . . . . . . . . . . . . . . . . . . . . . . . . . . . . . . . . . . . 77
6    Conclusions . . . . . . . . . . . . . . . . . . . . . . . . . . . . . . . . . . . . . . . . . . . . . . 78
References . . . . . . . . . . . . . . . . . . . . . . . . . . . . . . . . . . . . . . . . . . . . . . . . . . . . 78

**Translation of SLAs into Monitoring Specifications** . . . . . . . . . . . . . . . . . . . 79
Khaled Mahbub, George Spanoudakis, and Theocharis Tsigkritis
1    Introduction . . . . . . . . . . . . . . . . . . . . . . . . . . . . . . . . . . . . . . . . . . . . . . . 79
2    The Monitoring Infrastructure . . . . . . . . . . . . . . . . . . . . . . . . . . . . . . . 80
3    Overview of EC-Assertion . . . . . . . . . . . . . . . . . . . . . . . . . . . . . . . . . . 83
4    Parsing SLA Guarantee Terms . . . . . . . . . . . . . . . . . . . . . . . . . . . . . 86
5    Generation of Operational EVEREST Monitoring Specifications . . 88
     5.1    Templates for Basic QoS Terms . . . . . . . . . . . . . . . . . . . . . . 89
     5.2    Translation . . . . . . . . . . . . . . . . . . . . . . . . . . . . . . . . . . . . . . . 92
6    Limitations . . . . . . . . . . . . . . . . . . . . . . . . . . . . . . . . . . . . . . . . . . . . . . 98
7    Related Works . . . . . . . . . . . . . . . . . . . . . . . . . . . . . . . . . . . . . . . . . . . 98
8    Conclusions . . . . . . . . . . . . . . . . . . . . . . . . . . . . . . . . . . . . . . . . . . . . . 99
References . . . . . . . . . . . . . . . . . . . . . . . . . . . . . . . . . . . . . . . . . . . . . . . . . . . 100

**Part III   Scientific Innovations**

**Penalty Management in the SLA@SOI Project** . . . . . . . . . . . . . . . . . . . . . . . 105
Constantinos Kotsokalis, Juan Lambea Rueda, Sergio García Gómez, and
Augustín Escámez Chimeno
1    Introduction . . . . . . . . . . . . . . . . . . . . . . . . . . . . . . . . . . . . . . . . . . . . . 106
2    Business Considerations for Penalty Calculation and Reporting . . . 107
3    Business Terms Associated with Penalties . . . . . . . . . . . . . . . . . . . . 107
4    The SLA@SOI Penalty Management Architecture . . . . . . . . . . . . . 109
     4.1    Monitoring . . . . . . . . . . . . . . . . . . . . . . . . . . . . . . . . . . . . . . 109
     4.2    Reporting . . . . . . . . . . . . . . . . . . . . . . . . . . . . . . . . . . . . . . . 111
     4.3    Violations and Penalties Management . . . . . . . . . . . . . . . . 113
5    A Formal, Novel Penalty Model . . . . . . . . . . . . . . . . . . . . . . . . . . . . 116
6    Example Application . . . . . . . . . . . . . . . . . . . . . . . . . . . . . . . . . . . . . 118
7    Related Work . . . . . . . . . . . . . . . . . . . . . . . . . . . . . . . . . . . . . . . . . . . . 120
8    Summary and Conclusions . . . . . . . . . . . . . . . . . . . . . . . . . . . . . . . 121
References . . . . . . . . . . . . . . . . . . . . . . . . . . . . . . . . . . . . . . . . . . . . . . . . . . . 121

**Dynamic Creation of Monitoring Infrastructures** . . . . . . . . . . . . . . . . . . . . . 123
Howard Foster and George Spanoudakis
1    Introduction . . . . . . . . . . . . . . . . . . . . . . . . . . . . . . . . . . . . . . . . . . . . . 123
2    Architecture . . . . . . . . . . . . . . . . . . . . . . . . . . . . . . . . . . . . . . . . . . . . . 124
     2.1    Monitoring Features Specification . . . . . . . . . . . . . . . . . . . 126
3    Approach to Configuration . . . . . . . . . . . . . . . . . . . . . . . . . . . . . . . . 127
4    SLA Term Decomposition . . . . . . . . . . . . . . . . . . . . . . . . . . . . . . . . 129
5    Monitoring Configuration . . . . . . . . . . . . . . . . . . . . . . . . . . . . . . . . . 130
     5.1    Monitor Selection . . . . . . . . . . . . . . . . . . . . . . . . . . . . . . . . 130
     5.2    System Configuration . . . . . . . . . . . . . . . . . . . . . . . . . . . . 131
     5.3    Configuration Deployment . . . . . . . . . . . . . . . . . . . . . . . . . 132

6        Implementation and Validation ............................. 133
         6.1      The MonitoringManager Packages ................... 133
         6.2      Testing and Validation ........................... 134
7        Related Work.............................................. 135
8        Conclusions and Future Work .............................. 136
References ....................................................... 137

**Runtime Prediction** ................................................. 139
Davide Lorenzoli and George Spanoudakis
1        Introduction ............................................. 139
2        Related Work............................................. 141
3        Example Scenario ........................................ 141
4        Background: The EVEREST Monitoring Framework ........... 143
5        Prediction Specifications ................................ 146
         5.1      Predictor Configuration ......................... 146
         5.2      QoS Specification ............................... 147
6        Architecture Of EVEREST+ ............................... 148
         6.1      Prediction Manager .............................. 149
         6.2      Monitoring Specification Generator ................ 150
         6.3      Model Manager .................................. 150
         6.4      QoS Predictor ................................... 151
7        Conclusion............................................... 151
References ....................................................... 151

**Software Performance and Reliability Prediction** ..................... 153
Franz Brosch
1        Introduction ............................................. 153
2        Goals and Scope ......................................... 154
3        QoS Meta-Model ......................................... 155
4        Prediction Workflow...................................... 157
5        Prediction Realisation ................................... 159
         5.1      Overview ........................................ 159
         5.2      Prediction Engine Internals ....................... 160
         5.3      Prediction Process ............................... 161
6        Use Cases .............................................. 163
References ....................................................... 164

**Part IV   Core Components of the Service Level Agreements Framework**

**G-SLAM – The Anatomy of the Generic SLA Manager** ............... 167
Miguel Angel Rojas Gonzalez, Peter Chronz, Kuan Lu, Edwin Yaqub,
Beatriz Fuentes, Alfonso Castro, Howard Foster, Juan Lambea Rueda, and
Augustín Escámez Chimeno
1        Introduction ............................................. 167
2        Plug-in-based Approach to the G-SLAM Architecture........... 168
3        The G-SLAM Architecture ................................. 168

3.1    Technology Used by the Plug-in-based G-SLAM
       Architecture ........................................ 169
4    Generic Components ...................................... 170
     4.1    Core of the G-SLAM via Interfaces ................. 170
     4.2    Abstraction Layer for the Domain-Specific Components
            PAC and POC .................................... 172
     4.3    Main Bundle for the G-SLAM ...................... 172
     4.4    Syntax Conversion for Interoperability ............... 172
     4.5    Protocol Engine .................................. 173
     4.6    SLATemplateRegistry ............................. 174
     4.7    SLARegistry ..................................... 174
     4.8    MonitoringManager .............................. 175
     4.9    Authorisation ................................... 176
5    Advertisements System ................................... 176
6    Planning and Optimisation Component (POC) ................. 178
7    Provisioning and Adjustment Component (PAC) .............. 180
8    Skeleton SLAM .......................................... 181
     8.1    Maven Integration ............................... 184
9    Conclusions ............................................. 185
References ................................................... 186

**A Generic Platform for Conducting SLA Negotiations** ................. 187
Edwin Yaqub, Philipp Wieder, Constantinos Kotsokalis, Valentina Mazza,
Liliana Pasquale, Juan Lambea Rueda, Sergio García Gómez, and Augustín
Escámez Chimeno

1    Introduction ............................................. 187
2    State of the Art .......................................... 189
3    Protocol Engine ......................................... 191
     3.1    Design ......................................... 192
4    Protocol Description ..................................... 194
     4.1    Related Work .................................... 194
     4.2    Design ......................................... 195
     4.3    Bilateral Negotiations ............................ 198
5    Negotiation Rationality .................................. 200
     5.1    Profiles ........................................ 200
     5.2    Protocol Customisation Mechanism ................. 202
     5.3    Business Take-Up of Negotiations ................. 203
6    Conclusion .............................................. 204
References ................................................... 204

**Part V  Management of the Business Layer**

**Management of the Business SLAs for Services eContracting** ........... 209
Sergio García Gómez, Juan Lambea Rueda, and Augustín Escámez Chimeno

1    Introduction ............................................. 209
2    Business SLA Management in Current e-Contracting Proposals .. 210

    2.1     Information  .......................................  210
    2.2     Negotiation and Offer Building ......................  211
    2.3     Contracting.........................................  212
    2.4     Runtime  ...........................................  213
3       An SLA-Aware e-Contracting Proposal .......................  213
    3.1     Comprehesive SLA-Aware e-Contracting Suite.........  213
    3.2     Customisation of Business SLA Definitions  ...........  214
    3.3     Business SLA Post-Sale Management  ................  214
4       Business Layer Architecture ...............................  215
    4.1     Business Manager ..................................  215
    4.2     Business SLA Manager  ............................  216
5       Modelling SLA Business Terms ............................  217
    5.1     Business Terms Integration ........................  217
6       Future Work..............................................  221
7       Conclusions  .............................................  221
    References ....................................................  222

**Part VI  Management of the Software Layer**

**Model-Driven Framework for Business Continuity Management** ........  227
Ulrich Winkler and Wasif Gilani
1       Introduction ..............................................  227
2       Business Continuity Management...........................  229
3       Related Work..............................................  229
4       Model-Driven and Process-Centric BCM Framework ..........  231
    4.1     Requirements  .....................................  231
    4.2     Architecture .......................................  233
    4.3     Stakeholders.......................................  234
    4.4     Environment........................................  234
    4.5     Workflow and Methodology .........................  235
    4.6     Business Process Requirements Annotation............  236
    4.7     IT BCM Model Derivation ..........................  238
    4.8     BEAM Derivation ..................................  240
    4.9     Alpha BEAM.......................................  240
    4.10    Beta BEAM  ......................................  242
    4.11    Gamma BEAM ....................................  243
    4.12    Business Continuity Analysis ........................  244
    4.13    Analysis Result Presentation ........................  244
    4.14    Tracing ...........................................  245
    4.15    Context-Sensitive Presentation Mode .................  246
    4.16    Document-Oriented Presentation Mode ...............  246
5       Conclusions and Outlook  ...............................  248
    References ....................................................  249

**Managing Composite Services** ................................... 251
Sam Guinea, Annapaola Marconi, Natalia Rasadka, and Paolo Zampognaro
    1      Introduction .............................................. 251
          1.1     The Health and Mobility Use Case .................. 253
    2      Management Approach .................................... 254
    3      A Dynamic Orchestration Engine .......................... 256
    4      Dynamic Binding ........................................ 257
    5      Process Restructuring .................................... 260
    6      Related Work ........................................... 264
    7      Conclusions and Future Work ............................. 266
    References ..................................................... 267

**Part VII  Management of the Infrastructure Layer**

**SLA-Enabled Infrastructure Management** ......................... 271
John Kennedy, Andrew Edmonds, Victor Bayon, Pat Cheevers, Kuan Lu,
Miha Stopar, and Damjan Murn
    1      Introduction .............................................. 271
    2      SLA-Aware Infrastructure Architecture ...................... 272
    3      Infrastructure SLA Manager ............................... 273
    4      Infrastructure SLA Manager Implementation .................. 274
          4.1     Infrastructure Planning and Optimisation .............. 275
          4.2     Infrastructure Provisioning and Adjustment ............ 276
    5      Infrastructure Service Manager ............................ 277
          5.1     Open Cloud Computing Interface .................... 278
    6      Infrastructure Service Manager Implementation ............... 278
    7      Provisioning System ...................................... 279
          7.1     Scheduler ........................................ 280
          7.2     Re-provisioning ................................... 281
    8      Infrastructure Monitoring................................. 282
    9      Conclusions ............................................. 287
    References ..................................................... 287

**Part VIII  Selected Business Use Cases**

**Introduction to the SLA@SOI Industrial Use Cases** .................. 291
Joe M. Butler
    1      Introduction .............................................. 291
    2      Considerations for Use Case Selection ...................... 291
    3      Use Case Key Elements ................................... 293

**The ERP Hosting Use Case Scenario** ............................. 295
Wolfgang Theilmann, Jens Happe, and Ulrich Winkler
    1      Introduction .............................................. 295
    2      Business Context ........................................ 296

    2.1    Roles . . . . . . . . . . . . . . . . . . . . . . . . . . . . . . . . . . . . . . . . . . . 297
    2.2    Business Objectives . . . . . . . . . . . . . . . . . . . . . . . . . . . . . . 297
3   Foundations . . . . . . . . . . . . . . . . . . . . . . . . . . . . . . . . . . . . . . . . . . . 299
    3.1    Service Hierarchies for Business Applications . . . . . . . . . 299
    3.2    Related Work . . . . . . . . . . . . . . . . . . . . . . . . . . . . . . . . . . . . 300
4   SLA Management Architecture . . . . . . . . . . . . . . . . . . . . . . . . . . . . . 300
5   SLA Hierarchies . . . . . . . . . . . . . . . . . . . . . . . . . . . . . . . . . . . . . . . . 301
    5.1    SLA Terms and Translation . . . . . . . . . . . . . . . . . . . . . . . 302
    5.2    Integrated planning . . . . . . . . . . . . . . . . . . . . . . . . . . . . . . 304
6   Business Evaluation . . . . . . . . . . . . . . . . . . . . . . . . . . . . . . . . . . . . 306
    6.1    Improvements to enable dynamic service provisioning . . . 306
    6.2    Improvements to increase efficiency and reduce costs . . . 307
    6.3    Improvements to enhance transparency . . . . . . . . . . . . . . 307
7   Conclusions . . . . . . . . . . . . . . . . . . . . . . . . . . . . . . . . . . . . . . . . . . . 308
References . . . . . . . . . . . . . . . . . . . . . . . . . . . . . . . . . . . . . . . . . . . . . . . . 308

**The Enterprise IT Use Case Scenario** . . . . . . . . . . . . . . . . . . . . . . . . . . . . 311
Michael Nolan and Joe M. Butler
1   Introduction . . . . . . . . . . . . . . . . . . . . . . . . . . . . . . . . . . . . . . . . . . . 311
2   Business Context . . . . . . . . . . . . . . . . . . . . . . . . . . . . . . . . . . . . . . . 312
    2.1    Business Value . . . . . . . . . . . . . . . . . . . . . . . . . . . . . . . . . . 313
    2.2    Managing IT Like a Business . . . . . . . . . . . . . . . . . . . . . . 313
    2.3    The Provisioning Scenario . . . . . . . . . . . . . . . . . . . . . . . . . 315
    2.4    The Runtime Scenario . . . . . . . . . . . . . . . . . . . . . . . . . . . . 315
    2.5    The Investment Governance Scenario . . . . . . . . . . . . . . . . 318
    2.6    Business Objectives . . . . . . . . . . . . . . . . . . . . . . . . . . . . . 319
    2.7    Business Process Changes . . . . . . . . . . . . . . . . . . . . . . . . 320
    2.8    Integrating BLOs into the Digital SLA . . . . . . . . . . . . . . . 320
3   SLA Management Architecture . . . . . . . . . . . . . . . . . . . . . . . . . . . . . 322
4   Business Evaluation . . . . . . . . . . . . . . . . . . . . . . . . . . . . . . . . . . . . 325
    4.1    Improvements for IT Enabling the Enterprise . . . . . . . . . . 325
    4.2    Improvements to IT Efficiency . . . . . . . . . . . . . . . . . . . . . 325
    4.3    Improvements to IT Investment and Technology Adoption 326
5   Conclusions . . . . . . . . . . . . . . . . . . . . . . . . . . . . . . . . . . . . . . . . . . . 326
References . . . . . . . . . . . . . . . . . . . . . . . . . . . . . . . . . . . . . . . . . . . . . . . . 327

**The Service Aggregator Use Case Scenario** . . . . . . . . . . . . . . . . . . . . . . . 329
Juan Lambea Rueda, Sergio García Gómez, Augustín Escámez Chimeno
1   Introduction . . . . . . . . . . . . . . . . . . . . . . . . . . . . . . . . . . . . . . . . . . . 329
2   Business Context . . . . . . . . . . . . . . . . . . . . . . . . . . . . . . . . . . . . . . . 330
    2.1    Roles . . . . . . . . . . . . . . . . . . . . . . . . . . . . . . . . . . . . . . . . . . 332
    2.2    Business Objectives . . . . . . . . . . . . . . . . . . . . . . . . . . . . . 333
3   Foundations . . . . . . . . . . . . . . . . . . . . . . . . . . . . . . . . . . . . . . . . . . . 334
    3.1    Service Aggregation . . . . . . . . . . . . . . . . . . . . . . . . . . . . . 334
    3.2    Related Work . . . . . . . . . . . . . . . . . . . . . . . . . . . . . . . . . . . 335
4   SLA Management Architecture . . . . . . . . . . . . . . . . . . . . . . . . . . . . . 336

5       SLA Hierarchies .......................................... 338
        5.1     SLA Terms ....................................... 338
6       Business Evaluation ...................................... 339
        6.1     Improved Customer Satisfaction .................... 339
        6.2     Improved Dependability ........................... 340
        6.3     Improved End-To-End Manageability ................ 340
        6.4     Improved Decision-Making ........................ 340
        6.5     Improved Agility ................................. 340
        6.6     Improved Operational and Energy Efficiency ......... 341
7       Conclusions .............................................. 341
References .................................................... 341

**The eGovernment Use Case Scenario** ............................. 343
Giampaolo Armellin, Annamaria Chiasera, Ganna Frankova, Liliana
Pasquale, Francesco Torelli, and Gabriele Zacco

1       Introduction ............................................. 344
2       Business Context ........................................ 344
        2.1     Mobility and health care services ................... 344
        2.2     Roles ........................................... 345
        2.3     Business Objectives ............................. 346
3       Use Case Scenarios ....................................... 347
4       SLA Management Architecture ............................ 349
5       SLAs ................................................... 352
6       Evaluation: Practice and Experience ....................... 354
7       Conclusions .............................................. 357
References .................................................... 357

# List of Contributors

Giampaolo Armellin
GPI, Via Ragazzi del '99, 13, Trento 38123, Italy e-mail: achiasera@gpi.it

Victor Bayon
Intel Labs Europe, Collinstown Industrial Estate, Leixlip, Co. Kildare, Ireland,
e-mail: victorx.m.molino@intel.com

Franz Brosch
FZI Research Center for Information Technology, Haid-und-Neu-Str. 10-14, 76131
Karlsruhe, Germany, e-mail: brosch@fzi.de

Joe M. Butler
Intel Labs Europe, Collinstown Industrial Estate, Leixlip, Co. Kildare, Ireland,
e-mail: joe.m.butler@intel.com

Alfonso Castro
Telefonica I+D, Distrito-C. Ronda de la Comunicacin s/n. Edificio Oeste 1, planta
5. 28050 Madrid, Spain, e-mail: acast@tid.es

Pat Cheevers
Intel Labs Europe, Collinstown Industrial Estate, Leixlip, Co. Kildare, Ireland,
e-mail: patx.cheevers@intel.com

Peter Chronz
TU Dortmund University, Service Computing Group/ITMC, August-Schmidt-
Strasse 12, 44227 Dortmund, Germany, e-mail: peter.chronz@udo.edu

Annamaria Chiasera
GPI, Via Ragazzi del '99, 13, Trento 38123, Italy,
e-mail: achiasera@gpi.it

Augustín Escámez Chimeno
Telefonica I+D, c/Recogidas 24, Portal B, Escalera A, Planta 1, Puerta A, 18002
Granada, Spain, e-mail: escamez@tid.es

Beatriz Fuentes
Telefonica I+D, Distrito-C. Ronda de la Comunicacin s/n. Edificio Oeste 1, planta 5. 28050 Madrid, Spain, e-mail: `fuentes@tid.es`

Jens Happe
SAP Research, Vincenz-Priessnitz-Str. 1, 76131 Karlsruhe, Germany, e-mail: `jens.happe@sap.com`

Andrew Edmonds
Intel Labs Europe, Collinstown Industrial Estate, Leixlip, Co. Kildare, Ireland, e-mail: `andrewx.edmonds@intel.com`

Giovanni Falcone
FZI Research Center for Information Technology, Haid-und-Neu-Str. 10-14, 76131 Karlsruhe, Germany, e-mail: `falcone@fzi.de`

Ganna Frankova
GPI, Via Ragazzi del '99, 13, Trento 38123, e-mail: `gannafrankova@yahoo.com`

Sergio García Gómez
Telefonica I+D, c/Abraham Zacuto 10, Parque Tecnologico de Boecillo, 47151 Valladolid, Spain, e-mail: `sergg@tid.es`

Wasif Gilani
SAP Research, The Concourse, Queen's Road, Titanic Quarter, Belfast, BT3 9DT, United Kingdom, e-mail: `wasif.gilani@sap.com`

Sam Guinea
Politecnico di Milano, v. Golgi 42, Milano, Italy, e-mail: `guinea@elet.polimi`

Howard Foster
Department of Computing, City University London, Northampton Square, EC1V 0HB, London, e-mail: `howard.foster.1@city.ac.uk`

Keven T. Kearney
Engineering Ingegneria Informatica spa, Via Riccardo Morandi, 32, 00148 Roma, Italy, e-mail: `keven.kearney@eng.it`

John Kennedy
Intel Labs Europe, Collinstown Industrial Estate, Leixlip, Co. Kildare, Ireland, e-mail: `john.m.kennedy@intel.com`

Benjamin Klatt
FZI Research Center for Information Technology, Haid-und-Neu-Str. 10-14, 76131 Karlsruhe, Germany, e-mail: `klatt@fzi.de`

Constantinos Kotsokalis
TU Dortmund University, August-Schmidt-Strasse 12, 44227 Dortmund, Germany, e-mail: `constantinos.kotsokalis@udo.edu`

Davide Lorenzoli
School Of Informatics, Department Of Computing, City University, Northampton square, London, NW1 0TY, UK,
e-mail: Davide.Lorenzoli.1@soi.city.ac.uk

Kuan Lu
TU Dortmund University, Service Computing Group/ITMC, August-Schmidt-Strasse 12, 44227 Dortmund, Germany, e-mail: kuan.lu@tu-dortmund.de

Khaled Mahbub
Department of Computing, City University London, Northampton Square, London, EC1V 0HB, UK, e-mail: K.Mahbub@soi.city.ac.uk

Annapaola Marconi
Fondazione Bruno Kessler, via alla Cascata 56C, 38121 Povo, Trento, Italy, e-mail: marconi@fbk.eu

Valentina Mazza
Politecnico di Milano, piazza L. Da Vinci, 32 - 20133 Milano, Italy e-mail: pasquale@elet.polimi.it

Jessica McCarthy
Intel Labs Europe, Collinstown Industrial Estate, Leixlip, Co. Kildare, Ireland, e-mail: jessica.c.mccarthy@intel.com

Damjan Murn
XLAB d.o.o., Pot za Brdom 100, 1000 Ljubljana, Slovenia, e-mail: damjan.murn@xlab.si@xlab.si

Michael Nolan
Intel Labs Europe, Collinstown Industrial Estate, Leixlip, Co. Kildare, Ireland, e-mail: michael.nolan@intel.com

Liliana Pasquale
Politecnico di Milano, piazza L. Da Vinci, 32 - 20133 Milano, Italy e-mail: pasquale@elet.polimi.it

Natalia Rasadka
Fondazione Bruno Kessler, via alla Cascata 56C, 38121 Povo, Trento, Italy, e-mail: rasadka@fbk.eu

Christoph Rathfelder
FZI Research Center for Information Technology, Haid-und-Neu-Str. 10-14, 76131 Karlsruhe, Germany, e-mail: rathfelder@fzi.de

Miguel Angel Rojas Gonzalez
TU Dortmund University, Service Computing Group/ITMC, August-Schmidt-Strasse 12, 44227 Dortmund, Germany, e-mail: miguel.rojas@udo.edu

Juan Lambea Rueda
Telefonica I+D, Distrito-C. Ronda de la Comunicacin s/n. Edificio Oeste 1, planta

5, 28050 Madrid, Spain, e-mail: juanlr@tid.es

George Spanoudakis
Department of Computing, City University London, Northampton Square, London,
EC1V 0HB, UK, e-mail: g.spanoudakis@soi.city.ac.uk

Miha Stopar
XLAB d.o.o., Pot za Brdom 100, 1000 Ljubljana, Slovenia, e-mail: miha.
stopar@xlab.si

Wolfgang Theilmann
SAP Research, Vincenz-Priessnitz-Str. 1, 76131 Karlsruhe, Germany, e-mail:
wolfgang.theilmann@sap.com

Theocharis Tsigkritis
Dept. of Computing, City University London, Northampton Square, London, EC1V
0HB, UK, e-mail: t7t@soi.city.ac.uk

Francesco Torelli
Engineering Ingegneria Informatica Spa, Via Riccardo Morandi, 32, 00148 Roma,
Italy, e-mail: francesco.torelli@eng.it

Alexander Wert
SAP Research, Vincenz-Priessnitz-Str. 1, 76131 Karlsruhe, Germany, e-mail:
alexander.wert@sap.com

Philipp Wieder
TU Dortmund University, Service Computing Group/ITMC, August-Schmidt-
Strasse 12, 44227 Dortmund, Germany, e-mail: philipp.wieder@udo.edu

Ulrich Winkler
SAP Research, The Concourse, Queen's Road, Titanic Quarter, Belfast, BT3 9DT,
United Kingdom, e-mail: ulrich.winkler@sap.com

Ramin Yahyapour
TU Dortmund University, Service Computing Group/ITMC, August-Schmidt-
Strasse 12, 44227 Dortmund, Germany,
e-mail: ramin.yahyapour@tu-dortmund.de

Edwin Yaqub
TU Dortmund University, Service Computing Group/ITMC, August-Schmidt-
Strasse 12, 44227 Dortmund, Germany, e-mail: edwin.yaqub@tu-dortmund.
de

Gabriele Zacco
Fondazione Bruno Kessler, Via Santa Croce 77, 38122 Trento, Italy, e-mail:
zacco@fbk.eu

Paolo Zampognaro
Engineering, Engineering Ingegneria Informatica Spa, Via Riccardo Morandi, 32,
00148 Roma, Italy, e-mail: paolo.zampognaro@eng.it

# Part I
# Introduction to Service Level Agreements in Service Oriented Architectures

# Motivation and Overview

Joe M. Butler, Ramin Yahyapour, and Wolfgang Theilmann

**Abstract** Service-orientation is becoming the basic principle along which IT architectures and business structures are organised. It underlies all recent trends, including the Internet of Services, cloud computing, and Future Internet. However, to turn the promise of this principle into realised benefits, services must be accompanied by exact definitions as to the conditions of their usage. These conditions can be specified by Service Level Agreements (SLAs). A holistic SLA management framework allows SLAs to be consistently managed along a business/IT stack and also across different parties. This chapter introduces the underlying motivation for SLA management, exhibits the vision of the SLA@SOI project, and relates this vision to other key management approaches.

## 1 Socio-economic Context and Motivation

### 1.1 Towards a Service Economy

The ongoing transformation of a product-oriented economy into a service-oriented economy has come to a critical point. IT-supported service-provisioning has become of major relevance in all industries and domains. However, the nature of these ser-

Joe M. Butler
Intel Ireland Limited, Collinstown Industrial Park, Leixlip, Ireland,
e-mail: joe.m.butler@intel.com

Ramin Yahyapour
TU Dortmund University, August-Schmidt-Strasse 12, 44221 Dortmund, Germany,
e-mail: ramin.yahyapour@tu-dortmund.de

Wolfgang Theilmann
SAP Research, Vincenz-Priessnitz-Str.1, 76131 Karlsruhe, Germany,
e-mail: wolfgang.theilmann@sap.com

vices is typically quite static: the services take place in a predefined setup and well understood context.

However, since 2005, the future of the European knowledge economy has been identified as requiring services that can be dynamically provisioned to exactly meet the economic and technical characteristics required by the service customer (for example, as anticipated in the renewed Lisbon agenda [1], the i2010 initiative [2], the emerging field of Service Science [3] and the European technology platform NESSI [4]).

By fulfilling this vision the service economy can leverage its full potential, leading to a dynamic knowledge economy. Services shall be provided on-demand, according to conditions required by the consumers, and supported by a transparent and automated business process back-end. Eventually, dynamic value networks could be flexibly instantiated based on these services, thus driving innovation and competitiveness.

## 1.2 Cloud Computing

A major current industrial trend in this area emerged around the paradigm of cloud computing. Cloud computing is essentially a new business model for operating IT resources by providing them as common utility services that are offered and consumed by multiple stakeholders [5].

Cloud computing has gained significant attention and commercial uptake in many business scenarios. However, it also highlighted key challenges in IT-supported service provisioning. With more companies incorporating cloud-based IT services as part of their own value chain, reliability and dependability become a crucial factor in managing business.

## 1.3 Future Internet

A more recent related trend has emerged around the theme of the Future Internet. The Future Internet aims to offer integrated access to people, media, services and things, provided by one underlying platform. It seeks to enable new styles of societal and economic interactions on an unprecedented scale, offering both flexibility and quality. Besides being the constituting building block of the so-called Internet of Services, the Future Internet, through the metaphor of the Internet of Things, will provide location-independent, interoperable, scalable, secure and efficient access to a coordinated set of services [6].

However, such a broad vision demands a sound and well-defined approach to management and governance. This approach must harmonise with and bridge the various views and layers of the Future Internet following the subsidiary principle that as many issues as possible should be dealt with locally, while as few issues as possible will be managed in a more integrated way [7].

## 1.4 Business Need for Systematic SLA Management

The three perspectives introduced above all highlight key challenges and opportunities in IT-supported service provisioning. However, they also reveal a common characteristic: they will succeed if and only if the provisioning of services is done under clearly specified conditions. These conditions must be understood by service providers and service customers; they must be negotiable, so that services can meet customer requirements; and they must be manageable from a service provider's point of view.

Looking at the situation today, there are major risks and challenges to be solved. From a service consumer's point of view, the consumption of services can impose high risks; typically there are no formally agreed SLAs in place to specify the quality and delivery conditions for a service. Further, there are no standardised ways for customers to express and negotiate such non-functional conditions. From a service provider's perspective, creating customised service offerings, negotiating with individual customers, and translating from business requirements into specific internal provisioning manifestations consumes valuable time and resources. Internally, the economies of optimising deployment landscapes whilst maintaining all individual SLAs are largely unachievable. The potential of modern infrastructure technologies such as virtualisation is also untapped. Ultimately, the service marketplace is frustrating and cumbersome for both service providers and consumers.

A solution to these challenges can be found in addressing two needs: First, there is a need to express the exact conditions under which services are to be delivered. A common way to achieve this can be found in the notion of Service Level Agreements (SLAs). Second, there is a strong need to support the systematic management of SLAs, so that eventually customer and provider concerns are matched in a transparent way. This leads to the need of a holistic SLA-management framework which can be easily used in different scenarios and domains.

## 2 Vision

The vision of the SLA@SOI project [8] is an invigorated economy thriving in a market of dependable services empowered by SLAs.

To achieve this vision, the project delivered and showcased an innovative open SLA management framework that provides holistic support for service level objectives, enabling an open, dynamic, SLA-aware market for service providers. Under this framework, SLAs are managed autonomously throughout the complete service lifecycle, spanning the entire services stack from the business layer through to infrastructure. Arbitrary domains are supported, as demonstrated by evaluations in wide-ranging, grounded, use cases.

Specific benefits to expect from a holistic SLA management framework include improved service offerings that are:

- more dynamic (reduced preparation and setup time)
- more dependable (explicitly specified SLAs and the confidence to meet them)
- more automated and thus cost-efficient (automated service management procedures)
- more flexible (simplified adjustment or reprovisioning, possibly relying on third party providers)
- more transparent (clearer understanding the cost drivers and non-functional properties of their offering).

A motivating business scenario highlighting the project idea is that of a service provider who is able to offer services with differentiated, dependable and adjustable SLAs, and who can negotiate concrete SLAs with customers (individuals or groups) in an automated fashion. This business goal imposes additional requirements on software providers (who must provide components with predictable non-functional behaviour) and infrastructure providers (who must support an SLA-aware management of resources).

This vision maps to the overarching challenge for a service-oriented infrastructure (SOI) that supports consistent SLA management across all layers of an IT stack and across the various stakeholders' perspectives. In this vision, SLA characteristics may span multiple non-functional domains, including security, performance, availability and reliability.

Figure 5 gives an overview of how a systematic SLA management process might appear. As today's business systems typically consist of complex layered systems, user-level SLAs cannot be directly mapped onto the physical infrastructure. Services might be composed of other, more fundamental services that could be also provided by external parties. Consequently, a stepwise mapping of higher-level SLA requirements onto lower levels, and the aggregation of lower-level capabilities to higher levels, is crucial for grounding user-level SLAs to the infrastructure. This vertical information flow must carefully reflect service interdependencies as well as the original business context. In addition to SLAs, the vertical information flow also covers monitoring, tracking and accounting data, and must support brokering and negotiation processes at each layer. As shown in the figure, the overall SLA management process may include different stakeholders (namely customers, service providers and infrastructure providers), and various business steps (such as business assessment, contracting and sales). The overview is intentionally simplified in the sense that no service chains are visualised. Such chains would represent all cases where service providers rely on external providers.

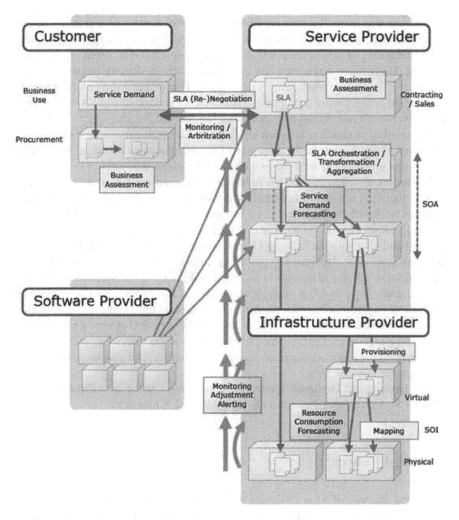

**Fig. 1** High-level interaction of the SLA@SOI framework.

## 3 Technical Perspective

SLAs are a common way to formally specify the exact conditions (both functional and non-functional) under which services are or shall be delivered. However, the SLAs currently in practice are only specified at the top-level interface between a service provider and a service customer. Top-level SLAs can be used by customers and providers to monitor whether an actual service delivery complies with the agreed SLA terms. In case of SLA violations, penalties or compensations can be directly derived.

However, top-level SLAs do not allow service providers to plan their IT land-scapes according to possible, planned or agreed SLAs. Further, they do not provide an understanding of why a certain SLA violation might have occurred. This is because SLA guarantee terms typically do not explicitly or directly relate to actual performance metrics or configuration parameters. This makes it difficult for service providers to derive proper configuration parameters from top-level SLAs and to assess (lower-level) monitoring metrics against top-level SLAs.

The missing connection between top-level SLAs and (lower-level) metrics and parameters is a major hurdle for managing IT stacks in terms of planning, predicting or adjusting processes in accordance with possible, planned or actual SLAs.

The technical vision of the SLA paradigm is the management of a complete IT stack in line with top-level SLAs that have been agreed at the business level. This complies well with the technical trend towards applying the paradigm of service-orientation across the complete IT stack (infrastructure, platform and software as a service), and also with the trend in IT companies towards organising different departments as service departments (providing infrastructure resources, middleware, applications or composition tools as a service). SLAs will be associated with multiple elements of the stack at multiple layers. For example, there will be SLAs for elements of physical infrastructure, virtualised infrastructure, middleware, applications and processes. Such internal SLAs describe the contract between a lower-level entity and a higher-level entity which consumes the lower one. More precisely, the SLAs specify the required or agreed performance metrics, and also the related configuration parameters.

The fundamental challenge for realising this vision is the coordination of the different SLAs such that they form a synchronised SLA hierarchy.

## 4 Related Concepts

A detailed analysis of SLA@SOI and related technical and scientific approaches can be found in [9] and [10]. However, we want to explicitly discuss the relationship between the SLA management framework and major management concepts.

### 4.1 ITIL

The Information Technology Infrastructure Library (ITIL) [11] is a set of concepts and policies for managing IT infrastructure, development and operations. ITIL is the most widely accepted approach to IT service management in the world. It provides a comprehensive and consistent set of best practices for IT service management, promoting a quality approach to achieving business effectiveness and efficiency in the support and maintenance of information systems.

SLA@SOI and the ITIL framework both aim to enable service providers to effectively manage service activities within their organisations. The two approaches share similarities and possess some distinct capabilities: For example, although the service lifecycles in each approach are conceptually equivalent, the phases are labelled differently. Further, some of the lifecycle phases in ITIL don't have a counterpart in the SLA@SOI lifecycle, but the activities carried out within these phases are covered in other phases of the SLA@SOI lifecycle. There is a good convergence between the two approaches in terms of service definition, broad applicability, the non-proprietary approach, and the concept of a configuration management database (CMDB). However, SLA@SOI and ITIL diverge at some important points: for example, SLA@SOI provides a full architecture (not just best practices), supports SLA/service negotiation (not covered by ITIL), supports a multi-provider focus (in contrast to ITIL's single provider view), has a notion of SLA translation (not addressed by ITIL at all), and includes mechanisms for predictive management (not addressed by ITIL).

A detailed comparison between SLA@SOI and ITIL can be found in [12].

## 4.2 Autonomic Management

SLA-driven system management is the primary approach discussed in this book. This approach aims to derive all kinds of management decisions from the requested or agreed SLAs. However, there are other management functions that are partially related to SLA management. As a reference structure for these functions, we use the four main categories of self-managing systems [13]: self-configuring, self-healing, self-optimising and self-protecting.

Configuration management is closely related to SLA management. Possible configuration options are captured in the service construction model and are considered during the planning phase. Once an SLA has been agreed and is to be provided, the configuration parameters derived during the planning phase are used to set up the system. The same holds for re-planning and adaptation cycles.

Self-healing is in the first place independent from SLA management: the detection and recovery from low-level unhealthy situations can be achieved completely independently from agreed SLAs. However, the detection of SLA violations and automated re-planning could be also be categorised as self-healing processes. Further, low-level unhealthy situations might be used for predicting possible future SLA violations.

Self-optimising is very closely related to SLA management and simply cannot be done without accounting for the respective constraints of the contracted SLAs.

Self-protecting is in the first place independent from SLA management; however, certain self-protecting mechanisms can be made part of an SLA

## 5 Conclusion and Book Overview

We are convinced that Service Level Agreements are an essential foundation for service oriented infrastructures and a society relying more and more on ICT services. Especially with the still growing provisioning and demand for Cloud-like services, frameworks like the one developed by SLA@SOI will become essential to deliver what has been promised. This is the reason why we regard this book as valuable for researchers as well as practitioners. It provides the results and lessons learned within the SLA@SOI project and prepares them for the community-at-large. Technical results — in particular the reference architecture and various models and mechanisms of our SLA management framework — are described in detail. We also show the results of a set of industrial use cases that were realised to test (a) the general value proposition of holistic SLA management and (b) the specific validation of our SLA@SOI framework.

## References

[1] European Council (Austrian Presidency Conclusion), *The renewed sustainable development strategy.* 16th June 2006 http://ec.europa.eu/sustainable/sds2006/index_en.htm

[2] European Commission, *i2010 - A European Information Society for growth and employment* COM(2005) 229

[3] IfM and IBM, *Succeeding through service innovation: A service perspective for education, research, business and government* White Paper, Univ. of Cambridge, 2008, URL: http://www.ifm.eng.cam.ac.uk/ssme/documents/080428cambridge_ssme_whitepaper.pdf

[4] NESSI (the European Technology Platform on Software and Services - the Networked European Software and Services Initiative), *Vision* 2005 http://www.nessi-europe.com/

[5] M. Armbrust, et al., *Above the Clouds: A Berkeley View of Cloud Computing.* Report, UC Berkeley Reliable Adaptive Distributed Systems Laboratory, February 10, 2009, URL: http://radlab.cs.berkeley.edu/

[6] Future Internet Assembly, *Bled Declaration on Future Internet* April 2008, http://www.future-internet.eu/index.php?id=47

[7] Theilmann, W., Baresi, L., *Multi-level SLAs for Harmonized Management in the Future Internet*

[8] SLA@SOI project: IST- 216556; Empowering the Service Economy with SLA-aware Infrastructures, http://www.sla-at-soi.eu/

[9] SLA@SOI project:, *State of the Art Analysis.* Technical Report, September 2010, http://sla-at-soi.eu/publications/deliverables/

[10] Li, H., Theilmann, W., and Happe, J., *SLA Translation in Multi-Layered Service Oriented Architectures: Status and Challenges.* Technical Report 2009-8, Universität Karlsruhe (TH) (April 2009)

[11] Office of Government Commerce, *The official introduction to the ITIL service lifecycle.* Stationery Office Books (TSO) (2007)

[12] SLA@SOI project:, *State of the Art Analysis.* Technical Report, July 2009, http://sla-at-soi.eu/publications/deliverables/

[13] Miller, B., *The autonomic computing edge: Can you CHOP up autonomic computing?* Whitepaper IBM developerworks, March 2008. URL: http://www.ibm.com/developerworks/autonomic/library/ac-edge4/

# A Reference Architecture for Multi-Level SLA Management

Jens Happe, Wolfgang Theilmann, Andrew Edmonds, and Keven T. Kearney

**Abstract** Service-orientation is the core paradigm for organising business inter-actions and modern IT architectures. At the business level, service industries are becoming the dominating sector in which solutions are flexibly composed out of networked services. At the IT level, the paradigms of Service-Oriented Architecture and cloud computing realise service-orientation for both software and infrastructure services. Service composition across different layers is a major advantage of this paradigm. Service Level Agreements (SLAs) are a common approach to specifying the exact conditions under which services are to be delivered, and thus are a pre-requisite for supporting the flexible trading of services. However, typical SLAs are only specified at a single layer and do not provide insight into metrics or parame-ters at the various lower layers of the service stack. Thus they do not allow service providers to manage their service stack optimally.

In this chapter, we present a reference architecture for a multi-level SLA manage-ment framework. We discuss fundamental concepts of the framework and detail its main architectural components and interactions.

Jens Happe
SAP Research, Vincenz-Priessnitz-Str.1, 76131 Karlsruhe, Germany,
e-mail: Jens.Happe@sap.com

Wolfgang Theilmann
AP Research, Vincenz-Priessnitz-Str.1, 76131 Karlsruhe, Germany,
e-mail: Wolfgang.Theilmann@sap.com

Andrew Edmonds
Intel Ireland Limited, Collinstown Industrial Park, Leixlip, Ireland,
e-mail: andrewx.edmonds@intel.com

Keven T. Kearney
Engineering Ingegneria Informatica spa, Via Riccardo Morandi, 32, 00148 Roma, Italy,
e-mail: keven.kearney@eng.it

# 1 Introduction

*Service Level Agreements* (SLAs) are a common way to formally specify the exact conditions (both functional and non-functional) under which services are or should be delivered. However, in practice, SLAs are only specified at the top-level interface between a service provider and a service customer. Customers and providers can use top-level SLAs to monitor whether their actual service delivery complies with the agreed SLA terms. In the case of SLA violations, top-level SLAs allow for penalties or compensations to be directly derived.

In a service-oriented world, services offered are (usually) composed of or built on a complete set of other services. These services may reside in the domain of the provider itself, or be hosted by external providers. Such services include business services, software services, and infrastructure services. The quality of an offered service depends heavily on the quality of the services it uses. Service quality also depends on the elements used and the structure of the underlying IT system realising the service. Currently, service providers cannot plan their service landscapes using the SLAs of dependent services. They have no means by which to determine why a certain SLA violation might have occurred, or how to express an associated penalty. SLA guarantee terms are not explicitly related to measurable metrics, nor is their relation to lower-level services clearly defined. As a consequence, service providers cannot determine the necessary (lower-level) monitoring required to ensure top-level SLAs. This missing relationship between top-level SLAs and (lower-level) metrics is a major hurdle to efficient service planning and prediction or adjustment processes in service stacks.

In this chapter, we present a reference architecture for a multi-level SLA management framework. The framework was built based on previous discussion of a purely conceptual architecture [1] and experimental analysis of a specialised showcase [2]. We also present underlying concepts of the architecture and its main building blocks (components and interactions).

The remainder of this chapter is organised as follows: Section 3 describes foundational concepts, Section 4 introduces the developed reference architecture, and Section 7 concludes with a brief summary and outlook.

# 2 Scope and Goals

The overall SLA@SOI Framework is conceived as a possibly distributed, hierarchical management system providing consistent SLA management across the service delivery stack. At the highest level, we assume operation of the SLA@SOI framework serves ultimately to satisfy the goals of some business entity. Consequently, all management activities supported by the framework should eventually relate to the needs of that business entity.

The primary goal of the framework is to provide a generic solution for SLA management that:

1. supports SLA management across multiple layers with SLA composition and decomposition across functional and organisational domains;
2. supports arbitrary service types (business, software, infrastructure) and SLA terms;
3. covers the complete SLA and service life cycle with consistent interlinking of design time, planning and runtime management aspects; and
4. can be applied to a large variety of industrial domains and use cases.

To achieve these goals, the reference architecture is based on three main design principles: First, we put a strong emphasis on clearly separating service management from SLA management and supporting a well-layered and hierarchical management structure.

Second, we included a solid foundation common to meta-models for SLAs, as well as their relation to services and the construction of actual service instances; such a foundation is essential to supporting clear semantics across the different framework components. Third, since design for extensibility and adaptability is key to addressing multiple domains, we clearly distinguished between generic solution elements and places where domain-specific logic/models need to be provided. We aim to achieve an architecture where even generic parts can be replaced by domain-specific versions, perhaps dictated by preexisting (legacy) management functionality.

## 3 Foundation Concepts

Before diving into the actual reference architecture, we will detail some of its fundamental concepts surrounding the notion of SLAs and the relationships between them. This includes the definition of SLA management, service and SLA life cycles, the SLA (template) model, and the service construction model (SCM).

### 3.1 Service Hierarchy

A first and fundamental concept for the architecture is the refinement of services into three specialisations, with respect to their concreteness:

- *Service Type:* Specifies the service as a fully abstract entity via its external interface.
- *Service Implementation:* Describes specific resources or artifacts (such as software components, or appliances) which allow for instantiating the service. Service implementations may still depend on other services. There can be different implementations of a given service type.
- *Service Instance:* Describes a running and accessible service which is ready for consumption by service users. It has one or more service endpoints (for service

consumption) and a management endpoint (for service monitoring and control). Service instances might have multiple service/management endpoints if their service type specifies a bundled service.

As an example of these concepts, we can take a database service: The abstract type of such a service is specified in that it is exposed via an SQL interface. Different service implementations may exist for such a database service; for example, a MySQL database or an IBM DB2 database. These implementations may rely on other services, such as a storage service. For each implementation, multiple service instances might be created and these may differ in their concrete configuration. For example, one instance might be configured for optimised read access, another one for fast write access.

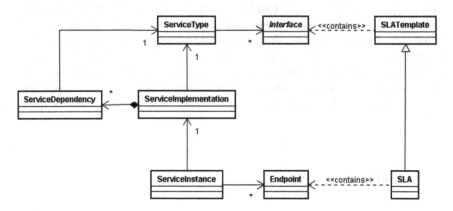

**Fig. 1** Service concepts and their relations to each other.

Figure 1 shows the main concepts coined for services and SLAs, as well as their relationships. SLA templates specify the types of SLA offerings a service provider is willing to accept. An SLA represents a potential agreement between a service provider and a customer that describes the service, documents service-level targets, and specifies the responsibilities of the service provider and the customer. An agreed SLA also refers to the endpoints of exactly one service instance. For example, an SLA for an instance of the address validation service contains the web-service endpoints for invoking the validation functionality.

Service dependencies relate to the service types that a given implementation relies on. To instantiate higher-level services, these dependencies must be resolved into concrete instances of the depending sub-service.

## 3.2 Management of Services and SLAs

Following the core concepts, we now briefly sketch our notion of management and the related lifecycles of SLAs and services.

### 3.2.1 SLA Management

The term management is interpreted here as "control" - in the classic control theory sense; synonymous with "applied constraint". We assume that the management actions enacted by the manager upon a system are goal-based; that is, that they serve to satisfy one or more management objectives, which are in some way dependent on the state of the system. To this end, the management relation is necessarily bidirectional: the application of management entails a continuous feedback loop in which the manager observes the dynamic state of the system, and acts upon it to constrain its state dynamics in some way. Both observation (sensing) and action are necessarily mediated by information exchange. Finally, management systems can be:

- *hierarchically organised* in that each level operates under the constraints imposed by higher levels, and serves in turn to constrain lower levels.
- *distributed* to the extent permitted by the communication channels supporting the management relation.

We interpret "SLA management" as the management of service delivery systems to meet the quality of service (QoS) objectives (goals) specified in SLAs. SLA management covers all stages in the SLA lifecycle:

- *SLA template design* ensures that offered QoS guarantees are realistic;
- *SLA negotiation* ensures that agreed QoS guarantees are realisable;
- *SLA runtime* ensures that QoS guarantees are satisfied; and
- *SLA (template) archiving* ensures that previous experience is available to future cycles.

### 3.2.2 Service Life cycle

The management of SLAs happens in the context of the overall service life cycle (Figure 2), which consists of the following stages:

- *Design and development:* development of artifacts needed for service implementation
- *Service offering (including SLA template design):* offering a service (type) to customers; results include specification of SLA templates
- *Service negotiation (including parts of SLA negotiation):* actual negotiation between customer and provider; results in an agreed SLA

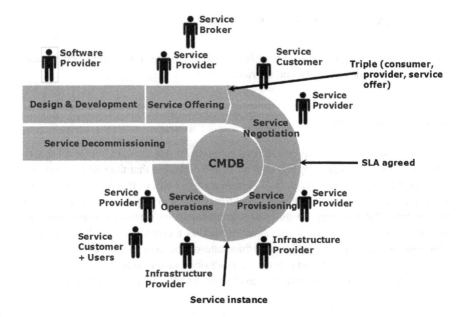

**Fig. 2** Service life cycle.

- *Service provisioning (including parts of SLA negotiation):* all activities required in system preparation and setup for allowing service operation, including booking, deployment (if needed), and configuration. Note that provisioning does not necessarily imply deployment, as, for example in a multi-tenant environment, the provisioning of a new tenant might be a simple reconfiguration of the running system.
- *Service operations (including SLA runtime):* an actual service instance is up and running; it might be adjusted to enforce an SLA
- *Service decommissioning:* the service instance is stopped and can no more be accessed by the service customer

### 3.2.3 Management Domains

Another important aspect of management is the notion of management domains. So far we distinguish two main kinds of domains: the first driven by business considerations, the second driven by technical considerations.

1. *Administrative domains* are areas of organisational coherence: for example, an independent organisation or a department that operates largely as a profit centre. Within an administrative domain, two main views can be considered:
   - The business view basically representing a sales department: that is, the activity of selling services via SLAs.

- The management view oversees all the offered or active SLAs within a certain domain and is responsible for the eventual SLA operation.

2. *Technical domains* are areas where certain kinds of resources or artifacts can be coherently managed: for example, domains for infrastructure artifacts, software artifacts, business artifacts or even subdivisions of these.

Technical domains can be understood as horizontal layers within a business/IT stack, while administrative domains relate more to vertical, cross-cutting pillars within an organisation (though they can form a hierarchy as well). Section 4 gives insight into how the notion of domains impacts the architecture.

## 3.3 Data Models

To communicate, the components of the SLA@SOI architecture make heavy use of two models that reflect the essential data structures in the system: The *SLA(T) model* (Chapter 'The SLA Model') describes SLAs for communication within and among SLA managers, as well with external providers. The *Service Construction Model* (SCM) (Chapter 'The Service Construction Meta-Model') provides and collects information necessary to create a new instance of a service (for a particular SLA). In the following, we provide a brief summary of both models.

### 3.3.1  SLA(T) model

The SLA and SLA template model (SLA(T) model) extends pure functional service descriptions to allow for the expression of non-functional service properties and QoS guarantees. The main body of the present specification defines the SLA(T) model, which allows the expression of non-functional service properties and QoS guarantees. The SLA(T) model leaves the specification of particular QoS terms open, supporting extension through standard vocabularies. A set of default QoS terms are provided as a standard vocabulary. An SLA is a set of agreements between two (or more) parties. These agreements are expressed using terms that each denote guarantees made by, or obligations on, the various parties.

### 3.3.2  Service Construction Model (SCM)

The SCM is inspired by the management of services and the SLA concepts sketched above. We introduced the SCM to ease communication between the different components responsible for core SLA management, service management, and quality evaluation of possible service offerings. Its core structure is the service hierarchy introduced in Section 3.1.

Service managers can use the SCM to manage multiple implementations of the same service. Further, the SCM allows different components to access and add information about a potential service instance.

In the following, we describe the architecture of the SLA management framework and how it makes use of the concepts presented in this section.

# 4 Architecture

## 4.1 Building Blocks

In this section, we introduce the main building blocks that constitute our framework, explain their responsibilities, show how they can be specialised for specific domains, and explain how they can be combined to serve different scenarios and setups.

**Overview**

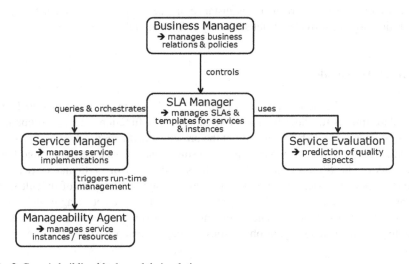

**Fig. 3** Generic building blocks and their relations.

Figure 3 gives an overview of the framework's main components and their relations. The leading component is the business manager, which is responsible for business-related information and business-driven decisions. It controls the SLA manager, which is responsible for SLA templates and actual SLAs. It uses the service manager for querying service implementations and orchestrating provisioning activities. The service manager is responsible for managing actual service implementation. It uses manageability agents to trigger runtime management activities. The SLA manager also relies on service evaluation for retrieving predictions of service qualities. More detailed discussions of these components and their relations follow below.

Taking the business-rooted ambition of an SLA management framework, the root of the management hierarchy is the *business manager* component. It is responsible for asserting overall business constraints on the system to meet business objectives and maintain customer and provider relations. To that extent, it captures knowledge about pricing schemes (including rewards, promotions and discounts), customer profile information, third-party service provider profiles and business rules for taking cost/profit-aware decisions. Business managers may contain sensitive data that must not be shared among components. The actual functionality of a business manager includes:

- searching and publishing of products
- management of customers and service providers
- negotiation and establishment of agreements/contracts with customers and service providers
- notification of bills and penalties to customers and service providers

The *SLA manager* component is responsible for managing a set of SLA templates and SLAs in its domain. It also captures knowledge about negotiation and planning goals (such as utility functions or policies). Depending on the specific context/requirements of a particular use case, a separate SLA manager may be set up for a complete organisation, a department, or for each individual service. The actual functionality of an SLA manager includes:

- searching and publishing of SLA templates
- negotiation of SLAs with customers and third parties, including conversion between different SLA formats
- SLA planning and optimisation
- SLA provisioning and adjustment

The *service manager* component is in charge of managing the elements necessary to instantiate a service. In particular, it knows about the structure of service implementations and keeps track of existing service instances. Service managers can be created for any technical domain which needs consistent management. The actual functionality of a service manager includes:

- publishing of service implementations
- maintenance of a service landscape, including elements required for instantiating a service implementation
- reservation and booking of service instances
- mediation of management/adjustment operations to service instances and manageability agents
- triggering of actual service provisioning

The *manageability agent* component acts as gateway to actual resources. It knows about the available sensors and effectors that can be used for managing a certain service instance and its resources. Manageability agents may exist per resource, per service instance, or per collection of these. The actual functionality of a manageability agent includes:

- sensing/monitoring the status of service instances and resources
- searching for and executing manageability actions

Finally, to support proactive management decisions at all levels, the framework also provides a *service evaluation* component. It relies on background information (from design-time, runtime or historical information) about the quality characteristics of services. It provides functionality for *a priori* quality evaluations of services, depending on influencing factors such as customer behavior or lower-level service qualities. Service evaluation components may exist per SLA manager or even for sets of these.

While all these components have clearly distinct responsibilities, they also need to have some common understanding of the overall problem domain.

- Service types must be commonly understood by SLA managers, service managers and service evaluation.
- The identity of service implementations must be commonly understood by service managers and service evaluation, though both components may rely on completely different data models to deal with service implementations.
- SLA terms and their quality aspects must be commonly understood by SLA managers and service evaluation.
- SLA terms and available monitoring handles must be commonly understood by SLA managers and service managers.
- The SLA negotiation process with customers and third parties must be commonly understood by business managers and SLA managers.

**Component Setups**

As stated in the design goals for the framework architecture (Section 2), a key goal is support for flexible configurations and setups where different domain cuts can be realised.

Our architecture supports cuts along the two main criteria mentioned in Section 3.2: that is, via administrative domains and technical domains. Administrative domains are characterised by having a dedicated SLA manager in charge of all the SLAs within that domain. Technical domains are characterised by having a dedicated service manager in charge of all the artifacts needed for a (set of) service implementation(s).

Figure 4 shows an example of how such a domain cut can be realised for a single service provider organisation that interacts with customers and third parties. Basically, the service provider organisation is split into two main administrative domains: one might be for application services, the other for infrastructure services.

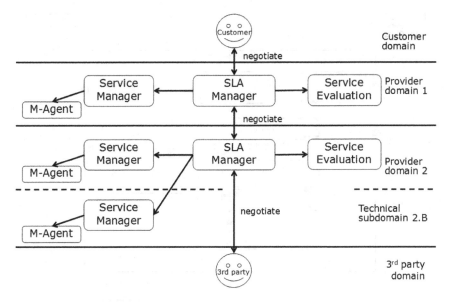

**Fig. 4** A possible domain split and component setup.

Further, there is a split into three technical domains, each represented by a service manager. For example, one might be for application artifacts, one for middleware artifacts, and one for infrastructure artifacts.

## 4.2 Top-Level Architecture

In the following, we present more detail of the top-level view of the SLA@SOI framework architecture. For its representation, we chose a simplified version of UML component diagrams. Boxes represent components and connections represent stereotyped dependencies that translate to specific sets of provided and required interfaces.

Figure 2 illustrates the main components of the SLA@SOI framework and their relationships. On the highest level, we distinguish between the core framework, service managers (infrastructure and software), deployed service instances with their manageability agents, and monitoring event channels. The core framework encapsulates all functionality related to SLA management. Infrastructure managers and software service managers contain all service-specific functionality. The deployed service instance is the actual service delivered to the customer, and is managed by the framework via manageability agents. Monitoring event channels serve as a flexible communication infrastructure that allows the framework to collect information about the status of the service instance. To achieve a good generalisation of the framework architecture, several components are realised as specialisations of

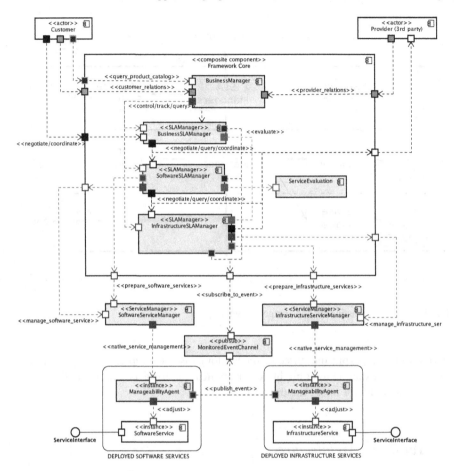

**Fig. 5** Top-level view of the SLA@SOI framework.

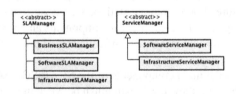

**Fig. 6** Component specialisation hierarchies.

abstract components, namely SLA manager components and service manager components. The component hierarchy assumed for the top-level view is depicted in Figure 6.

## *4.3 Main Components*

The top-level architecture comprises the building blocks introduced in Section 4.1. In the following, we describe the specific setup as well as the interactions shown in Figure 2.

The *business manager* is responsible for controlling all business information and communication with customers (<<customer_relations>>) and providers (<<provider_relations>>). For example, it realises the customer relationship management (CRM) necessary to efficiently sell the offered services. Further, the business manager governs the (business-, software-, and infrastructure-) SLA managers (<<control/track/query>>). For this purpose, SLA managers must adhere to business rules defined by the business manager (*control*) and must inform the business manager about their current status and activities (*track*).

The *(business-, software- and infrastructure-) SLA managers* are responsible for the management of all SLA-related concerns. The business SLA manager, software SLA manager, and infrastructure SLA manager are specialisations of an abstract generic SLA manager (Figure 6). SLA managers are responsible for the negotiation of SLAs, and for the management of services that are subject to the SLAs. All SLA managers can act as "service customers", negotiating SLAs with other SLA managers inside the same framework, or with external (third party) service providers (including other framework instances). As "service providers", all SLA managers can negotiate SLAs with other SLA managers in the same framework. Only the business SLA manager, however, can negotiate with customers who are external to the framework. To avoid confusion, we refer to external customers as "business customers", and use the term "product" to denote the (SLA-governed) services offered by the framework to business customers. Product descriptions are published in a "product catalogue" (accessible via <<query_product_catalog>>) maintained by the business manager. Once an SLA has been agreed with a customer, it is the responsibility of the business manager to send reports on SLA status to the customer. The <<negotiate/query/coordinate>> relation captures all framework-internal negotiation and querying interactions. These negotiations are equally used at business-level for customer interaction (<<negotiate/coordinate>>), where business-level considerations (e.g. billing) are intercepted by the business SLA manager into the negotiation protocol. Finally, all SLA managers can consult service evaluation to *a priori* evaluate the potential quality of a service (<<evaluate>>). This evaluation can be based on prediction, historical data, or predefined quality definitions, and supports the SLA manager in finding service realisations with an appropriate quality.

The *monitoring and adjustment management system* provides the underlying fabric across the different layers (i.e. across software and infrastructure layers), supporting the monitoring and management of actual service instances. The monitoring event channel is the basic component via which arbitrary monitoring events (e.g. SLO violations) can be propagated to relevant SLA managers. Access to this channel is realised via the <<publish_event>> and <<subscribe_to_event>> interaction stereotypes. Manageability agents support the actual configuration and management of service instances. Access to manageability agents for SLA managers is always mediated via a specific service manager. Due to their domain-specific nature, the interactions between service managers and manageability agents are represented by the <<native_service_management>> stereotype, which is not further refined by this architecture. It should be noted that manageability agents need not necessarily run within the same administrative domain as the service instance, but importantly, the sensors and effectors that are part of the manageability agent must reside in the same administrative domain of the service instance, and have access to their related manageability agent via some communication mechanism.

## 5 Conclusions

In this chapter, we presented a reference architecture for multi-level SLA management that supports the comprehensive management of possibly complex service stacks. SLAs are used for managing the nonfunctional aspects of the complete service life cycle. Further, SLA translations across different layers allow for consistent interlinking of complete service networks and hierarchies. The presented architecture is based on experiences gained from an SLA framework built around a specific reference application. The main achievement when compared to that work is the generalisation of concepts such that the architecture can serve a large variety of domains.

## References

[1] W. Theilmann, R. Yahyapour, and J. Butler, *Multi-level SLA Management for Service-Oriented Infrastructures.* Towards a Service-Based Internet (2008) 324–335
[2] M. Comuzzi, C. Kotsokalis, C. Rathfelder, W. Theilmann, U. Winkler, and G. Zacco, *A Framework for Multi-level SLA Management.* Proc. of 3rd Workshop on Non-Functional Properties and SLA Management in Service-Oriented Computing (NFPSLAM-SOC'09), November 23, Stockholm, Sweden

# The Open Reference Case
## A Reference Use Case for the SLA@SOI Framework

Christoph Rathfelder, Benjamin Klatt, and Giovanni Falcone

**Abstract** The Open Reference Case (ORC) is a Software as a Service (SaaS) solution supporting the sales process in supermarkets. Within the European research project SLA@SOI, the ORC is used as an open source demonstrator to highlight features offered by the SLA management framework. As per the vision of SLA@SOI, the ORC runs on a virtualised infrastructure operated by an infrastructure provider. The ORC also allows for the inclusion of services offered by external service providers, such as banks. Such external providers are used in this scenario to highlight the process of negotiating SLAs between the ORC and an external provider. More generally, the interactions defined in the ORC scenario cover the SLA negotiation phase as well as the automated provisioning of software and monitoring of SLA violations.

## 1 Background

The Open Reference Case (ORC) is used as an open source demonstrator to highlight the achievements of the European research project SLA@SOI, a key innovation of which was the SLA management framework. The ORC highlights use of the SLA management framework — including the process of SLA negotiation and renegotiation — in the context of a service-oriented retail solution that supports the sales

Christoph Rathfelder
FZI Research Center for Information Technology, Haid-und-Neu-Str. 10-14, 76131 Karlsruhe, Germany, e-mail: rathfelder@fzi.de

Benjamin Klatt
FZI Research Center for Information Technology, Haid-und-Neu-Str. 10-14, 76131 Karlsruhe, Germany, e-mail: klatt@fzi.de

Giovanni Falcone
FZI Research Center for Information Technology, Haid-und-Neu-Str. 10-14, 76131 Karlsruhe, Germany, e-mail: falcone@fzi.de

27

process in supermarkets. The ORC includes IT support for retail chains in general, covering enterprise headquarters (central management), stores (local management) and cash desks. Several shop providers, each with a certain number of stores, are connected to a single service provider, supporting the sales of goods with an IT system. This provider offers various services, such as the management of inventories, credit card payments, preferred customer club cards, and accounting. The ORC software can be operated on a virtualised infrastructure using tailored deployment options that cater to shops of varying size and with varying requirements regarding system performance.

The ORC extends the Common Component Modeling Example (CoCoME) [1], which was introduced to compare the facets of several well-known component models. CoCoME represents a trading system that deals with the various aspects of handling sales in a supermarket, including the customer interaction at the cash desk (including product scanning and payment), and registering the sale at the inventory. The CoCoME trading system also deals with ordering goods from wholesalers and generating reports.

In CoCoME, an enterprise is defined as consisting of several stores. Each enterprise has an enterprise server to which all stores are connected. An enterprise client is defined as part of the overall scenario, enabling the enterprise manager to generate several kinds of reports. To support and realise the sales process, a retail store operates a certain number of cash desks. Each store has its own central store server, which is connected to each cash desk of the store as well as to the enterprise server. The cash desk is the place where the cashier scans the goods that the customer wants to buy and where payment is made (either by credit card or cash). A number of hardware components are associated with a single cash desk (cash box, barcode scanner ... ). The central unit of each cash desk is the cash desk PC, which links all components to each other and calls the services provided by the retail solution provider.

## 2 Adapted ORC Use Case Scenario

The ORC is an extension of the CoCoME implementation, realising a service-oriented retail solution that can be used in a trading system of a supermarket to handle the sales and stocking processes. It includes IT support for retail chains in general, covering enterprise headquarters (central management), stores (local management) and cash desks. The use of the ORC as SaaS promises several benefits, including reduced operational costs for the supermarket and reduced customer waiting times at the cash desk. Thus the two most important quality characteristics to consider in SLAs are cost and the completion time of service invocations. The ORC supports the payment process at the cash desk; thus the reliability of services plays an important role and this should be reflected in the SLAs. From the service provider's point of view, the system load induced by a certain customer volume needs to be specified and limited. Thus knowledge of expected customer volume is required to determine the required infrastructure services. For this reason, an additional important quality characteristic is system load, which is measured in invocations per second. In using the ORC as SaaS, we use a slightly adapted scenario presented in more detail below.

## 2.1 Stakeholders

To highlight the features of the SLA@SOI framework, the original CoCoME scenario has been modified to create a SaaS scenario. An overview of the involved stakeholders and their bindings during runtime are given in Figure 1.

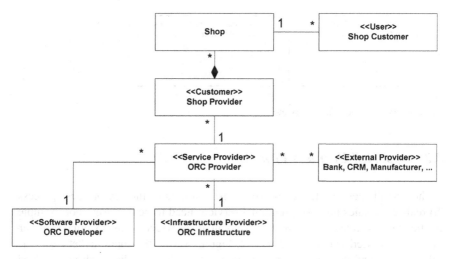

**Fig. 1** Adapted CoCoME scenario.

A key element — the ORC provider — is added as a single service provider and connected to several shop providers. The ORC provider (service provider) enables the shop providers to access several additional services, such as management of inventories, credit card payments, preferred customer club cards, accounting and so on. To provide services connected to banks, wholesale centers, or customer relationship management (CRM), the service provider can either use its own realisations or make use of external services. The ORC service is running on top of a virtualised IT infrastructure — the ORC infrastructure — that is offered by an additional provider. To complete the scenario, we assume the ORC has been designed and implemented by an independent software provider, namely, the ORC developer.

In Figure2, we present a view of the structure in a concrete scenario, where we assume that the service provider only makes use of a bank service as an external service. To provide other 'additional services' the service provider makes use of its own realisations.

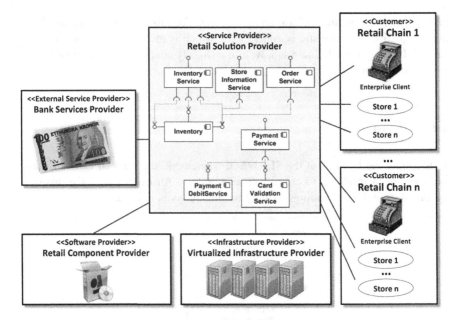

**Fig. 2** Open Reference Case overview.

## 2.2 Supported Business Process

In the overall scenario, the sales process is identified as the key business process. To realise the sales process, additional services need to be accessed. For example, the functions ValidateCard and DebitAmount are provided by the external bank service and accessed via the ORC service. Figure3 shows the supermarket cash desk sales process and its sub-processes. The process starts when the goods are scanned. The barcode of each good is scanned and the GetProductDetails operation of the InventoryService is called. If the detected product code is correct, the stock level is updated. If not, the product code must be entered manually. After that, payment by credit card is handled automatically. The card is first scanned and then validated using the CardValidationService. If the card is valid, payment is completed using the PaymentDebitService. If not, the card is rejected and the payment must be done manually using cash.

## 3 ORC Architecture and Services

The ORC architecture is described in more detail below, using the UML 2.0 syntax and giving a structural view. Figure 4 gives an overview of the implemented

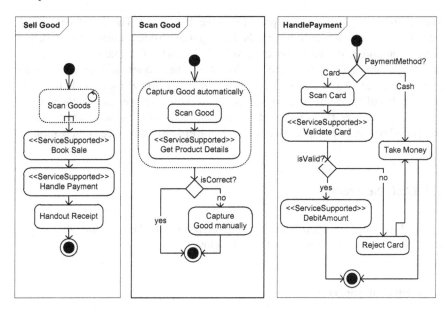

**Fig. 3** The sales process.

system, containing the legacy CoCoME components and the additional web-service components.

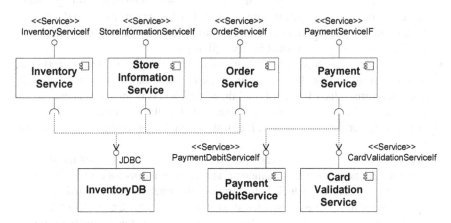

**Fig. 4** Architectural overview.

The five components `InventoryService`, `StoreInformation-Service`, `OrderService`, `PaymentDebitService` and `Card-ValidationService` implement web-service interfaces. `Inventory-Service`, `StoreInformationService`, and `OrderService` require the functionality provided by the legacy CoCoME component `Inventory`.

The `Inventory` component provides three interfaces: The interface `Cash-DeskConnectorIf` defines a method for getting product information (such as description and price) based on the product's barcode. The interfaces `StoreIf` and `ReportingIf` deliver the results of database queries. The components `PaymentDebitService` and `CardValidationService` provide functionality for handling credit card payments. These latter services are often provided by a bank; however, they can also be implemented locally. These two services are comprised within PaymentService, which is a BPEL-based service composition.

## 3.1 ORC Services

The web-services and their interfaces — which form the heart of the ORC implementation — are described in more detail below.

### 3.1.1 InventoryService

`InventoryServiceInterface` defines operations for getting product information and changing prices. It is used to get the current price of a product, check its availability in the inventory, and account for its removal from the inventory after sale. The interface consists of five operations:

- `getAllProductsWithOptionalStockItem` determines all products within the portfolio of a given store, the supplier for each of those products, and the number of each product in stock. It returns a list of products, their suppliers, and the number of each product in stock (if any).
- `getProductsWithLowStock` determines those products that are nearly out of stock, meaning that the number in stock is lower than 10% of the maximal stock. It returns a list of products and their stock levels in the given store.
- `getAllProducts` determines all products within the portfolio of a given store and the supplier for each of them. It returns a list of all products and their suppliers.
- `changePrice` updates the sales price of a stocked item. It needs the stocked item and the new price as parameters, and returns an instance of `Product-WithStockItemTO`, which holds product information and updated price information for the stocked item, identified by the parameter `StockItemTO`.
- `getProductDetails` uses a barcode to determine the products currently in the stock of the store. It returns a `ProductWithStockItemTO` instance, which contains the identified product linked to a stocked item in the store.

### 3.1.2 StoreInformationService

`StoreInformationServiceInterface` provides an operation for getting information about a store. The `getStoreInformation` operation returns a transfer object, which includes information about the store and the enterprise it belongs to. This information is stored within the system during the initialisation and setup phase.

### 3.1.3 OrderService

`OrderService` is used to control the ordering of products that run out of stock. It is also used to log the receipt of ordered products. The `OrderServiceInterface` consists of two operations:

- `rollInReceivedOrder` updates the store inventory after order delivery. It adds the number of ordered items to the number of stocked items, setting the delivery date as the date of method execution. It requires an instance of `Complex-OrderTO`, which contains the order that is rolled in as a parameter.
- `orderProducts` creates a list of orders from different suppliers for an initial list of products to be ordered by a store. The product order is kept and the ordering date is set as the date of method execution. The method requires an instance of `ComplexOrderTO`, which contains all products to be ordered and returns a list of orders, one for each supplier involved.

### 3.1.4 CardValidationService

`CardValidationService` is one of two services that might be provided by an external banking provider; its functionality is that of credit card validation. `CardValidationServiceInterface` comprises one operation, called `validateCard`, and requires a personal identification number (PIN) and some information about the card. The method returns a transaction ID that can be used to debit the payment.

### 3.1.5 PaymentDebitService

`PaymentDebitService` is the second service that might be offered by an external banking provider. `PaymentDebitServiceInterface` provides an operation `debitCard` for debiting payments. This operation is used to debit a bank account. Possible return values are OK, NOT_ENOUGH_MONEY and TRANSACTION_ID_NOT_VALID. Requires a `TransactionID` that is issued with a valid PIN.

### 3.1.6 PaymentService

PaymentService is a service composition which consists of the two services: Card-
ValidationService and PaymentDebitService, implemented as a WS-
BPEL [2] process. PaymentService is deployed on a runtime web-service composition middleware. The sub-process PaymentService includes card validation and
debit payment and is required to support the entire sale process.

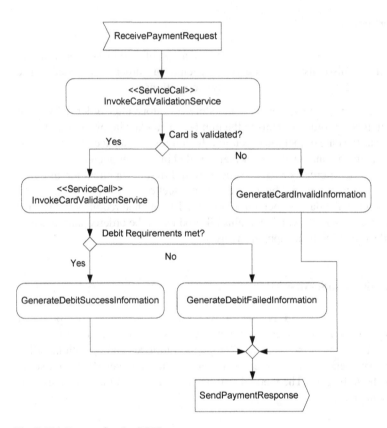

**Fig. 5** The PaymentService BPEL process.

As depicted in Figure 5, as soon as the payment request is received, an attempt
is made to validate the provided card information. If card validation fails, Card-
InvalidInformation is generated. If the card is validated, the next step is
to determine whether the debit requirement on the card is fulfilled. If the requirement is fulfilled, PaymentIsSuccessful information is generated. Otherwise,
DebitFailed information is generated. All generated information is sent to the
cashier as the PaymentResponse. Thus credit card payment requests can be automatically processed in this way.

# 4 ORC Deployment Options

The ORC software solution can be deployed on a single machine or distributed over two or three machines. This allows selection of the most appropriate option, depending on extra-functional requirements such as completion time, cost and the expected volume of customers. It is also possible to use the ORC as a multi-tenant system that handles several different shops on a single ORC instance. Figure 6 illustrates some of these deployment options. Although the services are quite independent, there are some constraints on deployment options. For example, the three services `InventoryService`, `StoreInformationServcie`, and `OrderService` must be deployed on the same machine, as they are service wrappers for software components running behind and share some functionality and configurations. The `CardValidationService` and `PaymentDebitService` are also bundled in one deployment unit, as card validation and debiting are always provided by the same institution and their separation makes no sense. Please note that in the SLA@SOI framework we use virtualised machines; this allows deployment of new instances by simply copying existing images and starting them, which is much easier than manual installation on real machines. However, it is possible to install the ORC manual without virtualisation.

- **AllInOne**: This deployment option comprises a single virtual machine image that contains the database (DB), the basic services, and the composite services (including the ORC application logic).
- **SeparatedDB**: This option comprises two virtual machine images: one provides an application server with all deployed services and the other hosts the DB.
- **SeparatedBPELEngine**: Since the DB consumes only a small part of the available CPU resources and most CPU power is consumed in the web-service container and BPEL engine, this deployment option separates the BPEL engine onto an individual virtual machine. Basic services and the DB are deployed on a second virtual machine.
- **ThreeLayer**: This deployment option combines the two previous ones, using three virtual machines to separate the DB, BPEL engine and basic services.
- **ExternalServices**: The ORC can also be used to demonstrate the involvement of an external service provider. The two services CardValidationService and PaymentDebitService can be transferred to an external virtual machine. In this way, they can be used as if they are being provided by an external service provider, including the negotiation of SLAs with this external service provider.

# 5 Interactions with the SLA@SOI Framework

In the ORC scenario, several interactions are defined to demonstrate the features of an SLA management framework. The interactions described below cover SLA

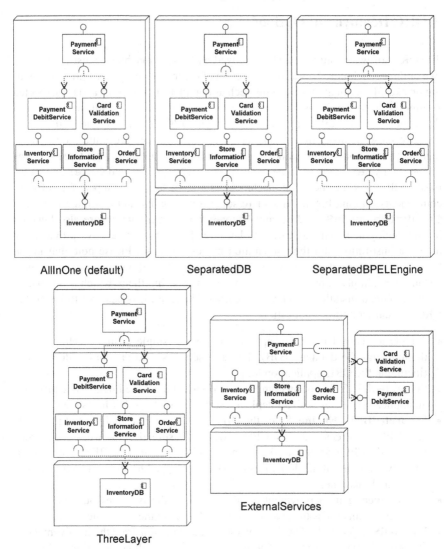

**Fig. 6** ORC deployment options.

negotiation, the automated provisioning of software, and the monitoring of SLAs and their violations.

## 5.1 Discovery Interaction

In the discovery interaction (Figure 7), a shop provider queries the framework to obtain products that satisfied his requirements. The shop provider must be registered into the framework, then he can interact with it for the operation `queryCatalogue`.

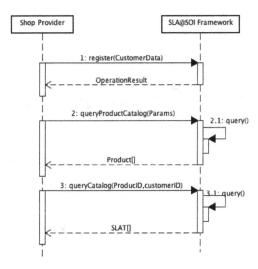

**Fig. 7** Product discovery interaction.

The discovery interaction contains the following steps:

- **customerRegister**: The framework receives customer data and registers it on the customer database of the framework.
- **queryProductCatalog**: The shop provider calls the framework with the request. The framework will search in the product catalogue for products that fulfill the requirements of the customer and will return them.
- **queryCatalog**: The framework searches within this catalogue for products that support the given customer requirements and returns a list of product SLA templates (SLATs).
- **customerStarts**: The customer begins the provisioning interaction to purchase products he is interested in.

## 5.2 Provisioning Interaction

The provisioning interaction (Figure 8) focuses on the negotiation and provisioning capabilities provided by the SLA@SOI framework.

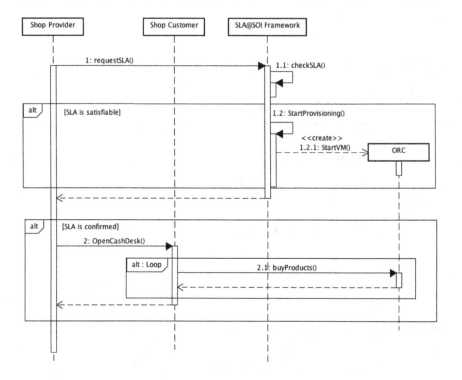

**Fig. 8** Provisioning interaction.

The provisioning interaction comprises the following steps:

- **requestSLA**: The shop provider sends a specific SLA request to the SLA@SOI framework. This step can be extended, for example, by browsing SLATs.
- **checkSLA**: The framework checks if the requested SLA can be fulfilled. This step can include different negotiation processes for other SLAs, planning or prediction invocations, and selection of deployment options. If the checkSLA step detects that the SLA cannot be fulfilled and should be rejected, the rejection message is sent back as a response to the requestSLA request.
- **StartProvisioning**: If the result of the previous step is that the SLA can be fulfilled, provisioning is started. This can include the confirmation of other software or infrastructure SLAs, or the planning of schedules.
- **StartVM**: The virtual machine with the deployed ORC instance is started and the endpoint address is returned to the shop provider.

To demonstrate that the provisioning process was executed successfully, this scenario includes two additional steps. If the SLA@SOI framework confirms the SLA, then normal usage of the ORC can start.

- **OpenCashDesk**: After a successful SLA negotiation, the shop provider can open the cash desks and customers can start buying products. The shop provider must control customer volume to ensure it does not exceed the maximal load specified in the SLA.
- **BuyProducts**: In an endless loop, customers wait in front of a cash desk and then buy and pay for their products using credit cards or cash (as previously explained in the overall ORC business process).

### 5.3 Monitoring Interaction

The monitoring interaction (Figure 5) focuses on the demonstration of capabilities that are useful when SLAs are already negotiated and the services are running. Different capabilities can be shown in this interaction (e.g. detection and prediction of different types of SLA violations, different adjustment actions, etc.).

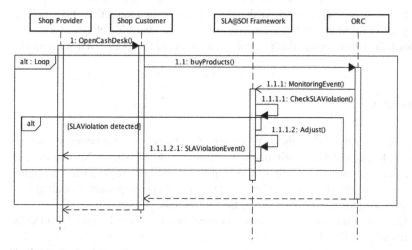

**Fig. 9** Monitoring interaction.

As per the provisioning interaction, this interaction includes customers buying products in the shop to induce a system load. In contrast to the provisioning interaction, the customers arrive at different rates, thus inducing different load situations on the ORC. This might be used to under- or overload the system.

The additional steps are:

- **MonitoringEvent**: The manageability instrumentation sends service invocation start and stop events to the monitoring infrastructure of the SLA@SOI framework.
- **CheckSLAViolation**: Based on the received events, the SLA is monitored and checked. If an SLA violation is detected, an adjustment within the SLA@SOI framework is started.
- **Adjust**: Based on the type of SLA violation and eventually additional information, a specific adjustment action is determined and performed.
- **SLAViolationEvent**: The shop provider is sent an event informing him of this violation and can view the penalty thus generated.


# 6 Conclusion

In this chapter we introduced the Open Reference Case, which is the reference use case of the SLA@SOI framework. The ORC is a Software as a Service (SaaS) solution that supports the sales process in supermarkets. Within this book, the ORC is used as a running example to explain different features of the SLA@SOI framework. The ORC consists of several services that can be combined in different deployment options. It is optimised for operation on virtualised on-demand images, which is the vision of the SLA@SOI project. With a description of the interactions between the ORC system, the SLA@SOI framework, and the customer, this chapter forms the basis for following chapters that present the internals of the SLA@SOI framework.


# References

[1] Herold, S., Klus, H., Welsch, Y., Deiters, C., Rausch, A., Reussner, R., Krogmann, K., Koziolek, H., Mirandola, R., Hummel, B., Meisinger, M., and Pfaller, C.: The Common Component Modeling Example, *Lecture Notes in Computer Science*, vol. 5153, chap. CoCoME – The Common Component Modeling Example, pp. 16–53. Springer-Verlag Berlin Heidelberg (2008)
[2] OASIS: Web services business process execution language version 2.0. OASIS Standard (2007). URL http://docs.oasis-open.org/wsbpel/2.0/OS/wsbpel-v2.0-OS.html

# Part II
# Foundations for Service Level Agreements

# The SLA Model

Keven T. Kearney and Francesco Torelli

**Abstract** This chapter describes the SLA model that has been developed by the SLA@SOI project. It defines a syntax for machine-readable Service Level Agreements (SLAs) and SLA templates (SLA(T)). Historically, the SLA was developed as a generalisation and refinement of the web service-specific XML standards: WS-Agreement, WSLA, and WSDL. Instead of web services, however, the SLA model deals with services in general, and instead of XML, it is language independent. The SLA model provides a specification of SLA(T) content at a fine-grained level of detail, which is both richly expressive and inherently extensible: supporting controlled customisation to arbitrary domain-specific requirements. The model has been applied to a range of industrial use-cases, including: ERP hosting, Enterprise IT, live-media streaming, and health-care provision. At the time of writing, the abstract syntax has been realised in concrete form as a Java API, XML-Schema, and BNF Grammar.

## 1 Introduction

This chapter describes the SLA Model employed within SLA@SOI. An SLA is an agreement between a service provider and service customer about the required quality-of-service (QoS) characteristics of some service(s) delivered by the provider to the customer. Properly speaking, the agreement *as such* is the intangible understanding, or accord, that exists between the provider and customer. The SLA Model is not concerned with the intentional aspects of an agreement. It is only concerned

Keven T. Kearney

Engineering Ingegneria Informatica spa, Via Riccardo Morandi, 32, 00148 Roma, Italy, e-mail: keven.kearney@eng.it

Francesco Torelli

Engineering Ingegneria Informatica spa, Via Riccardo Morandi, 32, 00148 Roma, Italy, e-mail: francesco.torelli@eng.it with modelling the *physical* document that serves as the formal, concrete representation of an agreement. The SLA Model is therefore a *document model*. In particular, it is an *abstract syntax*, specifying, in a language independent manner, the formal *serialised content* of SLA and SLA Template (SLAT) documents. The SLA Model assumes the basic domain concepts of 'SLA', 'SLA Template' and 'service' described elsewhere in this book, but it is *not* a conceptual model of this domain. For present purposes, an SLA is a document, the formal syntactic content of which is specified in an abstract way by the SLA Model presented here.

The key objective in developing the SLA Model is to meet two ostensibly conflicting requirements of SLA@SOI: On one side, the model needs to support the generic capabilities encapsulated by the 'Generic SLA Manager' (GSLAM; described in Chapter 'GSLAM – The Anatomy of the Generic SLA Manager'), requiring that QoS guarantees and party obligations be specified in a domain-*independent* manner at a fine-grained level of detail. On the other side, however, in order to meet the diverse domain-*specific* requirements of the SLA@SOI test-bed scenarios and real-world applications, the model must remain open to extension and customisation.

The domain-*independent* operations of the GSLAM span the entire SLA lifecycle and include:

- quality-of-service (QoS) based service discovery,
- SLA negotiation, planning and optimisation of service delivery systems to achieve the goals expressed in SLAs, and
- the subsequent monitoring and potential modification of these systems to ensure these goals are indeed satisfied.

While complex and diverse, these capabilities can all, in essence, be characterised as entailing some form of multiple constraint satisfaction, where the constraints to be satisfied are the QoS guarantees expressed in SLAs. Accordingly, the SLA Model must provide a common, domain-independent means for the detailed and precise expression of these *constraints*. At the same time, however, it is impossible to foresee and enumerate all the possible requirements of domain-*specific* applications. Thus the SLA Model also needs to support the definition and expression of custom constraints.

To meet these conflicting requirements, the SLA Model is designed as a domain-independent model of SLA(T)[1] content grounded in an *abstract constraint language*, the concrete elements of which are formally specified by 'plug-in' domain-specific vocabularies. The constraint language provides a consistent, fine-grained language supporting operations research, while the vocabularies provide for controlled extensibility.

Historically, the SLA Model has been developed as a generalisation and refinement of the web-service specific XML standards WS-Agreement [1], WSLA [2], and WSDL [3] abstracting the notion of 'web-service' to the more generic 'service', and eliminating the unnecessary restriction to XML as a representational format. The SLA Model thus supports the formulation of SLAs in *any* language for

---

[1] We use the acronym SLA(T) to refer collectively to SLAs and SLATs

*any* service. To support as wide a range of domain-specific scenarios as possible, the SLA Model only specifies the *minimal* content of SLA(T)s, encapsulating only those aspects of SLA(T)s necessary for the generic functions of the GSLAM.

This chapter is organised as follows: Section 2 introduces the basic modelling approach and provides foundational definitions. Sections 3 to 6 then describe, in order, the content of SLA(T)s, service interface specifications, the abstract constraint language, and domain-specific vocabularies. Section 7 closes the chapter with a detailed walk-through of an example SLA Template represented in concrete XML syntax.

## 2 Basic Concepts

The SLA Model is an abstract syntax specifying the formal content of serialised SLA(T) documents. In purely formal terms, we define a document in generic terms as *an hierarchical organisation of symbols*. This book, for example, is a document comprised of a sequence of letters and punctuation marks (the symbols), hierarchically divided into chapters, sections, subsections, paragraphs, and so on. The SLA Model is a *syntax* because it serves to specify the *organisation of symbols* in an SLA document, but it is *abstract* in that it leaves unspecified the particular symbols used to instantiate this organisation.

We will refer to any organisation of symbols as an *expression* (this sentence, for example, is an expression), and to classes of expressions as *expression-types*. The SLA Model is specified in terms of expression-types. Formally, we treat each expression-type as a *set* whose members are the expressions which instantiate that type. In the remainder of this chapter, we will use the terms *type* and *expression-type* interchangeably. To avoid ambiguity, we will also use *token* (meaning an 'instance of a type') as synonymous with *expression*.

The SLA Model also draws a distinction between tokens *per se* and tokens that are *references to tokens*. Specifically, if $\mathbf{T}$ is an expression-type, then:

- $\mathbf{T}$ : denotes the set of tokens of type $\mathbf{T}$,
- $\uparrow\mathbf{T}$ : denotes the set of references to tokens of type $\mathbf{T}$,
- $\Uparrow\mathbf{T}$ : denotes the set of references to (subtypes of) type $\mathbf{T}$, while
- $(\uparrow)\mathbf{T}$ : denotes either a token, or a reference to a token, of type $\mathbf{T}$.

The universal type, which is the set of all possible expressions, is denoted by the symbol $\mathbf{L}^*$ (where 'L' may be read as 'legal expressions', or simply 'language'). The asterix is used here, and in subsequent type names, to indicate that the type is abstract (meaning that it cannot be directly instantiated).

To capture the hierarchical organisation of documents, we introduce a first high-level expression-type, $\mathbf{E}^* \subset \mathbf{L}^*$, denoting a class of *entity expressions*, each token of which is just a collection of key/value attribute pairs. Attribute values can be any kind of expression, including other entity expressions, which thus permits the hierarchical nesting of entities. Formally:

**E\*** ⊂ **V\*** : each token is an unordered collection of ordered key/value attribute pairs $<k,v>$, where: $k$ ∈ **NAME** is the name (key) of the attribute, and $v$ ∈ **L\*** gives the attribute's value.

The **NAME** type referred to in this definition is a *datatype*, in this case denoting a class of *simple names*. All datatypes belong to a second high-level expression-type, **V\*** ⊂ **L\***, denoting a class of *value* expressions. In particular, a datatype is a specialisation of a generic **Constant\*** ⊂ **V\*** type denoting constant values (e.g. Boolean values ('true' or 'false') or metric quantities ('4 s', '10 bytes', etc.), web and e-mail addresses, and so on). We will describe **V\***, and explain datatypes in more detail, in Section 5. Additional datatypes will be introduced in the text as the need arises.

Every document is an entity expression, that is, a token of type **E\***. From the definition above, this means that a document is just an ordered collection of key/value attributes. In order to specify a document, therefore, we need to specify the particular *entity-expression-types* — i.e. subtypes of **E\***, henceforth just 'entity-type' — from which the document is composed. As a first step, we introduce a generic *document*-type, encapsulating the common attributes of all documents. We define this document-type as follows (the notation is explained below):

**Document\*** ⊂ E\*
   *vocabularies* ⊂ (↑)Vocabulary $_{[0+]}$

The first line of this definition declares **Document\*** as an expression-type that specialises (i.e. is a subset of) the type **E\***. Each subsequent line defines a key/value attribute pair, or *attribute-type*. In this case, there is only one attribute-type, whose key is 'vocabularies' and whose value-type (denoted by the ⊂ relation) is an array of 0+ (*zero or more*) (↑)**Vocabulary** expressions (i.e. either tokens or references to tokens of the type **Vocabulary**). The type **Vocabulary** is the generic entity-type for all vocabulary documents, and will be explained in detail in Section 6. For now, it suffices to state that a vocabulary is a collection of expression-type definitions. Semantically, the *vocabularies* attribute of a **Document\*** token lists all the vocabularies required to specify, and hence validate, the content of that **Document\*** token.

To specify an SLA, we will also require two further entity-types — **NamedEntity\*** and **Macro** — which have the following definitions:

**NamedEntity\*** ⊂ E\*
   *name* ⊂ NAME $_{[1]}$

**Macro** ⊂ NamedEntity\*
   *expression* ⊂ V\* $_{[1]}$

A **NamedEntity\*** token is simply an entity expression which carries a single *name* attribute, the value of which can be used to refer to the token from other parts of the document. **Macro** inherits the *name* attribute from **NamedEntity\***, and also carries a second *expression* attribute, whose value can be any token of type **V\***. A **Macro** token serves a similar purpose to a **NamedEntity\*** token, but this time its *name* value, when used as a reference, is always interpreted as referring to the value of the token's *expression* attribute, rather than the token itself. A **Macro** token with the *name* 'X' and *expression* 'abcdef', for example, permits the expression 'X' to be used in place of 'abcdef'. Macros are essentially a convenience feature, providing a means to decompose complex value expressions, and hence improve readability.

The next section builds on these basic definitions to specify the content of SLA(T) documents.

# 3 SLAs and SLA Templates

Historically, the high-level structure of an SLA(T), as defined by the SLA Model, has its roots in, and still maintains much in common with, WS-Agreement. Briefly, an SLAT is a document which comprises three sections, describing:

- the *parties* to the agreement,
- the relevant services, specified in terms of their functional *interfaces*, and
- the *agreement terms*, including *quality-of-service* (QoS) guarantees and other party obligations.

In formal terms, this document structure is captured by the following entity-type definition:

> **SLAT** $\subset$ Document*
>    *parties* $\subset$ Party $_{[2+]}$
>    *interfaceDeclrs* $\subset$ InterfaceDeclr $_{[1+]}$
>    *agreementTerms* $\subset$ AgreementTerm $_{[1+]}$
>    *macros* $\subset$ Macro $_{[0+]}$

The types **Party**, **InterfaceDeclr** (interface declaration) and **AgreementTerm** are all entity-types which we will define formally in the subsections below.

The SLAT entity-type also includes an optional *macros* attribute. Although macros are essentially a convenience feature (as described earlier), their essentially symbolic (referential) properties can be exploited to serve more significant purposes. In SLA(T)s we exploit *macros* in order to encode customer *options*. This is done by introducing a **Macro** subtype, **Customisable**, defined as follows:

> **Customisable** $\subset$ Macro
>    *domain* $\subset$ Domain $_{[1]}$

The **Domain** type is part of the abstract constraint language and will be defined formally in Section 5.1. For now, it suffices to state that the *domain* attribute specifies a set of alternative values, with the value of the *expression* attribute then denoting a particular selection from these alternatives. In an SLAT this selection is interpreted as the 'default option', while in SLAs it is interpreted as the 'option chosen by the customer'. The example SLAT in Section 7 illustrates this use of the **Customisable** macro.

An SLA document has the same structure as an SLAT, but with additional attributes giving the time at which the SLA was agreed, its effective lifespan, and a reference to the template (if any) from which it was derived. To denote a specific point-in-time, or time-stamp (e.g. 'Wed Dec 15 18:38:0.0 CET'), we introduce a **DATETIME** datatype. For the template reference we use a reference type (as explained in the previous section), in this case ↑**SLAT**. An SLA document can then be modelled formally as:

> **SLA** ⊂ SLAT
>    *agreedAt* ⊂ DATETIME $_{[1]}$
>    *effectiveFrom* ⊂ DATETIME $_{[1]}$
>    *effectiveUntil* ⊂ DATETIME $_{[1]}$
>    *template* ⊂ ↑SLAT $_{[0..1]}$

These two definitions completely capture the high-level structure of SLAs and SLATs. In the following subsections we move stepwise through the document hierarchy to specify SLA(T) content in more detail.

## 3.1 SLA(T) Parties

Information about a particular agreement party (e.g. the service provider, or the service customer) is captured using a **Party** entity-type, which is a concrete specialisation of a more generic **Actor*** entity-type. The relevant definitions are:

> **Actor*** ⊂ NamedEntity*
>
> **Party** ⊂ Actor*
>    *role* ⊂ ENUM $_{[1]}$
>    *operatives* ⊂ Operative $_{[0+]}$

The *role* attribute of **Party** serves to identify the role played by the party in the agreement. Typically, this role will be either 'service provider' or 'service customer', but there may be other roles peculiar to specific domains. Within any given domain, however, there will only be a handful of valid roles. As such, we need a mechanism by which we can state that the value of an attribute will be drawn from a limited set of *domain-specific* alternatives. The **ENUM** datatype, denoting an *enumerated* list, serves this purpose (the enumerated items themselves are specified in domain-specific vocabularies using **DataValue** tokens, described in Section 6).

Conceptually, each party to an SLA may be acting as an agent, or proxy, *on behalf of others*. A company executive, for example, can sign a contract for a catering service on behalf of the company's employees, who are the end consumers proper of the service. In the SLA Model, the individuals, if any, represented by a party are referred to as 'operatives'. A single SLA(T) may offer different QoS guarantees to different categories of operative, with each category described by an **Operative** entity-type expression:

**Operative** ⊂ Actor*

Note that both **Party** and **Operative** specialise the abstract **Actor\*** type, and thus describe SLA 'actors'. As with all definitions in the SLA\* model, the **Party** and **Operative** definitions are intended to capture only the minimal information and/or distinctions required to specify the agreement terms. It is expected that domain-specific vocabularies will extend these actor definitions to add more detailed information.

## 3.2 SLA(T) Interface Declarations

All information about the functional capabilities of a service is captured in the form of an **Interface** entity-type, a detailed description of which will be given later in Section 4. For the moment, it is sufficient to note that the **Interface** type essentially encapsulates the information found in traditional 'service descriptions' (in particular, WSDL documents). What is important in an SLA(T) is that all the relevant interfaces are *declared*, and this is achieved using an **InterfaceDeclr** entity-type, which has the following definition (the parent **Service\*** type will also be defined in Section 4):

**InterfaceDeclr** ⊂ Service*
  *provider* ⊂ ↑Actor* $_{[1]}$
  *consumers* ⊂ ↑Actor* $_{[1+]}$
  *endpoints* ⊂ Endpoint $_{[1+]}$
  *interface* ⊂ (↑)Interface $_{[1]}$

Each **InterfaceDeclr** entry in an SLA(T) asserts an obligation on the part of one of the SLA(T) actors, as given by the *provider* attribute, to provide specific functional capabilities to one or more other actors, given by the *consumers* attribute. Note that both *provider* and *consumers* attributes accept references to *any* actor — i.e. to *any* **Party** or **Operative** — regardless of that actor's role in the agreement. It may be, for example, that we wish to oblige a service provider to send regular status reports to the service customer, a prerequisite for which is that the *customer* provides a suitable interface for receiving these reports.

In addition to specifying the relevant actors, each **InterfaceDeclr** also enumerates one or more *endpoints*, each of which provides a *location* (address) and a communications *protocol* by which interface operations may be invoked:

**Endpoint** ⊂ NamedEntity*

$protocol \subset$ ENUM $_{[1]}$
$location \subset$ TEXT $_{[0..1]}$

Just as with the **Party** *role* attribute (Section 3.1 above), the **ENUM** value-type defined for the *protocol* attribute indicates that values will be drawn from some limited set of *domain-specific* alternatives, such as 'SOAP', 'HTTP', 'e-mail', 'voice-telephony', 'SMS', and so on. The choice of protocol also determines the appropriate form for *location* values. For example, for 'e-mail', an e-mail address is required, while for 'voice-telephony', the location would be a telephone number. Accordingly, we define the value-type of the *location* attribute as **TEXT**, a datatype denoting some opaque string constant. Note that the *location* attribute is optional, since it is not necessarily the case that locations can be fixed in advance.

Finally, the interface that is the subject of the declaration is given by the *interface* attribute, whose value may be an embedded **Interface** document, or more typically, a reference to an **Interface** document accessible from some external source. Note that several endpoints may be defined for a single interface, and that the same interface may appear in multiple interface declarations.

## 3.3 SLA(T) Agreement Terms

The agreement terms section of an SLA(T) specifies the QoS guarantees and other party obligations that form the substantive content of the agreement. An SLA(T) may contain multiple agreement terms, each of which can define multiple guarantees effective under varying conditions. The **AgreementTerm** entity-type is defined as follows:

**AgreementTerm** $\subset$ NamedEntity*
    *pre* $\subset$ Constraint* $_{[0..1]}$
    *macros* $\subset$ Macro $_{[0+]}$
    *guarantees* $\subset$ Guarantee* $_{[1+]}$

The *pre* attribute specifies (optional) *pre*-conditions on the agreement term, defining the conditions under which the agreement term is effective. (If none are given the agreement term is always effective.) These *pre*-conditions take the form of a **Constraint*** expression, which is part of the *abstract constraint language* and will be explained in detail in Section 5.1. The *macros* attribute is provided for convenience or for encoding agreement-term-specific options (*cf.* the use of the **Customisable** macro described earlier).

The most significant part of an agreement term are its guarantees, which come in two forms: guaranteed *states* and guaranteed *actions*. Formally, we first define an abstract **Guarantee*** type to capture the common attributes of both states and actions; namely, these are a reference to the actor obligated to ensure the guarantee is satisfied, and an optional **Constant\*** (described in Section 5.2) serving as a domain-specific indication of the guarantee's priority:

> **Guarantee\*** $\subset$ NamedEntity\*
>    *priority* $\subset$ Constant\* $_{[0..1]}$
>    *obligated* $\subset$ ↑Actor\* $_{[1]}$

A guaranteed *state* describes some state of affairs that the obligated actor is responsible for maintaining. Typically, this will be a QoS constraint, such as *completion time of service X is less than 5 s* or *service X has greater than 90% availability*. We refer to this state of affairs as the guarantee's *post*-condition (since it represents the desired effect of the guarantee). To allow for multiple guaranteed states effective under different contingencies, an optional *pre*-condition is also permitted. Thus a guaranteed state is a **Guarantee\*** with additional *pre* and *post* constraints:

> **State** $\subset$ Guarantee\*
>    *pre* $\subset$ Constraint\* $_{[0..1]}$
>    *post* $\subset$ Constraint\* $_{[1]}$

A guaranteed *action*, instead, describes an obligation on an actor to perform (or refrain from performing) some specific action under specific conditions. Simple examples include obligations on the service provider to send periodic reports to the customer, or to pay penalties in the case of SLA violations. The description of a guaranteed action entails four elements:

- a 'policy' stating whether the action is mandatory, forbidden or optional,
- a specification of the (class of) events which *trigger* (or, depending on policy, *inhibit*) the action, referred to as the guaranteed action's *pre*-condition,
- a *time limit* within which the action must be performed (or during which the action is prohibited),
- a description of the action itself, which leads to the guaranteed action's *post*-condition,

The entity-type definition encapsulating this information is as follows:

> **Action** $\subset$ Guarantee\*
>    *policy* $\subset$ ENUM $_{[1]}$
>    *pre* $\subset$ ↑EventClass\* $_{[1]}$
>    *limit* $\subset$ DURATION $_{[1]}$
>    *post* $\subset$ ActionDef\* $_{[1]}$

Formally, the action's *pre*-condition (trigger) is given as a *reference to* an **EventClass\***, identifying a class of events. The SLA Model defines several classes of event, the simplest of which are **DATETIME** constants (i.e. time-stamps). Additional classes of event can be defined by domain-specific vocabularies (Section 6).

The action's *post*-condition, instead, is given as an **ActionDef\***, which is essentially an empty placeholder to be filled by domain-specific action descriptions:

> **ActionDef\*** $\subset$ E\*

By way of illustration, the SLA Model defines an **ActionDef\*** subtype representing a 'payment', i.e. a transfer of economic value. Since the actor obliged to make the payment is already given (see *Guarantee\**), the formal definition of a payment need only identify the recipient and the value:

> **Payment** $\subset$ ActionDef\*
>    *recipient* $\subset$ ↑Actor\* $_{[1]}$
>    *value* $\subset$ V\* $_{[1]}$

Other action **ActionDef\*** subtypes defined by the SLA Model are:

- **Invocation** : denoting the invocation of a specific interface operation,
- **Termination** : denoting the termination of an SLA,
- **Workflow** : denoting a composition of actions.

The example SLA Template presented in Section 7 illustrates the use of both guaranteed states and actions.

# 4 Interface Specifications

The functional capabilities of services are captured as functional interface specifications. The notion of 'interface' employed in the SLA Model is essentially a generalisation of WSDL 2.0, abstracting from web-service to 'service', and from the use of XML as concrete syntax. Accordingly, an interface is essentially a collection of named *operations*. For modularity, each interface specification may be a document in its own right, and interfaces may obtain specialisation hierarchies (i.e. extension, with operation inheritance). The **Interface** entity-type is defined as follows:

> **Interface** $\subset$ Document\*
>    *extended* $\subset$ ↑Interface $_{[0+]}$
>    *operations* $\subset$ Operation $_{[0+]}$

An interface operation is effected by a choreographed exchange of messages, specified by assigning appropriate message *types* to particular roles, or slots, in a standard exchange *pattern*. Potential faults (or exceptions) are specified in a similar fashion (we refer readers to the WSDL 2.0 specification for a more detailed explanation of these concepts). The **Operation** entity-type is defined as follows, with the value of the *message_label* attribute identifying the relevant pattern slot:

**Operation** $\subset$ Service*
  *pattern* $\subset$ UUID [1]
  *messages* $\subset$ Message [0+]
  *faults* $\subset$ Message [0+]

**Message** $\subset$ E*
  *message_label* $\subset$ NAME [1]
  *valuetype* $\subset$ ⇑MessageType* [1]

**MessageType*** $\subset$ E*

**Service*** $\subset$ NamedEntity*

Note that the **MessageType*** entity-type is defined as an empty specialisation of **E***, which means that messages may have arbitrary content. **MessageType*** subtypes are defined in vocabularies (Section 6) in just the same way that any domain-specific entity-type is defined (an example is given in Section 7).

The parent type of **Operation** is the abstract entity-type **Service***, which we first encountered in the previous section as the parent of **InterfaceDeclr**. To recap, an **InterfaceDeclr** comprises an **Interface**, which in turn comprises a set of **Operations**. The **Service*** type can therefore be understood as encapsulating (through its subtypes) a collection of service **Operations**.

In formal terms, an **Operation**, as we have just defined it, is essentially a prescription, or protocol, for exchanging messages. In contrast, when we speak of the *invocation* of an **Operation**, we are instead referring to the *execution* of this protocol; that is, we refer to a particular exchange of particular messages. In other words, an *invocation* is a specific *physical event* occurring at a specific point in space in time. Distinct invocations of the same **Operation** will thus have idiosyncratic properties (e.g. time and place) which are not represented at the level of protocol description. To describe such *event properties*, the SLA Model provides a dedicated **EventClass*** type (see also guaranteed actions in the previous section). For invocation events in particular, the model provides **InvocationClass***, the formal definition of which is as follows:

**InvocationClass*** $\subset$ EventClass* $\Longleftrightarrow$ Service*
  *invocation_uuid* $\subset$ UUID [1]
  *request_time* $\subset$ DATETIME [1]
  *reply_time* $\subset$ DATETIME [1]
  *endpoint_uuid* $\subset$ UUID [1]
  *consumer_uuid* $\subset$ UUID [1]

The attributes of **InvocationClass*** denote properties of invocation events. The value of *request_time*, for example, gives the point in time at which an invocation request was received, while the value of *endpoint_uuid* identifies the endpoint at which the request was received. As such, it should be clear that tokens of the **Invocation-Class\*** type, or indeed of any **EventClass\*** type, always constitute descriptions of *particular* events.

This, however, constitutes a problem. Since the purpose of a SLA(T) is to constrain *future* events (those constituting the service *to be* delivered), it is unlikely that **EventClass\*** tokens will ever appear in SLA(T)s. Nevertheless, it is useful to refer to event properties. We may wish, for example, to define different QoS guarantees for a given service according to the *request_time*, or *endpoint_uuid* of invocations. To permit this, the SLA Model requires that each **EventClass\*** type is associated with a corresponding entity-type. In the case of **InvocationClass\***, the associated entity-type is **Service\*** (indicated by the $\iff$ symbol in the formal definition). This association permits **InvocationClass\*** attributes to be referenced *as if* they were attributes of a **Service\*** token.

This completes the SLA Model specification of **SLA**, **SLAT** and **Interface** document types. As stated in the introduction, all these definitions are *minimal*, encapsulating only the common, domain-independent content of SLA(T) documents. As we will see in Section 6, all the entity-types defined here may be arbitrarily extended by domain-specific vocabularies.

## 5 Value Types (the abstract constraint language)

The entity-type definitions presented in preceding sections made use of two important — but as yet undefined — expression types, namely: **Constraint\*** (used for specifying QoS guarantees) and **Constant\*** (the abstract supertype of all datatypes). These types both specialise the high-level type $V^* \subset L^*$, which denotes a class of 'value types'. A third value-type, thus far unmentioned, is **Parametric** $\subset V^*$, denoting an extensible set of expressions with a parametric, or functional, form. Examples include arithmetic and set operators ($+$, $\times$, $\subset$, $\in$, etc), and QoS 'metrics' (e.g. *completion_time*, *arrival_rate*, *availability*, etc). Taken together, these types constitute an *abstract constraint language*, which we describe in the following subsections.

## 5.1 Constraint Expressions

The starting point in the abstract constraint language, is the **Constraint\*** expression type. A constraint expression is some statement, or formula, which places bounds on the permitted value of some variable. A constraint may be *atomic* or *compound*. Examples of atomic constraints include the following:

- $X < 4$,
- $X + Y >= Z$,
- *foo*$(Y) \mathrel{!} = goo(Z)$,
- $Z \in \{ a, b, c \}$,

- *completion_time*(S) < 10 s,

In general, an atomic constraint could be defined as an ordered relation between a variable and a value. The expression 'X < 4', for example, would comprise the relation '<' between values 'X' and '4'. In the SLA Model, however, we take a slightly more convoluted approach, and define an atomic constraint as a variable (e.g. 'X') bound to lie in some *domain* (e.g. '< 4'). This approach allows the domain part of the expression to be employed independently of constraints.

A compound constraint is some logical combination of *sub*-constraints. For maximum flexibility we also allow both atomic and compound domains, where a compound domain is some logical combination of *sub*-domains (e.g. the conjunction '> 4 and < 10').

To model constraints, we first introduce the following abstract types:

**Constraint\*** ⊂ **V\*** : the abstract supertype of constraints,

**Domain\*** ⊂ **V\*** : the abstract supertype of domains,

**Constant\*** ⊂ **V\*** : the abstract supertype of constants,

The concrete atomic and compound versions of constraints and domains are then given by the following expression type definitions:

**AtomicConstraint** ⊂ **Constraint\*** : each token is an ordered pair <*c,d*>, where *c* is a non-empty array (an ordered list) of **Constant\*** values, each member of which is constrained to lie in the domain *d* ∈ **Domain\***.

**CompoundConstraint** ⊂ **Constraint\*** : each token is an ordered pair <*o,C*>, where *o* ∈ **UUID** uniquely identifies a compound operator (e.g. 'and', 'or', or 'not'), and *C* ⊂ **Constraint\*** is an unordered set of *sub*-constraints.

**AtomicDomain** ⊂ **Domain\*** : each token is an ordered pair <*o,c*>, where *o* ∈ **UUID** uniquely identifies a domain operator (e.g. <, >=, ! =, etc), and *c* ∈ **Constant\*** specifies a domain boundary (according to the semantics of the domain operator).

**CompoundDomain** ⊂ **Domain\*** : each token is an ordered pair <*o,D*>, where *o* ∈ **UUID** uniquely identifies a compound operator (e.g. 'and', 'or', or 'not'), and *D* ⊂ **Domain\*** is an unordered set of *sub*-domains.

Note that the constrained variable in an **AtomicConstraint** is defined as an array. So, for example, the constraint 'X < 4' would represent '[X] < 4' (where '[..]' denotes an array). Semantically, a constraint such as '[X,Y] < 4' could equally be expressed as a conjunction '(X < 4) and (Y < 4)'. Constraints are defined in this way to ensure a consistent semantics for **EventClass\*** types (Section 4), a full discussion of which is beyond the scope of this chapter.

The SLA Model predefines several domain operators, namely: the standard comparison operators (<, >, <=, >=, = and ! =), a 'matches' operator for comparing character strings against regular expressions, and a set membership operator ('member_of'). Three compound (logical) operators are also defined: 'and' (conjunction), 'or' (disjunction) and 'not' (negation). If required, additional, domain-specific operators can be specified using vocabularies, as described in Section 6.

## 5.2 Constants and Datatypes

Constant expressions, encapsulated by the abstract type **Constant\***, are the most primitive expressions of the SLA Model, constituting the terminal nodes in document content hierarchy. Constant expressions include such things as metric quantities (e.g. '4 s', '10 MB', '90%', etc.), e-mail and web addresses (e.g. 'http://sla-at-soi.eu/'), Boolean values (e.g. 'true' and 'false'), time-stamps (e.g. 'Wed Dec 15 18:38:0.0 CET'), and others. The term *datatype* is used informally to refer to any subtype of **Constant\***.

We have already encountered some of the datatypes built-in to the SLA Model. The complete list is as follows:

- **TEXT** : opaque (unparsed) character strings,
- **REGEX** : regular expressions (explained below),
- **ENUM** : enumerations (e.g. Section 3.1),
- **PATH** : typically takes the form of a navigable route through the document hierarchy, identifying some target expression token,
- **UUID** : a universally unique identifier (e.g. a URI),
- **NAME** : used in particular as the name of a **NamedEntity\***,
- **CARD** : cardinality constraints (e.g. '0..1', '1+'), etc.
- **BOOL** : Boolean values,
- **STND** : standard forms (explained below),
- **NUMERIC\*** : abstract supertype of numeric quantities.

The **NUMERIC\*** datatype is an abstract supertype encapsulating numeric constants, and, in particular, metric quantities. The SLA Model provides the following built-in specialisations:

- **QUANTITY** : non-metric real values, e.g. '1.435', 'pi',
- **COUNT** : non-metric integer values,
- **PERCENT** : percentiles, e.g. '90%',
- **DURATION** : periods of time, e.g. '4 s', '2 days',
- **CURRENCY** : e.g. '10 Euros',
- **DATASIZE** : e.g. '5 bytes', '100 GB',
- **DATARATE** : e.g. '1 GB_per_s' (gigabytes per second),
- **TXRATE** : transaction rates, e.g. '2 tx_per_day' (transactions per day),
- **LENGTH** : e.g. '4 m', '10 cm',
- **AREA** : e.g. '10 m2' (metres squared),
- **FREQUENCY** : e.g. '200 Hz', '33 rpm',
- **WEIGHT** : e.g. '25 kg',
- **POWER** : e.g. '300 mW',
- **ENERGY** : e.g. '37 KWh',

To compare and validate constant expressions, we require a means to determine the datatype of any given constant token. To determine that the phrase '4 kg < 10 J' is invalid, for example, we need to know that '4 kg' and '10 J' denote measures with different (and incomparable) datatypes (**WEIGHT** and **ENERGY** *respectively*). To achieve this, datatypes can be associated with regular expressions, which constrains the format of tokens, and allows for the determination of type by pattern matching. The **WEIGHT** datatype, for example, has an associated regular expression '[x] kg', where '[x]' is interpreted as a placeholder for a number, such that any character sequence matching '[x] kg' will be interpreted as a **WEIGHT** token. The built-in **REGEX** datatype denotes the class of such regular expressions.

The **STND** datatype extends this use of regular expressions to also allow definitions of data-conversion formula. The **REGEX** token '[x] hrs', for example, is mapped onto the **STND** token '[x*3600] s' (which is referred to as its *standard form*), and serves to encode the formula required to convert a duration expressed in hours into the equivalent duration expressed in seconds.

All the datatypes listed above are defined as part of the SLA Model. In Section 6 we will see how vocabularies can be used to define additional datatypes to meet domain-specific requirements.

## 5.3 Parametrics

The third, and final class of value tokens is the **Parametric** $\subset$ **V\*** type, denoting expressions which have a parametric, or functional, form. Common examples include:

- arithmetic operations, e.g. '$X + 4$', '$8 \times 12$',
- aggregate operations, e.g. '*sum*( [1,2,3] )', '*mean*( [4,5,6] )'
- set operators, e.g. '$X \in$ [a,b,c] $\cup$ [d,e,f]',
- QoS metrics, e.g. '*completion_time(S)*', where $S$ denotes a set of service invocations.

The formal definition of **Parametric** type is as follows:

**Parametric** $\subset$ **V\*** : each token is an ordered pair $<f,P>$, where $f$ uniquely identifies an operator (i.e. a 'function' or 'predicate' name), and $P \subset$ **V\*** is an ordered set of parameters.

For validation purposes, we also need a means to specify, for each function name (i.e. $f$ in the preceding definition) the required arity and types of its parameters. In addition, **Parametric** expressions have the special property that, as well as conforming to a syntactic type, they also obtain a *semantic 'role'*, which is defined as the syntactic type to which the expression *evaluates* when interpreted. The token '*sum*([2 mins, 3 s])', for example, denotes the summation over the durations '2 mins' and '3 s' which evaluates to the single duration '123 s'. The semantic role of the token '*sum*([2 mins, 3 s])' is the type of this evaluated result, namely, the datatype **DURATION**. The significance of the semantic role is that **Parametric** expressions may be used anywhere that tokens with their semantic role are permitted. If a **DURATION** constant is required, for example, then *any* **Parametric** expression which evaluates to a **DURATION** constant may be used instead.

The SLA Model allows all this information to be captured formally in vocabularies (Section 6). The *sum* operator, for example, is formally defined as a single non-empty array of some numeric type $N \subset$ **NUMERIC** as parameter, and as evaluating to a single value of the same type. We can express this concisely with the following notation:

- $sum(N_{[1+]}) \rightarrow N_{[1]} \subset$ **NUMERIC**.

The SLA Model defines many built-in **Parametric\*** types covering, among others, the common arithmetic, aggregation and set operators as well as QoS metrics. A complete description of all the parametric types would require more space than is available here. To give some flavour of the model, however, the following is a complete list of formal definitions for the built-in QoS metrics:

- *accessibility*($\uparrow$**InvocationClass\***$_{[1]}$) $\rightarrow$ **QUANTITY**$_{[0+]}$.
- *arrival_rate*($\uparrow$**InvocationClass\***$_{[1]}$) $\rightarrow$ **TXRATE**$_{[0+]}$.
- *availability*($\uparrow$**InvocationClass\***$_{[1]}$) $\rightarrow$ **QUANTITY**$_{[0+]}$.
- *completion_time*($\uparrow$**InvocationClass\***$_{[1]}$) $\rightarrow$ **DURATION**$_{[0+]}$.
- *isolation*($\uparrow$**InvocationClass\***$_{[1]}$) $\rightarrow$ **BOOL**$_{[0+]}$.
- *mttf*($\uparrow$**InvocationClass\***$_{[1]}$) $\rightarrow$ **DURATION**$_{[1]}$.
- *mttr*($\uparrow$**InvocationClass\***$_{[1]}$) $\rightarrow$ **DURATION**$_{[1]}$.
- *non_repudiation*($\uparrow$**InvocationClass\***$_{[1]}$) $\rightarrow$ **TEXT**$_{[1]}$.
- *regulatory*($\uparrow$**InvocationClass\***$_{[1]}$) $\rightarrow$ **TEXT**$_{[1+]}$.
- *supported_standards*($\uparrow$**InvocationClass\***$_{[1]}$) $\rightarrow$ **TEXT**$_{[1+]}$.
- *throughput*($\uparrow$**InvocationClass\***$_{[1]}$) $\rightarrow$ **TXRATE**$_{[1]}$.

To close this section, we should mention two additional **Parametric** types that will be used in the example SLAT in Section 7:

- *violation*($\uparrow$**Guarantee\***$_{[1]}$) $\rightarrow$ **E**$_{[1]}$ $\subset$ $\uparrow$**EventClass\***.
- *union*(**E**$_{[2+]}$) $\rightarrow$ **E**$_{[1]}$ $\subset$ $\uparrow$**EventClass\***.

The first of these, *violation*, is used to specify a class of events whose members are the individual occurrences of the violation of some guarantee. The second, *union*, serves to combine diverse classes of event into a single event class. By combining the two, we can specify a class of events whose members are the occurrences of violations of any of a given set of guarantees.

Additional domain-specific **Parametric** types can be specified using vocabularies, which we describe in the next section.

# 6 Domain-Specific Vocabularies

The previous sections outlined the basic content of the SLA Model, which, by way of summary, comprises an abstract constraint language (Section 5), a document model for **Interface** specifications (Section 4), and, building on these, document models for SLAs and SLATs (Section 3). Many aspects of the SLA Model, however, are open and extensible, supporting customisation to domain-specific requirements. Extensions to the model are specified using vocabularies, which we describe in this section.

A vocabulary is a document comprising a list of vocabulary terms, each of which specifies a particular extension to the SLA Model. Formally, a vocabulary is encapsulated by the entity-type **Vocabulary**:

**Vocabulary** $\subset$ Document\*
  *terms* $\subset$ Term\* $_{[1+]}$

The type **Term\*** is the abstract supertype of all vocabulary terms, of which there are seven concrete specialisations, each serving a different purpose. For reasons of space we can not present their complete formal definitions, but the following list provides brief informal descriptions:

**Term\*** $\subset$ **E\*** : abstract supertype of vocabulary terms.

**EntityType** $\subset$ **Term\*** : each token provides a formal definition of an entity-type (i.e. a subtype of **E\***). All the formal entity-type definitions provided in this chapter — for example, the **Vocabulary** definition above — are perfectly valid examples of **EntityType** tokens.

**DataType** $\subset$ **Term\*** : each token provides a formal definition of a datatype (i.e. a subtype of **Constant\***), which comprises a unique identifier (**UUID**) and supertype.

**DataValue** $\subset$ **Term\*** : each token associates a datatype with a regular expression (**REGEX**) and optional standard form (**STND**), the purposes of which are explained in Section 5.2.

**ParametricType** $\subset$ **Term\*** : each token specifies a parametric operator (**UUID**), together with its required arity and parameter types, and its semantic role. The 'QoS metrics' listed in Section 5.3 are all valid examples of **ParametricType** tokens.

**DomainOp** $\subset$ **ParametricType** : each token specifies a domain operator (*cf* the definition of **AtomicDomain** in section 5.1).

**CompoundOp** $\subset$ **Term\*** : each token specifies a compound operator (*cf.* the definitions of **CompoundConstraint** and **CompoundDomain** in Section 5.1).

**EventClass\*** $\subset$ **Term\*** : each token specifies a class of events, defining a unique identifier (**UUID**) for the class, the entity-type with which it is associated, and a list of monitorable attributes. The **InvocationClass\*** defined in Section 4 is a valid example of an **EventClass\*** token.

Vocabulary documents thus allow for a considerable degree of domain-specific customisation, supporting the definition of new entity-types, datatypes and data-formats, parametric, domain and compound operators, and classes of event. Domain-specific applications may pick and choose from existing vocabularies, or create entirely new ones, as per their needs, thus supporting a modular approach to development. Individual vocabularies are identified by a URI, which also constitutes a *namespace* (in the manner of XML) for the terms defined in that vocabulary.

Thus the SLA Model itself can in large part be specified using vocabularies. The SLA Model is specified in four distinct parts: The first, referred to as the 'core', comprises all the basic definitions given in Section 2, the abstract constraint language (Section 5), and the definition of vocabulary documents (this section). Interface specifications (Section 4), SLAs and SLATs (Section 3), and QoS Metrics (Section 5.3) are then each specified in distinct vocabularies. The namespace URIs of these vocabularies are as follows:

- *Core* : http://www.slaatsoi.org/coremodel#
- *Interfaces* : http://www.slaatsoi.org/interfaces#
- *SLA(T)s* : http://www.slaatsoi.org/slamodel#
- *QoS Metrics* : http://www.slaatsoi.org/commonTerms#

For simplicity, we have until now ignored these namespace URIs. It should be borne in mind, however, that all the expression types defined by the SLA Model are formally identified by URIs. The formal identifier for the **NamedEntity\*** entity-type, to take a random example, is the URI http://www.slaatsoi.org/coremodel#NamedEntity.

In the final section, below, we provide an example SLAT which illustrates how the SLA Model is applied, and how diverse vocabularies work together.

# 7 An Example SLA

We close this chapter on the SLA Model with a concrete example of an SLA Template. Since the SLA Model is an *abstract* syntax, the first task is to choose an appropriate concrete syntax for the example. For simplicity, we will use XML[1], assuming that it is familiar to most readers. Line numbers are added to facilitate description. The content of the SLAT will be described as the example progresses.

We start by describing the service that is the subject of the SLAT. Since our focus is the SLAT itself, we will keep the service simple and intuitive: a *product purchasing service* comprising a single operation, 'BuyProduct', offered by a provider 'Fred'. The interface for the service is specified as an *interface document*, i.e., an instance (token) of the entity-type **Interface** (described in Section 4). The complete document is as follows:

```
1: <iface:Interface
2:  xmlns:iface = "http://www.slaatsoi.org/interfaces#"
3: >
4:   <vocabularies>
5:     http://www.fred.com/freds_vocab
6:   </vocabularies>
7:   <operations>
8:     <iface:Operation>
9:       <name>BuyProduct</name>
10:       <pattern>http://www.w3.org/ns/wsdl/in-out</pattern>
11:       <messages>
12:         <iface:Message>
13:           <message_label>In</message_label>
14:           <valuetype>
15:             http://www.fred.com/freds_vocab#BuyProduct.In
16:           </valuetype>
17:         </iface:Message>
18:       </messages>
19:     </iface:Operation>
20:   </operations>
21: </iface:Interface>
```

---

[1] For reasons of space we do not provide an XML Schema. The mapping from the abstract syntax to XML should be, however, self-evident.

The opening element (lines 1–3) announces the document to be an instance (to-ken) of the entity-type **iface:Interface**, where 'iface' denotes the URI namespace 'http://www.slaatsoi.org/interfaces#', defined by the SLA Model for interface document terms. The first child element (lines 4–6) lists the various vocabularies against which the document content must be validated. In this case, just one vocabulary is used (available at the URI 'http://www.fred.com/freds_vocab'), which we will describe shortly.

The remaining content (lines 7–20) defines an interface operation with the name 'BuyProduct' (line 9), and standard 'in-out' messaging pattern, as identified by the URI 'http://www.w3.org/ns/wsdl/in-out' (line 10). Lines 12–17 then assign a message-type, identified as 'http://www.fred.com/freds_vocab#BuyProduct.In' (line 15), to the pattern role 'In' (line 13). For modularity, the message type is defined in the imported domain-specific vocabulary (line 5). This vocabulary is a distinct document, whose content is as follows:

```
1:  <core:Vocabulary
2:     xmlns:core = "http://www.slaatsoi.org/coremodel#"
3:     xmlns:iface = "http://www.slaatsoi.org/interfaces#"
4:  >
5:     <vocabularies>
6:        http://www.slaatsoi.org/interfaces
7:     </vocabularies>
8:     <terms>
9:      <core:EntityType>
10:         <uuid>
11:            http://www.fred.com/freds_vocab#BuyProduct.In
12:         </uuid>
13:         <supertype>
14:            http://www.slaatsoi.org/interfaces#MessageType
15:         </supertype>
16:         <concrete>yes</concrete>
17:         <definition>
18:            defines the 'In' message of 'BuyProduct'
19:         </definition>
20:         <attributeTypes>
21:           <core:AttributeType>
22:              <name>product_id</name>
23:              <valuetype>
24:                 http://www.slaatsoi.org/coremodel#TEXT
25:              </valuetype>
26:              <cardinality>1</cardinality>
27:              <definition>
28:                 identifies the product to buy
29:              </definition>
30:           </core:AttributeType>
31:         </attributeTypes>
32:      </core:EntityType>
33:     </terms>
34:  </core:Vocabulary>
```

As before, the opening element announces the document entity-type, which is now **core:Vocabulary**, with 'core' denoting 'http://www.slaatsoi.org/coremodel#',

the URI namespace of the core SLA Model terms. Since the purpose of this vocabulary is to define the message-type used by the 'BuyProduct' operation, we first need
to import (in lines 5–7) the 'http://www.slaatsoi.org/interfaces' vocabulary in which
'iface:MessageType' is defined (the core vocabulary is imported automatically and
does not need to be included). Vocabulary imports are transitive in the SLA Model,
which means that the interfaces vocabulary is also automatically available to the
interface specification document.

The message-type required for the interface is specified using an
**core:EntityType** vocabulary term (lines 9–32). This term defines
a new concrete (line 16) subtype of **iface:MessageType** (line 13),
'http://www.fred.com/freds_vocab#BuyProduct.In' (line 11), whose purpose
is described in the scope-note (lines 17–19). It has a single attribute, defined in
lines 20–31, with the name 'product_id' (line 22), whose value is a single (line
23) opaque character string (datatype **core:TEXT**; line 24). Using the notation
introduced in Section 2, we would write this entity-type definition as:

**http://www.fred.com/freds_vocab#BuyProduct.In** $\subset$ iface:MessageType*
   *product_id* $\subset$ core:TEXT $_{[1]}$

These two documents fully specify the service interface. The last step is to create an SLAT to specify quality constraints and party obligations in respect of this
service.

In outline, the SLAT will provide customers the option of two 'service levels':
*basic* and *premium*. At the *basic* level, the customer is guaranteed a completion
time for service invocations of less than 2 hours, while at the *premium* level, this is
improved to less than 30 minutes. Each time a guarantee is violated, the provider,
'Fred', is given two weeks to pay a penalty of 10 Euros. The complete SLAT is
given by the remaining XML listings below, which for ease of description we will
explain section by section.

The opening XML elements are straightforward, announcing that the document
is an SLAT, and enumerating namespace abbreviations. In addition, for convenience
only, we have also added XML entity declarations (lines 1–6) denoting the core,
interface, SLA(T) and QoS Metric URIs. The SLAT also needs to explicitly import
the SLA(T) and QoS Metric vocabularies (lines 13–16).

```
 1: <!DOCTYPE E [",
 2: <!ENTITY core "http://www.slaatsoi.org/coremodel#">
 3: <!ENTITY iface "http://www.slaatsoi.org/interfaces#">
 4: <!ENTITY sla "http://www.slaatsoi.org/slamodel#">
 5: <!ENTITY qos "http://www.slaatsoi.org/commonTerms#">
 6: ]>",
 7: <sla:SLAT>
 8:    xmlns:core = "&core;"
 9:    xmlns:iface = "&iface;"
10:    xmlns:sla = "&sla;"
11:    xmlns:qos = "&qos;"
12: >
13:    <vocabularies>
```

```
14:        <item>http://www.slaatsoi.org/commonTerms</item>
15:        <item>http://www.slaatsoi.org/slamodel</item>
16:    </vocabularies>
```

The first content proper of the SLAT is a *parties* section (lines 17–26), which in this case distinguishes just two SLA actors: the provider, 'Fred', and customer, 'TheCustomer'. Note that the SLA Model requires merely that relevant parties are distinguished and assigned SLA(T) roles. Additional party information can be included, but is treated as domain-specific; that is, additional party information needs to be specified by domain-specific extensions to the basic SLA(T) document definition.

```
17:    <parties>
18:      <sla:Party>
19:        <name>Fred</name>
20:        <role>provider</role>
21:      </sla:Party>
22:      <sla:Party>
23:        <name>TheCustomer</name>
24:        <role>customer</role>
25:      </sla:Party>
26:    </parties>
```

Having identified the key actors, we next declare (in lines 27–43) all the service interface(s) which are the subject of the SLAT. In this case, there is only the *product purchase interface* defined earlier, whose interface specification document we will reference (line 40) using the URI 'http://www.fred.com/freds_service'. Note, however, that the use of a URI here is not obligated by the SLA Model. References may take any form, and the mechanism(s) by which references are resolved is application-specific. The SLA@SOI implementation assumes the use of URIs mapped to URLs.

The **sla:InterfaceDeclr** entity token specifies that this interface is to be provided by 'Fred' (line 30), that the intended consumer is 'TheCustomer' (line 31), and that it is accessible only by 'e-mail' (line 36) at the address 'fred@xyz.com' (line 35). We employ an e-mail protocol here for no other reason than to emphasise that the SLA Model is not restricted to standard web-service protocols. For internal reference, both the **sla:InterfaceDeclr** and **sla:Endpoint** token are assigned identifiers: 'IF1' and 'EPR1' (*resp.*).

```
27:    <interfaceDeclrs>
28:      <sla:InterfaceDeclr>
29:        <name>IF1</name>
30:        <provider>Fred</provider>
31:        <consumers>TheCustomer</consumers>
32:        <endpoints>
33:          <sla:Endpoint>
34:            <name>EPR1</name>
35:            <location>fred@xyz.com</location>
36:            <protocol>e-mail</protocol>
37:          </sla:Endpoint>
38:        </endpoints>
```

```
39:        <interface>
40:           http://www.fred.com/freds_service
41:        </interface>
42:      </sla:InterfaceDeclr>
43:    </interfaceDeclrs>
```

In the next section, *macros* (lines 44–63), we introduce the 'service level' options together with any other macros that may be useful. The 'service level' options are encoded in lines 45–56 as a **sla:Customisable** macro 'X' (line 46), denoting an expression whose value must be either 'premium' (line 51) or 'basic' (line 52), with 'premium' as the default option (line 47). For convenience, we also define a second macro 'S' (line 58), denoting the expression 'IF1/interface[0]/BuyProduct' (line 60). This expression is a **core:PATH** token which resolves to the 'BuyProduct' **iface:Operation** entity in the embedded interface document. (As with all references, the particular format of the path is application-specific.) As such, the value 'S' can from now on be used to refer to the 'BuyProduct' operation.

```
44:    <macros>
45:      <sla:Customisable>
46:        <name>X</name>
47:        <expression>premium</expression>
48:       <domain>
49:          <core:AtomicDomain op="&core;member_of">",
50:            <array>
51:              <item>premium</item>
52:              <item>basic</item>
53:            </array>
54:          </core:AtomicDomain>
55:        </domain>
56:      <sla:Customisable>
57:      <core:Macro>
58:        <name>S</name>
59:        <expression>
60:          IF1/interface[0]/BuyProduct
61:        </expression>
62:      </core:Macro>
63:    </macros>
```

The final section of the SLAT details the agreement terms. For the present example, there is only one agreement term, given the name 'AT1'. The opening elements are as follows (lines 64–67):

```
64:    <agreementTerms>
65:      <sla:AgreementTerm>
66:        <name>AT1</name>
67:        <guarantees>
```

The required completion time and penalty guarantees (see above) will be encoded as two guaranteed states and a guaranteed action, named 'G1', 'G2' and 'G3' (*respectively*). The first guaranteed state (lines 68–89) encodes an obligation on 'Fred' (line 70) to ensure that, in the case that the 'basic' service level is selected, the completion time of any invocation of the 'BuyProduct' operation (line 82) is less than

2 hours (line 85). In a more concise form, we may express this guarantee as the following rule: *if X = 'basic', then completion_time( S ) < 2 hrs.*

```
 68:              <sla:State>
 69:                <name>G1</name>
 70:                <obligated>Fred</obligated>
 71:                <pre>
 72:                  <core:AtomicConstraint>
 73:                    <item>X</item>
 74:                    <core:AtomicDomain op="&core;equals">
 75:                       basic
 76:                    </core:AtomicDomain>
 77:                  </core:AtomicConstraint>
 78:                </pre>
 79:                <post>
 80:                  <core:AtomicConstraint>
 81:                    <core:Parametric op="&qos;completion_time">
 82:                       S
 83:                    </core:Parametric>
 84:                    <core:AtomicDomain op="&core;less_than">
 85:                       2 hrs
 86:                    </core:AtomicDomain>
 87:                  </core:AtomicConstraint>
 88:                </post>
 89:              </sla:State>
```

In the same manner, the second guaranteed state (lines 90–111) encodes the following rule: *if X = 'premium', then completion_time( S ) < 30 mins.*

```
 90:              <sla:State>
 91:                <name>G2</name>
 92:                <obligated>Fred</obligated>
 93:                <pre>
 94:                  <core:AtomicConstraint>
 95:                    <item>X</item>
 96:                    <core:AtomicDomain op="&core;equals">
 97:                       premium
 98:                    </core:AtomicDomain>
 99:                  </core:AtomicConstraint>
100:                </pre>
101:                <post>
102:                  <core:AtomicConstraint>
103:                    <core:Parametric op="&qos;completion_time">
104:                       S
105:                    </core:Parametric>
106:                    <core:AtomicDomain op="&core;less_than">
107:                       30 mins
108:                    </core:AtomicDomain>
109:                  </core:AtomicConstraint>
110:                </post>
111:              </sla:State>
```

The third and final guarantee encodes the penalty action. The trigger (precondition) for the action (lines 112–135) is the occurrence of a violation of either of the guaranteed states 'G1' and 'G2' (Section 5.3 for an explanation of the *union* and *violation* parametrics). The guarantee specifies that, in case of such a violation, there is a 'mandatory' (line 115) obligation on 'Fred' (line 114) to make a payment of '10 Euros' (line 1132) to 'TheCustomer' (line 131), with a payment deadline of '2 weeks' (line 128) from the violation trigger event. The guarantee is violated if 'Fred' fails to make this payment within this time-frame.

```
112:            <sla:Action>
113:              <name>G3</name>
114:              <obligated>Fred</obligated>
115:              <policy>mandatory</policy>
116:              <pre>
117:                <core:Parametric op="&core;union">
118:                  <array>
119:                    <core:Parametric op="&sla;violation">
120:                      G1
121:                    </core:Parametric>
122:                    <core:Parametric op="&sla;violation">
123:                      G2
124:                    </core:Parametric>
125:                  </array>
126:                </core:Parametric>
127:              </pre>
128:              <limit>2 weeks</limit>
129:              <post>
130:                <sla:Payment>
131:                  <recipient>TheCustomer</recipient>
132:                  <value>10 Euros</value>
133:                </sla:Payment>
134:              </post>
135:            </sla:Action>
```

The remaining lines of XML (lines 136–139) close the agreement terms section, and complete the SLAT.

```
136:            </guarantees>
137:          </sla:AgreementTerm>
138:        </agreementTerms>
139: </sla:SLAT>
```

To convert this SLA Template into an SLA, we just need to add values for the mandatory SLA attributes *agreedAt*, *effectiveFrom* and *effectiveUntil*.


# 8 Conclusion

The SLA model meets the project requirements and has been tested in practical application. The model offers a language-independent specification of SLA(T) content at a fine-grained level of detail, which is both highly expressive and inherently extensible. The model has been applied to the business use cases of the SLA@SOI project (see also Chapter 'Introduction to the SLA@SOI Industrial Use Cases') and is already used by a number of European projects, for example Contrail[2].

# References

[1] A. Andrieux, K. Czajkowski, A. Dan, K. Keahey, H. Ludwig, T. Nakata, J. Pruyne, J. Rofrano, S. Tuecke, and M. Xu, Web services agreement specification (ws-agreement). Grid Forum Document GFD.107, The Open Grid Forum, Joliet, Illinois, United States, 2007

[2] A. Keller and H. Ludwig, The WSLA Framework: Specifying and Monitoring Service Level Agreements for Web Services. *Journal of Network and Systems Management*, 11(1):57–81, 2003.

[3] E. Christensen, F. Curbera, G. Meredith, and S. Weerawarana, Web Services Description Language (WSDL) 1.1 W3C Note, World Wide Web Consortium, 15 March 2001

---

[2] Contrail – Open Computing Infrastructures for Elastic Services: http://contrail-project.eu

# Service Construction Meta-Model

Jens Happe, Wolfgang Theilmann, and Alexander Wert

**Abstract** Dynamic negotiation, quality assessment, and provisioning of services all require means for expressing information about the kind of service, its quality characteristics and dependencies, and its configuration and deployment. The Service Construction Meta-model (SCM) provides the necessary means for describing services in their different stages. As such, it represents a core concept in SLA@SOI for communication between SLA managers, service managers, and service evaluators. In this chapter, we present the core elements of the SCM and their interdependencies.

## 1 Introduction

The Service Construction Meta-model (SCM) is motivated by the need to store and manage information about services inside the SLA@SOI framework. Service managers must provide data about the types of services offered, about alternative realisations of these service types, and about the service instances that have already been provisioned. Further, SLA managers require information about the dependencies of a service on other services, about features of the service itself, and about features of its associated monitoring system. Based on this information, SLA managers can

Jens Happe
AP Research, Vincenz-Priessnitz-Str. 1, 76131 Karlsruhe, Germany,
e-mail: Jens.Happe@sap.com

Wolfgang Theilmann
SAP Research, Vincenz-Priessnitz-Str. 1, 76131 Karlsruhe, Germany,
e-mail: Wolfgang.Theilmann@sap.com

Alexander Wert
AP Research, Vincenz-Priessnitz-Str. 1, 76131 Karlsruhe, Germany,
e-mail: Alexander.Wert@sap.com

plan and negotiate SLAs with their customers and acquire other (external) services as required.

The SCM is driven by the information necessary to create, evaluate, and maintain services and their associated SLAs. As such, it is essential to the communication of SLA managers, service evaluators, and (software-)service managers. With the SCM, (software-)service managers can maintain information about provided and required service types, available service implementations, and running service instances. SLA managers and service evaluators can retrieve information about service dependencies, about features of the service, and about its monitoring system. Further, they can resolve dependencies to external services and provide particular configurations of the service and its monitoring system in a generic way. Service managers instantiate services that have been negotiated by the SLA manager based on their configuration.

In this chapter, we introduce the basic elements of the SCM and describe their purpose. In Section 2, we introduce the hierarchical structure of service types, service implementations, and service instances. Section 3 illustrates how the different elements of the SCM are stored and maintained inside the service landscape. Section 4 introduces all elements of the SCM in more detail. In Section 5, we illustrate these concepts and their usage by means of an example. Section 6 concludes this chapter.

## 2 Service Hierarchy

During its life cycle, a service exists in different aggregate states that must be reflected inside the SLA@SOI framework. The service hierarchy shown in Figure 1 reflects the different states a service can assume during its life cycle: service types, service implementations, and service instances.

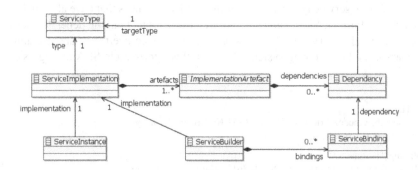

**Fig. 1** Service hierarchy and the relations of the different layers

A *service type* describes the functionality that a service provides. For example, it contains pointers to the WSDL definitions of the service's interfaces. The same service type can be realised by multiple service implementations.

A *service implementation* consists of a set of *implementation artefacts* (such as software components, or appliances for virtual machines) that are required to instantiate the service. Each implementation artefact has a set of *dependencies* to other services. For example, a software service that is realised by an appliance depends on an infrastructure service that can host that particular appliance. As in the relationship between implementation and instance in object-oriented languages, an arbitrary number of service instances can be created for each service implementation.

A *service instance* describes the properties of a service that is (about to be) provisioned and accessible. For example, a service instance contains the endpoint of a particular service. The endpoint either refers to a running service instance or points to the location where the service will be available, according to the time constraints defined in the corresponding SLA.

To instantiate a service for a customer, various degrees of freedom must be resolved. For example, all dependencies of an implementation on other services need to be bound to offers of an external service provider or of another SLA manager. The *service builder* provides a generic way to resolve service dependencies and provide custom configurations for a service and its associated monitoring system. For each dependency, the service builder holds a *service binding* that maps the dependency to an SLA template (Chapter 'The SLA Model') or one of its specialisations (SLAs or business products). The SLA template contains all information necessary to assess and access a service outside the current SLA manager's domain. It includes quality constraints and, after the SLA has been agreed, endpoints of the service.

In the following section, we describe how the elements introduced above are maintained inside a software landscape. Even though this can be considered an implementation detail of service managers, it supports understanding of the overall model.

# 3 Software Landscape

Inside the service manager, the *landscape* is the central element holding and managing all elements introduced in the previous section (service types, service implementations, service instances, and service builders). The landscape contains and organises the various services being offered by a service provider. As such, the landscape is the SCM's root element and can only exist once in each service manager. Figure 2 shows the landscape and its relations.

A landscape contains a set of provided and required service types, a set of implementations of these types, and all instances that are (about to be) provisioned. We explicitly distinguish between service types that are offered to customers and service types that are required to fulfill their functionality. Further, the landscape holds all service builders that have been used to provision a service instance. These

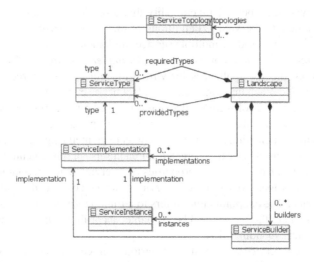

**Fig. 2** Structure of the SCM's elements inside a landscape

service builders allow retrieval of information about the service's configuration at runtime. In addition to the elements of the SCM, the landscape contains a service topology which specifies how different software elements are connected.

## 4 Core elements of the SCM

Thus far we have examined the broader context of the SCM, and more specifically, the service hierarchy (Figure 1) and software landscape 2. In the following, we describe the SCM's core elements in more detail.

### 4.1 ServiceType

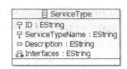

**Fig. 3** Attributes of a service type

A service type (Figure 3) specifies the externally accessible interfaces of a service. It basically describes what functionality a service provides. For this purpose, a service type contains a set of interfaces that specify its exact functionality using a set of operations it makes available. A detailed specification of interfaces can be found in Chapter 'The SLA Model'. Service types establish a link to particular interfaces by means of a unique identifier encoded in a string. The identifier can either contain a full interface reference as specified in the SLA model (Chapter 'The SLA Model'), or be a unique name for an interface without a formal definition. An example of the latter would be the user interface of an ERP system.

The remaining attributes serve the purpose of identification by machines (ID) and humans (service type name and description).

## 4.2 Service Implementation

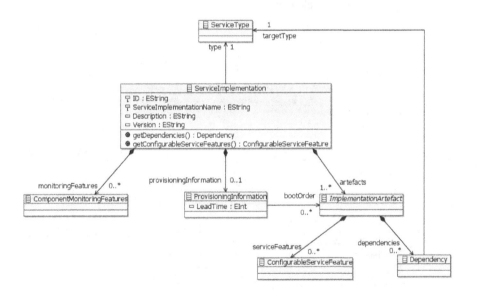

**Fig. 4** Internals of the service implementation

*Service implementations* (Figure 4) realise a specific service type. They describe i) specific artefacts and assets (such as software components or appliances) that are required to instantiate a service, ii) the dependencies of assets and artefacts on other services, and iii) the configurable features of the particular service implementation and its associated monitoring system. For example, an "all-in-one" implementation of the ORC's services depends on one infrastructure service that hosts its appliance. The threadpool size of its ActiveBEPL engine can be adjusted according to the service's usage and deployment. Further, the monitoring system allows for instrumenting each service operation and extracting response times and throughput.

To express such properties, service implementations contain a set of *component monitoring features*, some provisioning information, and a set of implementation artefacts. Component monitoring features specify the capabilities of the monitoring system associated with a service. They contain information about the available sensors, effectors and reasoners. Chapter 'Dynamic Creation of Monitoring Infrastructures' provides further details on the monitoring system's meta-model.

Provisioning information and implementation artefacts hold the information necessary to plan and execute the provisioning of a service. *Provisioning information* contains the lead time needed to start a particular software system. Further, it specifies the boot order in which multiple implementation artefacts are to be started. Each implementation artefact represents a single unit, such as appliances or software archives, that must be deployed separately. The meta-model of an *implementation artefact* contains information about its dependencies and the configurable service features associated with this artefact. Figure 5 presents a detailed view of implementation artefacts and their elements.

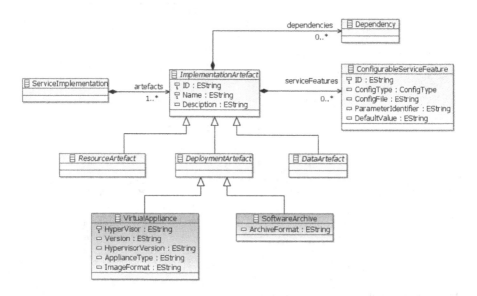

**Fig. 5** Detailed view of implementation artefacts

A *dependency* refers to service types that are necessary to instantiate a given service implementation. Dependencies are part of implementation artefacts to allow a direct association of a dependency to the artefact that requires it. This is necessary if multiple artefacts require the same service type with different quality characteristics. In this case, multiple SLAs need to be established for the same service type. A typical example of such a scenario is that of multiple dependencies to infrastructure services. If a service implementation comprises multiple appliances (e.g. one for the application server and one for the database), the model needs to reflect which appliance is to be hosted on which virtual machine.

Further, *configurable service features* describe those properties of a service that can be adjusted for each instance. Again, configurable service features are directly associated to implementation artefacts to avoid ambiguity. Configurable service features comprise a unique identifier (ID), a configuration type (e.g. property file or environment variable), a pointer to a file (ConfigFile), and an identifier of the parameter to be adjusted (ParameterIdentifier). Identifiers depend on the configuration and file type considered. For example, the identifier of a parameter in an XML file can be an XPath expression.

Implementation artefacts are abstract entities that must be specialised for different domains. In Figure 5, we show subclasses for resource artefacts, deployment artefacts, and data artefacts. Deployment artefacts are further refined to virtual appliances and software archives. These elements contain the detailed information necessary to deploy the artefact.

Please note that implementation artefacts are only used inside a service manager. Thus, information about the internal structure of a service implementation does not have to be understood by SLA managers and service evaluators. For this purpose, service implementations contain explicit operations that aggregate the dependencies and configurable service features for external processing.

## 4.3 ServiceBuilder

*Service builders* serve as a communication data structure to be used by SLA managers, (software-)service managers and service evaluators. Service builders are associated with a service implementation for which they construct a new service instance. They are used throughout the entire negotiation and provisioning process and are stepwise enriched with information. Basically, service builders serve as configuration objects for new service instances. SLA managers, service evaluators, and service managers exchange information on potential services using service builders. The implementation of a service builder follows the builder pattern of Gamma et al. [1]. Multiple service builders can exist and be associated with a single service implementation.

A service builder (Figure 6) is responsible for i) resolving dependencies of a service implementation by offers of an external service provider or another SLA manager, ii) the configuration of specific service features, and iii) the configuration of specific monitoring features. For each dependency of a service implementation, the service builder can hold a *service binding* that maps the dependency to an SLA template or one of its specialisations (SLAs or business products). The SLA template

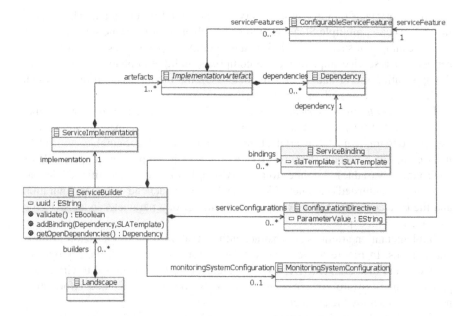

**Fig. 6** Service builder and its associated elements

represents a contract for a service of the required type. It contains all information necessary to assess and access a service outside of the current SLA manager's domain. It includes quality constraints and, after the SLA has been agreed, endpoints of the service.

For purposes of configuring a service, *configuration directives* assign new values to configurable service features. The setup of the monitoring system is given in the *monitoring system configuration*. Details of monitoring features and configurations can be found in Chapter 'Dynamic Creation of Monitoring Infrastructures'.

## 4.4 Service Instance

A *service instance* (Figure 7) refers to the instantiated version of a service implementation. As such, it contains information about runtime aspects of the deployed services. For example, it contains the endpoints of a particular service. The endpoints either refer to a running and accessible service or point to locations where the service will be available, according to the time constraints defined in the corresponding SLA. Each service instance can contain multiple endpoints. Additionally, a service instance contains information about the date and time of its creation (InstantiatedOn) and the usual means for identification by machines (ID) and humans (service instance name, description).

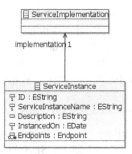

**Fig. 7** Attributes of a service instance

# 5 Example

In the following, we give a simple example of service implementations, dependencies, service builders, service bindings and their usage in the overall system.

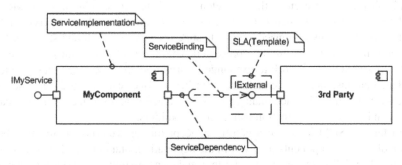

**Fig. 8** Illustration of the different concepts

Figure 8 shows a service implementation called "MyComponent" with an explicit dependency on an external service type called "IExternal". The service implementation is depicted as a component that provides a service of type "IMyService". The link between the implementation and the service type reflects the dependency of the meta-model. This concept is analogue to (required) roles in common component models. In Figure 8, the dependency is resolved by a service binding that links the dependency to the SLA template of an external provider. The SLA template contains the specification of interface "IExternal". The external service type can again be realised by a service implementation.

In the following, we illustrate how the service builders can be used for communication between SLA managers, (software-)service managers, and service evaluators.

1. The SLA manager requests the service implementations of a particular service type from the service manager
2. For each service implementation

    a. the SLA manager creates a service builder

    b. the SLA manager resolves the dependencies of the service implementation using available SLA templates, SLAs, and business products

    c. when all dependencies have been resolved, the service builder is passed to service evaluators which assess the expected quality of the setting given by the service builder, and

    d. the above steps may be repeated several times

3. When a particular service builder is to be instantiated, the SLA manager (tries to) agree on the selected SLA templates (or SLAs) of the depending services and adds the corresponding endpoints to the SLA templates. The resulting object is passed to the service manager, which instantiates the requested service based on the settings given in the service builder.

# 6 Conclusions

In this chapter, we presented the core elements of the Service Construction Meta-model and their dependencies. The SCM structures the life cycle of a service into a set of hierarchically organised aggregate states of services. Different stages of the service's life cycle are explicitly represented. This approach allows the components of the SLA@SOI framework to exchange information about service types, service implementations, and service instances. Further, services can be build stepwise using service builders. Service managers, SLA managers, and service evaluators can obtain and add their information using service builders.

So far, the SCM has been a helpful concept for fostering communication between different components involved in the negotiation, planning, and provisioning process. The SCM is a general model that makes no assumption about the type of service (e.g., infrastructure, platform, or software) that is to be provisioned or negotiated. However, until now we have mainly applied the SCM in the context of software services. In the future, we plan to extend application of the SCM to infrastructure and human services as well.

# References

[1] Gamma, E., Helm, R., Johnson, R., and Vlissides, J.: Design Patterns: Elements of Reusable Object-Oriented Software. Addison-Wesley, Reading, MA, USA (1995)

# Translation of SLAs into Monitoring Specifications

Khaled Mahbub, George Spanoudakis, and Theocharis Tsigkritis

**Abstract** The general architecture of the SLA@SOI framework supports the integration of different types of generic or special-purpose monitoring engines. While internally these engines may realise different monitoring approaches (or reasoning mechanisms), externally they support the same common interface. This interface enables the reasoning engines to receive the SLA guarantee terms that need to be monitored and to report monitoring results to the SLA@SOI framework. However, due to differences in the languages that the monitoring engines use to express operational monitoring specifications, the monitoring of SLAs expressed in the SLA specification language of SLA@SOI requires the translation of these SLAs into operational monitoring specifications. This chapter describes the translation scheme developed for the monitoring engine EVEREST, which has been used in the SLA@SOI framework for monitoring SLAs at the software service layer.

## 1 Introduction

To monitor SLAs expressed in the SLA specification language of SLA@SOI, these SLAs must be translated into operational monitoring specifications, i.e., specifications that can be checked by a low-level monitor plugged into the SLA@SOI framework. The general architecture of this framework supports the integration of differ-

Khaled Mahbub
Dept. of Computing, City University London, Northampton Square, London, EC1V 0HB, UK
e-mail: K.Mahbub@soi.city.ac.uk

George Spanoudakis
Dept. of Computing, City University London, Northampton Square, London, EC1V 0HB, UK
e-mail: G.Spanoudakis@soi.city.ac.uk

Theocharis Tsigkritis
Dept. of Computing, City University London, Northampton Square, London, EC1V 0HB, UK
e-mail: t7t@soi.city.ac.uk

ent types of generic or special-purpose monitoring engines. Internally, these engines may realise different monitoring approaches (or reasoning mechanisms), but externally they support the same common interface.

The established interface fixes the form in which the different monitoring engines receive the guarantee terms of the SLAs that require monitoring and the monitoring results that they report back to the SLA@SOI framework, thus enabling the basic interoperability aimed for in the design of the monitoring infrastructure of SLA@SOI. However, due to differences in the languages that the monitoring engines use to express operational monitoring specifications, it is not possible to devise a common translation scheme for all of them. To address this problem, the architecture of the monitoring infrastructure of SLA@SOI uses wrappers for the monitoring engines, called Reasoning Component Gateways (RCGs), which are responsible for translating: (a) the SLAs expressed in the common language of the SLA@SOI framework into the language of the particular engine that they support, and (b) the results produced by the particular engine into the common monitoring schema used by the framework.

This chapter describes the RCG developed for the monitoring engine used in the SLA@SOI framework for monitoring SLAs at the software service layer. This engine is called EVEREST and is a general-purpose engine for monitoring the behavioural and quality properties of distributed systems based on events captured from them during the operation of these systems at runtime [1]. The properties that can be monitored by EVEREST are expressed in a language based on Event Calculus [2], called *EC-Assertion*. EC-Assertion realises a form of Event Calculus in which the properties to be monitored are expressed in terms of monitoring rules that specify patterns of events that should (or should not) occur within specific periods of time, and may be related to each other and/or the state of the system that is being monitored with temporal or other data dependencies.

This chapter also describes the translation of SLAs expressed in the common SLA specification language of SLA@SOI into EC-Assertion. The rest of the chapter is structured as follows: In Section 2, we provide an overview of the SLA@SOI architecture to establish the context within which the RCG for EVEREST and the translation that it performs take place. Section 3 outlines EC-Assertion, the language in which the operational monitoring specifications are expressed, and Section 4 describes the translation scheme realised by EVEREST's RCG. In Section 5, we discuss the overall limitations of the current translation scheme. In Section 6, we provide an overview of related work. Section 7 provides concluding remarks and outlines directions for future work.

## 2 The Monitoring Infrastructure

The SLA@SOI monitoring infrastructure adopts an event-based architecture with three main layers: the sensing and adjustment layer, the monitoring layer, and the monitoring management layer. Sensing and adjustment form the bottom layer that includes sensors and effectors, which have responsibility for capturing runtime events during the operation of the services that an SLA covers, and for adjusting their operation if an SLA violation occurs (or is forecast to occur (see Chapter 'Runtime Prediction'). Runtime events from the lowest layer are communicated to the monitoring layer, which includes the reasoning engines that perform the actual SLA monitoring and store monitoring results.

Within the monitoring layer are the RCGs, which translate the SLAs to be monitored into the operational monitoring specifications of the specific reasoning engines, and translate the monitoring results generated by these engine into the common representation schema used by the infrastructure for monitoring data.

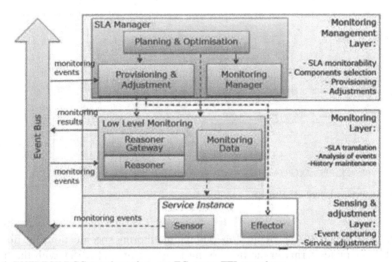

**Fig. 1** EVEREST RCG translator that uses EC-aware FTL templates

The top layer of the architecture is the monitoring management layer. This component includes a *Monitoring Manager*. This component checks the monitorability of an SLA given the available sensors and reasoning engines of the managed services, and produces a *monitoring system configuration* that indicates the reasoning engines and sensors that will be used to monitor the different guarantee terms of an SLA. To check the monitorability of an SLA, the Monitoring Manager parses an SLA and checks whether the available sensors and reasoning engines are sufficient to monitor the managed services (Chapter 'Dynamic Creation of Monitoring Infrastructures'). The monitoring management layer also includes components for planning and setting up the monitoring infrastructure (*Planning and Optimisation*), and, as shown in Figure 1, for making decisions for service adjustment on the basis of monitoring results (*Provisioning and Adjustment*).

Figure 2 shows the internal architecture of the monitoring layer of the EVEREST system. Within this architecture, the RCG provides the interface for accessing the

EVEREST reasoning engine. More specifically, the RCG receives the monitoring system configuration generated by the Monitoring Manager and produces operational monitoring specifications for the EVEREST reasoning engine. It also translates the monitoring results produced by EVEREST into the common event schema that is used to encode such results within the EVEREST infrastructure.

The RCG contains a *monitoring template repository*, a *parser*, an *ASTTranslator*, an *instantiator* and a *results generator*.

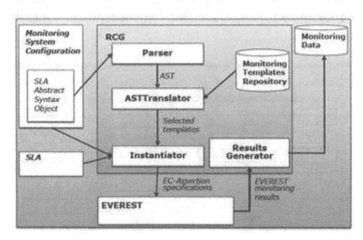

**Fig. 2** Monitoring layer for EVEREST

The EVEREST RCG generates operational monitoring specifications for different SLA guarantee terms in the monitoring language of EVEREST with the help of a set of predefined parametric *monitoring templates*. These templates enable the generation of the complex monitoring formulae required to check guarantee terms requiring the computation of aggregate information from complex patterns of events at runtime.

The RCG parser transforms SLA expressions — represented by abstract syntax Java objects in the monitoring system configuration — to Abstract Syntax Trees (ASTs), which are used by the *ASTTranslator* to select appropriate monitoring templates from the template repository. From the selected templates, the *instantiator* generates operational EVEREST monitoring specifications by analysing the monitorable SLA expressions assigned to EVEREST by the Monitoring Manager. The operational monitoring specifications are subsequently sent to the EVEREST reasoning engine as illustrated in Figure 2. Finally, the EVEREST RCG includes a results generator that transforms the results generated by EVEREST into the common schema used to represent monitoring results in the SLA@SOI infrastructure.

# 3 Overview of EC-Assertion

To be monitored by the EVEREST monitoring engine, SLA guarantee terms need to be expressed as *monitoring rules* and *assumptions* of EC-Assertion, which is the operational monitoring specification language of EVEREST. EC-Assertion is based on Event Calculus and is accompanied by an XML schema that enables the representation of monitorable properties in a system-exchangeable format.

Event Calculus (referred to below as EC) is a first-order temporal logic language that expresses properties of dynamic systems (i.e., systems that can consume and generate events in ways that depend on and can alter their internal state) in terms of two basic modelling constructs, namely *events* and *fluents*. An event in EC is something that occurs at a specific instance in time, has instantaneous duration, and may cause some change in the state of the reality (system) being modelled. This state is represented by fluents.

The occurrence of an event in EC is represented by the predicate *Happens(e, t, $\Re(t1,t2)$)*. This predicate represents the occurrence of an event *e* at some time point *t* that is within the time range $\Re(t1, t2)$ and is of instantaneous duration. The boundaries of $\Re(t1, t2)$ can be specified by using either time constants or arithmetic expressions over time variables of other predicates in the EC formula that include the *Happens* predicate. Events in EC can affect the overall state of a system by either initiating or terminating a specific state within that system. To represent these effects, EC uses two specific predicates: *Initiates(e,f,t)* and *Terminates(e, f, t)*. The predicate *Initiates(e,f,t)* signifies that a fluent *f* starts to hold after event *e* occurs at time *t*. The predicate *Terminates(e, f, t)* signifies that a fluent *f* ceases to hold after event *e* occurs at time *t*. EC also uses two additional predicates, namely *Initially(f)* and *HoldsAt(f, t)*. The first of these predicates signifies that a fluent *f* holds at the start of operation of a system. The second predicate signifies that a fluent *f* holds at time *t*.

---

(EC1)    $Clipped(t1,f,t2) \Leftarrow (\exists e,t) \, Happens(e,t,\Re(t1,t2)) \wedge Terminates(e,f,t)$

(EC2)    $HoldsAt(f,t) \Leftarrow Initially(f) \wedge \neg Clipped(0,f,t)$

(EC3)    $HoldsAt(f,t) \Leftarrow (\exists e,t1) \, Happens(e,t,\Re(t1,t)) \wedge Initiates(e,f,t1) \wedge \neg Clipped(t1,f,t)$

(EC4)    $Happens(e,t,\Re(t1,t2)) \Rightarrow (t1 < t) \wedge (t \leq t2)$

---

**Fig. 3** Axioms of Event Calculus

EC defines a set of axioms that can be used to determine when a fluent holds based on initiation and termination events that regard it. These axioms are listed in Figure 3. Axiom *EC1* states that a fluent *f* is clipped (i.e., ceases to hold) within the time range from *t1* to *t2*, if an event *e* occurs at some time point *t* within this range and *e* terminates *f*. Axiom *EC2* states that a fluent *f* holds at time *t*, if it held at time *0* and has not been terminated between *0* and *t*. Axiom *EC3* states that a fluent *f* holds at time $t$, if an event $e$ has occurred at some time point $t1$ before $t$, which initiated $f$ at $t1$ and $f$ has not been clipped between $t1$ and $t$. Finally, axiom *EC4* states that the time range in a Happens predicate includes its boundaries.

EC-Assertion adopts the basic representation principles of Event Calculus and its axiomatic foundation, but introduces special terms to represent the types of events and conditions that are needed for runtime monitoring. More specifically, given its focus on monitoring the operation of software systems at runtime, events in EC-Assertion can be invocations of system operations, responses to such operations, or exchanges of messages between different system components. To represent these types of events, EC-Assertion defines a specific event structure that is syntactically represented by the event term

$$event(\_id, \_sender, \_receiver, status(\_sig), \_source)$$

In this event term:

- *_id* is a unique identifier of the event;
- *_sender* is the identifier of the system component that sends the message/operation call/response;
- *_receiver* is the identifier of the system component that receives the message/operation call/response;
- *status* is the processing status of an event (i.e., *Call* if the event represents an operation invocation and Response if the event represents an operation response);
- *_sig* is the signature of the dispatched message or the operation invocation/response that is represented by the event, comprising the operation name and its arguments/result; and
- *_source* is the identifier of the component where the event was captured.

Further, fluents in EC-Assertion are defined as relations between arguments represented as terms of the form *relation(e1, , en)*. In a fluent term *relation(a1, , an)*, *relation* is the name of a relation that associates the fluent arguments *a1, , an*. These arguments can be constants, variables, or mathematical functions and arithmetic expressions defined over other arguments. EC-Assertion extends standard Event Calculus by supporting relational predicates over constants, defining object and time variables in formulae, and using arithmetic and mathematical expressions in place of variables (the latter expressions must be defined over other time variables in this case).

EC-Assertion specifies the properties to be monitored at runtime in terms of monitoring specifications that consist of *monitoring rules* and *assumptions*. Monitoring rules and assumptions are expressed in terms of the predicates listed above and have the general form *body* $\Rightarrow$ *head*. The meaning of a monitoring rule is that if its *body* evaluates to *True*, its *head* must also evaluate to *True*, whilst the meaning of the assumption is that when its *body* evaluates to *True*, its *head* can be deduced from this. Given this general interpretation, EC-Assertion uses a monitoring rule to express a property that needs to be monitored at runtime, and uses assumptions to express how event occurrences (and/or absences) affect the state of the monitored system.

An example of an SLA property that can be expressed in EC-Assertion is that the average response time of any operation of a service *srvID* should always be less than N milliseconds. This SLA property can be expressed in EC-Assertion using the following formulae:

## Monitoring rule R1[1]:

```
Happens(e(_id1,_snd, srvId, Res(_O), _sns),
_t1, [_t1,_t1]) ∧ (∃ _NoC: Int, _MSRT: Real)
HoldsAt(MSRT(srvId, _NoC,
_MSRT), _t1) ⇒ _MSRT < N
```

## Assumption R1.A1:

```
(∀ t1: Time) Happens(e(_id1, _snd, srvId, Response(_O),
_sns),_t1,[_t1,_t1]) ∧ Happens(e(_id2, _snd, srvId,
Call(_O), _sns), _t2,[_t2,_t1]) ∧ (∃ _NoC: Int, _MSRT:
Real) HoldsAt(MSRT(srvId,_NoC,_MSRT), _t1) ⇒
Terminates(e(_id1,), MSRT(srvId, _NoC, _MSRT), _t1) ∧
Initiates (e(_id1,), MSRT(srvId, _NoC+1, (_MSRT*_NoC
+(_t1-_t2))/(_NoC+1)), _t1)
```

According to rule *R1*, when a response from the execution of an operation *_O* of the service *servId* occurs at some time point *_t1*, the value of the variable *_MRST* must be less than N. The variable *_MSRT* in *R1* keeps the current value of the mean response time of service *servId* as part of the fluent *MSRT(srvId, _NoC, _MSRT)*. This value is updated by the assumption *R1.A1*.

According to this assumption, the mean response time of the service is updated every time an event representing the response from the execution of a service operation happens. More specifically, *R1.A1* states that when an event *e(_id1, _snd, srvId, Response(_O), _sns))* representing the response from the execution of an operation *_O* of the service *servId* happens at a time point *_t1*, and another event *e(_id2, _snd, srvId, Call(_O), _sns)* representing the call of the same operation has also happened at some time point *_t2* before *_t1*, and a fluent *MSRT(srvId,_NoC,_MSRT)* keeping a record of the current MSRT of the service and the number of its calls (*_NoC*) holds at *_t1*, the value of *_MSRT* will be updated by the response time of the latest call. This update is expressed by terminating the fluent *MSRT(srvId,_NoC,_MSRT)* and initiating the fluent *MSRT(srvId, _NoC+1,(_MSRT*_NoC +(_t1-_t2))/(_NoC+1)), _t1)*.

---

[1] In the EC-Assertion syntax, variable names are preceded by '_' but constants are not (i.e., _a is a variable but a is a constant). Also, all variables in formulae are assumed to be universally quantified unless their quantification is explicitly given in the formula.

## 4 Parsing SLA Guarantee Terms

The guarantee terms in an SLA are parsed to the EVEREST RCG as Java objects. These objects need to be translated in an abstract intermediate representation notation before being translated into the actual EVEREST monitoring rules and assumptions that will constitute the corresponding EVEREST monitoring specification in EC-Assertion. The intermediate notation used by the translator is an abstract syntax tree (AST). The AST is created to provide an intermediate representation that simplifies adaptation of the translation process if the SLA model or EC-Assertion language are extended in the future.

The SLA parsing algorithm is shown in Figure 4. This algorithm takes as input a Java object encoding an *agreement term, state* or *constraint expression* (i.e., *AgreementTerm, State,* or *ConstraintExpr*) in the SLA model (as described in Chapter 'The SLA Model') and generates as output the AST used subsequently for the selection and instantiation of the parametric EC-Assertion templates, and the generation of the EC-Assertion monitoring specifications.

The general form of an agreement term in the SLA model is:

*AgreementTerm := (Precondition, GuaranteeStates)*

In this form, the *preconditions* and *guaranteed states* of an *agreement term* are defined by constrained expressions (*ConstraintExpr*). When an agreement term's precondition is satisfied, its guaranteed states should also hold.

For each inputted *AgreementTerm*, the parsing algorithm creates an AST node labelled *IMPLIES*. An IMPLIES node is a binary node with two children: a left child node and a right child node.

The left child of an IMPLIES node represents the *precondition* of the corresponding term, if any. The right child is an AND-node representing the conjunction of the *guaranteed states* of the parent *agreement term*. The algorithm takes into account whether the *ConstraintExpr* that defines the guaranteed states of an agreement term is a *CompoundConstraintExpr* or a *TypeConstraintExpr*. The former of these types of constraint expressions is used for defining logical sub-expressions whilst the latter is used for defining relational comparison expressions. Based on this type, the algorithm generates the corresponding sub-trees. The sub-trees of a *ConstraintExpr* node end up in leaf nodes representing standard QoS terms for the SLA model or constants (or else the provided SLA would not be valid).

```
Parsing(inputObject)
 /*inputObject can be an AgreementTerm,
     State or ConstraintExpression */
1. node: ASTNode
2. node = null
3. node.Object = inputObject
4. IF node.Object is an AgreementTerm THEN
5.      node.Label = IMPLIES
6.      IF node.Object.Precondition is NOT empty THEN
7.          bodyNode = parse(inputObject.Precondition)
8.          node.addLeftChild(bodyNode)
9.      ELSE
10.         node.addLeftChild(null)
11.     END IF
12.     headNode.Object = LogicalOperator.AND
13.     headNode.Label = AND
14.     FOR each guaranteedState in
                   input.Object.Guaranteed.States[] DO
15.          guaranteeStateNode = parse(guaranteedState)
16.          headNode.addChild(guaranteeStateNode)
17.     END FOR
18.     node.addRightChild(headNode)
19. ELSE IF node.Object is a ConstraintExpr THEN
20.     IF node.Object is a CompoundConstrainrExpr THEN
21.         nodeLabel =
                   inputObject.LogicalOperator.STND.Value
22.         FOR each subExpression in
                       inputObject.SubExpressions DO
23.             subExpressionNode = parse(subExpression)
24.             node.addChild(subExpressionNode)
25.         END FOR
26.     ELSE IF node.Object is a TypeConstraintExpr THEN
27.         IF node.Object.DomainExpr is a
                             SimpleDomainExpr THEN
28.             node.Label = node.Object.DomainExpr.
                         ComparisonOperator.STND.Value
29.             LHSNode.Object = node.Object.ValueExpr
30.             node.addLeftChild(LHSNode)
31.             RHSNode.Object =
                           node.Object.DomainExpr.Value
32.             node.addRightChild(RHSNode)
33.         ELSE IF node.Object.DomainExpr is a
                             CompounDomainExpr THEN
34.             node.Name = inputObject.DomainExpr.
                             LogicalOperator.STND.Value
35.             FOR each subExpression in
                       node.Object.DomainExpr.SubExpressions DO
36.                 subExpressionNode = parse(subExpression)
37.                 node.addChild(subExpressionNode)
38.             END FOR
39.         END IF
40.     END IF
41. END IF
42. return node
END Parse
```

**Fig. 4** Parsing algorithm

To further illustrate the output of the parsing algorithm, assume the following agreement term:

```
AT1:
AT1.Precondition: Throughput ≥ T
AT1.Guaranteed.States = MTTR < M
```

For this term, the algorithm will generate the tree illustrated in Figure 5.

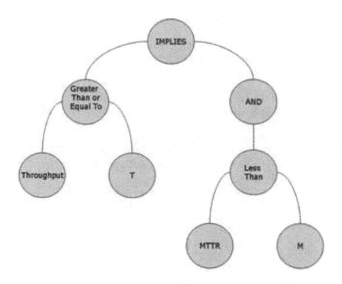

**Fig. 5** Abstract Syntax Tree for agreement term AT1

# 5 Generation of Operational EVEREST Monitoring Specifications

Once the AST for an SLA guarantee term has been generated, the next step in the translation process is to generate its operational EC-Assertion specification. This translation is based on the use of parametric templates for the basic guarantee terms defined in the SLA model.

## 5.1 Templates for Basic QoS Terms

The generation of EC-Assertion monitoring specifications is based on predefined monitoring templates. These templates are required since the SLA model does provide formal definitions of standard QoS terms in a form that enables the processing and generation of corresponding EC-Assertion formulae from basic EC predicates and fluents.

For example, the definition of the standard QoS term *mean-time-to-repair* (MTTR) for a service in the SLA model is underpinned by three basic concepts — *failed service operation call*, *service availability period* and *service unavailability period* — that are not defined such that EC-Assertion formulae could be automatically generated from the primitive EC predicates to represent event patterns for expressing these concepts and enabling their capture, which is needed for the computation of MTTR.

To address this limitation, we have defined sets of parametric EC-Assertion monitoring formulae, called *monitoring templates*. These templates are indexed by the standard QoS term that they refer to in the SLA model, and are retrieved and instantiated during the translation process when the relevant standard QoS term is encountered in a node of the AST generated for an SLA guarantee term.

A monitoring template consists of one parametric *monitoring rule* and zero or more *assumptions*.

To automate the process of template selection and instantiation, the monitoring templates are described using *Formal Template Language* (FTL) [3, 4]. FTL is a generic formal language for expressing templates of any target language. FTL is generative: it describes sentences of a target language (in this case, EC-Assertion) and can generate sentences when provided with an instantiation. A brief introduction to FTL, as well as a detailed description of the process of generating EVEREST monitoring specifications using EC-aware FTL templates, is provided in [3].

The main constructs used in the definition of FTL templates are *placeholders, lists, choice, template definitions* and *template references*. The syntax and role of these constructs in the definition of templates is summarised below:

Placeholders: Placeholders denote one variable occurrence and are substituted by the value assigned to the variable when the template is instantiated. Placeholders are represented by enclosing one variable within "$\langle\rangle$". The FTL template $\langle X\rangle=\langle Y\rangle$, for instance, includes two placeholders (i.e., $\langle X\rangle$ and $\langle Y\rangle$) and two variables (i.e., X and Y) and can be instantiated with the substitution set $\{X\mapsto$ "A", $Y \mapsto$ "1"$\}$, generating the formula A=1.

Lists: A list comprises a list term, a list separator (the separator of the instantiated list terms), and a string representing the empty instantiation of the list. A list is represented by enclosing the list term within []. The list term is a combination of text, placeholders and possibly other lists.

A placeholder within a list denotes an indexed set of variable occurrences, i.e., $[\langle V\rangle]$ denotes the occurrence of the indexed set of variables $V_1,...,V_n$.

The template $[\langle X\rangle=\langle Y\rangle]_{(v,\lambda)}$ can be instantiated with the sequence of substitution sets $\langle\{X\mapsto$ "A", $Y \mapsto$ "1"$\}, \{X\mapsto$ "B", $Y \mapsto$ "2"$\}\rangle$ generating A=1 $\vee$ B=2.

Choice: The FTL choice construct enables choices to be made between alternative template expressions. A choice in FTL can be optional or multiple. The former choice is represented by enclosing a template expression in $()^?$ and signifies that the expression might be present in the instantiation or not. Multiple choice is represented by enclosing the choice expressions within () and separated by [] (see below); this means that one of the choice expressions must be present in the instantiation. Choices are instantiated with a choice-selection; a natural number indicates the selected choice and non-selection takes the value zero.

The template $(\langle X \rangle = \langle Y \rangle)^?$ can be instantiated with $(1, \{X \mapsto \text{"A"}, Y \mapsto \text{"1"}\})$ to yield A = 1. To avoid the presence of the expression in the instantiation, the template can be instantiated with $(0\ \{\})$, which simply yields the empty string. In the multiple-choice template $(\langle X \rangle = \langle Y \rangle [] \langle X \rangle = \{\langle Z \rangle\})$, the first choice is instantiated with $(1, \{X \mapsto \text{"A"}, Y \mapsto \text{"1"}\})$ to yield A = 1; the second with $(2, \{X \mapsto \text{"A"}, Z \mapsto \text{"2"}\})$ to yield A = 2.

Template Definitions:A template definition in FTL associates some template name with the FTL expressions defining the template. For example, the templates named "FluentInitiation" and "FluentTermination" below are defined as EC-Assertion formulae where an event X initiates and terminates a list of fluents, respectively:

$\langle \text{FluentInitiation} \rangle_{tdef} ==$ Happens($\langle X \rangle$,_t1,[_t1,_t1]) $\Rightarrow$ [Initiates($\langle X \rangle$,$\langle F \rangle$,_t1)]

$\langle \text{FluentTermination} \rangle_{tdef} ==$ Happens($\langle X \rangle$,_t1,[_t1,_t1]) $\Rightarrow$ [Terminates($\langle X \rangle$,$\langle F \rangle$,_t1)]

Template Reference: In FTL it is possible to refer to a template using its name as defined in a template definition and the template reference construct $\langle \rangle_{tdef}$. The following template definition, for instance, the template X, is defined as a choice of fluent initiation or termination:

$\langle \text{FluentInitiationOrTermination} \rangle_{tdef} ==$
$\langle \text{FluentInitiation} \rangle_{tref} [] \langle \text{FluentTermination} \rangle_{tdef}$.

To illustrate the FTL, consider the template $\langle \text{FluentInitiation} \rangle$ above. This template can be instantiated by the substitution set $\{E \mapsto \text{"e(_eId1,_snd,_srv,Call(_o),_src)"}, F \mapsto \text{"called(_O)"}\}$ and generates the EC-Assertion rule:

*Happens(e(_eId1,_snd,_srv,Call(_o),_src),_t1,[_t1,_t1])* $\Rightarrow$
*Initiates(e(_eId1,_snd,_srv,Call(_o),_src),called(_O),_t1)]*

Figure 6 shows an example of the monitoring templates used to support the translation of guarantee terms expressed in the SLA model into EC-Assertion. This template corresponds to the standard QoS term *throughput* in the SLA model.

Throughput is the number of consecutive operation calls of a service that are served before a service operation call is not served (or is dropped).

$\langle$Throughput$\rangle_{tdef}$==

**A0.Throughput.$\langle$CaseId$\rangle$: Initially**(Served(0,$\langle$_SrvId$\rangle$,0,0))

**A1.Throughput.$\langle$CaseId$\rangle$: Initially**($\langle$CaseId$\rangle$.Throughput(0))

**A2.Throughput.$\langle$CaseId$\rangle$:**
**Happens**(e(_id1, _Snd, $\langle$_SrvId$\rangle$, Call(_O), $\langle$_SensorId$\rangle$)), _t1, [_t1,_t1]) $\wedge$
**Happens**(e(_id2,$\langle$_SrvId$\rangle$, _Snd, Response(_O), $\langle$_SensorId$\rangle$)), _t2, [_t1,_t1+$\langle$d$\rangle$]) $\wedge$
($\exists$_t3: **HoldsAt**(Served(_P, $\langle$_SrvId$\rangle$, _N1, t3), _t1) $\wedge$(_t3 _t1)) $\wedge$ ($\neg\exists$_t4, _P2, _N2:
(_P1$\neq$_P2) $\wedge$ (_t4 $\geq$ _t3) $\wedge$ (_t4 < _t1+ $\langle$D$\rangle$) $\wedge$ **HoldsAt**(Served(_P2 $\langle$_SrvId$\rangle$,
_N2, _t4), _t1+$\langle$d$\rangle$))) $\Rightarrow$
**Terminates**(e(_id1, $\langle$_SrvId$\rangle$, _Snd, Response(_O), $\langle$_SensorId$\rangle$)), Served(_P1,
$\langle$_SrvId$\rangle$, _N1, _t3), _t1) $\wedge$ **Initiates**(e(_id1, $\langle$_SrvId$\rangle$, _Snd, Response(_O),
$\langle$_SensorId$\rangle$)), Served(_P1, $\langle$_SrvId$\rangle$, _N1+1, _t3), _t1)

**A3.Throughput.$\langle$CaseId$\rangle$:**
**Happens**(e(_id1, _Snd, $\langle$_SrvId$\rangle$, Call(_O), $\langle$_SensorId$\rangle$)), _t1, [_t1,_t1]) $\wedge$
$\neg\exists$**Happens**(e(_id2,$\langle$_SrvId$\rangle$, _Snd, Response(_O), $\langle$_SensorId$\rangle$)), _t2,
[_t1,_t1+$\langle$D$\rangle$]) $\wedge$ ($\exists$_t3: **HoldsAt**(Served(_P, $\langle$_SrvId$\rangle$, _N1, t3), _t1) $\wedge$(_t3
_t1)) $\wedge$ ($\neg\exists$_t4, _P1, _N1: (_P$\neq$_P1) $\wedge$ (_t4 $\geq$ _t3) $\wedge$ (_t4 < _t1+ $\langle$CaseId.d$\rangle$) $\wedge$
**HoldsAt**(Served(_P1 $\langle$_SrvId$\rangle$, _N1, _t4), _t1+$\langle$D$\rangle$))) $\Rightarrow$
**Initiates**(e(_id1, $\langle$_SrvId$\rangle$, _Snd, Response(_O), $\langle$_SensorId$\rangle$)), Served(_P1+1,
$\langle$_SrvId$\rangle$, 0, _t1), _t1)

**A4.Throughput.$\langle$CaseId$\rangle$:**
**Happens**(e(_id1, _Snd, $\langle$_SrvId$\rangle$, Call(_O), $\langle$_SensorId$\rangle$)), _t1, [_t1,_t1]) $\wedge$
$\neg\exists$**Happens**(e(_id2,$\langle$_SrvId$\rangle$, _Snd, Response(_O), $\langle$_SensorId$\rangle$)), _t2,
[_t1,_t1+$\langle$D$\rangle$]) $\wedge$ ($\exists$_t3: **HoldsAt**(Served(_P, $\langle$_SrvId$\rangle$, _N1, t3), _t1) $\wedge$(_t3
_t1)) $\wedge$ ($\neg\exists$_t4, _P1, _N1: (_P$\neq$_P1) $\wedge$ (_t4 $\geq$ _t3) $\wedge$ (_t4 < _t1+ $\langle$D$\rangle$) $\wedge$ **HoldsAt**(Served(_P1 $\langle$_SrvId$\rangle$, _N1, _t4), _t1+$\langle$D$\rangle$))) $\Rightarrow$
**Initiates**(e(_id1, $\langle$_SrvId$\rangle$, _Snd, Response(_O), $\langle$_SensorId$\rangle$)),
$\langle$CaseId$\rangle$.Throughput( _N), _t1)

**R.Throughput.$\langle$CaseId$\rangle$:**
**Happens**(e(_id1, _Snd, $\langle$_SrvId$\rangle$, Call(_O), $\langle$_SensorId$\rangle$)), _t1, [_t1,_t1]) $\wedge$
$\neg\exists$**Happens**(e(_id2,$\langle$_SrvId$\rangle$, _Snd, Response(_O), $\langle$_SensorId$\rangle$)), _t2,
[_t1,_t1+$\langle$D$\rangle$]) $\wedge$ ($\exists$_t3: **HoldsAt**(Served(_P, $\langle$_SrvId$\rangle$, _N1, t3), _t1)$\wedge$(_t3
_t1)) $\Rightarrow$
_N > $\langle$ThroughputThreshold$\rangle$

**Fig. 6** Monitoring template for *Throughput*

To keep track of the served operation calls of a service, the fluent *Served* is specified as having several parameters: the identifier of the throughput period that refers

to the period between two consecutive dropped operation calls of the monitored service (_P), the unique ID of the monitored service (_SrvId), the number of consecutive service operation calls that are served during the throughput period (_N), and the starting time point of the aforementioned period (t). By processing the formulae in Figure 6, EVEREST manages — by initiating and terminating — instances of the fluent *Served* whenever an operation call of the monitored service is served or dropped.

To reason whether the operation calls of the monitored service are served or dropped, EVEREST should receive primitive call and response events from the sensor that has been selected by the Monitoring Manager to provide such events for the particular service. Therefore, a call to the monitored service that occurred at *t* is considered as served if a corresponding response occurs within a predefined time range between *t* and *t+d*.

Finally, EVEREST generates and instantiates the fluent *Throughput( ThroughputValue)* — specified as having the variable *ThroughputValue* as a parameter — whenever an operation call of the monitored service is dropped. It should be noted that the value of the ThroughputValue variable equals the number of consecutive service operation calls that are served within the current throughput period (_N).

The assumption formulae used to monitor the Throughput of a monitored service are presented in Figure 6.

The assumption formulae A0 and A1 initiate the *Served* and ⟨*CaseId*⟩.*Throughput* fluents for first time. The assumption A2 increases the number of served calls for a given throughput period, after an operation call has been served. The assumption formula A3 starts a new throughput period, after an operation call has been dropped. Finally, A4 initiates the Throughput fluent, after an operation call of the monitored service has been dropped.

In the above template form, ⟨*SrvId*⟩ is the unique identifier of the service that the throughput expression refers to, and ⟨*CaseId*⟩ refers to the unique IDs of the SLA and SLA objects that were assigned to EVEREST.

Thus far, EVEREST supports the following QoS terms: *Throughput, MTTR, MTTF, Availability, Completion_Time, Accessibility, Arrival_Rate,* and *Reliability.* In the following, we present the parametric EVEREST monitoring template for *Throughput.*

## 5.2 Translation

The algorithm *Translate* (Figure 7) is used to select the parametric FTL templates that must be used for the monitoring of the assigned SLA expressions. This algorithm takes as input the AST of the parsed SLA expression that is assigned to EVEREST. By recursively traversing the given AST, the algorithm compiles a set of parametric FTL templates (*ECFormulasList*). The compiled list contain templates for each QoS term the assigned SLA expression includes, as well as a parametric

EC-Assertion monitoring rule (*monitoringRule*) that is necessary for the runtime check of the assigned SLA expression as a whole. It should be noted that the EC monitoring rule that is built up on the fly, as well as all the formulae that EVEREST checks, are specified as *body→head*, where body and head are conjunctions of EC-Assertion predicates. Therefore, the monitoring rule is constructed by analysing the visited nodes and then adding predicates in the conjunctions of the monitoring rule body and head.

```
Translate(node, initialNode, ParametricECFormulasDB,
          ParametricECPredicatesDB,QoSTermECConditionsDB,
          ECFormulasList, monitoringRule)
1. IF node.Object is an AgreementTerm THEN
2.    body = node.LeftChild
3.    IF body is NOT null THEN
4.        Translate(body, initialNode,
                      ParametricECFormulasDB,
                      ParametricECPredicatesDB,
                      QoSTermECConditionsDB,
                      ECFormulasList, monitoringRule)
5.    END IF
6.    head = node.RightChild
7.    Translate(head,initialNode,ParametricECFormulasDB,
                      ParametricECPredicatesDB,
                      QoSTermECConditionsDB,
                      ECFormulasList, monitoringRule)
8. ELSE IF node is a LogicalOperator THEN
9.    FOR each child in node.Children DO
10.       Translate(child, initialNode,
                      ParametricECFormulasDB,
                      ParametricECPredicatesDB,
                      QoSTermECConditionsDB,
                      ECFormulasList, monitoringRule)
11.   END FOR
12. ELSE IF node is a ComparisonOperator THEN
13.    relationalPredicate =
         ParametricECPredicatesDB.getPredicate(Relational,
                                                node)
14.    FOR each child in node.Children
15.        IF child.Object is a ValueExpr THEN
16.          IF child.Object.Value is QoSTerm THEN
17.            childTemplates =
                   ParametricECFormulasDB.getTemplates
                                    (child.Object.Value)
18.            appendAll(ECFormulasList, childTemplates)
19.            QoSTermHoldsAtPredicate =
                   ParametricECPredicatesDB.getPredicate
                                  (HoldsAt, child.Object.Value)
20.            IF child is node.LeftChild
21.              relationalPredicate.LHSOperand =
                   QoSTermHoldsAtPredicate.QoSTermVariable
22.            ELSE
23.              relationalPredicate.RHSOperand =
                   QoSTermHoldsAtPredicate.QoSTermVariable
```

```
24.                 END IF
25.                 IF initialNode is an AgreementTerm THEN
26.                   IF child is at
                                 initialNode.LeftSubtree THEN
27.                     QoSTermECConditions =
                        QoSTermECConditionsDB.getPredicates
                                      (child.Object.Value)
28.                     FOR each predicate in
                                      QoSTermECConditions DO
29.                       IF predicate is NOT contained
                                  in monitoringRule.Body THEN
30.                         append(monitoringRule.Body, predicate)
31.                       END IF
32.                     END FOR
33.                   END IF
34.                   IF child is at
                                 initialNode.LeftSubtree THEN
35.                       append(monitoringRule.Body,
                                        QoSTermHoldsAtPredicate)
36.                   ELSE
37.                       append(monitoringRule.Head,
                                        QoSTermHoldsAtPredicate)
38.                   END IF
39.                 ELSE
40.                   IF monitoringRule.Body does NOT contain
                                      any predicate THEN
41.                     QoSTermECConditions =
                        QoSTermECConditionsDB.getPredicates
                                      (child.Object.Value)
42.                     appendAll(monitoringRule.Body,
                                        QoSTermECConditions)
43.                   END IF
44.                     append(monitoringRule.Head,
                                        QoSTermHoldsAtPredicate)
45.                 END IF
46.                END IF
47.         ELSE IF child.Object.Value is a CONST THEN
48.            IF child is node.LeftChild
49.                 relationalPredicate.LHSOperand =
                                  child.Object.Value
50.            ELSE
51.                 relationalPredicate.RHSOperand =
                                  child.Object.Value
52.            END IF
53.         END IF
54.     END FOR
55.     IF initialNode is an AgreementTerm THEN
56.         IF child is at initialNode.LeftSubtree THEN
57.             append(monitoringRule.Body,
                                  relationalPredicate)
58.         ELSE
59.             append(monitoringRule.Head,
                                  relationalPredicate)
60.         END IF
```

```
61.    ELSE
62.       append(monitoringRule.Head,
                               relationalPredicate)
63.    END IF
64. END IF
65. append(ECFormulasList, monitoringRule)
66. returnECFormulasList
67. END Translate
```

**Fig. 7** The template selection algorithm

For each visited node N$_i$, the algorithm checks whether N$_i$ represents an agreement term, a logical operator or a comparison operator. If N$_i$ represents an agreement term, the algorithm processes its precondition (if any) recursively and its guaranteed states, by visiting the left and right child nodes of Ni respectively (lines 1–7 in Figure 7). Otherwise, if N$_i$ represents a logical operator, the algorithm processes recursively the children of N$_i$ (lines 8–11 in Figure 7).

For each AST node N$_i$ that represents a comparison operator (lines 12–13 in Figure 7), the algorithm generates an EC-Assertion relational predicate (*relation-Predicate*) of the same type as the comparison operator in N$_i$ by retrieving a parametric EC-Assertion relational predicate from the corresponding repository (*ParametricECPredicatesDB*). The operands of the relational predicate are specified in accordance to the left and right child nodes of Ni. The algorithm considers that both the left and right child of N$_i$ can be either a QoS term (lines 15–16 in Figure 7) or a constant (line 47 in Figure 7).

When the algorithm visits a N$_i$ child node that represents a QoS term (lines 16–64 in Figure 7), it retrieves the parametric EC FTL templates — which are necessary for monitoring the QoS term — from the corresponding repository (*ParametricEC-FormulasDBs*) and adds them to the *ECFormulaList*. Moreover, for each QoS term node, the algorithm creates a HoldsAt predicate (*QoSTermHoldsAtPredicate*) that should contain a fluent for the translated QoS term by retrieving a parametric EC Assertion *HoldsAt* predicate from *ParametricECPredicatesDB* (line 19 in Figure 7). It should be noted that the QoS term fluent is initiated by the formulae specified in the corresponding parametric FTL templates for the translated QoS term. The algorithm uses the QoS term fluent variable to set the corresponding operand of the *relationalPredicate*, depending on the relative position of the QoS term node (lines 20–24 in Figure 7). More specifically, the algorithm decides whether to set the left (LHS) or right (RHS) operand with respect to the relative position of the QoS term node. If the QoS term node is the left child of Ni, then the LHS operand is set. The RHS operand is set otherwise.

To further resume the *monitoringRule* buildup, the algorithm checks whether the *initialNode* is an *AgreementTerm* (line 25 in Figure 7). If it is, and the QoS term node is in the left sub-tree of the *initialNode*, the algorithm resumes by adding the parametric EC-Assertion predicates *QoSTermECConditions*, which are compulsory for triggering QoS term monitoring in the *monitoringRule*(lines 26–33 in Figure 7). It should be noted that for each QoS term supported by EVEREST, there is a predefined set of parametric EC-Assertion predicates that represent the necessary conditions for the QoS term computation.

For instance, the predefined set for Throughput is as follows:

```
(∀case : ⟨CaseId⟩; srvId: ⟨_SrvId⟩; sensorId: ⟨_SensorId⟩;
d: ⟨D⟩; t1, t2, t3, t4 : Time)
ThroughputECConditions = {
Happens(e(_id1, _Snd, srvId, Call(_O), sensorId),
t1, [t1,t1]), ¬Happens(e(_id2, srvId, _Snd,
Response(_O),
sensorId), t2, [t1, t1+d]), (∃ t3: HoldsAt(Served(_P,
srvId, _N1, t3), t1) ∧ (t3 ≤ t1)), (¬ ∃ t4, _P2, _N2:
(_P1 ≠ _P2) ∧ (t4 ≥ t3) ∧ (t4 < t1+d) ∧ HoldsAt(Served(
_P2, srvId, _N2, t4), t1+d)) }
```

The predefined condition predicate sets are stored in the repository *QoSTermECConditionsDB*. Thus, the algorithm retrieves the QoS term condition predicates from *QoSTermECConditionsDB*. For each parametric condition predicate p, the algorithm checks whether the body of *monitoringRule* contains p. If p is not included, the algorithm adds p to the conjunctive list of the *monitoringRule* body. Regarding the generated *QoSTermHoldsAtPredicate*, the algorithm adds the predicate to the *monitoringRule* body when the *initialNode* is an *AgreementTerm* and the current node $n_i$ is located in the left sub-tree of *initialNode*; if this is not the case, the predicate is added to the *monitoringRule* head (lines 34–38 in Figure 7).

When a child of the comparison operator node ni represents a constant, the algorithm uses the constant value to set the appropriate operand of the *relationaPredicate* that is generated because of $n_i$ (lines 47–52 in Figure 7). Again, the algorithm determines whether to set the LHS or RHS operand with respect to the relative position of the constant node. If the constant node is the left child of ni, then the LHS operand is set. Otherwise, the algorithm sets the RHS operand.

Once both the LHS and RHS nodes of the comparison operator node are visited and translated, the generated *relationalPredicate* is added to the *monitoringRule* (lines 47–52 in Figure 7). In particular, when the *initialNode* is an *AgreementTerm* and the current node $n_i$ is located in the left sub-tree of *initialNode*, the *relationalPredicate* is added to the *monitoringRule* body. If this is not the case, the predicate is added to the *monitoringRule* head. Finally, when all *initialNode* child nodes are visited, *monitoringRule* is appended to the final output of the algorithm, i.e. to the *ECFormulaList* (lines 45–46 in Figure 7).

To give an illustrated example of the monitoring rules that the Translate algorithm generates, we use as an example the AST in Figure 5. The given AST is translated into:

```
(∀case : ⟨CaseId⟩; srvId: ⟨_SrvId⟩; sensorId: ⟨_SensorId⟩;
```

```
d: ⟨D⟩; t1, t2, t3, t4 : Time)
Rule.case:
Happens(e(_id1, _Snd, srvId, Call(_O), sensorId),
t1, [t1,t1]) ∧ ¬Happens(e(_id2, srvId, _Snd,
Response(_O),
sensorId), t2, [t1, t1+d]) ∧ (∃ t3: HoldsAt(Served(_P,
srvId, _N1, t3), t1) ∧ (t3 ≤ t1)) ∧ (¬ ∃ t4, _P2, _N2:
(_P1 ≠ _P2) ∧ (t4 ≥ t3) ∧ (t4 < t1+d) ∧ HoldsAt(Served(
_P2, srvId, _N2, t4), t1+d)) ∧ HoldsAt(case.Throughput(
ThroughputValue),t1) AND ThroughputValue ≥ T ⇒
HoldsAt(case.MTTR(MTTRValue),t1) ∧ MTTRValue < M
```

Once the *ECFormulaList* is compiled, the *instantiator* of the EVEREST RCG Translation component processes the parametric *ECFormulaList* templates and transforms them to operational EVEREST monitoring specifications. Besides the compiled *ECFormulaList*, the *instantiator* component takes as input the Java SLA object containing the SLA@SOI object assigned to EVEREST for monitoring by the Monitoring Manager [5], as well as, the monitoring configuration generated by the Monitoring Manager. The parametric templates contained in *ECFormulaList* are instantiated to operational EVEREST monitoring specifications by making the appropriate substitutions according to the following look up table.

**Table 1** Instantiation look up table

| FTL EC Template Placeholders | SLA@SOI SLA and SLA Template Abstract Syntax Equivalent Terms |
| --- | --- |
| _CaseId | SLA.UUID+AssignedSLAObject.Id |
| _SrvId | InterfaceRef.UUID ↦ service URL |
| _SensroId | The ID of the sensor ID that provides the primitive request and response events of the monitored service |
| _D | Represents a time period |

More specifically the following substitutions are made:

- Each appearance of _CaseId in a selected parametric template is substituted by a string that contains the unique ID of the monitored SLA plus the unique ID of the Java SLA@SOI object assigned to EVEREST for monitoring by the Monitoring Manager.

- Each appearance of _SrvId is substituted by the unique ID of the interface reference of the monitored service. Note that the substitution string should be identical to the value of the receiver and sender parameters of the request and response SLA@SOI primitive events that are generated by the monitored service [6].

- Each appearance of _SensorId is substituted by the unique ID of the sensor that provides the request and response SLA@SOI primitive events that are generated by the monitored service. Note that substitution string should be again identical to the source parameter of the aforementioned primitive events.

- Each appearance of _D is substituted by the constant that represents the time period within which a request to the monitored service is considered served or dropped, upon the occurrence or non-occurrence of a response from the service respectively.

## 6 Limitations

The translation of the SLA model into EC-Assertion has some limitations. These limitations are summarised below:

- Guaranteed actions in SLA agreement terms — that is, the actions that one of the parties of the SLA is obligated to perform if the precondition of the agreement term is satisfied — are not supported by the translation process. This is because guaranteed actions do not constitute monitoring actions. Guaranteed actions are control measures that the SLA@SOI monitoring infrastructure should take under specific conditions, and they therefore fall under the remit of the Provisioning and Adjustment and effector components in the architecture of Figure 1.

- Periodic events — used in the SLA model to denote the "trigger" conditions in time-series functions and guaranteed actions — are not currently supported.

## 7 Related Works

Service monitoring has been the focus of several strands of work that have developed standards and languages for specifying monitorable service and service-based system properties, and methods for monitoring these properties ([7] and [8]). Runtime monitoring has also focused on monitoring SLAs ([9] and [10], for example).

The approach presented in [11] supports the monitoring of a BPEL process according to certain QoS criteria; if an existing partner fails to satisfy QoS criteria, the services of that partner may be replaced using various replacement strategies.

There have also been several approaches that verify the runtime behavioural correctness of service-centric systems using formal verification approaches; these approaches include, for example, [12] and [13]. In [12], safety and liveness properties of service-centric systems are expressed using a subset of UML sequence diagrams. These diagrams are transformed into automata applying some formal translation patterns. During the execution of service-centric systems, the messages exchanged between the participating services are captured and used to update the states of the automata to verify the correctness of the execution.

In [13], a formal model of a web-service is constructed using a variant of a finite state machine and test cases are generated from this formal model. Generated inputs are fed to the web-service to verify that its implementation conforms to the formal model. The approaches described in [14] and [15] apply aspect-oriented programming for runtime monitoring of service-centric systems. In [14], monitorable properties of statefull services are expressed as algebraic specifications. Following a mapping of the operations of such services onto the operations in the corresponding algebraic specification, an evaluator with the algebraic specification is dynamically attached to a service execution engine and it observes the execution of the web-service at runtime, checking if the algebraic specification is preserved.

In [16], service choreography constraints are expressed in Linear Temporal Logic (LTL) and translated into XQuery expressions applying some transformation patterns. The generated XQuery expressions are then verified against the runtime XML messages exchanged with the web-service using a standard XML streaming engine.

# 8 Conclusions

In this chapter, we described the integration of the EVEREST monitor into the SLA@SOI monitoring framework. We also described the process of translating SLAs expressed in the SLA model (as described in Chapter 'The SLA Model') into EC-Assertion, where EC-Assertion is the formal first-order temporal logic language that EVEREST uses to specify service monitoring conditions.

The translation of SLAs expressed in the SLA model into the formal EC-Assertion language gives an unambiguous meaning to SLA guarantee terms expressed in the former language, and this is important given the semi-formal nature of the former. The current translation scheme has certain limitations — for example the lack of support for periodic triggering conditions for monitoring SLA guarantee terms — and these constitute the focus of ongoing work.

# References

[1] Spanoudakis G, Kloukinas, and C. Mahbub K.: The SERENITY Runtime Monitoring Framework, In Security and Dependability for Ambient Intelligence, In Security and Dependability for Ambient Intelligence, Information Security Series, Springer, pp. 213-238.

[2] M. Shanahan.: The event calculus explained, In M. J. Wooldridge and M. Veloso, editors, Articial Intelligence Today, Vol. 1600 of LNCS, pages 409–430. Springer, 1999

[3] Amalio N., Di Giacomo V., Kloukinas C., and Spanoudakis G. Mechanisms for detecting potential S&D Threats. Deliverable A4.D4.1, SERENITY Project, 2008.

[4] Amlio N., Stepney S., and Polack F. A formal template language enabling meta-proof. In Proceedings of Formal Methods 2006, 2006.

[5] Ellahi T. et al., SLA-Aware Service Management, Deliverable D.A3b, SLA@SOI Project, September 2010. URL: http://sla-at-soi.eu/wp-content/uploads/2009/07/D.A3a-M26-SLAAwareServiceManagement.pdf

[6] H. Li et al., SLA-Aware Service Management, Deliverable D.A3a, SLA@SOI Project, June 2009. URL: http://sla-at-soi.eu/wp-content/uploads/2009/10/D.A3a-M12_SLA-aware_Service_Management.pdf

[7] Baresi, L. and Guinea, S.: Dynamo: Dynamic Monitoring of WS-BPEL Processes, ICSOC 05, 3rd International Conference On Service Oriented Computing, Amsterdam, The Netherlands, 2005.

[8] K. Mahbub and G. Spanoudakis, A framework for Requirements Monitoring of Service Based Systems, 2nd International Conference on Service Oriented Computing (ICSOC 2004), pp 84 – 93, November 2004.

[9] Ghezzi C. and Guinea S., Runtime Monitoring in Service Oriented Architectures, In Test and Analysis of Web Services, (eds) Baresi L. & di Nitto E., Springer, 237-264, 2007.

[10] Mahbub K. and Spanoudakis G., Monitoring WS-Agreements: An Event Calculus Based Approach, In Test and Analysis of Web Services, (eds) L.Baresi, E. diNitto, Springer Verlag, 2007.

[11] O. Moser, F. Rosenberg, and S. Dustdar: Non-intrusive monitoring and service adaptation for WS-BPEL, WWW 2008, pp. 815–824

[12] J. Simmonds, Y. Gan, M. Chechik, S. Nejati, B. O'Farrell, E. Litani, and J. Waterhouse, Runtime Monitoring of Web Service Conversations, IEEE Transactions on Services Computing, 29 Jun 2009. IEEE Computer Society Digital Library. IEEE Computer Society.

[13] D. Dranidis, E. Ramollari, and D. Kourtesis, Run-time Verification of Behavioural Conformance for Conversational Web Services, European Conference on Web Services, Eindhoven, November 2009.

[14] D. Bianculli and C. Ghezzi. Monitoring Conversational Web Services. In IW-SOSWE '07, 2007.

[15] S. Halle and R. Villemaire, Runtime Monitoring of Message-Based Work-flows with Data, 12th International IEEE Enterprise Distributed Object Computing Conference, 2008.

[16] S. Hall and R. Villemaire, Runtime monitoring of web service choreographies using streaming XML, Proceedings of the 2009 ACM symposium on Applied Computing (SAC '09), 2009.

# Part III
# Scientific Innovations

# Penalty Management in the SLA@SOI Project

Constantinos Kotsokalis, Juan Lambea Rueda, Sergio García Gómez, and Augustín Escámez Chimeno

**Abstract** One important differentiation of SLAs from best-effort service provisioning requests is the annotation with penalties: all those provisions that define what will happen in the case that a provider fails to deliver the agreed service. The consequences of such failures may be some kind of refund, additional (free) service points, and so on. This chapter explores this topic, starting from a business perspective. It reviews the current implementation of the SLA@SOI project capabilities for monitoring and reporting SLA violations, and eventually proposes a new formalisation for penalty definition. This formal model takes into account requirements for fairness and business value. Following the model's definition, an example is provided that links the model to SLA hierarchies.

Constantinos Kotsokalis
TU Dortmund University, August-Schmidt-Strasse 12, 44227 Dortmund, Germany,
e-mail: constantinos.kotsokalis@udo.edu

Juan Lambea
Telefónica Investigación y Desarrollo, Madrid, Spain, e-mail: juanlr@tid.es

Sergio García Gómez
Telefónica Investigación y Desarrollo, c/Abraham Zacuto 10, 47151 Valladolid, Spain,
e-mail: sergg@tid.es

Augustín Escámez Chimeno
Telefónica Investigación y Desarrollo, c/Recogidas 24, 18002 Granada, Spain,
e-mail: escamez@tid.es

# 1 Introduction

*Penalties* are as essential to SLAs as guarantees, a notion essential to the very concept of using SLAs as instruments for providing some level of determinism in business relations. Thus SLAs also describe what must happen when something goes wrong and the SLA cannot be honored and is violated. The section of an SLA that describes these penalties is typically of concern to businesses and company legal departments.

Penalties requested by customers during a negotiation process emphasise the importance of SLA compliance to those customers. In a similar way, the penalties acceptable to a service provider indicate their risk strategy: namely, how far they are willing to go to make their customer feel safe while minimising the risk to their business. In addition, penalties may be defined for cases in which customers do not respect certain obligations agreed to in the SLA (for example, when exceeding the invocation rate may lead to additional costs).

Penalty *fairness* is important to maintaining stable business relationships, and to preserving SLAs as a useful and meaningful instrument for defining such business relationships. Fairness refers to reasonable and proportional royalties returned when the SLA is violated. This kind of proportionality is of interest to both the customer and the provider.

The penalties ideally reflect business value of the SLA to the customer, yet the provider does not usually wish to risk its complete business over a single contract. Further, to achieve proportionality, penalties should reflect how far from the agreed QoS level an SLA has drifted. By way of an example, one may consider an SLA where 95% of invocations of some operation are guaranteed to complete within 5 seconds. If 94.9% did so during the accounting period, the SLA is violated, but the penalty will typically be smaller than if only 80% of the invocations completed within 5 seconds.

Usually, an offered service aggregates many 'atomic' services; thus, the individual SLAs for each atomic service must be taken into account in the offered service's SLA [1]. Composing SLAs and their respective terms — such as QoS and penalty expressions — can be very challenging. A dynamically composed offer can include not only the bundling of services, but also the current supply and demand, historical data [2], and the parameters defined above. Thus, one of the most complex issues that must be faced when defining service prices and penalties is their relationship to QoS levels. That relationship can be expressed in various ways (absolute values, percentages, etc) and is part of ongoing research [3].

## 2 Business Considerations for Penalty Calculation and Reporting

Calculating the penalties derived from SLA breaches is an important SLA management process, as is the process of adjusting the resources involved to avoid those violations and their consequences. Some methods that take into account financial penalties resulting from SLA violations have been proposed, like the one in [4] by Macias and Guitart, where the authors enforce the maximisation of a single Service Level Objective (SLO): the provider's revenue based on resource allocation monitoring.

The main innovation of SLA@SOI is the adoption of an architecture that separates SLA monitoring from SLA reporting and evidence representation. The architecture makes it possible to monitor different guarantee terms that in turn have different associated reporting requirements. This means that a customer may decide to be informed periodically about a certain average QoS parameter (*push* model), or could prefer to obtain a report on a specific moment (*pull* model).

The SLA@SOI Business Manager's SLA reporting module (Figure 1), which sits on top of the framework's monitoring infrastructure, addresses all reporting requirements.

This reporting module receives low-level information from the SLA@SOI monitoring infrastructure, and (being aware of the relation between agreements and reporting requirements) creates the corresponding business (BSLAM) reports. It is driven by policies specifying the SLA terms that should be included in a BSLAM report, the types of monitoring results, and the required frequency of report generation. On a practical level, the former policies are described by an XML schema that includes the terms and parameters that should be included in the report. A second XML schema defines the formatting and appearance details of such reports.

## 3 Business Terms Associated with Penalties

The generic SLA model of SLA@SOI includes several extension mechanisms to describe domain-specific information (Chapter 'The SLA Model'). Here we present the extension for penalty- and reporting-related terms.

An SLA is a set of agreements between two parties expressed using *terms*, each of which denotes *guarantees made by*, or *obligations on* the parties, and may have an expression specifying the conditions that must be met to consider the agreement as valid (i.e. preconditions). If there is no precondition for a certain term, then it applies for the entire lifecyle of the SLA. Each one of these agreements has a set of *guarantees* of two types: *states* and *actions*. In short, an SLA is an agreement between a service provider and a service customer, where the agreement describes the service, documents the service-level targets, and specifies the responsibilities of the service provider and customer.

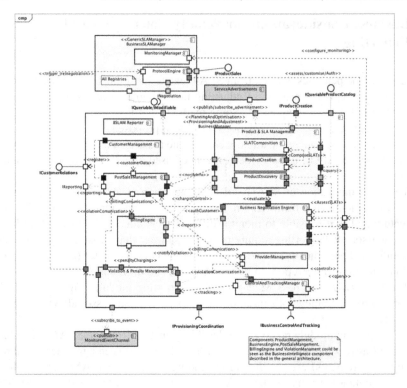

**Fig. 1** Business Manager components

Guaranteed states:    These constitute acceptance by one of the parties that a certain
parameter value will hold, e.g. Service Level Objectives (SLOs) or targets for
Key Performance Indicators (KPIs).

Guaranteed actions:    They are activities that, under certain circumstances, one of
the parties:

- may perform; or
- is required to perform; or
- is not allowed to perform.

On the business layer, the following guaranteed actions have been defined:

Monitoring:    This specifies which SLA parameters must be continuously monitored to control the information retrieved by the parties. Includes the units and
frequency of monitoring.

Reporting:    This represents the desire of the customer to be informed, automatically (*push*) or on demand (*pull*), about service usage and SLA status over time.
Since the information is sent as a report, this term includes information regarding
the report format, the frequency (only push) and the exact delivery method.

Termination and TerminationClause:    These represent the conditions under which one of the parties may terminate an SLA. A clause may include a notification method and a fee in case of unexpected cancellation.

Penalty:    This is the amount of money to be paid in case of a breach of a specific SLA term. A penalty may also be used to trigger an SLA termination clause.

*Rewards* are not addressed in the model; rather, it is assumed that in a realistic scenario, better service is more expensive by default.

# 4 The SLA@SOI Penalty Management Architecture

## 4.1 Monitoring

Figure 2 illustrates the main components of the SLA@SOI architecture and their relationships. On the highest level, we distinguish between the core framework, service managers (infrastructure and software), deployed service instances with their manageability agents, and monitoring event channels. The core framework encapsulates all functionality related to SLA management. Infrastructure and software service managers contain all service-specific functionality. The deployed service instance is the actual service delivered to the customer, and is managed by the framework via manageability agents. Monitoring event channels serve as a flexible communication infrastructure that allow the framework to collect information about the status of the service instance.

In the SLA@SOI framework, business-level SLA reporting is separated from SLA monitoring because SLA guarantee terms might need to be monitored for different purposes and have different reporting requirements. The primary function of these components is to receive low-level monitoring information from the SLA@SOI monitoring infrastructure, and to transform this into business SLA monitoring reports, including descriptions of SLA breaches, if any, and the penalty.

For example, the average response time of services in an SOA might need to be monitored continuously to enable automatic replacement of services that fail to satisfy the thresholds set for this guarantee term, as well as to provide evidence of the breaches. At the business layer, it might be necessary to report only the weekly or monthly average response time of a service, as well as the response time in specific days within the relevant period where the average response time significantly exceeded the threshold value. This is especially important in those cases where aggregated services exist and the penalty must therefore be divided between different third party providers.

The business component in charge of receiving violations from the lower level components is the *Provisioning and Adjustment Component* (PAC). The PAC makes decisions based on business criteria, including renegotiating agreements with end-customers, terminating offered services, or even, in a multi-provider environment, changing the third party provider providing a given service.

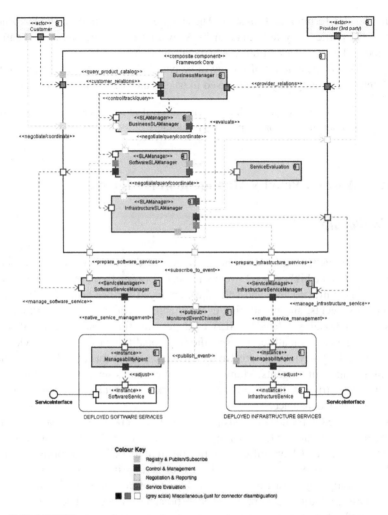

**Fig. 2** SLA@SOI framework

Thanks to the $<<$ control/track $>>$ interaction, business-level criteria can be taken into account within the lower levels of the SLA@SOI architecture. For instance, a service provider can decide that it is better to accept violations in some SLAs to give priority to others, based on business impact. The service provider may also decide to prevent breaches to some SLAs or specific QoS metrics while applying reaction upon violations to others. To this end, the $<<$ control $>>$ interaction allows the Business Manager component to retrieve the current adjustment policies and to set a new list of policies. The $<<$ track $>>$ interaction allows the communication of violations from the software and infrastructure levels to the Business Manager. This informs the business layer of problems in the underlying levels, and allows it to calculate and apply penalties derived from the malfunctioning of services under its control. The $<<$ query $>>$ interaction is implemented in the software and infrastructure PACs and allows an external entity, namely the Business Manager, to query SLA violations and historical monitoring information.

## 4.2 Reporting

### 4.2.1 BSLAM Reporter Architecture

In the SLA@SOI platform, the *BSLAM reporter* is responsible for generating BSLAM reports. Its main functionality is to get basic monitoring results from the SLA@SOI monitoring subsystem, and use them to generate and provide BSLAM reports to the *business intelligence* component of the Business Manager. These reports will be assembled and structured according to BSLAM reporting policies, which are also specified within the business intelligence component.

The BSLAM Reporting Manager is functionally divided in five components (Figure 3):

- The *Manager* coordinates reporting activities (e.g., reporting specification parsing, reporting scheduling, building reports).
- The *SchedulerManager* creates jobs and executes them at specific time points
- The *Communication* component provides the means for retrieving data required to create reports.
- The *Storage* component stores job results to be subsequently fetched for report generation.
- The *Parser* converts XML artefacts to Java objects (since reporting requests come as XML strings).

A number of interactions take place between the Reporting Manager and the outer world, as well as between components of the Reporting Manager:

- *reporting_request*: external components request the Reporting Manager to generate reports. Passing to Reporting Manager an XML string representation of a business SLA performs the request.
- *reporting_response*: a report result is delivered to a requester component. Business SLA contains chosen delivery methods.
- *parser*: prior to any other tasks, the XML string representation of a business SLA need to be converted into a suitable Java object representation. Parser component performs the conversion.
- *schedule_job*: a job is uniquely associated to a reporting specification. A scheduler, according to reporting policies contained in a business SLA, triggers respective jobs.
- *fetch_data*: data needed to accomplish a job is fetched by querying Communication component which knows how to retrieve requested data.
- *store_job_result*: job results are stored to be later processed to build reports.

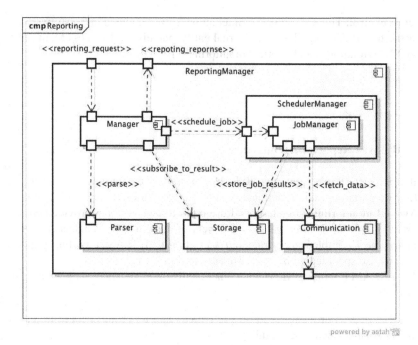

**Fig. 3** BSLAM reporter architecture

- *subscribe_to_result*: Manager and Storage components implement the producer/-consumer paradigm. Manager subscribes to Storage to be notified when a job result is stored.

A monitoring policy refers to guarantee terms and business monitoring parameters in particular SLAs. Hence the related SLA guarantee terms and any required events related to these terms can be extracted from the policy by the BSLAM reporter and passed to the *SoftwareLandscape* component. This component is aware of the exact monitors responsible for monitoring the particular SLA items required for a BSLAM report, and is able to subscribe the BSLAM reporter as a listener to monitor result events. These events carry monitoring information about particular SLA items and are generated by reasoning components that have been assigned the responsibility of checking the relevant items. The latter components are indirectly accessible through the *ServiceManager* component. Note that the SLA@SOI monitoring subsystem may deploy different reasoning components to monitor different SLAs or even different items within the same SLA[1].

---

[1] The assignment of different SLAs or items of a single SLA to different reasoning components might be dictated by the need to use the specialised capabilities of individual reasoning components or other requirements (e.g. load balancing across these components).

### 4.2.2 Push/Pull Penalties Reporting

The BSLAM reporter has been specifically implemented as a report generator for customers and service providers. This component offers a web-service interface through which on-demand reports can be requested. Reports can be retrieved by product and client, by SLA ID, or by a GuaranteeTerm specific to a given SLA. Aggregated reports for a specific product can also be requested. The output includes information on the associated SLA and the performance of the service *in terms of violations and penalties*.

While the methods described above can be considered as a *pull* interface, the BSLAM reporter component also implements a *push* approach, providing an automatic mechanism for sending reports to the customer. These reports indicate periodicity in the SLA and when a violation occurred. To this end, an e-mail is sent to the contact email address of the customer.

The content of the report is retrieved from the business database, where all the business information is stored, including product descriptions, business SLAs, prices, violations and penalties. If more detail is needed, the reporting component can use the $<<$ control/track $>>$ interaction to retrieve this information from the registries in the underlying SLAMs and from the low-level monitoring system database.

All this information is structured into reports in PDF format. On-demand reports can be viewed using a web browser; otherwise, the file is attached to the e-mail.

## 4.3 Violations and Penalties Management

From a real business perspective scenario (Figure 4), the importance of violation management is clear. Most guarantee terms set in an SLA are subject to direct financial penalties or indirect financial repercussions if not met. Hence in business interactions it is essential that all violations occurring in the service lifetime are detected, analysed against the corresponding SLAs, and relevant penalties calculated.

Inside the SLA@SOI framework, the business layer takes care of the economic impact derived from the performance of the service. The violation and penalty management component of the Business Manager must analyse and correlate information from two sources: the signed business SLAs, and runtime information on service performance.

Within signed business SLAs, the agreement terms may have a penalty attached when a given guarantee term is breached. In the current SLA@SOI implementation, this penalty requires a financial amount to be paid by the service provider (e.g. when the bad performance is caused by a failure of software or infrastructure resources) or by the customer(e.g. when the number of requests exceeds the maximum threshold indicated in the SLA).

The violation and penalty management component must implement a mechanism to receive runtime information about each SLA from the software and infrastructure

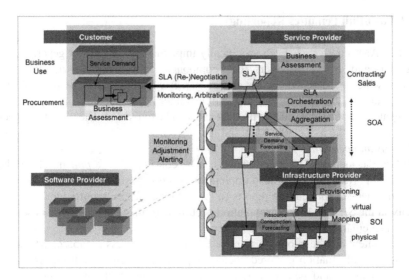

**Fig. 4** SLASOI use case scenario

levels. The incoming data, namely SLA violations, must then be checked against the conditions signed in the SLA. When a violation notification is received, the violation and penalty management component must evaluate whether the corresponding SLA foresees a penalty for the violation. If it does, then it must calculate the exact penalty and apply it, through communication with the billing engine.

Further, a mechanism must be implemented to allow persistent storage of the information generated: the violations of each SLA, the duration of the malfunction, and the penalties attached. This information will be used by the reporting component to generate the corresponding reports, making the data available both internally to the service provider, and externally to the customer.

On the software and infrastructure levels, the low-level monitoring system continuously supervises parameters that characterise the service. The collected information is then fed into the SLA-level monitoring system, which compares the instrumentation data with the conditions specified in the SLA as guarantee terms. When a violation of one of those terms is detected, a specific *SLAViolation event* is triggered and captured by the adjustment component of the corresponding layer. The information flows to the business layer through the << control/track >> interaction, where the economic impact of the underlying problem is evaluated by the violation and penalty management system. The output of this analysis will be used at the business layer in the post-sale subcomponent, and should be permanently stored in the database.

The violations and penalties management system is embedded in the *business adjustment* component in view of the close relationship between both functionalities: the input data for both concerns violation events produced at the software and infrastructure layers, and both modules aim to analyse those events and take corresponding action (a recovery action or penalty application).

Thus the manageability agent and monitoring system continuously observe the quality of a service. If the observed quality is less than that agreed to in the SLA, the resulting violation is published on an event channel. In the scenario depicted in Figure 4, the SLA manager retrieves the notification and initiates countermeasures (i.e. calls to the right service from infrastructure or software). If successful, the countermeasures allow the framework to restore the quality of service agreed upon in the SLA. The violation — and the countermeasures taken — are reported to the business manager via the ¡¡tracking¿¿ interaction. The business manager records the violation and decides — based on the severity of the violation and the success or failure of the countermeasures taken — whether to report the violation to the customer. Such a report would include the associated penalties.

In Section 3, guarantee states and actions were introduced. The *penalty action* is another relevant SLA term. When the monitoring component receives an SLA breach (e.g. failing a KPI target), the associated penalty is thrown and then captured by the violations and management module, which in turn loads the associated SLA that has the corresponding penalty description and fee.

The *termination action* is another guarantee action for cases where repeat violations occur. It is associated with a *termination clause*, which records when an SLA should be deemed invalid and be cancelled. For example:

```
guaranteed_action{
    id = PenaltyAction_SMS_ProviderConstraintAvailability
    actor = http://www.slaatsoi.org/slamodel#provider
    policy = mandatory
    trigger = violated[SMSAvailabilityConstraint]
    penalty{
        price = "0.1" EUR
    }
}
```

We can see that this block includes a policy associated with the penalty and economic fee. The former penalty example has an associated *termination action*:

```
guaranteed_action{
    id = TerminationAction_SMS_ProviderConstraintAvailability
    actor = http://www.slaatsoi.org/slamodel#provider
    policy = mandatory
    trigger = violated[violation_count ( \
      PenaltyAction_SMS_ProviderConstraintAvailability) < "3"]
    termination{
        name = Termination Action
        terminationClauseId = 2
    }
}
```

This includes the ID of the *termination clause*: terminationClauseId = 2.

For aggregated services, the different SLAs are joined and the penalties are redefined. Thus the old penalties are not used and new penalties are calculated specific to the composite service.

The implementation of the violations and penalty management module declares specific rules that have been added to the rule engine. When a violation arrives, the following actions are performed:

1. The corresponding SLA is retrieved from the SLARegistry.
2. The SLA is checked to establish whether there is a penalty charge for the guarantee term that has been violated.
3. If such a penalty exists, then information corresponding to the penalty is extracted and its value evaluated.
4. Information regarding application of the penalty is stored in the database for inclusion in generated reports and billing procedures.
5. Regardless of whether the violation had a penalty attached, it is recorded in the database for reporting purposes.

### 4.3.1 Current Penalty Model

The SLA model from Chapter 'The SLA Model' has been extended to include business-related terms. This extension establishes two business terms associated with penalties: *penalty count* and *violation count*. Penalty count is the number of penalties applied to a service upon violation of the signed conditions of that service; violation count is the number of notifications received of violations to an agreement term, guaranteed state or guaranteed action of a service.

In the next section we present a proposal for a unique (albeit as yet unimplemented) model for defining penalties within an SLA, taking into account business considerations and requirements as part of the contract negotiation. This new model has been designed to be flexible, adaptable to different scenarios, and expressive enough to accommodate complex expressions (e.g. penalties for when combinations of different guarantees are violated). An example of this penalty model is given, customised to a simple application such as the Open Reference Case (ORC) (Chapter 'The Open Reference Case').

## 5 A Formal, Novel Penalty Model

Currently, there are various ways to express penalties, some simpler (e.g. a flat rate for the entire SLA, or a linear proportionality per guarantee) and others more complex (such as those in Section 7). These various approaches, however, do not satisfy *all* of the following requirements for formulating complex penalty expressions in a single unambiguous model:

- Able to describe associative penalties, where the penalty for failing one SLA guarantee depends on the state (failed or satisfied) of other guarantee(s)
- Full flexibility regarding QoS levels agreed and/or achieved, without being constrained (e.g. by pre-specified classes of service)

- Openness and applicability to different domains, without dependence on specific languages, taxonomies or technologies.

Motivated by this identified gap, we propose a new, formal penalty model, outlined below:

Let us assume service $S$, and an SLA that governs consumption of this service by a certain customer. Also, assume that the total cost for consumption of the service under this SLA is $C$, and that the agreed QoS is given as a set of guarantees $(Q_1, Q_2, ..., Q_n)$ for the various supported quality metrics and properties. Then, a *set of penalty functions* is defined as:

$$P_m(Q_{1_m}, ..., Q_{N_m}) = C \cdot PW_m \cdot \sum_k QW_k \cdot FR_k \qquad (1)$$

where $m > 0$ and $1_m \leq k \leq N_m$.

$Q_{1_m}, ..., Q_{N_m}$ represents a combination of guarantees that depend on each other, and the violation of one may affect, under specific circumstances, the others. This is a way to express correlations of fine granularity. Thus, a customer can express statements wherein the violation of one guarantee becomes more relevant if another guarantee is also violated.

$P_m$ is a penalty function that corresponds to the above combination $Q_{1_m}, ..., Q_{N_m}$ of guarantees. The sum of all penalty functions during one reporting period represents the total penalties for this SLA during that period.

$PW_m$ is the *weight* of penalty function $P_m$. It indicates how important a function is to the total calculated penalty, and may aid the service provider in making decisions regarding the deployment and implementation of the SLA. The sum of all weights is equal to 1.

$QW_k$ is the weight of one specific guarantee being violated, *for this specific combination* of guarantees. *This value may be arbitrarily high.* It allows the negotiating customer to express the importance of honoring certain guarantees in this penalty function. Take, for example, a case where the guarantees concern the availability of two load-balancing servers. If the availability guarantee for one server is violated, its weight (and hence, the penalty) is kept small. If, however, the availability guarantee of the other server is violated at the same time, there may be a very high weight to suggest an equally high penalty as a result of the system becoming unavailable as a whole.

Finally, $FR_k$ is the failure ratio: the relationship between achieved quality and planned quality. It indicates how far the offered quality has drifted from the agreed quality of a specific service parameter. For instance, if 100% service availability was agreed to but only 90% is achieved, then the failure ratio is 0.1; if a 5 second average response time was agreed but a 6 second average response time is achieved, then the failure ratio is 0.2. By definition, $FR_k$ may also model possible rewards for performing better than agreed.

Previous chapters have discussed the top-down construction of subcontracts from a higher-level contract. In this process, proper values for service properties of the SLAs must be decided and suitable penalties for non-compliance deduced. Thus penalty calculation for subcontracts is part of the SLA negotiation/translation process. Since service properties depend on each other in domain-specific ways, generic analytical expressions of penalties for antecedent services/SLAs cannot be provided. Instead, the next section illustrates how this process would work, by means of an example.

## 6 Example Application

This section provides an example use of the penalty model, roughly based on the Open Reference Case (Chapter 'The Open Reference Case') scenario. It illustrates how the model is applied for a service *PS*, and how it is translated to calculate penalties for antecedent services in this context. Let us assume that the negotiable properties for the payment service are:

- *Availability*, defined as the ratio of service uptime to total monitoring time, over a certain predefined time period (e.g. one month); and
- *Response time*, defined as the time duration from the moment a message is received to the moment a response is generated and put on the wire, for a specific percentage of all invocations.

The customer wants to express that availability must be over 99%, and the penalty for availability dropping to 90% increases up to the full cost. For response time, the customer desires that 98% of invocations return in less than five seconds. The response time penalty increases linearly towards 85% of the calls; at that point, full SLA cost is claimed back. Network delays are not considered in this example. The customer expresses these penalty terms as follows:

$$P(A) = C \cdot 1 \cdot \left( \frac{99}{99 - 90} \cdot FR_A \right) \qquad (2)$$

$$P(R) = C \cdot 1 \cdot \left( \frac{98}{98 - 85} \cdot FR_R \right) \qquad (3)$$

$P(A)$ and $P(R)$ are the penalties for availability and response time respectively. $C$ is the total SLA price. For all penalty functions, a maximum penalty equal to the SLA price is requested ($PW_A = PW_R = 1$). (Note that this may equate to more than the SLA price if more than one parameter is 'sufficiently violated'. The provider may not accept this and may choose instead to set a maximum aggregate penalty. This is something to be negotiated between the two parties and its expression is a syntactical matter mostly related to Chapter 'The SLA Model'.)

The weight for violation of each guarantee is set such that each unit of additional failure from an agreed target contributes linearly to a total failure at the agreed threshold. Thus, $99/(99 - 90)$ is the necessary number to reach a value of 1 when multiplied by the threshold failure ratio of $(99 - 90)/99$ for availability (where 99%

is the planned availability and 90% is the actual availability). Similarly, $98/(98 - 85)$ is required for the response time threshold of 85% (down from 98%).

The planning component of the ORC service provider knows that availability of the payment service $A_g$ depends on availability of the infrastructure on which the service executes. Service response time $R$ depends on use of the infrastructure being sufficiently low. Equations 4 and 5 describe the availability and response time of the payment service in relation to the availability and use of the supporting virtual machines (VMs). Coefficients $k$ and $l$ are specific to the software used, and are known to the planning component via software modeling, monitoring, or other means. A constant $c$ denotes the response time for near-zero use of the VMs. Based on these formulae, the payment service provider deduces the required guaranteed properties and constructs an SLA offer for the infrastructure provider.

$$A_g = min(A_{VM1}, A_{VM2}) \tag{4}$$

$$R = k \cdot U_{VM1} + l \cdot U_{VM2} + c \tag{5}$$

$$A_{VM1}, A_{VM2}, U_{VM1}, U_{VM2} \in [0, 1] \tag{6}$$

The policy of the payment service provider is to ensure that full infrastructure SLA costs will be refunded if the infrastructure provider fails to such an extent that *profit* from the payment service SLA is affected. Thus, although availability of the payment service can be as low as 90% before a full refund is issued — and service availability relates to VM availability as shown in Equation 4 — the payment service provider will ask that it converges sooner to values that constitute 'complete failure' to deliver. As such, the failure multipliers must be larger, to reflect this financial difference. The same applies to response time, and the penalties for infrastructure use levels. (For the purposes of this example, we have assumed that the payment service provider has no implementation costs and that the difference between software SLA price $C$ and infrastructure SLA price $C^*$ is all profit.)

Eventually, this penalty can be formulated as in Equations 7 and 8.

$$P(A_{VM1}, A_{VM2}) = C^* \cdot 1 \cdot \left( \frac{C}{C^*} \cdot \alpha \cdot FR_{A_{VM1}} + \frac{C}{C^*} \cdot \alpha \cdot FR_{A_{VM2}} \right) \tag{7}$$

$$P(U_{VM1}, U_{VM2}) = C^* \cdot 1 \cdot \left( \frac{C}{C^*} \cdot \beta \cdot FR_{U_{VM1}} + \frac{C}{C^*} \cdot \beta \cdot FR_{U_{VM2}} \right) \tag{8}$$

where $\alpha = 99/(99 - 90)$ and $\beta = 98/(98 - 85)$.

These equations can be simplified as follows:

$$P(A_{VM1}, A_{VM2}) = C \cdot \alpha \cdot (FR_{A_{VM1}} + FR_{A_{VM2}}) \tag{9}$$

$$P(U_{VM1}, U_{VM2}) = C \cdot \beta \cdot (FR_{U_{VM1}} + FR_{U_{VM2}}) \tag{10}$$

Taking into account Equations 2 and 3, it holds that:

$$\frac{P(A)}{P(A_{VM1}, A_{VM2})} = \frac{FR_A}{FR_{A_{VM1}} + FR_{A_{VM2}}} \tag{11}$$

$$\frac{P(R)}{P(U_{VM1}, U_{VM2})} = \frac{FR_R}{FR_{U_{VM1}} + FR_{U_{VM2}}} \tag{12}$$

However, it must be underlined that this applies only because of the assumption that the payment service provider has no implementation costs other than the infrastructure for service execution.

## 7 Related Work

In [5], Becker et al. propose a price function over achieved QoS. Subtracting from the agreed price provides the penalty, so the price function can also be considered to be the penalty function. Rewards are also possible using their approach. The main difference between this and the approach presented in this chapter is that in [5], it is not possible to express penalties that involve more than one QoS property or these properties being correlated. That is, quality is seen as a unidirectional aggregated measure for a service, while in fact there may be quality characteristics that cannot be aggregated without preference information and also without property interdependence information.

In [6], Jurca and Faltings suggest a method for calculating penalties based on a reputation mechanism, where all customers evaluate the quality of the service they received. The authors take measures to avoid false voting for price reduction or other fraud. This approach, however, can only be combined with classes of service.

In [7], Rana et al. discuss monitoring and reputation mechanisms for SLAs. The authors look into EU contract law, taking relevant points into account, and then define three broad penalty categories: *all-or-nothing*, *partial* and *weighted partial*. However, a complete mathematical model is not present. The work they present is then related to WS-Agreement, so the relevant negotiation concepts are also discussed.

Finally, Kosinski et al. present in [8] a mathematical formulation of penalty functions that is fairly similar to that presented here (although applied specifically to networking). The paper *does* capture the relationships between different properties, and policies are defined depending on such relationships and their respective combinations. These policies are captured within 'subcontracts' (Kosinski et al. use this term to refer to sections of a single SLA). Kosinki et al. calculate failures using a pre-specified taxonomy (number of violations, amount of violations, etc), while in this paper, failure ratios are considered domain-specific and calculations are left open. In addition, the model from Section 5 assigns a weight not only to each violation, but also to each penalty function (or 'subcontract', using the terminology of [8]).

# 8 Summary and Conclusions

In this chapter, we introduced penalty-related business terms defined within SLA@SOI, as well as capabilities for monitoring and reporting SLA violations. A novel, complete mathematical penalty model was then discussed. Expressions compliant to this model can be integrated within SLAs to define unambiguously the penalties that accompany SLA failures. The model takes into account concepts of fairness, business value and quality parameter interdependencies.

An example application of the model to SLA hierarchies was demonstrated, showing that the model can be applied using domain-specific (and perhaps use-case-specific) knowledge to build analytical penalty expressions at negotiation time, dynamically and according to top-down or bottom-up hierarchy construction.

# References

[1] Cheng S, Chang C, Zhang L, Kim T (2007) Towards competitive web service market. In: 11th IEEE International Workshop on Future Trends of Distributed Computing Systems, p 213219

[2] Hasselmeyer P, Koller B, Kotsiopoulos I, Kuo D, Parkin M (2007) Negotiating slas with dynamic pricing policies. In: Proceedings of the SOC@ Inside07

[3] Marchione F, Fantinato M, de Toledo M, Gimenes I (2009) Price definition in the establishment of electronic contracts for web services. In: Proceedings of the 11th International Conference on Information Integration and Web-based Applications & Services,, ACM, p 217224

[4] Macias M and Guitart J (2010) Maximising revenue in cloud computing markets by means of economically enhanced sla management. In: Tech. Rep. UPC-DAC-RR-CAP-2010-22, Universitat Politecnica de Catalunya, Computer Architecture Department

[5] Becker M, Borrisov N, Deora V, Rana O, Neumann D (2008) Using k-Pricing for Penalty Calculation in Grid Market. In: Hawaii International Conference on System Sciences, Proceedings of the 41st Annual, pp 97–97, DOI 10.1109/HICSS.2008.485

[6] Jurca R, Faltings B (2005) Reputation-Based Service Level Agreements for Web Services. Service-Oriented Computing - ICSOC 2005 pp 396–409, DOI 10.1007/11596141{\_}30

[7] Rana O, Warnier M, Quillinan T, Brazier F (2008) Monitoring and Reputation Mechanisms for Service Level Agreements. Grid Economics and Business Models pp 125–139, DOI 10.1007/978-3-540-85485-2{\_}10

[8] Kosinski J, Radziszowski D, Zielinski K, Zielinski S, Przybylski G, Niedziela P (2008) Definition and Evaluation of Penalty Functions in SLA Management Framework. Networking and Services, International conference on pp 176–181, DOI http://doi.ieeecomputersociety.org/10.1109/ICNS.2008.32

# Dynamic Creation of Monitoring Infrastructures

Howard Foster and George Spanoudakis

## 1 Introduction

As a key part of monitoring and management, systems developed with a Service-Oriented Architecture (SOA) design pattern should utilise negotiated agreements between service providers and requesters. Typically, the results of these negotiations are specified in Service Level Agreements (SLAs), which are then used to monitor key levels of service provided, and to optionally specify preconditions and actions in case these levels are violated. Responsibility for monitoring SLAs (and often individual parts within them) must be dynamically allocated to different monitoring components, since SLAs — and the components available for monitoring them — may change during the operation of a service-based system [4]. The complexity of SLA terms, however, often means that several monitoring components may need to be selected for a single SLA-guaranteed term expression (e.g. availability > 90%), since each part of the expression may be reasoned by a physically different provider. Existing work has shown examples of decomposition based upon simple decomposition of expressions [4], but there is also a need to consider variations between different monitors (e.g. trustworthiness or access constraints) in a dynamic monitoring configuration process.

In this chapter, we show how complex SLA terms specified in the SLA@SOI SLA (Chapter 'The SLA Model') can be decomposed into manageable monitoring configurations, and include a mechanism to support the selection of preferred monitoring components. Advanced configuration is supported by a *MonitoringManager* component which mechanically parses an SLA, generates a formal Abstract Syntax Tree (AST) and decomposes the terms of the AST into expressions for monitoring. Each expression is then used to select appropriate reasoning or service sensor monitoring components. The main contribution of this work is that both the monitoring

Howard Foster, George Spanoudakis,
Department of Computing, City University London, Northampton Square, EC1V 0HB, London.
e-mail: {howard.foster.1,g.e.spanoudakis}@city.ac.uk

configurator and the monitoring configuration specification are generic, reusable artifacts able to be incorporated into other frameworks where configuration of monitoring components is required. The monitoring configurator is already offered as a reusable service that uses standard web-service protocols to enable the use of replaceable selection criteria for candidate monitors; selection criteria can be driven from preferences for monitor provider and/or offered features.

The chapter is structured as follows: Section 2 illustrates the service monitoring architecture and components, whilst Section 3 describes the overall approach to monitoring configuration. In Section 4 we describe the parsing and decomposition of SLAs, and in Section 5, the monitoring component selection algorithms. In Section 6 we discuss implementation and testing of the approach, and in Section 7 we briefly discuss related work. Section 8 concludes the chapter with a discussion of present and future work.

## 2 Architecture

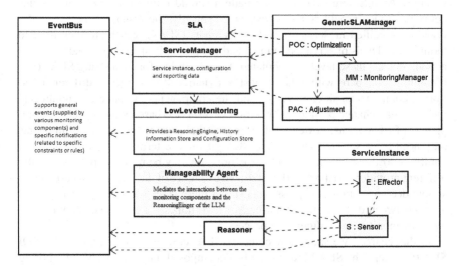

**Fig. 1** A Service Monitoring Architecture

An overview architecture for service monitoring in the SLA@SOA project is illustrated in Figure 1. In this chapter, we focus on the GenericSLAManager (providing generic support for planning, optimisation, adjustment and configuration of monitoring) and monitoring component features (such as reasoners, sensors and effectors). The Planning and Optimization Component (POC) is a local executive controller for a service manager. It is responsible for assessing and customising SLA offers, evaluating available service implementations, and planning optimal service provisioning and monitoring strategies. The POC generates a suitable execution plan for monitoring (based upon a configuration obtained from the MonitoringManager component) and passes this to the Provisioning and Adjustment Component (PAC). The PAC collects information from the Low Level Monitoring System, analyses the incoming events, decides if a problem has occurred or is about to occur, identifies the root cause, and then (if possible) decides on and triggers the best corrective or proactive action. If the problem cannot be solved at a local level, the PAC escalates the issue to a higher level component, namely the POC. In the case of an SLA violation, such an adjustment can trigger re-planning and reconfiguration, and/or alert higher-level SLA monitoring. These capabilities are considered important in order to assure preservation of service provision and resource quality.

The MonitoringManager (MM) coordinates the generation of a monitoring configuration for the system. The MM uses configurable selection criteria to determine which is the most appropriate monitoring configuration for each SLA specification instance it receives. Each monitoring configuration describes which components to configure and how their configurations can be used to best monitor guaranteed states. The Low Level Monitoring Manager is a central entity for storing and processing monitoring data. It collects raw observations, processes them, computes derived metrics, evaluates the rules, stores the history, and offers all this data to other components (accessible via the service manager). It also implements the monitoring part of a ProvisioningRequest, containing constraint-based rules (time- and data-driven evaluations) and ServiceInstance-specific sensor-related configurations. It is general by design, and thus capable of monitoring software services, infrastructure services and other resources. Since POC and PAC functionality is very closely related to domain-specific requirements, they are provided as extendible components. For SLA@SOI case studies, they are already extended for either software service monitoring or infrastructure service monitoring. The MM aims to be generic for all solutions and is provided as one solution.

There are three types of monitoring feature in the monitoring system: First, *sensors*, which collect information from a service instance. Their designs and implementations are domain-specific. Sensors can be injected into the service instance (e.g., service instrumentation), or can be outside the service instance (e.g. intercepting service operation invocations). A sensor can send the collected information to a communication infrastructure (e.g. an Event Bus), or other components can request (query) information from it. There can be many types of sensors, depending on the type of information they are designed to collect, but they all implement a common sensor interface. The interface provides methods for starting, stopping, and configuring a sensor. The second type of monitoring feature is an *effector*. Effectors are components for configuring service instance behaviour. Their designs and implementations are also domain-specific. Like sensors, effectors can be injected into a service instance or can interface with a service configuration. There can be many types of effectors, depending on the service instance to be controlled, but they all implement a common effector interface. The interface provides methods for configuring a service. The third type of monitoring feature is a *reasoner* (also known as a Reasoning Engine), which performs a computation based upon a series of inputs provided by events or messages sent from sensors or effectors. An example reasoner may provide a function to *compute the average completion time* of a service request. In this case, it accepts events from sensors detecting both requests for and responses to a service operation, and computes an average over a period of time. Reasoners also provide access to generic runtime monitoring frameworks, such as EVEREST [15].

## 2.1 Monitoring Features Specification

In addition to an SLA specification (Chapter 'The SLA Model'), the Monitoring-Manager requires a set of feature specifications for monitoring feature types (introduced at the beginning of this section). Component monitoring features are specified for a type of monitoring component and offered for a type of service (Chapter 'The Service Construction Meta-Model' for details of the Service Construction Meta-Model). A feature specification has two instance variables: The *type* variable holds the type of the component, and the permitted types are sensor, effector and reasoner. A sensor provides information about a service, an effector changes the properties of a service, and a reasoner processes information to produce a monitoring result (for example, it consumes information provided by sensors and reports whether or not an SLA is violated). The second instance variable is the *UUID* variable, which uniquely identifies the component with the monitoring features. This variable has the same value as the service UUID. Furthermore, each component feature contains a list of monitoring features. The example in Figure 2 illustrates the component features of an example service. In this example, the sensor component has two monitoring features: one for events reporting *cpu-load*, and another for reporting the number of *logged-users*. The example also illustrates a reasoner component with two monitoring features: one providing a *greater-than* comparison of two input parameter numbers, and the other providing an *MTTR* (Mean Time To Repair) computation output based upon request and response input events.

*Basic* monitoring features are used to distinguish between 'event' and 'primitive' monitoring features. There is a single parameter *type* for the type of basic monitoring feature. In the case of primitive monitoring features, allowed types correspond to the Java primitive types (e.g., Long, Boolean, String, etc). In the case of an event monitoring feature, allowed types are currently request, response and computation (as a result of a function). A basic monitoring feature with a sub-type of *primitive* is used to advertise an ability to report about primitive service information (e.g., cpu_load, logged_users, available_memory, etc). Sensors are the typical components with this kind of feature. A primitive feature has two instance variables: First, a *type* holds the variable type. This can be, for instance, one of the Java standard primitive types. It can also be any other type defined in an SLA vocabulary. The second instance variable is a *unit*, which holds the monitoring feature unit of measurement (e.g., mt, km, kg, etc.). *Event* monitoring features are used to advertise an ability to report about service interactions or service states (e.g., service operation requests and responses, service failures, etc.). Sensors and reasoners are the typical compo-

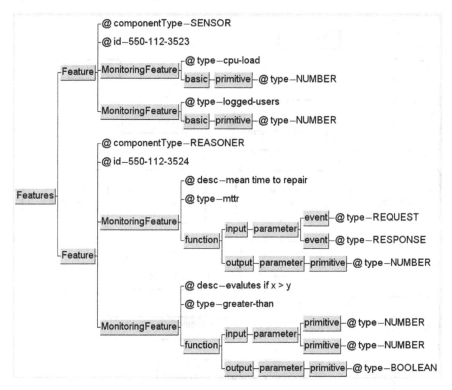

**Fig. 2** Component Monitoring Features as XML Elements

nents with this kind of feature. An event basic sub-type has one instance variable: a *type*. This *type* holds the event type as either request, response or computation. Domain-specific event types can also be defined and used here.

*Function* monitoring features are used to advertise an ability to perform a computation and report its result (e.g., availability, throughput, response_time). Reasoners are the typical components with this kind of feature. The class *Function* has two instance variables: the first is *input*, which holds the list of function input parameters. The second is *output*, which holds the output parameters. Reasoner features are described by a type (the term or operator performed), one or more input parameters, and one output parameter.

## 3 Approach to Configuration

Given an SLA specification and a set of component monitoring features, our approach to dynamic configuration of monitoring infrastructures is based on the process illustrated in Figure 3.

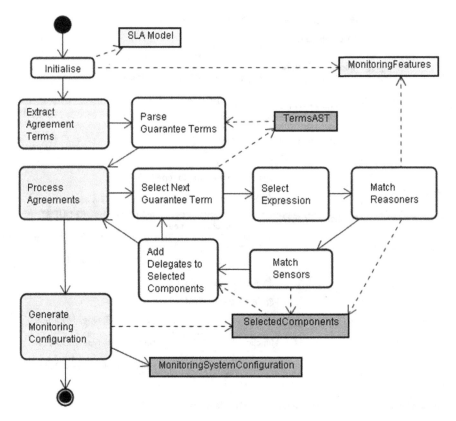

**Fig. 3** SLA Monitoring Configuration Activities

The process starts by extracting the guaranteed states from AgreementTerms of the SLA specification. The terms are then parsed into a formal Abstract Syntax Tree (AST) for the expression of the states. The AST is then used as input to select each expression of each state (by traversal of the AST), and to match each left-hand-side (lhs), operator, and right-hand-side (rhs) of the expression with appropriate component monitoring features. The matching algorithms are discussed in Section 5. Following selection, the delegate components form a Selected Components list, which is used to generate a complete Monitoring System Configuration (MSC) for an SLA. If no suitable monitoring configuration can be formed (i.e. all monitoring requirements could not be matched), then an empty configuration is returned for a particular agreement term. This approach can be used in two types of situation: firstly, to configure the monitoring system when a new SLA needs to be monitored, and secondly, to perform adjustments to an existing configuration when requirements change or violations are detected. The main focus in this chapter is the first of these situations: we assume a new SLA is to monitored and therefore do not consider how this would affect the current state of monitoring.

# 4 SLA Term Decomposition

The MM abstracts the guaranteed states (guarantees made by any of the parties involved in the agreement) that certain states of affairs will hold for the service. We
abstract these states from the agreement terms and parse the terms using a grammar
based upon the Backus Normal Form (BNF) specification of the SLA specification [14]. The grammar for the parser is currently based only upon the agreement
terms and guaranteed state expressions. A sample part of the grammar is listed in
Figure 4.

```
/1****************************************************************************
*2SLA: The Specification of agreement terms
*3***************************************************************************/
void SLA() : {} {
  5AgreementTerm()* }
/6****************************************************************************
*7Agreement: AgreementTerms in SLA Model
*8***************************************************************************/
void AgreementTerm() : {} {
10GuaranteeTerm()((TermOperator()) GuaranteeTerm())* }
11***************************************************************************
12GuaranteeTerm: A guaranteed state expression
13***************************************************************************/
void GuaranteeTerm() : {} {
15QUOTED_STRING> (Term())(Comparator())(Term())}
16***************************************************************************
17Term: One or more TermFunctions or Identifier
18***************************************************************************/
void Term() : {} {
20LOOKAHEAD(TermFunction()) TermFunction() | <STRING> | <QUOTED_STRING> }
21***************************************************************************
22Comparator: Operators in Term expression
23***************************************************************************/
void Comparator() : {} {
25 <EQUALS> | <NOTEQUAL> | <LTHAN> | <GTHAN> | <LEQUAL> | <GEQUAL> |
26 <ISEQUALTO> ) }
```

**Fig. 4** Partial JavaCC Grammar for SLA Term Decomposition

The grammar is used as input to the Java Compiler Compiler (JavaCC) [16],
which generates compiler source code to accept and parse source files specified in a
defined grammar language. The resulting AST is built to represent the SLA specification terms and expressions. Beginning with the SLA declaration (lines 4–5), one
or more AgreementTerms are parsed. Each AgreementTerm (lines 9–10) is parsed
as one or more GuaranteeTerms, separated by a comparison operator. Each GuaranteeTerm (lines 14–15) is then parsed as an Identifier (which holds the ID label
of the GuaranteeTerm), and a basic Term followed by a comparison operator and
then followed by another basic Term. Each basic Term (lines 19–20) is represented
by either one or more TermFunctions (similar to a normal function call syntax), a
string Identifier (representing a variable of the SLA specification. The JavaCC function *LOOKAHEAD* informs the parser to check whether the next symbol to parse is

a function or string. Finally, the Comparator operators (lines 24–26) list the acceptable types of operators that can be used between GuaranteeTerms.

Since Term decomposition is based upon a generated parser, other SLA specification formats may generate their own parsers and transform their SLA specification to the AST input required by the MonitoringManager. In this way, the implementation of the configurator is generic and reusable. In addition, the generated AST compiler can be reused by monitorability agents (which accept the monitoring system configuration as a result of matching monitoring components). These Agents can translate the SLA terms into their own language specification. As an example, we have performed such a translation for the EVEREST monitoring language [15], which is based on Event Calculus and is used to analyse expressions in use cases of the SLA@SOI project SLA (Chapter 'Introduction to the SLA@SOI Industrial Use Cases').

# 5 Monitoring Configuration

## 5.1 Monitor Selection

A main configuration algorithm *MonitorConfig* (illustrated in Figure 5) is responsible for selecting all the term expressions from the prepared SLA term tree (Terms AST), obtaining a match for the expression terms with available monitoring component features, and then building a suitable monitoring system configuration. The algorithm begins by selecting the root of each AgreementTerm expression, which in turn holds one or more guaranteed state expressions (GuaranteeTerms). An AgreementTerm expression is predefined as a set of Boolean expressions (where all must result in *true* for the AgreementTerm to be upheld). Each GuaranteeTerm has a left-hand-side term, a right-hand-side term, and an operator. From these terms, a set of input types is determined. Two term monitors (M1 and M2) are set to analyse the terms, and a reasoner monitor is set to analyse the entire expression. If the left-hand-side of the expression is itself an expression, then the second monitor (M2) is recursively configured using the same algorithm (MonitorConfig). If this is not the case, then the value of the right-hand-side of the expression is used as the monitor. Furthermore, a reasoner monitor is assigned to select a monitor appropriate to the input types, operation, and required monitor features .

The MonitorConfig algorithm uses a *SelectMonitor* algorithm (Figure 5) to match the required types and operations (or term names) to the monitoring component features. The algorithm begins by iterating the monitoring component features available and building an appropriate feature list, (FeaturedMonitors), by selecting the monitors that match the type of term or operator. Each FeaturedMonitor is then selected and checked for appropriate input types. For example, the operator < (less than) can be provided for numeric input types. If the feature and types match, the FeaturedMonitor is added to a list of selected monitors (SelectedMonitors). In the

| **Function:** | **MonitorConfig**. Given an agreement, select the most appropriate monitoring components. | **SelectMonitor**. Given a set of input types and a monitor term, select the first monitor that matches the term or event types required. |
| --- | --- | --- |
| **Input(s):** | 1) Terms AST: an AST of the Guaranteed Agreement Terms. 2) Features: a list of service monitoring features. | 1) Input Types: a set of types (e.g. Number, Event, etc.). 2) Term: a term or operation to be monitored (e.g. completion-time or ¡ (operator)). 3) Features: a list of service monitoring features. |
| **Output(s):** | a set of monitoring components with configurations. | A monitoring component offering the types and operation/term. |
| **Algorithm:** | Given the Terms AST and a set of monitoring features<br>1) **select** root of AST and extract *expressions*<br>2) **extract** lhs, rhs, operation and **select** input-types<br>3) **set** M1 to **MonitorConfig(***lhs***)**<br>4) **if** *node.lhs* is **expression** then<br>  (a) **set** M2 to **MonitorConfig(***rhs***)** **otherwise set** M2 to *rhs.value*<br>5) **set** RM to **SelectMonitor(***input-types***,***operation***,***Features***)**<br>6) **store** delegate for expression | Given the input types, MonitoringFeatures and Term:<br>1) **for each** MonitoringFeature in Features **do**<br>  (a) **select** FeaturedMonitors where *type* **equals** the Term<br>2) **for each** Monitor in FeaturedMonitors **do**<br>  (a) **for each** *type* in input types **do**<br>    (i) **if** Monitor has *Type*, then<br>      (ia) **add** Monitor to SelectedMonitors<br>3) **select** the first Monitor in SelectedMonitors *(*replaceable selection criteria)*<br>4) **return** *SelectedMonitor* |

**Fig. 5** Algorithms for MonitorConfig (left) and SelectMonitor (right)

current implementation of the work, we simply select the first monitor matched. It is envisaged that an enhanced implementation will use some optimisation algorithm (at step 3. of the SelectMonitor algorithm), which will be based on criteria specified by the user (or indeed, specified as part of the overall SLA). This could also include assessing use of the same provider of features to group related monitors, reduce financial cost and optimise messaging.

## 5.2 System Configuration

As briefly discussed in Section 2, the MSC defines an entire configuration for monitoring an SLA within the monitoring system. An example MSC is illustrated in Figure 6, showing a reasoner component (for monitoring a guaranteed state), and a set monitoring feature components for each part of the guaranteed state expressions.

The MSC contains a list of components representing sensors, effectors or reasoners selected to support the GuaranteeTerms of agreements in an SLA.

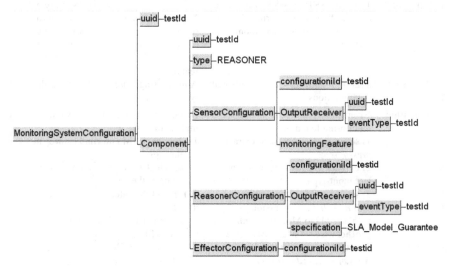

**Fig. 6** A Monitoring System Configuration

Each component in an MSC contains one or more component configurations for each of the different components. For example, an MSC can contain a reasoner component that has component configurations for two sensor components and one additional reasoner component. The sensor component configuration contains a MonitoringFeature (that used to advertise features during selection of the sensor component) and one or more OutputReceiver(s). An OutputReceiver is another component which expects the result (as an event or value) to perform its own function. A reasoner component configuration also specifies one or more OutputReceivers, but a *specification* component replaces the MonitoringFeature component. The specification component lists the guaranteed states required by the component for reasoning.

## 5.3 Configuration Deployment

Here we briefly outline configuration deployment as an aid to the reader in understanding how the output is leveraged in the environment. As illustrated in Figure 1, a generated MSC is passed to a *service manager*, which links a service instance with a service *manageability agent*. The manageability agent exposes a method to accept a configuration and then, on behalf of the service under agreement, starts dependent components to monitor the service activities and to generate any notifications as part of that agreement. For example, each AgreementTerm has a reasoner (the sum of evaluating all guaranteed states in the SLA). Each GuaranteeTerm also has a reasoner (to evaluate the expression of each guaranteed state). Once the service manageability agent is initialised, each reasoner is configured with the appropriate part of the MSC (e.g. for a cpu_load evaluation). The results generated by the reasoners and sensors in this configuration will be monitored by the manageability agent and appropriately routed from the Event Bus.

## 6 Implementation and Validation

### 6.1 The MonitoringManager Packages

The approach and algorithms discussed in this chapter are supported by a number of implementation packages. In particular the *MonitoringManager* component is available as an OSGI-enabled [10] JAVA package and can also be hosted as a web-service. In this section, we describe each of these packages with classes and their relationships (as depicted in Figure 7).

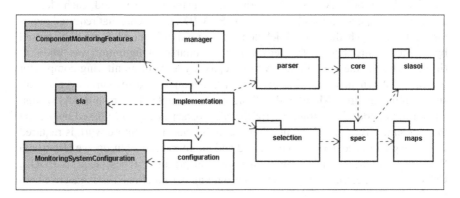

**Fig. 7** Core Implementation Packages of the MonitoringManager

The MonitoringManager module is split into a number of packages: The core package *implementation* supports the MonitorConfig algorithm (as described in Section 5) provided by a *checkMonitorability* method, which accepts an SLA model (Chapter 'The SLA Model'), and a set of monitoring features (Chapter 'The Service Construction Meta-Model'). In turn, the implementation package depends initially on a *parser* package to support parsing of each AgreementTerm in the SLA model. The parser package provides an *AgreementTerm* class containing a *parse* method which accepts an AgreementTerm of the SLA and produces an expression AST (as described in Section 4). A sub-package of the parser package is the core parser itself, built from the compilation of a JavaCC grammar for the SLA agreements.

The implementation package also references the methods of a *SelectionManager* class contained within the *selection* package. This class provides methods and an overall framework for matching and selecting the most appropriate monitoring feature components with that of the expressions parsed previously (i.e. the SelectMonitor algorithm). To enable future dynamic configuration of selection algorithms, the SelectionManager refers to an extendable *ComponentSelector* module, offering a flexible *selectAppropriateComponent* method which may be redefined for preferred component selection strategies. Finally, the *configuration* package is used by the *checkMonitorability* method to configure the component selections into a required MonitoringSystemConfiguration format (Chapter 'The Service Construction Meta-Model' for format specification).

## 6.2 Testing and Validation

To thoroughly test the implementation scope and suitability of configurations produced, we devised an SLA coverage test based upon each of the model elements described in the SLA@SOI SLA Model and the features available using a monitoring engine. Aligned with the work on translation and monitoring of SLAs (Chapter 'Translation of SLAs into Monitoring Specifications'), we listed: each element along with its specifications in a test SLA (SLA-ID), the events that required monitoring (Events), whether the model element expression in the SLA could be parsed by the MonitoringManager (Parsed), whether a suitable configuration was produced (MSC), whether the configuraton was accepted by a client monitoring component (Client), and whether any violation or service request and response events were successfully captured (Monitored). (Table 1 lists a sample of the results.) As we discussed in Section 4, the grammar for the SLA parser is currently based only upon the AgreementTerm and GuaranteeTerm expressions. Thus future work is required to enable guaranteed actions to be parsed and monitored. In addition, we also tested SLA model metrics (such as units of time) and primitive types (such as BOOL, CONST, TIME, etc.), mixing them and providing permutations for exhaustive testing.

The other main tests that have been carried out related to the use cases featured in the SLA@SOI project; The SLA specifications for both B4 (Chapter 'The Enterprise IT Use Case Scenario') and B6 (Chapter 'The eGovernment Use Case Scenario') have been fully covered in testing. We also expect to continue testing with other monitoring engines, for example, the ASTRO Project's [11] SLA monitoring tools can be tested with infrastructure monitoring components.[1]s

---

[1] The MonitoringManager implementation, EVEREST monitoring framework, and SLA@SOI test cases are an integrated part of the SLA@SOI project platform showcase and are available from: http://sourceforge.net/projects/sla-at-soi/

**Table 1** Sample Test Cases for SLA Elements, Parsing, Configuration and Monitoring

| Model | SLA-ID | Events | Parsed | MSC | Client | Monitored |
|---|---|---|---|---|---|---|
| InterfaceDeclrs | ID1 | None | Yes | Yes | Yes | No |
| AgreementTerms | AT1 | Violation | Yes | Yes | Yes | Yes |
| Guaranteed Actions[a] | GA1 | Violation | No | No | No | No |
| Guaranteed States | GS1 | Violation | Yes | Yes | Yes | Yes |
| VariableDeclrs | VD1 | Computation | Yes | Yes | Yes | Yes |
| Terms | SLA-ID | Events | Parsed | MSC | Client | Monitored |
| core:and | GS1 | Computation | Yes | Yes | Yes | Yes |
| core:equals | GS1 | Computation | Yes | Yes | Yes | Yes |
| core:sum | GS1 | Computation | Yes | Yes | Yes | Yes |
| core:series | GS2 | Computation | Yes | Yes | Yes | Yes |
| core:availability | GS1 | Request-Response | Yes | Yes | Yes | Yes |

[a] The element is not currently supported

# 7 Related Work

Background and related work in this chapter falls within two areas: First, we consider the definition and translation of SLAs, and second, the runtime monitoring of service-based systems based upon monitoring features.

Several projects have focused on SLA definitions and provisioning in the context of both web and grid services. The Adaptive Services Grid (ASG) project, for example, has designed an architecture for establishing and monitoring SLAs in grid environments [8]. In this architecture, the monitoring rules and parameters as well as the architecture for SLA monitoring are statically defined and cannot be updated at runtime. The TrustCOM project has also produced a reference implementation for SLA establishment and monitoring [17]. This implementation, however, does not involve the dynamic setup of monitoring infrastructures. The SLA Monitoring and Evaluation architecture presented within the IT-Tude project [7] has several similarities with the approach presented in this chapter, such as the need to separate SLAs from service management. This work focuses, however, on statically binding services and monitors, whilst the SLA@SOI work focuses on dynamically allocating monitors to SLA parts, based upon matching the exact terms that need to be monitored and the monitoring capabilities available for different services. Further, in the IRMOS project architecture [19], service monitors are used to gather information about QoS levels. The SLA@SOI approach splits these monitors into three types, providing greater flexibility and catering for changing services (with effectors) as the need arises. With regards to SLA translation, in [18, 12], the authors describe decomposing an SLA of resource requirements (with the purpose of building a system that represents the SLA required). This approach is focused more on building a system rather than monitoring existing services; however, it also employs techniques to optimise and arrange efficient configurations based upon the SLA expressions stated. In [13], the authors consider evaluating expressions for conditions of properties of services (e.g. response time), however, their SLA format appears to offer only single assertions rather than complex expressions.

Work on runtime monitoring of service-based systems has resulted in the development of different types of monitors. These monitors realise either intrusive or event-based monitoring. Intrusive monitoring relies on weaving the execution of monitoring activities at runtime using code that realises the service itself or the orchestration process. In the case of composite services, this can be done directly in a process engine, by interleaving monitoring code with the process executable code as in [2, 3, 1, 9]. The assessment of monitoring service properties required by SLAs cannot be easily achieved through this paradigm, since the properties to be monitored and the actions required for monitoring must be interleaved with service execution code, and therefore known *a priori* by the system designer.

The work described in this chapter extends existing approaches to dynamic generation of monitoring system configurations [4, 5, 6]. Specifically, we consider individual agreement terms within an SLA by decomposition of complex guarantee expressions, utilise a wider spectrum of monitoring components (e.g. sensors and effectors), and support complex monitoring configurations that can engage different monitoring components for checking the same SLA term if necessary.

# 8 Conclusions and Future Work

In this chapter we have described an approach to advanced configuration of service systems, in particular, systems in which an SLA agreement has been established and concerns services that require monitoring. The work aims to provide a generic module, applicable not only to the architecture illustrated, but also to other architectures (although still based upon SLAs and monitoring component features). This work will be extended to cover further elements of the SLA specification (such as guaranteed actions, which are not presently considered), and also to include preferential selection of monitoring components. Preferential selection of components is useful where there are multiple monitoring components offered for the same term. Preferences could be based upon monitoring cost (either in terms of computing resources or financially) or non-functional requirements. The existing implementation is already part of the wider SLA@SOI project monitoring platform, providing integration and validation testing, and we are keen to seek other environments in which to test it.

# References

[1] Baresi, L., Bianculli, D., Ghezzi, C.: Validation of Web Service Compositions. IET Software **1**(6), 219–232 (2007)

[2] Baresi, L., Guinea, S.: Towards Dynamic Monitoring of WS-BPEL Processes. In: International Conference on Service-Oriented Computing (ICSOC) (2005)

[3] Bianculli, D., Ghezzi, C.: Monitoring Conversational Web Services. In: 2nd International Workshop on Service Oriented Software Engineering (IW-SOSWE) (2007)

[4] Comuzzi, M., Spanoudakis, G.: Dynamic Set-up of Monitoring Infrastructures for Service-Based Systems. In: 25th Annual ACM Symposium on Applied Computing, Track on Service Oriented Architectures and Programming (SAC 2010). ACM, Sierre, Switzerland (2010)

[5] Foster, H., Spanoudakis, G.: Model-Driven Service Configuration with Formal SLA Decomposition and Selection. In: The 4th International Symposium On Leveraging Applications of Formal Methods, Verification and Validation (ISoLA). Crete, Greece (2010)

[6] Foster, H., Spanoudakis, G.: Advanced Service Monitoring Configurations with SLA Decomposition and Selection. In: 26th Annual ACM Symposium on Applied Computing (SAC) Track on Service Oriented Architectures and Programming (SOAP). ACM, TaiChung, Taiwan (2011)

[7] IT-Tude: SLA Monitoring and Evaluation Technology Solution. Available from: http://www.it-tude.com/?id=gridipedia (2009)

[8] Jank, K.: Reference Architecture: Adaptive Services Grid Deliverable D6.V-1. Available from: http://asg-platform.org/twiki/pub/Public/ProjectInformation (2005)

[9] Lazovik, A., Aiello, M., Papazoglou, M.: Planning and Monitoring the Execution of Web Service Requests. International Journal of Digital Libraries (2006)

[10] OSGi Alliance: OSGi Service Platform Core Specification Version 4.2. Available from: http://www.osgi.org/Download/Release4V42 (2011)

[11] Pistore, M., Barbon, F., Bertoli, P., Shaparau, D., Traverso, P.: Planning and Monitoring Web Service Composition. In: AIMSA, pp. 106–115 (2004)

[12] Richter, J., Baruwal, C., Kowalczyk, R., Quoc Vo, B., Adeel Talib, M., Colman, A.: Utility Decomposition and Surplus Redistribution in Composite SLA Negotiation. In: IEEE International Conference on Services Computing (2010)

[13] Sahai, A., Machiraju, V., Sayal, M., Jin, L.J., Casati, F.: Automated SLA Monitoring for Web Services. In: IEEE/IFIP DSOM, pp. 28–41. Springer-Verlag (2002)

[14] SLA@SOI: Deliverable D.A1a: Framework Architecture. Available from: http://sla-at-soi.eu/publications/deliverables (2009)

[15] Spanoudakis, G., Kloukinas, C., Mahbub, K.: The SERENITY Runtime Monitoring Framework. In: Security and Dependability for Ambient Intelligence,Information Security Series. Springer (2009)

[16] Sun Microsystems: The Java Compiler Compiler (JavaCC). Available from: https://javacc.dev.java.net/ (1999)

[17] TrustCOM: Deliverable 64: Final TrustCoM Reference Implementation and Associated Tools and User Manual. Available from: http://www.eu-trustcom.com/ (2007)

[18] Yuan, C., Iyer, S., Liu, X., Milojicic, D., Sahai, A.: SLA Decomposition: Translating Service Level Objectives to System Level Thresholds. In: Fourth International Conference on Autonomic Computing (ICAC) (2007)

[19] Menychtas, A., Gogouvitis, S., Katsaros, G., Konstanteli, K., Kousiouris, G., Kyriazis, D., Oliveros, E., Umanesan, G., Malcolm, M., Oberle, K., Voith, T., Boniface, M., Bassem, M., Berger, S.: Deliverable D3.1.3: Updated version of IRMOS Overall Architecture. Available from: http://www.irmosproject.eu/Deliverables/ (2010)

# Runtime Prediction

Davide Lorenzoli and George Spanoudakis

**Abstract** Monitoring the preservation of quality of service (QoS) properties during the operation of service-based systems at runtime is an important verification measure for determining whether current service usage is compliant with agreed SLAs. Monitoring, however, does not always provide sufficient scope for taking control actions against violations, as it only detects violations after they occur.

This chapter describes a model-based prediction framework for detecting potential violations of QoS properties *before* they occur to enable the undertaking of control actions that could prevent the violations. EVEREST+ receives prediction specifications expressed in Event Calculus and automatically identifies relevant monitoring data that should be collected at runtime to infer QoS property prediction models. It then analyses runtime monitoring data to infer statistical prediction models for the relevant properties, and uses the models to detect potential violations of QoS properties and the probability of such violations.

## 1 Introduction

Monitoring the preservation of quality of service (QoS) properties during the operation of service-based systems at runtime is an important verification measure for determining whether current usage and behaviour of the services deployed by the system is compliant with Service Level Agreements (SLAs) set for these services. Monitoring of SLA-specified QoS properties has received significant attention in the literature, and several approaches and monitoring systems have been developed to support it: for example, [10], [8], [1], and [5]. Most of these approaches and systems, however, can only support the detection of a QoS property violation once it has occurred. Thus, they do not provide sufficient scope for taking control actions

Davide Lorenzoli, George Spanoudakis
Department of Computing, City University London, Northampton Square, EC1V 0HB, London.
e-mail: {davide.lorenzoli.1,gespan}@soi.city.ac.uk

that could prevent violations, or that could warn relevant parties that violations are likely to occur.

This chapter describes EVEREST+, a new prediction framework for predicting potential violations of QoS properties in SLAs. EVEREST+ addresses three limitations that cause existing techniques to fall short of providing adequate support for runtime prediction of SLA violations: generality, integration, and focus.

*Generality*. Existing techniques tend to focus on the prediction of specific types of properties, without providing a more generic framework for building predictors that can cover a wide or even an entire spectrum of service properties that can be part of an SLA. EVEREST+ has been designed to be an extensible prediction framework. Users can implement their own prediction algorithms and plug them into the framework to extend its prediction capabilities.

*Integration*. Existing techniques do not allow for integration with environments for monitoring SLAs for service-based systems. EVEREST+, however, integrates EVEREST into its design. EVEREST currently allows properties to be monitored by simply writing a monitoring specification; no code needs to be written. However, EVEREST+ is not chained to EVEREST; it allows users to develop their own modules to interface with their own monitoring frameworks.

*Focus*. Existing techniques tend to focus on system infrastructure properties (e.g., network and server properties) rather than service-level application-based properties (e.g., service throughput, mean-time-to-failure). EVEREST+, however, can monitor properties at different levels: for example, infrastructure and application levels. Moreover, thanks to its specification-driven monitoring, it allows for a user-defined monitoring specification to extend its default set of monitoring capabilities.

The EVEREST+ integrated monitoring-prediction framework addresses a lack of integration between monitoring and prediction systems, and the tendency to provide specific prediction algorithms instead of a generic framework for building predictors. The EVEREST+ framework provides a coherent approach to data collection and analysis, both for monitoring and prediction purposes. Moreover, it supports the development of algorithms designed for use in monitoring and prediction, which can be used to extend its framework abilities. Also, it defines a single point of access for configuring the integrated framework.

Below we examine EVEREST+ in more detail: Section 2 compares EVEREST+ with existing work; Section 3 introduces an example scenario; Section ?? presents EVEREST, the monitoring framework used by EVEREST+; Section 5 describes the prediction specification, a document used to request predictions in EVEREST+; Section 6 illustrates the EVEREST+ architecture and gives insights into its most significant components; and Section 7 summarises the EVEREST+ peculiarities and gives a roadmap for future developments.

## 2 Related Work

Several different approaches to QoS monitoring have been proposed in the literature (e.g. [10], [8], [1]) and recommendations about QoS metrics measurement for web services have been described in [12].

Michlmayr et al. [8] present an event-based QoS monitoring and SLA violation detection framework. They developed client- and service-side monitoring and integrated these into VRESCo [9], a runtime environment for service-oriented computing. At the moment, VRESCo supports a limited list of QoS properties. Our approach, like that of [8], can monitor both client- and server-side, but it does not have a fixed list of supported QoS properties. Indeed, users can specify new properties to be monitored as EC-Assertions.

Sahai et al. [10] present an automated and distributed SLA monitoring engine. They use both client- and service-side collected information. There is not a fixed set of monitorable properties, but to add a new property, a new SLA evaluator component must be developed and deployed into the framework. Our approach does not require any new components to be developed or deployed in this case. All that is required is to write a new AC-Assertion specification.

De Luc et al. [1] present a middleware component for monitoring services and service delivery and providing coherent monitoring data to businesses using them in runtime decision making settings. This work focuses on data collection and how to efficiently deliver that data to other components. Our approach also detects when monitored data violates QoS requirements.

Leitner et al. [5] present an approach for predicting SLA violations at runtime. This prediction approach requires the definition at design-time of checkpoints for each property being predicted. Moreover, it does not support the prediction of aggregate properties. Our approach does not require the definition of any checkpoints; in fact, a prediction can be requested at any time. Our approach also allows prediction of aggregate properties.

All the approaches described above focus on monitoring or prediction only. However, our approach integrates monitoring *and* prediction within the same coherent framework. Moreover, we provide a more generic framework for building predictors that can cover a wide or even an entire spectrum of service properties able to be included in an SLA.

## 3 Example Scenario

The scenario described in this section, and shown in Figure 1, has three actors: a service provider *Srv*, a set of users contractually engaged to *Srv* by agreed SLAs, and EVEREST+, which users utilise to predict SLA violations.

The service provider *Srv* makes available several services (e.g., *Srv.s*1 and *Srv.s*2), and defines service unavailability as follows: a service is unavailable when the time elapsed between a service call and its expected response is greater than a

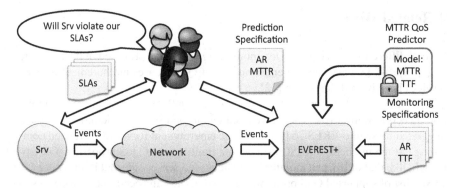

**Fig. 1** Scenario in which users request EVEREST+ to predict violations of SLAs they agreed to with their service provider *Srv*

threshold $d$. The meaning of $d$ should not be confused with the concept of service *response time* (RT), which might be defined between the parties in agreed SLAs. To guarantee correct service utilisation, between RT and $d$ values should hold the relation $d \gg \overline{RT}$, where $\overline{RT}$ is the service's average response time.

Users are interested in knowing whether their SLAs will be violated; both users and *Srv* can violate SLAs. In this scenario, they are concerned about violations of two QoS terms: *arrival rate* (AR) and *mean time to repair* (MTTR). In our example, arrival rate measures the mean number of new calling units arriving at the service provider *Srv* per unit time, whilst mean time to repair measures the average time a service operation on *Srv* takes to repair after a failure. Predicting AR allows users to tune their service usage such that it will not exceed agreed thresholds. Also, predicting *Srv* MTTR allows users to plan their *Srv* service usage after considering predicted *Srv* service availability. Users agreed with the service provider *Srv* on the following constraints: $AR \leq 20r/s$ and $MTTR \leq 40s$, where $r$ is the requests and $s$ is the seconds. Prediction requests are made by providing EVEREST+ with prediction specifications. A *prediction specification* is a document containing the QoS term constraints being predicted, e.g., $MTTR \leq 40s$, and settings to customise the prediction task, e.g., when to perform the prediction, the time the prediction refers to, QoS predictor settings, and monitoring settings. In the example, the users provide EVEREST+ with prediction specifications for predicting AR and MTTR.

EVEREST+ is invoked by users wanting to receive predictions about SLA violations; more specifically, predictions about violations of guaranteed states. A *guaranteed state* is the SLA part in which QoS terms and their constraints are defined. EVEREST+ exposes monitoring and prediction capabilities: that is, those states that can be monitored and predicted. Its monitoring capabilities are given by its set of monitoring specifications, whilst its prediction capabilities are given by its set of QoS predictors. A *monitoring specification* is a document interpreted by the EVEREST monitoring framework, part of EVEREST+, containing directives about how to monitor specific properties, i.e., how to set up EVEREST. In the example, EVER-

EST+ already has monitoring specifications for monitoring arrival rate and *time to fail* (TTF). A *QoS predictor* is an EVEREST+ software component implementing a prediction algorithm. In the example, EVEREST+ already has the QoS predictor for predicting MTTR violations.

At runtime, once all SLAs between users and services have been established and EVEREST+ has been provided with prediction specifications, users begin to receive violation predictions. EVEREST monitors services provided by *Srv* by collecting events sent by *Srv*. EVEREST processes these events to compute the values of the QoS specified in its monitoring specification. In the example, the monitoring event calculates QoS values about MTTR and AR and stores these in its historical database. EVEREST+ computes statistical models by analysing the QoS historical database for the QoS terms specified in the prediction specification. In the example, it computes models for AR and MTTR. On top of these activities, QoS predictors execute their algorithms and compute predictions.

Generally, prediction algorithms rely on historical data and/or models representing properties about historical data, e.g., statistical models obtained by analysing historical data. EVEREST+ provides QoS predictors with both *raw* historical data and inferred statistical models. Data required by QoS predictors might change with respect to the algorithms they implement. In the example, Figure 1 shows a lock on MTTR QoS predictor; this means that it requires some data to operate. In fact, it requires two statistical models: the probability distribution function of MTTR and TTF historical QoS values. When a QoS predictor depends on some data to operate, there can be two possibilities:

1. EVEREST has the monitoring specifications for collecting the needed data, and therefore models can be derived, or
2. EVEREST does not have the needed monitoring configurations, and EVEREST+ cannot supply the QoS predictor with the needed data.

In the example, the MTTR QoS predictor requires MTTR and TTF models, but EVEREST+ only has monitoring specifications for computing AR and TTF QoS values. In this case, together with a prediction specification, EVEREST+ can be provided with the monitoring specification for computing the required QoS terms, e.g., the monitoring specification for computing MTTR values. This mechanism, together with the possibility of extending the default set of QoS predictors with user-developed ones, allows users to predict their own defined QoS terms.

## 4 Background: The EVEREST Monitoring Framework

EVEREST [11] is a generic monitoring engine for runtime checking of violations of software system properties expressed in an Event Calculus (EC) [3]-based language called EC-Assertion. EVEREST has been used to monitor different types of properties of software systems, including functional security and dependability properties [11]. It has also been applied to monitoring of SLA guarantee terms for service-based systems [7]. Whilst a full description of EVEREST is beyond the scope of this paper, in this section we provide an overview of the language it uses to express monitorable SLA guarantee terms to enable the reader to understand how the prediction specifications used by the prediction framework relate to specifications of these terms.

More specifically, the SLA terms that can be checked by EVEREST are expressed as EC-Assertion monitoring rules and/or assumptions of the form: $body \Rightarrow head$. The semantics of a monitoring rule of this form is that when the body of the rule evaluates to *True*, its head must also evaluate to *True*. The semantics of assumption of this form is that when the body of the rule evaluates to *True*, its head is deduced by EVEREST. The body and head of EC-Assertion rules and assumptions are defined in terms of standard EC predicates:

- $Happens(e,t,\Re(lb,ub))$ - This predicate denotes that an instantaneous event $e$ occurs at some time $t$ within the time range $\Re(lb,ub)$, where $lb \leq ub$ are $\Re$ lower and upper bounds.
- $HoldsAt(f,t)$ - This predicate denotes that a state (a.k.a. fluent) $f$ holds at time $t$.
- $Initiates(e,f,t)$ and $Terminates(e,f,t)$ - These predicates denote the initiation and termination of a fluent $f$ by an event $e$ at time $t$ respectively, and
- $Initially(f)$ which denotes that a fluent $f$ holds at the start of the operation of a system.

An example of an SLA term specified in EC-Assertion is shown in Figure 2. The formulas in the table check whether the mean time to repair (MTTR) of a service _Srv (i.e. the mean length of the periods of time over which the service does not respond to operation calls and is therefore unavailable) is always below a given threshold $K$; i.e., $MTTR \leq K$.

More specifically, rule (1) in Figure 2 checks for $MTTR$ violations when a call of an operation of the service _Srv is served after a period of unavailability. The first two conditions in the rule check whether a served operation call has occurred. The latter two conditions check whether this happened at a time when the service was unavailable.

The first assumption (2) in Figure 2 initiates the fluent *Unavailable(_PeriodNumber* $+1, \_Srv, t_1)$ to represent a period of service unavailability. This fluent is initiated when a service call occurs (i.e., the call represented by the event _id1), and no response to this call is produced within $d$ time units, and at the time of the call, the service was not already unavailable (i.e., no fluent of the form *Unavailable(_PeriodNum, _Srv, _STime)* already holds). The number of the new unavailability period is determined by increasing the variable _PeriodNumber whose current value is extracted from the fluent $MTTR(\_Srv, \_PeriodNum, \_MTTR)$ which keeps a record of the number of the past periods of unavailability of the service (i.e., _PeriodNumber) and the mean length of time during which the service remained unavailable in each of these periods (i.e., the value of the variable _MTTR). As a new period of unavailability is initiated for the service,

**Rule R1:**

$$Happens(e(\_id1, \_Snd, \_Srv, Call(\_O), \_Srv), t_1, [t_1, t_1]) \;\wedge$$
$$Happens(e(\_id2, \_Srv, \_Snd, Response(\_O), \_Srv), t_2, [t_1, t_1 + d]) \;\wedge$$
$$\exists \_PeriodNumber, \_STime, MTTR : HoldsAt(Unavailable(\_PeriodNumber, \_Srv, \_STime), t_1) \;\wedge$$
$$HoldsAt(MTTR(\_Srv, \_PeriodNumber, \_MTTR), t_1) \Rightarrow$$
$$\_MTTR < K$$

(1)

**Assumption R1.A1:**

$$Happens(e(\_id1, \_Snd, \_Srv, Call(\_O), \_Srv), t_1, [t_1, t_1]) \;\wedge$$
$$\neg Happens(e(\_id2, \_Srv, \_Snd, Response(\_O), \_Srv), t_2, [t_1, t_1 + d]) \;\wedge$$
$$\neg \exists \_PeriodNumber, \_STime, MTTR : HoldsAt(Unavailable(\_PeriodNumber, \_Srv, \_STime), t_1) \;\wedge$$
$$\exists periodNumber, \_MTTR : HoldsAt(MTTR(\_Srv, periodNumber, MTTR), t1) \Rightarrow$$
$$Initiates(e(\_id1, \_Snd, \_Srv, Call(\_O), \_Srv), Unavailable(\_PeriodNumber + 1, \_Srv, \_STime), t_1) \;\wedge$$
$$Terminates(e(\_id1, \_Snd, \_Srv, Call(\_O), \_Srv), MTTR(\_Srv, \_PeriodNumber, \_MTTR), t_1) \;\wedge$$
$$Initiates(e(\_id1, \_Snd, \_Srv, Call(\_O), \_Srv), MTTR(\_Srv, \_PeriodNumber + 1, \_MTTR), t_1)$$

(2)

**Assumption R1:A2**

$$Happens(e(\_id1, \_Snd, \_Srv, Call(\_O), \_Srv), t_1, [t_1, t_1]) \;\wedge$$
$$Happens(e(\_id2, \_Srv, \_Snd, Response(\_O), \_Srv), t_2, [t_1, t_1 + d]) \;\wedge$$
$$\exists \_PeriodNumber, \_STime : HoldsAt(Unavailable(\_PeriodNumber, \_Srv, \_STime), t_1) \Rightarrow$$
$$Terminates(e(\_id1, \_Snd, \_Srv, Call(\_O), \_Srv), Unavailable(\_PeriodNumber, \_Srv, \_STime), t_1)$$

(3)

**Assumption R1:A3**

$$Happens(e(\_id1, \_Snd, \_Srv, Call(\_O), \_Srv), t_1, [t_1, t_1]) \;\wedge$$
$$Happens(e(\_id2, \_Srv, \_Snd, Response(\_O), \_Srv), t_2, [t_1, t_1 + d]) \;\wedge$$
$$\exists \_PeriodNumber, \_STime : HoldsAt(Unavailable(\_PeriodNumber, \_Srv, \_STime), t_1) \;\wedge$$
$$\exists \_PeriodNumber, \_MTTR : HoldsAt(MTTR(\_Srv, \_PeriodNumber, \_MTTR), t_2) \Rightarrow$$
$$Terminates(e(\_id1, \_Snd, \_Srv, Call(\_O), \_Srv), MTTR(\_Srv, \_PeriodNumber, \_MTTR), t_2) \;\wedge$$
$$Initiates(e(\_id1, \_Snd, \_Srv, Call(\_O), \_Srv), MTTR(\_Srv, \_PeriodNumber, MTTR_{new}), t_2)$$

*where*

$$MTTR_{new} = \frac{\_MTTR(\_PeriodNumber - 1) + (t_1 - \_STime)}{\_PeriodNumber}$$

(4)

**Assumption R1:A4**

$$Happens(e(\_id1, \_Snd, \_Srv, Call(\_O), \_Srv), t_1, [t_1, t_1]) \;\wedge$$
$$\neg Happens(e(\_id1, \_Snd, \_Srv, Response(\_O), \_Srv), t_1, [t_1, t_1]) \;\wedge$$
$$\neg \exists \_PeriodNumber1, \_STime : HoldsAt(Unavailable(\_PeriodNumber1, \_Srv, \_STime), t_1) \;\wedge$$
$$\exists \_PeriodNumber2, \_TTF \_ITF : HoldsAt(TTF(\_PeriodNumber2, \_Srv, \_TTF, \_IFT), t_1) \Rightarrow$$
$$Terminates(e(\_id1, \_Snd, \_Srv, Call(\_O), \_Srv), TTF(\_PeriodNumber2, \_Srv, \_TTF, \_ITF), t_1) \;\wedge$$
$$Initiates(e(\_id1, \_Snd, \_Srv, Call(\_O), \_Srv), TTF(\_PeriodNumber2 + 1, \_Srv, t_1 - \_ITF, t_1), t_1)$$

(5)

**Fig. 2** EC formula for monitoring MTTR. Please note, $MTTR_{new}$ is just a placeholder created for readability purposes. EC requires $MTTR_{new}$ formula to be written in-line in the fluent declaration.

the assumption also reinitiates the fluent $MTTR(\_Srv, \_PeriodNumber, \_MTTR)$ to increase the number of unavailable periods $\_PeriodNumber$.

The second assumption (3) in Figure 2 terminates the fluent that represents a currently active period of service unavailability (i.e., the fluent $Unavailable(\_PeriodNum, \_Srv, \_STime)$) when a served service call occurs (i.e., the call represented by the event $\_id1$), and at the time of this call, the service is not unavailable (i.e., a fluent of the form $Unavailable(\_PeriodNum, \_Srv, \_STime)$ holds).

The third assumption (4) in Figure 2 updates the fluent that represents the mean length of consecutive periods of service unavailability (i.e., the value stored in the variable $\_MTTR$ of the fluent $MTTR(\_Srv, \_PeriodNumber, \_MTTR)$) when a served service call occurs (i.e., the call represented by the event $\_id1$), and at the time of this call the service is not unavailable (i.e., a fluent of the form $Unavailable(\_PeriodNum, \_Srv, \_STime)$ holds). The new mean value is computed as the mean of the mean of the previous $\_PeriodNumber - 1$ observations that is stored as the current value of $\_MTTR$ and the new period of unavailability $(t_1 - \_STime)$.

# 5 Prediction Specifications

A prediction specification is a user-defined document that tells the prediction framework what to predict. To express the prediction specification we use the high-level SLA specification language SLA* (read SLA star) [2], and we extended it to support the specification of prediction requirements.

An example of a prediction specification is given in Listing 1. It specifies i) the constraint that holds for the QoS specified in the guaranteed state whose violation will be the subject of prediction and ii) the window of the prediction, i.e., the time period in the future that the prediction should be concerned with. In the scenario, the guaranteed state value is $MTTR < 40$ and the prediction window is set to ten minutes. Thus, EVEREST+ will compute the probability of observing an MTTR value of greater than 40 seconds in ten minutes time.

Besides the *agreement_term* element, which is inherited from [2] and specifies the QoS terms to be guaranteed by an SLA, a prediction specification also includes the following elements: *predictor_configuration*, and *qos_specifications*.

## 5.1 Predictor Configuration

EVEREST+ provides mechanisms for extending its default set of QoS predictors with used-developed predictors. For this reason, the framework does not know *a priori* which QoS predictions might be available or their configurations. A prediction configuration provides a general way for configuring QoS predictor components.

```
 1          prediction_specification {
 2              service.id = Srv
 3              operation.id = Ping
 4              prediction.window.value = 10
 5              prediction.window.unit = minute
 6              agreement_term {
 7                  guaranteed_state {
 8                      expression.qos = MTTR
 9                      expression.operator = less_than
10                      expression.value = 40
11                      expression.unit = second
12                  }
13              }
14              predictor_configuration {
15                  predictor.id = MTTR_CITY
16                  prediction_parameters {
17                      property {
18                          name = "EVEREST+.model.distribution"
19                          value = "MTTR"
20                      }
21                      property {
22                          name = "EVEREST+.model.distribution"
23                          value = "TTF"
24                      }
25                  }
26              }
27              qos_specification {
28                  specification.name = MTTR
29                  specification.value = <EC_assertion_formula>
30              }
31          }
```

**Listing 1** Prediction specification example

A predictor configuration has a mandatory field *predictor.id*, indicating which QoS predictor to use when predicting violations about the guaranteed state in the *guaranteed_state* element. For example, the predictor configuration in Listing 1 specifies use of the *MTTR_CITY* QoS predictor.

The *MTTR_CITY* QoS predictor depends on MTTR and TF distribution models to function. QoS predictor dependencies are declared in the *prediction_parameter* element as key/value properties.

## 5.2 QoS Specification

In this scenario, the *MTTR_CITY* QoS predictor depends on MTTR and TTF distribution models. Since EVEREST does not know how to monitor MTTR term values, it does not have a monitoring specification for computing these same, and thus additional monitoring specifications can be included in a prediction specification by using the *qos_specification* element.

For instance, the prediction specification in Listing 1 includes a QoS specification named *MTTR* whose value consists of an EC formula for monitoring the

MTTR QoS term. The actual EC formula, omitted from the specification, is shown in Figure 2.

The *qos_specification* element not only contains dependency but is also used to declare any configuration properties required by a QoS predictor. There is a set of reserved key names that have special meaning. All key names beginning with *EVEREST+* are used by the framework for configuration purpose, e.g., the key-pair *EVEREST + .model.distribution, MTTR* instructs the framework to provide a QoS predictor with the best-fit distribution computed over past MTTR values.

## 6 Architecture Of EVEREST+

EVEREST+ has been designed with the general goal of providing a framework for developing QoS predictors quickly and easily by focusing only on prediction algorithm implementations without the need for concern about collection or retrieval of historical data. The architecture of EVEREST+, shown in Figure 3, includes two main components: (1) the EVEREST monitoring framework, and (2) the new prediction framework.

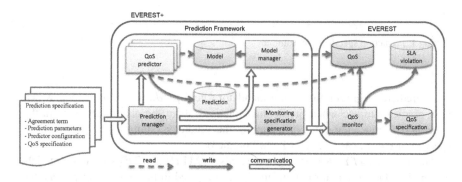

**Fig. 3** Everest+ main components and their interactions

As discussed earlier, the EVEREST monitoring framework checks services at runtime to determine whether they behave according to SLA QoS terms set for them. EVEREST checks QoS terms based on events intercepted from services by internal or external event captors. Whilst monitoring QoS terms, EVEREST stores QoS-related information, including computed QoS term values, instances of QoS term violations and satisfactions, and the values of any other state variables (fluents) that have been taken into account in checking QoS terms (Section 4). This information is available through an API that allows its retrieval from the internal EVEREST monitoring database (see *QoS* store in Figure 3).

The *prediction framework* (PF) fits statistical distribution functions to different types of historical QoS data generated by EVEREST, selects the distribution functions that have the best fit with the data, and makes these functions and the *raw* QoS data available to different QoS predictors deployed in EVEREST+ as plug-ins. The prediction framework has three main components: the *model manager*, *QoS predictor*, and *prediction manager*. These components are described below.

## 6.1 Prediction Manager

The prediction manager component coordinates and supervises prediction tasks by managing prediction specifications, triggering components, and reporting prediction results. The operations of the prediction manager are driven by prediction specifications.

The prediction manager analyses information contained in prediction specifications and dispatches it to the relevant components. Information on the relationships between prediction specification parts and the components they are dispatched to is summarised in Table 6.1.

|                         | QoS Predictor | Model Manager | Mon. Spec. Generator |
|-------------------------|:-------------:|:-------------:|:--------------------:|
| agreement_term          |               |               | X                    |
| prediction_parameters   |               | X             | X                    |
| predictor_configuration | X             |               |                      |
| qos_specifications       |               |               | X                    |

**Table 1** Prediction specification elements and the components they are dispatched to

In this scenario, the prediction manager parses the prediction specification in Listing 1. It dispatches the MTTR monitoring specification contained in the *qos_specifications* to EVEREST via the monitoring specification generator. Also, it instructs the monitoring specification generator to create two monitoring specification instances for monitoring *Srv* MTTR and TTF. The prediction manager also triggers the model manager by passing it the list of models requiring computation: the MTTR and TTF statistical distribution functions. Finally, it creates an instance of the chosen QoS predictor.

Once the above components are configured, QoS predictors begin producing prediction results. The prediction manager stores prediction results into the *prediction database*. It is the prediction manager's responsibility to fetch and report these results as required.

## 6.2 Monitoring Specification Generator

The monitoring specification generator is the framework component responsible for creating the monitoring specifications used to set up the monitoring framework. EVEREST+'s default monitoring specification generator creates monitoring specifications expressed in EC-Assertion: the language used by the EVEREST monitoring framework.

In the scenario, the monitoring specification generator receives an input—the element *agreement_term* of the prediction specification in Listing 1—and creates an instance of the monitoring specification in Figure 2. The MTTR monitoring specification variables, which are EC-Assertion formula parameters prefixed by the underscore symbol, are replaced with actual values from the *agreement_term* element. For instance, the first predicate in rule (1) becomes:

$$Happens(e(\_Id1, Srv, Srv, Call(Ping), Srv), t_1, [t_1, t_1]) \tag{6}$$

The predicate (6) instructs EVEREST to listen for events from *Srv* about the *Ping* operation invocations. Since the event timestamp $t_1$ has not been specified, as well as the event time range $[t_1, t_1]$, EVEREST will accept events occurring anytime.

## 6.3 Model Manager

The model manager is the framework component responsible for computing the data models that EVEREST+ makes available to QoS predictors. By default, the model manager fits statistical distribution functions to different types of historical QoS data generated by EVEREST, selects the distribution functions that have the best fit with the data, and makes these functions available to QoS predictors. For each data set, the fit suitability of over 44 different distribution functions is measured using the non-parametric Kolmogorov-Smirnov (K-S) goodness-of-fit test, and the probability distribution with the smallest goodness-of-fit (GoF) value is selected.

In the scenario, the model manager fits statistical distribution functions for MTTR and TTF historical values. These models are made available to QoS predictors as instances of classes implementing the *Distribution* interface. The model manager uses SSJ [4], a framework for stochastic simulation in Java, to fit up to 44 continuous distributions at runtime. Each distribution function implementation provides methods for computing several statistical measurements: for example, density function and cumulative distribution function.

## 6.4 QoS Predictor

The QoS predictor is the framework component that implements a prediction algorithm; it is triggered by the prediction manager once all other components have been configured. EVEREST+ has its own default set of QoS predictors for predicting MTTR, mean time to failure (MTTF), and other QoS terms. For information about the implemented prediction algorithms, see [6].

EVEREST+ allows users to implement their own QoS predictors so as to extend EVEREST+'s prediction capabilities. To implement a QoS predictor, it is necessary to extend the *QoSPredictor* class; in this way, the new QoS predictor inherits functionalities allowing it to access historical data as well as to automatically access runtime computed models.

## 7 Conclusion

EVEREST+ is a framework for detecting potential violations of QoS properties. The key properties of the proposed approach are generality and extensibility. EVEREST+ is general because it does not support only a limited set of QoS values, and it is extensible because the definition of which data to collect and how to analyse this data can be specified using models (QoS specifications) and pluggable components (QoS predictors).

To proof the validity of our approach, we are designing prediction models for predicting MTTR and MTTF QoS terms values, to be implemented in QoS predictors.

We are also planning to extend the set of built-in QoS predictors to include generic MT* predictors (i.e., predictors able to predict generic mean-time-related properties); for example, the mean time to completion of an operation.

## References

[1] Duc, B.L., Châtel, P., Rivierre, N., Malenfant, J., Collet, P., Truck, I.: Non-functional data collection for adaptive business processes and decision making. In: Proceedings of the 4th International Workshop on Middleware for Service Oriented Computing, MWSOC '09, pp. 7–12. ACM, New York, NY, USA (2009)

[2] Kearney, K., Torelli, F., Kotsokalis, C.: SLA*: An abstract syntax for service level agreements (2010). Developed by the the FP7 EU project SLA@SOI. To be published

[3] Kowalski, R., Sergot, M.: A logic-based calculus of events. New Gen. Comput. **4**(1), 67–95 (1986)

[4] L'Ecuyer, P., Meliani, L., Vaucher, J.: Ssj: a framework for stochastic simulation in java. Winter Simulation Conference **1**, 234–242 (2002)

[5] Leitner, P., Wetzstein, B., Rosenberg, F., Michlmayr, A., Dustdar, S., Leymann, F.: Runtime prediction of service level agreement violations for composite services. In: A. Dan, F. Gittler, F. Toumani (eds.) Service-Oriented Computing – Revised Selected Papers of ICSOC/ServiceWave 2009 Workshops, Stockholm, Sweden, November 23-27, 2009, *Lecture Notes in Computer Science*, vol. 6275, pp. 176–186. Springer, Berlin / Heidelberg (2010)

[6] Lorenzoli, D., Spanoudakis, G.: EVEREST+: run-time sla violations prediction. In: Proceedings of the 5th International Workshop on Middleware for Service Oriented Computing, MW4SOC, pp. 13–18. ACM, New York, NY, USA (2010)

[7] Mahbub, K., Spanoudakis, G.: Monitoring ws-agreements: An event calculus based approach. In: In Test and Analysis of Web Services, (eds) Baresi L. & di Nitto E, pp. 265–306. Springer Verlang (2007)

[8] Michlmayr, A., Rosenberg, F., Leitner, P., Dustdar, S.: Comprehensive qos monitoring of web services and event-based sla violation detection. In: Proceedings of the 4th International Workshop on Middleware for Service Oriented Computing, MWSOC '09, pp. 1–6. ACM, New York, NY, USA (2009)

[9] Michlmayr, A., Rosenberg, F., Leitner, P., Dustdar, S.: End-to-end support for qos-aware service selection, binding, and mediation in vresco. IEEE Transactions on Services Computing **3**, 193–205 (2010)

[10] Salfner, F., Schieschke, M., Malek, M.: Predicting failures of computer systems: a case study for a telecommunication system. In: Parallel and Distributed Processing Symposium, 2006. IPDPS 2006. 20th International, p. 8 (2006)

[11] Theocharis Tsigkritis George Spanoudakis, C.K., Lorenzoli, D.: Diagnosis and Threat Detection Capabilities of the SERENITY Monitoring Framework, *Advances in Information Security*, vol. 45, chap. 14, pp. 239–271. Springer US (2009)

[12] Thio, N., Karunasekera, S.: Automatic measurement of a qos metric for web service recommendation. Software Engineering Conference, Australian **0**, 202–211 (2005)

# Software Performance and Reliability Prediction

Franz Brosch

## 1 Introduction

In the vision of SLA@SOI, providers of software services give guarantees as to the specific quality of service (QoS) properties for the services they offer. These properties may relate to performance, reliability, or to other quality characteristics of the offered services. Service level agreements (SLAs) capture the QoS guarantees and represent a contract between service providers and service customers. To this end, the providers need to create general offers for services (called *SLA templates* in SLA@SOI), and react to the individual SLA requests of potential customers. General offers and individual requests must be based on sound data to ensure that services will show the quality that has been negotiated.

This chapter describes an approach to predicting the performance and reliability of software services: this approach helps software providers to create feasible SLA templates, and to determine a proper reaction to SLA requests from potential customers. More concretely, the approach predicts completion time distributions and success probabilities for service execution. The prediction method is based on a model of service implementation and evaluates this model to determine the expected service quality. The use of a model in this way allows for early quality prediction, without requiring the service to already be in place. The required input data for the model is collected during service design and implementation. Model parameters related to performance and reliability properties may be obtained by estimation, historical data or measurement.

Once a service implementation model has been created, it can be used to evaluate expected service quality. To this end, the SLA management framework (see Chapter 'Reference Architecture for Multi-Level SLA Management') developed in the context of SLA@SOI is enriched by a service evaluation (SE) component, which

Franz Brosch

FZI Research Center for Information Technology, Haid-und-Neu-Str. 10–14, 76131 Karlsruhe, Germany, e-mail: brosch@fzi.de provides the prediction functionality and is used by the SLA manager components throughout the service negotiation process. The SE component predicts the quality of service for different service configurations and usage profiles, and integrates the quality impact of required external services into its evaluation. Thus, it helps to automate negotiation activities across multiple provider boundaries, which is one of the envisioned SLA@SOI goals.

The remainder of this chapter illustrates these concepts and the realisation of this approach in greater detail. The following Sections 2, 3 and 4 discuss the general scope of this approach, the nature of the created service models, and the envisioned prediction workflow. Following this, Sections 5 and 6 discuss the technical realisation, integration into the SLA management framework, and application to SLA@SOI use cases.

## 2 Goals and Scope

The applicability of a software service to different usage scenarios is not only determined by the functionality that the service provides, but also the provided quality of service (QoS). For example, a ticket reservation service designed for up to 50 concurrent users will not fit the needs of a large international airline; equally, a data retrieval service with weak protection against data loss or corruption is not appropriate for supporting financial transactions. These examples show that successful adoption of service-oriented architectures across multiple provider boundaries needs stable agreements regarding QoS properties, which are established in terms of service level agreements (SLAs). As a basis for such agreements, service providers need to be aware of the QoS properties expected of their services before their actual operation in the field. Predictive approaches can deliver such information based on an existing or envisioned service design as well as estimations, historical data or measurements.

The prediction approach presented in this chapter allows the expected performance and reliability of a *target software service* to be evaluated before its operation. The obtained prediction results offer valuable support to service providers in two ways: First, the providers need to create general SLA offers (*SLA templates*) at the service-offering stage. SLA templates constitute the envisioned way in SLA@SOI of promoting services to potential customers. They relate service usage parameters (such as a maximal number of invocations per minute) to QoS parameters (such as a maximal service completion time). Thus the templates indicate what QoS properties can be expected under which conditions. The second major need for service quality prediction arises during the service negotiation stage. At this stage, to arrive at a concrete SLA, parameter ranges and choices in an SLA template must be narrowed down to single values and selections. The negotiation may be a complex process, especially if it spans multiple provider boundaries. Each party may take multiple roles, being a provider of certain target services, and a customer of required services at the same time. Multiple prediction iterations may be necessary to determine the quality of target services when different assumptions are made about the quality of required services, until finally, SLAs can be established across the whole provider chain. In both situations (SLA template creation and SLA establishment), the approach presented herein allows service providers to investigate what levels of quality can be expected from their provided services, and which QoS customer requirements can be met.

To yield realistic and relevant predictions, this approach must account for a complex interplay of factors that influence the quality of target services. The first major influencing factor is service usage: the performance and reliability of a service depends on the intensity of service usage (measured using parameters such as the number of invocations per minute), the invoked service operations, and the input data given to service calls. A further influencing factor is the internal structure of the service, which may consist of multiple — and possibly hierarchically composed — service components. The internal structure of the service is known only to the service provider, who provides this as input information for the prediction approach. Finally, the QoS properties of required external services are an influencing factor for the quality of the target service. Such external services may be software services or infrastructure services that provide a physical or virtualised software execution environment.

The explicit consideration of all mentioned quality-influencing factors creates a highly beneficial and innovative prediction approach, which has the potential to substantially enhance SLA negotiation processes. Further benefits of the approach when compared to related work (e.g. [3, 6]) lie in the separation of modelling responsibilities between software providers and service providers (supporting a distributed development process), the prediction of complete probability distributions for service performance (instead of only mean-value analysis), and the adoption of one common modelling language for performance and reliability prediction (providing a foundation for trade-off analyses). Within SLA@SOI, a concrete implementation of the approach has been created in terms of the service evaluation component (Section 4), and the approach has been demonstrated in several industrial use cases within the project (Section 6). The encouraging results from this practical experience underline the role of this approach as an important contribution to the overall SLA@SOI goal of empowering the service economy in a flexible and dependable way.

## 3 QoS Meta-Model

In order to enable the prediction of service performance and reliability, service providers need to create a model of the service-based system under study. To this end, the approach defines a QoS meta-model, which may be instantiated as a *prediction model* to describe the performance- and reliability-relevant aspects of the system. The QoS meta-model is based on the *Palladio Component Model* (PCM) [4],

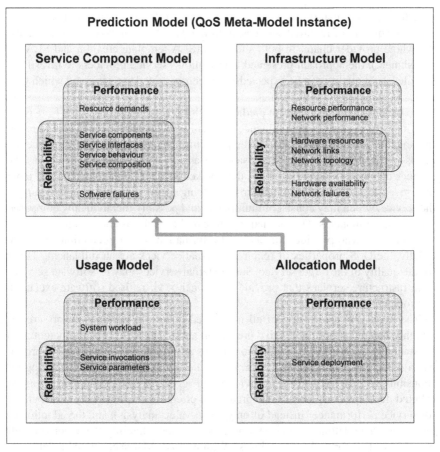

**Fig. 1** QoS Meta-Model for Performance and Reliability Prediction

which has been developed for performance modelling and prediction of component-based software architectures.

Figure 1 gives an overview of the structure of a prediction model. The figure consists of four parts, each describing different aspects of a service-based architecture. Each part has an individual impact on the overall performance and reliability of the service:

- The **Service Component Model** specifies the service components of the architecture, their interfaces, and their hierarchical composition. A high-level behavioural specification captures the relevant aspects of control and data flow, without unveiling details of the underlying implementation. Service Component Model information is provided by software providers who implement service components and offer them to software service providers.
- The **Infrastructure Model** specifies the execution environment of the architecture in terms of computing nodes (containing hardware resources, e.g. CPUs)

and network links. The relevant information comes from infrastructure service providers, who offer their infrastructures to software service providers.

- The **Usage Model** specifies a usage profile for the provided services of the system. It indicates: usage intensity (specified as a system workload); which services are invoked; and what kind of input data can be expected. This information is either specified directly by the software service provider (anticipating a certain usage profile), or can be deduced from a concrete customer request at service negotiation time.

- The **Allocation Model** provides a link between a given service component model and an infrastructure model. It maps service components to computing nodes and thus determines the actual topology of the distributed service-based system. The allocation is generally decided and specified by the software service provider.

To predict the performance or reliability of services provided by the system, a complete prediction model is required, containing all four parts described above. However, the individual parts may be created independently, and several variants for a part may exist (for example, several deployment variants may be specified through multiple allocation models). The software service provider is free to examine different system configurations by exchanging individual parts, and can perform predictions for each configuration. This way, the provider can identify the most beneficial configuration without deploying and executing all configuration variants in a real system.

# 4 Prediction Workflow

Performance and reliability prediction of software services follows a general workflow, performed by the software service provider. The workflow can be categorised into three individual phases, depicted in Figure 2: (i) model creation, (ii) identification of system configurations, and (iii) prediction of performance and reliability. The three phases are basically sequential, but can interfere with each other. Providers are able to step back and forth between the phases as required.

The first phase is *model creation*. In this phase, software service providers collect information from other roles and create parts of the prediction model as described in Section 3. Existing PCM tools — including graphical model editors — are used to provide an integrated environment that allows software service providers to create parts of their prediction model. The software service providers can map multiple choices regarding service components, infrastructure services, and external software services to multiple variants of the corresponding prediction model parts. They may also anticipate information that it is not yet available, such as an assumed usage profile. The model creation requires several parameters to be determined, including resource demands, software failure probabilities, and the frequencies of service invocations. The collection of these parameters is not actively supported by the approach itself, but can be based on estimations, historical data or measurements, as proposed in the literature [7, 9, 10].

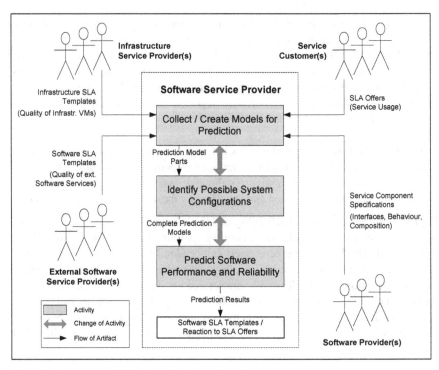

**Fig. 2** Performance and Reliability Prediction Workflow

The model creation phase is followed by *identification of system configurations*. Here, the software service providers determine possible and feasible system configurations. They decide how to compose the available service components, which infrastructure and external software services to use, and how to allocate service components to infrastructure (virtual) machines. Thus, possible solutions depend on the offers available from infrastructure and external service providers, but also on other factors that the software service providers might take into account (for example, legal restrictions or best practice for component deployment). For each system configuration, the software service providers can adjust and combine the existing prediction model parts to create a complete prediction model, including a specification of the intended system usage. This prediction model serves as an input for prediction of actual performance and reliability. If these predictions are performed automatically during service negotiation, they rely on the feasible system configurations that have been predetermined by the software service providers. However, the choice between these configurations is automated and performed by the SLA manager components.

Following creation and assembly of all model parts, the prediction itself takes place in the *performance and reliability prediction* phase. Prediction results are used either to determine feasible parameters for initial SLA templates, or to determine an appropriate reaction when concrete SLA offers are made by customers. In the former case, software service providers carry out the prediction manually using the PCM tooling environment. In the latter case, prediction is invoked programmatically and is carried out by the service evaluation components. In both cases, prediction may be carried out repeatedly in order to evaluate several system configurations and to enable selection of the best alternative. To this end, various search strategies and heuristics for finding good alternatives have been proposed in the literature (for example, see the solution and related work survey in [8]).

# 5 Prediction Realisation

To realise software performance and reliability prediction in the context of SLA@SOI, a set of tools and components have been created, supporting service providers with an integrated environment for modelling service-based systems, and enabling manual or programmatic quality prediction. This section discusses the technical realisation of such predictions, as well as their programmatic execution within the SLA negotiation process.

## 5.1 Overview

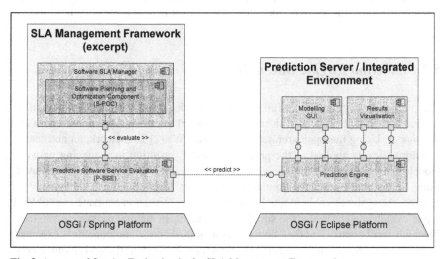

**Fig. 3** Automated Service Evaluation in the SLA Management Framework

Figure 3 shows the architecture of the available prediction tools and their integration into the SLA management framework. This architecture has been chosen such that (i) the solution can benefit from the existing PCM infrastructure, and (ii) predictions can be applied manually (during service offering) or automatically (during service negotiation).

In the service offering scenario, a software service provider uses prediction to determine feasible quality parameters for the software services to be offered. Prediction results are used for the creation of corresponding software SLA templates. The software service provider uses an integrated environment for the graphical creation of prediction models, the prediction itself, and the graphical visualisation of prediction results (Figure 3, right-hand-side). This prediction environment is realised as a set of Eclipse plug-ins running on an OSGi platform, based on existing PCM tooling. It is a self-contained tool that allows the software service provider to perform the prediction.

In the service negotiation scenario, prediction is performed automatically as part of the SLA negotiation workflow conducted by the SLA management framework. To this end, the prediction engine has been extended with a web-service interface. Thus, the environment becomes a prediction server application, and prediction can be triggered programmatically, supporting an automated negotiation process. Within the SLA management framework, prediction is offered as an implementation of the service evaluation component for the special case of *predictive software service evaluation* (P-SSE). It is invoked through the *software planning and optimisation* sub component (S-POC) of the *software SLA manager* component, in order to determine a proper reaction to a concrete SLA request from a potential customer. P-SSE invokes the prediction engine with a prediction model and retrieves the prediction result as an output.

Both scenarios use the same prediction engine, ensuring consistent results independent from the phase of application (service offering or service negotiation).

## 5.2 Prediction Engine Internals

The prediction engine takes a full QoS meta-model instance as input, including a service component model, an infrastructure model, an allocation model and a usage model. Using the openArchitectureWare (OAW) [2] framework, an automated transformation is applied to the prediction model, resulting in a queuing network model realised as a Java implementation. This queuing network is then simulated, using the discrete-event Java simulation framework SSJ [1].

From the system workload specification, the transformation generates a workload driver, which spawns threads to simulate arriving users that invoke system services. The high-level control and data flow throughout the service components is executed as specified in the prediction model. Furthermore, network traffic and resource consumption are considered by the simulation. Contention effects caused by concurrent service execution and resulting waiting times can be observed. Whenever a probabilistic decision has to be made (e.g. to determine the arrival time of the next user, the size of a resource demand, or which branch in the control flow to take), a sample is drawn from the specified probability distribution, and the decision is based on the sample. This way, it is ensured that the simulation follows the distributions that have been specified in the prediction model.

Throughout the simulation, sensors are placed that record the simulated start and end times of each service invocation, as well as the history of resource demands and waiting times for resources. After the simulation, these data are available for visualisation (e.g. time series diagrams or histograms) or further aggregation (e.g. determining the 90% percentile of service completion time). The integrated prediction environment provides capabilities for such visualisation of results, allowing the software service provider to derive the relevant information about feasible quality parameters, or to make a sophisticated choice between multiple system configurations.

For reliability prediction, another procedure is applied, transforming the prediction model into a discrete-time Markov Chain (DTMC) that represents the possible execution paths through the service-based architecture and their probabilities. Based on existing results from Markov theory, a *service success probability* is calculated, denoting the probability that a service call is completed without failure — finishing successfully, delivering a correct result, and not triggering any unwanted side effects. The approach takes into account failures due to implementation faults (software level), unavailability of physical resources (hardware level), and communication errors (network level). It has been described in detail in [5].

## 5.3 Prediction Process

Figure 4 illustrates the prediction process that is executed when the predictive software service evaluation (P-SSE) component is invoked via the evaluate interaction during service negotiation. The invocation comes from the software planning and optimisation (S-POC) component, which in turn has been triggered by a customer SLA offer with the goal of establishing an SLA as per the offer, to reject the offer, or to create a counter-offer. P-SSE helps S-POC in this decision-making by evaluating performance and reliability for individual system configurations and usage profiles. S-POC can compare the predicted quality of a given system configuration with the customer request, decide if the configuration satisfies all given requirements, and then determine if the SLA can be established based on this configuration.

The actors shown in Figure 4 are a running instance of the S-POC, as well as several entities belonging to a P-SSE instance. The sequence diagram shows an invocation of P-SSE by S-POC, with the following steps:

1. S-POC issues an `evaluate()` request to P-SSE, containing information about the system configuration(s) to evaluate, as well as service usage and external service quality parameters. The request is received by the `PredictiveSoftwareServiceEvaluator`.
2. The `PrectiveSoftwareServiceEvaluator` checks whether the input is valid (i.e. consistent and complete). If the input is invalid, an `IllegalArgumentException` is thrown.

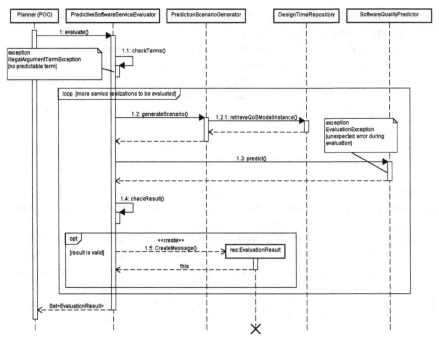

**Fig. 4** Evaluation of Software Services

3. A given `ServiceRealisation` (i.e. system configuration) is forwarded to the `PredictionScenarioGenerator`, which retrieves the corresponding `QoSModelInstance` (the prediction model) from a `DesignTimeRepository`, creates a `PredictionScenario` (i.e. a complete and adjusted prediction model that considers service usage and external service quality parameters), and returns this scenario to the `PredictiveSoftwareServiceEvaluator`.

4. The generated `PredictionScenario` is given as an input via a web-service interface to the `SoftwareQualityPredictor`, which is part of the prediction server. The `SoftwareQualityPredictor` performs a simulation and/or analysis to evaluate the expected performance and/or reliability of the target service. The evaluated quality parameters are returned to the `PredictiveSoftwareServiceEvaluator`. If the `PredictionScenario` cannot successfully be evaluated because of an unexpected error, an `EvaluationException` is generated and returned to the S-POC (as the caller of the `evaluate()` operation).

5. The `PredictiveSoftwareServiceEvaluator` checks whether the evaluation result is valid. This includes adherence to the usage bounds of required software services, as well as an indication that the system will not be overloaded by the envisioned target service usage.

6. If the result is valid, the `PredictiveSoftwareServiceEvaluator` creates an `EvaluationResult` instance and stores the results for the current
   `PredictionScenario` there.
7. Steps 3–6 are repeated until all given `ServiceRealisations` have been
   evaluated.
8. The list of evaluated results is returned to S-POC (as the caller of the
   `evaluate()` operation).

## 6 Use Cases

This approach to software performance and reliability prediction has been applied
to multiple use cases in the SLA@SOI project, including the Open Reference Case
(ORC) (Chapter 'The Open Reference Case'), a service-based ERP hosting solution
(Chapter 'The ERP Hosting Use Case Scenario'), and an eGovernment use case
featuring health care and mobility services (Chapter 'The eGovernment Use Case
Scenario'). Prediction models for these use cases have been created, and predictions have been performed to determine the expected performance and reliability of
different system configurations.

In the ORC scenario, this approach has been used to predict the completion time,
throughput, and success probability of the sales process at individual cash desks in a
supermarket, as well as the utilisation of back-end servers involved in this process.
Prediction has been performed for the *inventory service* and the *payment service*,
where the latter is a composition of two basic services for *card validation* and *payment debit*. The prediction results show how an increasing system workload leads to
lower service quality and eventually to a point where the system is overloaded and
no longer available.

Prediction for the ERP hosting use case focuses on the *sales and distribution*
(SD) application, which covers a sell-from-stock business process. The process includes the creation of a customer order with five items and the corresponding delivery of those items, with subsequent good movements and invoicing. It consists of
six individual transactions, involving multiple service components and operations.
Prediction results may be used to indicate how varying infrastructure characteristics
(such as CPU speeds or network bandwidth) influence the throughput and completion time of the business process transactions.

The e-government use case constitutes a special application of this prediction
approach, extending its scope beyond pure software services towards human services and resources. Instead of reflecting a software architecture as a composition
of software service components, the prediction model reflects a health care system,
where the 'components' are call centres that provide 'services' (in this case, booking capabilities). Thus in this scenario, instead of predicting demand for computing
resources during software service execution, the approach predicts the number of
human operators required to serve the booking requests of calling customers. The
performance predictions show how long calls take for different types of customer

request and assuming different call centre capabilities. It is also possible to deduce how many operators would be busy at a time, and how many would be required to serve customer requests without waiting times. The results of this application are of special interest as they point towards a new domain of application for this approach to performance and reliability prediction.

# References

[1] SSJ: Stochastic Simulation in Java. `http://www.iro.umontreal.ca/ \~simardr/ssj/indexe.html` (2010). Last retrieved 2010-12-30

[2] Eclipse Modeling Project. `http://www.eclipse.org/modeling/` (2011). Last retrieved 2011-01-03

[3] Balsamo, S., Di Marco, A., Inverardi, P., Simeoni, M.: Model-based performance prediction in software development: A survey. IEEE Transactions on Software Engineering **30**, 295–310 (2004)

[4] Becker, S., Koziolek, H., Reussner, R.: The Palladio Component Model for Model-Driven Performance Prediction. Journal of Systems and Software **82**(1), 3–22 (2009)

[5] Brosch, F., Koziolek, H., Buhnova, B., Reussner, R.: Parameterized Reliability Prediction for Component-based Software Architectures. In: G. Heineman, F. Kofron, Jan; Plasil (eds.) International Conference on the Quality of Software Architectures (QoSA), vol. 6093, pp. 36–51. Springer (2010)

[6] Immonen, A., Niemel, E.: Survey of reliability and availability prediction methods from the viewpoint of software architecture. Journal on Software and Systems Modeling **7**(1), 49–65 (2008)

[7] Koziolek, H., Schlich, B., Bilich, C.: A Large-Scale Industrial Case Study on Architecture-based Software Reliability Analysis. In: IEEE International Symposium on Software Reliability Engineering (ISSRE), pp. 279–288. IEEE (2010)

[8] Martens, A., Koziolek, H., Becker, S., Reussner, R.: Automatically improve software architecture models for performance, reliability, and cost using evolutionary algorithms. In: International Conference on Performance Engineering (WOSP/SIPEW), pp. 105–116. ACM (2010)

[9] Menasce, D.A., Almeida, V.A., Dowdy, L.W.: Performance by design : Computer capacity planning by example. Prentice-Hall (2004)

[10] Musa, J.D.: Operational profiles in software-reliability engineering. IEEE Softw. **10**, 14–32 (1993). DOI http://dx.doi.org/10.1109/52.199724. URL `http://dx.doi.org/10.1109/52.199724`

# Part IV
# Core Components of the Service Level Agreements Framework

# G-SLAM – The Anatomy of the Generic SLA Manager

Miguel Angel Rojas Gonzalez, Peter Chronz, Kuan Lu, Edwin Yaqub, Beatriz Fuentes, Alfonso Castro, Howard Foster, Juan Lambea Rueda, and Augustín Escámez Chimeno

## 1 Introduction

The Generic SLA Manager, also known as the G-SLAM, provides a generic architecture that can be used across different domains and use cases to manage the entire SLA life cycle, including activities such as negotiating SLAs, provisioning resources, monitoring and adjustment. A first approach to this architecture is described in [7]. The key feature of this approach is the high degree of flexibility provided for dynamic behavior (assisted by OSGi), customisable system deployment, and the ability to reconfigure individual pieces comprising the G-SLAM. Each concrete SLAM implementation can customise or reuse components, integrate new components or replace others with minimal effort, and even swap components at runtime. The G-SLAM kernel orchestrates the general purpose components, which are the SLATemplateRegistry, SLARegistry, SyntaxConverter, MonitorManager and ProtocolEngine. This set of generic components is referred to as the G-Components.

Miguel Angel Rojas Gonzalez, Peter Chronz, Kuan Lu, Edwin Yaqub
TU Dortmund University, August-Schmidt-Strasse 12, 44227 Dortmund, Germany, e-mail: {miguel.rojas,peter.chronz,kuan.lu,edwin.yaqub}@tu-dortmund.de

Beatriz Fuentes, Alfonso Castro, Juan Lambea Rueda, Augustín Escámez Chimeno
Telefónica Investigación y Desarrollo, Spain,
e-mail: {fuentes,acast,juan.lambea,escamez}@tid.es

Howard Foster
Department of Computing, City University London, Northampton Square, EC1V 0HB, London,
e-mail: Howard.Foster.1@city.ac.uk

## 2 Plug-in-based Approach to the G-SLAM Architecture

The SLA@SOI framework is designed to be extensible by mechanisms called plug-ins or bundles that can be dynamically added to and removed from any SLA@SOI framework instance. In the SLA@SOI framework, every plug-in component amends the functionality of other plug-ins. This is achieved using the underlying OSGi [1, 2] framework, which defines the dependencies between plug-ins, and how and when additional plug-ins are activated. The target platform for G-SLAM support is based on the OSGi R4 Reference Implementation. G-SLAM defines a set of generic components, known as G-Components, which are collected into an entity named SLAManagerContext. Any SLAM implementation requires the G-SLAM service to initialise its own context. This context will then allow the interaction of each of the generic components in a light manner, without having strong interdependencies. This way of building the SLA manager leads to an extensible architecture with well-defined interfaces, and makes programming and testing of new SLAMs much easier.

The use of OSGi brings with it the following advantages: long classpaths are no longer required, the modules' life cycles are fully handled by the platform, dynamic updates can be performed without rebooting the application, and the package visibility of bundles enables the dynamic sharing of classes across components, reflecting a high decoupling of modules through interfaces and services. Public third parties (normally published as JAR files) can be also used, but are included as bundles in OSGi. The Spring Source website provides a repository of libraries ready for use as bundles [10]). Note that maintenance and update of these libraries for any OSGi application is quite transparent and does not require major changes at the application-side.

OSGi declarative services — Service Binder, Spring Dynamic Modules (Spring DM) and other existing component models — enable the handling of dynamic aspects, service location, dependency injection, and manage all the dynamic linking. The hard manual work required by other platforms when bringing components together in a dynamic fashion is not required under OSGi. Nevertheless, a minimal effort is required to create the plugins or bundles, a task that is assisted by Maven.

## 3 The G-SLAM Architecture

The G-SLAM is the orchestrator of the generic components and creates on-demand new instances of these components for the DS-SLAMs in question. Figure 1 shows the dynamic interaction between the DS-SLAM and the G-SLAM when obtaining its own instances of the G-Components. On demand, any DS-SLAM is able to contact the G-SLAM via the OSGi-services to request a new set of G-Components. The G-SLAM creates each generic component, then creates a SLAMContextManager that includes these recently created objects, and gives this to the DS-SLAM.

From there, the DS-SLAM is responsible for those instances, making each SLAM independent of the G-SLAM service.

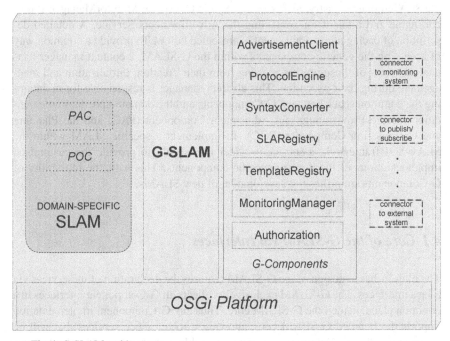

**Fig. 1** G-SLAM architecture

## 3.1 Technology Used by the Plug-in-based G-SLAM Architecture

As noted above, the SLA@SOI framework is targeted to the OSGi platform. This allows a modular and pluggable way of implementing each of the G-Components. The G-SLAM takes especial advantage of the OSGi Spring DM framework. Spring DM simplifies the creation and management of bundles and makes use of an injection mechanism to share OSGi service references. This injection mechanism is supported using Java annotations, which makes the development simple and flexible; thus the integration and maintenance of existing components does not require extra configuration.

# 4 Generic Components

G-SLAM encapsulates the generic components that are responsible for handling SLAs within the SLA@SOI framework. Its most important generic components are the SLATemplateRegistry, SLARegistry, SyntaxConverter, MonitorManager, ProtocolEngine and a client for contacting the Advertisements Service. A detailed description of each generic component is presented below. To provide a common way of accessing the generic components within the G-SLAM, a context manager handles instances of those objects, starting from their creation, initialisation and management during their execution. This abstract manager is responsible for maintaining the common space between G-Components and the domain-specific implementations of the Provisioning and Adjustment Component (PAC) and the Planning and Optimisation Component (POC). To implement a specific SLAM within the SLA@SOI framework, a service provider needs only to provide the customised implementations of the domain-specific components. This way, the reusability of G-Components simplifies the development of new SLAMs.

## 4.1 Core of the G-SLAM via Interfaces

The plug-in-based design of the G-SLAM requires the declaration of its services via a Java interfaces. The G-SLAM exclusively collects all G-Component interfaces in a common place, named the G-SLAM core. Thus any G-Component implementation imports the bundled G-SLAM core, allowing it to reference services that will be exposed by other G-Components in runtime. Table 2 enunciates some of interfaces included in the G-SLAM core.

| Generic Component | Interfaces |
|---|---|
| *ProtocoEngine* | **INegotiation**<br>initiateNegotiation(SLATemplate slaTemplate)<br>SLATemplate[] negotiate(String negotiationID, SLATemplate slaTemplate)<br>SLA createAgreement(String negotiationID, SLATemplate slaTemplate)<br>cancelNegotiation(String negotiationID)<br>renegotiate(UUID slaID)<br>terminate(UUID slaID)<br>**IControl**<br>setPolicies( String policyClass, Policy[] policies )<br>Policy[] getPolicies( String policyClass ) |
| *SyntaxConverter* | Object parseSLA(String slaObject)<br>Object parseSLATemplate(String slaTemplateObject)<br>Specification[] parseWSDL(String wsdlString) |
| *SLARegistry* | **IRegister**<br>UUID register(SLA agreement, ...)<br>UUID update(UUID id, ...)<br>**IQuery**<br>SLA[] getSLA(UUID[] ids)<br>UUID[] getDependencies(UUID id)<br>UUID[] getSLAsByState(SLAState[] states)<br>SLA[] getSLAsByTemplateId(UUID slatId) |
| *SLATemplateRegistry* | addSLATemplate(SLATemplate)<br>removeSLATemplate(UUID templateId)<br>SLATemplate getSLATemplate(UUID templateId)<br>ResultSet query(SLATemplate query) |
| *MonitoringManager* | MonitoringSystemConfiguration checkMonitorability(SLA slaModel,<br>ComponentMonitoringFeatures[] componentMonitoringFeatures) |
| *POC* | SLATemplate[] negotiate(String negotiationID, SLATemplate slaTemplate)<br>SLA createAgreement(String negotiationID, SLATemplate slaTemplate)<br>terminate(UUID slaID)<br>SLA provision(UUID slaID) |
| *PAC* | executePlan(Plan plan)<br>cancelExecution(String planId) |
| *Authorization* | checkAccess(SLATemplate template) |

**Fig. 2** G-Component services

## 4.2 Abstraction Layer for the Domain-Specific Components PAC and POC

The G-SLAM core also interfaces with the domain-specific components PAC and POC. Their minimal behavior and interaction with the G-Components is declared here. If customised services are needed, they can be defined within the domain-specific core (Section 7).

## 4.3 Main Bundle for the G-SLAM

The G-SLAM implementation consists of a set of bundles and Java third-party libraries for OSGi. Those bundles represent each G-Component and are bound to the main G-SLAM bundle. Based on Spring DM, the main bundle exposes a service called createContext. This service allows any SLAManager to dynamically create its G-Components. The main bundle internally invokes a builder service for each G-Component. A builder service is exposed by each G-Component and is responsible for the instantiation of its required objects such that it can be executed independently within the DS-SLAM. Thanks to these builder services, the G-SLAM can create a SLAManagerContext, where all G-Components are grouped and returned to the DS-SLAM. Note that the domain-specific components PAC and POC can be linked to this context before any SLA operation takes place.

## 4.4 Syntax Conversion for Interoperability

The syntax-converter is a component of the GSLAM that provides interoperability and separates the SLAMS from specific representations of an SLA or SLA template. Supported representations are the XML representation of SLA@SOI's SLA model (SLA*) (Section 2) and the WS-Agreement [3]. The GSLAM's internal interface with the syntax-converter provides its related components with means to execute operations using the SLA*'s Java representation. The syntax-converter provides external components with various interactions as web-services, including an interface for negotiation. As such, the syntax-converter is a central communication point for the GSLAM, acting as a facade that allows GSLAM's internal components to be independent from specific representations.

The syntax-converter's purpose is to convert between various SLA representations. Internally, the GSLAM uses a Java-based representation of SLA*, while external parties use either a direct XML representation of SLA* or the WS-Agreement. When communicating with outside parties, the syntax-converter also represents a central entry point for negotiations. SLA* is defined using an abstract syntax expressed with a Backus Normal Form (or Backus-Naur Form; BNF) [4] and textual descriptions. To apply the model in a use case, a concrete implementation is required. One such implementation is the Java-representation, which is used by components within the GSLAM. For on-the-wire communication purposes, two XML-representations exist. One — referred to as the XML-representation of the SLA* — directly implements the abstract syntax in XML. The other embeds SLA*'s expressions in the WS-Agreement. This extended WS-Agreement representation directly uses the SLA*'s XML-representation within the WS-Agreement. Those textual representations are mostly used whenever an SLA needs to be serialised and reread by a machine at a later stage. Example uses are serialisation for communication over-the-wire, such as using web-services, and serialisation for storing SLA documents in the SLA registry and the SLA template registry. In addition, a textual representation of the SLA-model exists (in a notation resembling JSON [5]) that is conveniently readable by humans. This representation, however, is for a human reader's convenience and cannot be parsed by the syntax-converter.

The syntax-converter is also able to convert between SLA*'s interface specification and WSDL 2.0 [6], in both directions. This feature is needed when an externally provided interface is described in WSDL. Conversely, this mechanism is required to provide external parties who do not know SLA*'s interface specification model with a commonly understood description of a web-service interface.

The syntax-converter's external interface provides the means for the SLAM's internal components to communicate with external components. Those external components may belong to the SLA@SOI framework or to components implemented by third parties. Components within the framework that interact using the syntax-converter's external interfaces are the SLA-Managers, which are based on the GSLAM. As such, a GSLAM will communicate with another GSLAM using the syntax-converter as if it were any other external component.

## 4.5 Protocol Engine

Negotiations are of fundamental interest in service-oriented systems. Two or more parties negotiate SLAs based on their individual goals. Service level guarantees are bargained during the negotiation process. Negotiations may last several rounds until an agreement is reached. In each round, several counter-offers can be generated by the recipient of an offer. The customer and the provider both try to maximise their individual utilities, and if the customer's request matches the provider's capabilities, negotiation can converge on an agreement.

In SLA@SOI, the negotiation model is represented as a state machine. The state machine captures 1) the states in the model, 2) the sequence of messages, and 3) restrictions on a state. This also introduces a taxonomy of events. Additionally, there are trigger conditions that control transitioning logic and may be extrapolated to make additional checks. In the SLA@SOI project, these elements are composed into a Negotiation Protocol. Technically, a protocol is filed as a collection of rules and different versions are available via a public repository/registry. Negotiating parties run the same protocol. In the SLA@SOI project, the software machinery that executes the protocol is called a Protocol Engine. The Protocol Engine is stateful and maintains a session per negotiation. At any time, the state machines of negotiating parties are synchronised until one transits, triggering the other to attempt the same. The main interaction over which the Protocol Engine provides its functionality is the *negotiate/renegotiate* interaction. A bilateral protocol has been developed to allow two SLA managers to negotiate with each other; multiple bilateral negotiations can also be conducted to allow for multiplicity. Future extensions will allow multilateral protocols as well.

## 4.6 SLATemplateRegistry

The SLATemplateRegistry is a persistent queriable store for SLA templates (SLATs). Architecturally, there is one registry for customer-facing (offered) SLATs, and another for provider-facing SLATs. The customer-facing registry can be queried by external actors and is maintained by an external registry (an actor responsible for deciding which SLATs should be offered to customers). SLATs offered by external providers are cached locally in the provider-facing registry.
The SLATemplateRegistry publishes and subscribes to the Advertisements Service (Section 5) under the policy control of the external registrar. Mediating the interaction with the pss4slam bus are a number of syntax-converters that transparently convert SLAT serialisations in various formats into the internal SLA Model (and *vice versa*).

From the DS-SLAM perspective, the SLATemplateRegistry is a private and persistent store of SLATs. If an entity external to this DS-SLAM needs to query the registry, it must send query sentences to the syntax-converter of the associated SLAM (see Section 2 or the API documentation at [11]).

## 4.7 SLARegistry

The SLARegistry is a persistent store for SLAs and historical SLA-state information. It is maintained directly by the Protocol Engine and can be queried by all internal SLA manager components. It can also query web-services via the syntax-converter.

Architecturally, there is one registry for customer-facing SLAs, and another for provider-facing SLAs. As well as the SLAs themselves, the registry also maintains historical SLA status information (for auditing). The registries serve as an archive for completed SLAs as well as those currently in effect.

The SLARegistry is defined by two interfaces that provide access to implementation of the *query* and *register* stereotype interactions. The *register* interaction stores an SLA in the registry, with pointers to dependent/depending SLAs. The second interaction, *query*, retrieves a SLA, its status, its status history, and the dependent/depending SLAs.

As for the SLATemplateRegistry, the SLARegistry is a private and persistent store of SLAs from the DS-SLAM's perspective. If any entity external to the SLA manager needs to query the registry, it must send query sentences through the syntax-converter of the associated SLAM (Section 2 or the API documentation at [12]).

## 4.8 MonitoringManager

The MonitoringManager (MM) coordinates generation of a monitoring configuration for the Monitoring System (2). For each SLA specification instance it receives, the MM decides which monitoring configuration would best fit configurable selection criteria. A monitoring configuration describes which components to configure and how their configurations can be used to obtain results of monitoring guaranteed states. The Low Level Monitoring Manager is a central entity for storing and processing monitoring data. It collects raw observations, processes them, computes derived metrics, evaluates the rules, stores the history and offers all this data to other components (accessible through the ServiceManager). It implements the monitoring part of a ProvisioningRequest, containing constraint-based rules (time- and data-driven evaluations) and ServiceInstance-specific sensor-related configurations. It is generic by design, and thus capable of supporting the monitoring of infrastructure, software, services and other use cases.

The Monitoring System has three types of monitoring feature: First, *sensors* collect information from a service instance. Their design and implementation is very much domain-specific. A sensor can be injected into the service instance (e.g., service instrumentation), or it can be outside the service instance intercepting service operation invocations. A sensor can send the collected information to the communication infrastructure or other components can request (query) information from it. There can be many kinds of sensors, depending on the kind of information they want to collect, but all of them should implement a common interface. The interface provides methods for starting, stopping, and configuring a sensor. Second, Effectors are components for configuring service instance behaviour. Their design and implementation are very much domain-specific. An effector can be injected into a service instance, e.g., service instrumentation, or can interface a service configuration interface. There can be many kinds of effectors, depending on the service instance to be controlled, but all of them should implement a common interface. The interface should provide methods for configuring a service. The third type of monitoring feature is a Reasoning Component Gateway (RCG). An RCG provides the interface for accessing a Reasoning Engine. A Reasoning Engine (or short name as Reasoner) performs a computation based upon a series of inputs provided by events or messages sent from a sensor or an effector. An example RCG may provide a function to compute the average completion time of service requests. In this case the RCG accepts events from sensors detecting both request and responses to a service operation. RCGs also provide access to generic runtime monitoring frameworks such as EVEREST. For more details see the monitoring features specification (Section 2.1).

## 4.9 Authorisation

During the negotiation interaction, parties involved in the negotiation need to be identified. The outcome of a negotiation is the contracting of a product and included services; thus, prior to any order, existing customer relationships (if any) should be checked along with the validity of the customer's economic status. More customer-related checks may be required depending on the environment, domain, or business support systems in which the SLA@SOI framework will be integrated. It must also be possible to determine whether the customer can make an order; thus the framework must be able to check the customer's validity for each customer-initiated negotiation interaction. If the validation and negotiation has finished successfully, the customer signs the product's SLA (or orders a product). There should be another economic check of the order before the SLA is signed and returned, but this check will appear at the final step of the negotiation, and will take into account the final agreement. Whenever a new negotiation starts, the authorisation operation must be able to be invoked; thus the beginning of the negotiation must be able to be intercepted such that different questions about the customer can be answered. In the SLA@SOI framework, this validation was implemented by default in the Business SLA Manager, since this component is in charge of customer relationships; however, it could be added to any SLAM as required.

## 5 Advertisements System

To address the service discovery and remote services issues, G-SLAM architecture includes a universal publish/subscribe system. The Advertisements System is a Java message system (based on the Apache Message Broker [8]) for the exchange of SLATs among several SLA managers in a distributed environment. It allows the sharing of new SLATs in a reliable and asynchronous manner. Apache ActiveMQ is an open source message broker which fully implements Java Message Service 1.1 (JMS). The publish and subscribe model provided by ActiveMQ enables the publishing of SLA templates to multiple subscribers (in this case SLAMs). Subscribers may register interest in receiving SLATs on a particular topic. In this model, neither the publisher nor the subscriber know about each other. In the SLA@SOI framework, the publisher (a SLAM) is able to publish templates in any time. The subscriber must remain continuously active to receive templates, unless it has established a durable subscription. In this case, templates published while the subscriber is not connected will be redistributed whenever it reconnects. The durability feature of a subscription is configured at the initialisation of client.

The Advertisements System includes inherited features; for example, the system supports very fast persistence using JDBC along with a high performance journal, pluggable transport protocols such as in-VM, TCP, SSL, NIO, UDP, multicast, JGroups and JXTA transports, and a collection of JMS brokers, to which clients will connect. It also provides load balancing of templates across consumers, supports master/slave configuration to provide high availability, and fault tolerance of brokers for delivering SLATs.

A broker component in the Advertisements System allows the exchange of templates between two or more SLA managers. A broker can be aligned with others into a cluster or hierarchy, allowing the configuration of complex structures for increasing reliability and redundancy of the Advertisements System in the SLA@SOI framework. A set of brokers can be specified in design time via a configuration file, or discovered dynamically, as depicted in Figure 3. Broker 1 is pre-configured in the SLA@SOI framework while the other brokers (2, n and m) join together dynamically. The SLATs published by Publisher-X will be propagated across any known broker. Each subscriber (A, B and C) will get a copy of the published templates.

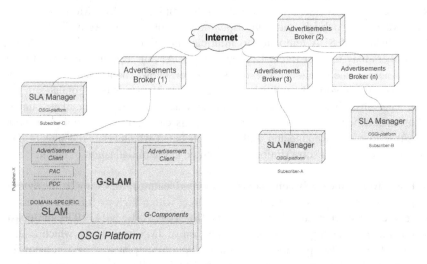

**Fig. 3** Advertisements System

The Advertisements System actually supports two channels for the protocols WSAgreement and SLAModel. Those channels enable interoperability between the SLA@SOI framework and legacy systems, allowing publishers and subscribers to share templates in two different formats (Section 4.4).

The SLA@SOI framework provides a plug-in-based client for interacting with any available broker. The client offers the basic functionality for subscribing to a specific channel, as well as facilities for publishing SLATs. The client is configured by default to connect to a predefined broker in the SLA@SOI framework. The publish/subscribe client is integrated by the G-SLAM, enabling access to each component from any DS-SLAM.

The Advertisements System is modeled on the following interfaces: IPublishable,which sends SLATs via an internal broker to current subscribers, and ISubscribable, which notifies the internal broker of new subscribers or agents and links it to the specified channel.

# 6 Planning and Optimisation Component (POC)

In general terms, the POC is responsible for assessing and customising a customer's SLA. It is an intelligent component that evaluates the feasibility of provisioning the requested service by considering the availability of the service as well as other Quality of Service (QoS) terms, and it plans optimal service provisioning and monitoring strategies.

The POC is an abstract component and its service is domain-specific with a unique service type and QoS terms. Therefore, software POCs and infrastructure POCs share a common interface design but domain-specific implementation. For instance, they can have different policies and strategies for processing a domain-specific SLA. Mechanisms such as a binary decision diagram can be used within a POC to facilitate the process of negotiating SLAs, subcontracting their parts, optimising their utility, and managing them during runtime for monitoring and enforcement [9]. Figure 5 indicates the general architecture diagram of G-SLAM, in which the interactions between POC and other components are illustrated.

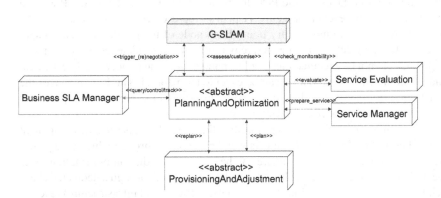

**Fig. 4** POC interactions inside G-SLAM

The POC interfaces include the following:

| Interface | Description |
|---|---|
| <<IAssessmentAndCustomize>> | *negotiate*: starts the negotiation between customer and service provider.<br>*createAgreement*: establishes a final agreement (SLA) between customer and service provider.<br>*terminate*: cancels an agreement after the SLA is established. |
| <<INotification>> | *activate*: starts to prepare a plan for provisioning the service. |
| <<IPlanStatus>> | *planStatus*: gets the current status of a specific plan. |
| <<IReplan>> | *rePlan*: starts to generate an alternative plan, when a violation is detected by the other component. |

**Fig. 5** POC interactions inside G-SLAM

## 7 Provisioning and Adjustment Component (PAC)

The Provisioning and Adjustment Component (PAC) has, as its name suggests, a two-pronged mission. First, it plays a crucial role at provisioning time, effectively executing the optimised provisioning plans — provided by the POC — on the service manager. Second, SLA enforcement ensures continual identification, monitoring and reviewing of the optimally agreed service levels required by the business, and ensures that given SLAs are fulfilled such that previous performance estimates equal final performance of the running services. The PAC will dynamically readjusts the service if given quality levels cannot be met.

A planned interaction subsumes the functionality needed for service provisioning, providing interfaces for the POC to submit an optimised plan to the PAC, and to inform it of the execution status. A plan is represented as a Directed Acyclic Graph (DAG) with a unique entry point. Each node of the graph represents a specific task to be executed, and the hierarchy represents dependencies; for example, a child node cannot be executed unless all its parent nodes have successfully executed, and children of the same parent can be executed in parallel. The PAC manages the synchronisation and parallelisation of different tasks in the provisioning plan, and an appropriate rollback if an execution fails.

The runtime role of the PAC is primarily adjustment. For this role, the component subscribes to the MonitoringEventChannel, an event bus through which data generated by the monitoring infrastructure can be received. Prediction information gives the probability of an SLA breach, and can also be received through a dedicated channel. Low-level domain-specific PACs (namely, software and infrastructure) react on the available information; for example, they may force reallocation of dynamic resources on the infrastructure, substitute a service, or increase a service level. The manage_T_service interaction allows the execution of these actions to be triggered by the corresponding service manager (Figure 6).

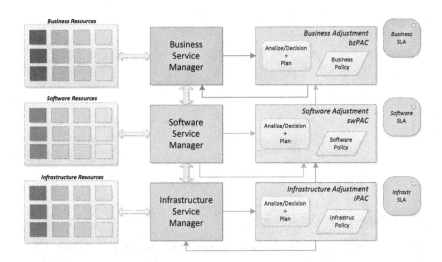

**Fig. 6** Three-level adjustment

However, not all exceptions can be solved locally. In this case, decisions may need to be escalated to the highest SLA management level, that is, the business manager. These notifications, together with economic information that resides on the business level, allow the business adjustment to analyse the situation and decide, plan and execute the necessary actions, aiming to minimise the penalties paid to the customer and therefore maximising benefits and revenue. Actions at this level include renegotiation of the agreement or, in the case of multi-provider environments, modification of the conditions of a third party service (for example, selecting a new third party to deliver the service).

# 8 Skeleton SLAM

One of the most important features of G-SLAM is that is can be reused by new SLA managers with minimal effort during implementation. The Skeleton SLAM (SK-SLAM) aims to define basic structure and components, so the development of new SLAMs is faster and simpler. The SK-SLAM not only contains classes and resources, but also includes the skeleton (ready to be filled) of domain-specific components (PAC and POC), so the programmer can take care of implementation details of the concrete SLAM. Configuration files and building maven files are also included for the generation of bundles for the new SLAM.

Figure 7 shows the basic structure of the Skeleton-SLAM directories.

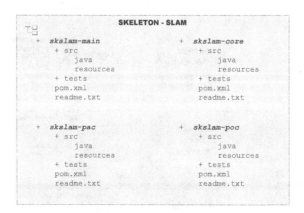

**Fig. 7** Skeleton directories structure

The SK-SLAM consists of four sub-projects. The main project, called skslam-main, initialises the SLAMManagerContext via the G-SLAM service, and links the domain-specific implementation of PAC and POC with the generic components. Sub-projects skslam-pac and skslam-poc define the PAC and POC respectively. The fourth sub-project, called skslam-core, defines new interfaces and services to be shared within the SK-SLAM. Note that this design allows independence across components within the SLAM and enables new entities to be plugged in and out.

The DS-SLAM obtains generic components from the G-SLAM using OSGi services, thus creating a new SLAMManagerContext. This SLAMManagerContext initialises references to the new generic components that will be part of the concrete SLAM. Figure 8 depicts how the SLA manager uses the G-SLAM service to obtain its own generic components.

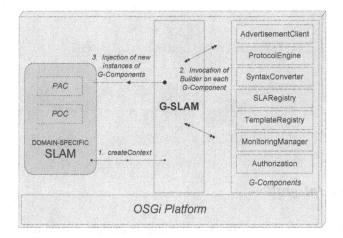

**Fig. 8** SLA Manager Context

The following Java snippet shows how to easily obtain a new set of G-Components using G-SLAM services exposed via OSGi. Spring DM provides ServiceReference annotation, which enables the signed method to get the G-SLAM service 'gslamServ' by injection.

```
@ServiceReference
public void setGslamServices( GenericSLAManagerServices gslamServ )
{
   SLAMAnagerContext context = gslamServ.createContext();
}
```

**Fig. 9** Getting a context from G-SLAM

The object *context* contains references to G-Components attached to the DS-SLAM. For instance, if the recently created SLAM needs to access its SLARegistry or ProtocolEngine, the required code is as below.

```
{
    ...
    context.getProtocolEngine().initiateNegotiation( ... );
    ...

    context.getSLARegistry().getSLAs( ... );
}
```

**Fig. 10** Injection of G-Components

## *8.1 Maven Integration*

The skeleton component provides a maven plug-in implementation called *maven-slam-plugin*. This plug-in enables the generation of a basic DS-SLAM based on the SK-SLAM (Figure 7) via simple maven commands.

```
script
@echo off
SET PLUGIN=org.slasoi.slam.factory:maven-slam-plugin:0.1-SNAPSHOT
SET PARAM0=generate
SET PARAM1=-Dskeleton.directory.generate=/repository
SET PARAM2=-Dskeleton.dsslam.name=b3slam
SET PARAM3=-Dskeleton.dsslam.namespace=org.slasoi.usecases.b3

mvn %PLUGIN%:%PARAM0% %PARAM1% %PARAM2% %PARAM3%
```

**Fig. 11** Maven integration of Skeleton-SLAM

Figure 11 shows the steps required to generate a new DS-SLAM. Note that the plug-in parameters allow specification of the *directory* where the SLAM will be generated, the *name* of the SLAM and the *namespace* for all classes and references that will be part of the generated SLAM.

After running this script, the DS-SLAM will contain following directories.

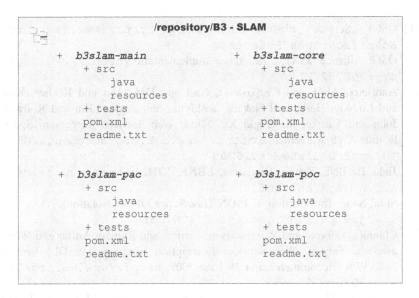

**Fig. 12** B3-SLAM example

# 9 Conclusions

In this chapter, we have described the plug-in-based architecture of the Generic SLA Manager, also known as G-SLAM. This SLA manager offers a set of generic components for managing the entire SLA life cycle and these can be easily reused by a domain-specific SLA manager. The dynamic features of G-SLAM are assisted by the OSGi platform with SpringDM, and enable the customisation or reuse of components, the integration of new components with minimal effort, and even swapping of components at runtime. Components such as the SLA Registry and Template Registry offer a consistent mechanism for storing SLAs and maintaining their historical information.

The Skeleton SLA manager provides a tool that assists with the initial phase of the implementation of a new domain-specific SLAM. Because this tool is integrated as a maven plug-in, its invocation is highly flexible with few parameters.

# References

[1] OSGi Service Platform Release 4 `http://www.osgi.org/Specifications/Reference`

[2] OSGi Alliance, JSR232 Reference Implementation `http://www.osgi.org/JSR232/RI`

[3] Andrieux, Alain and Czajkowski, Karl and Dan, Asit and Keahey, Kate and Ludwig, Heiko and Nakata, Toshiyuki and Pruyne, Jim and Rofrano, John and Tuecke, Steve and Xu, Ming: Web Services Agreement Specification (WS-Agreement), `http://www.ogf.org/documents/GFD.107.pdfPublishedMay252007`

[4] Jinks P.: BNF, Syntax Diagrams, EBNF. 2004, `http://www.cs.man.ac.uk/~pjj/bnf/bnf.html`.

[5] Shin, Sang: Introduction to JSON (JavaScript Object Notation), `http://www.javapassion.com/ajax/JSON.pdf`

[6] Chinnici, Roberto and Weerawarana, Sanjiva and Ryman, Arthur and Weerawarana, Sanjiva: Web Services Description Language (WSDL) Version 2.0 - W3C Recommendation 26 June 2007, `http://www.w3.org/TR/wsdl20/wsdl20.pdf`

[7] Kotsokalis, C. and Yahyapour, R. and Rojas-Gonzalez, M.A.: SAMI: The SLA Management Instance. Fifth International Conference on Internet and Web Applications and Services (ICIW), Barcelona, Spain

[8] Snyder, Bruce and Davies, Rob and Bosanac, Dejan: ActiveMQ in Action `http://www.manning.com/snyder/snyder\_meapch1.pdf`

[9] Kotsokalis, C and Yahyapour, R. and Rojas-Gonzalez, M.A.: Modeling Service Level Agreements with Binary Decision Diagrams. ICSOC-ServiceWave '09 7th International Joint Conference on Service-Oriented Computing.

[10] SpringSource Enterprise Bundle Repository `http://ebr.springsource.com/repository/app/`

[11] SLA@SOI Framework: SLATemplate Registry, `http://sourceforge.net/apps/trac/sla-at-soi/wiki/SlaTemplate`

[12] SLA@SOI Framework: SLA Registry, `http://sourceforge.net/apps/trac/sla-at-soi/wiki/GenericSlaManager/SLARegistry`

# A Generic Platform for Conducting SLA Negotiations

Edwin Yaqub, Philipp Wieder, Constantinos Kotsokalis, Valentina Mazza, Liliana Pasquale, Juan Lambea Rueda, Sergio García Gómez, and Augustín Escámez Chimeno

**Abstract** In service-oriented systems, negotiating service level agreements (SLAs) occupies a central role in the service usage cycle. It is during negotiations that parties are brought together in an interactive mechanism determined by the negotiation protocols. The choice and description of negotiation protocol determines the scope of information flow which in turn influences convergence upon an agreement. In this chapter, we observe the state of the art on negotiations and introduce the generic negotiation platform developed for the SLA@SOI framework. We strive for a generic approach for protocol description and execution that also caters for domain-based rationality and ease of adoption.

## 1 Introduction

Procuring software as a negotiated service is gaining popularity for various business and technological reasons [7, 9]. Various offshoots of this paradigm include Software as a Service (SaaS), Infrastructure as a Service (IaaS) and Platform as a Service (PaaS). These emerging business models have an inherent potential to reduce the Total Cost of Ownership (TCO) and improve Return on Investment (ROI). Traditionally, software is purchased under a license and used accordingly. Under the

Edwin Yaqub, Philipp Wieder, Constantinos Kotsokalis
TU Dortmund University, August-Schmidt-Strasse 12, 44227 Dortmund, Germany, e-mail: {edwin.yaqub,philipp.wieder,constantinos.kotsokalis}@ tu-dortmund.de

Valentina Mazza, Liliana Pasquale
Politecnico di Milano, piazza L. Da Vinci, 32, 20133 Milano, Italy, e-mail: {vmazza,pasquale}@elet.polimi.it

Juan Lambea Rueda, Sergio García Gómez, Augustín Escámez Chimeno
Telefónica Investigación y Desarrollo, Madrid, Spain, e-mail: {juanlr,sergg,escamez}@tid.es

new "aaS" models, the user subscribes to a software [17]. This is determined by a process of negotiation expected to converge on an agreement between the service customer and the service provider. During negotiation, the software is tailored to a consumer's needs and provider's capabilities.

Hence, the "as a service" paradigm injects flexibility to the notion of software usage. In an open market, as envisaged by service-oriented computing, this flexibility becomes a necessity, as usage aspects like cost and quality cannot be fixed beforehand; rather, they depend on the current situation of supply and demand in the market [12]. Analogies to the stock exchange market are often made to explain this paradigm.

Negotiating parties are brought together through negotiation protocols, which determine the rules of engagement. Various styles have been observed, varying from simple take-it-or-leave-it to multi-round negotiations and even more complex auction-like interactions. These have been studied extensively in the literature under the context of automated negotiations, as we present in Section 2.

A negotiation protocol determines the cardinality of parties involved, their roles, the visibility of the offers exchanged, session management, bounds for negotiation rounds, and so on. Usually, a dedicated software machinery is required to execute negotiation protocols, so that the negotiating agent may perform its domain-specific functionality either as a client or provider of the service under negotiation. In SLA@SOI, this software machinery is developed as a generic negotiation platform. The platform is designed to abstract from the lower-level functionality, which tends to get domain-specific, by allowing a loose coupling with the planning and optimisation component (see Chapter 'GSLAM – The Anatomy of the Generic SLA Manager'), such that a strategy is used to evaluate each proposal to maximise a utility function.

To enter the market, providers often advertise their services using publishing templates. Templates express the functional and non-functional properties of a service, along with the necessary constraints to tailor it as a concrete offer. A single service may be advertised through multiple templates. Customers shortlist providers based on templates of interest and use template(s) to initiate a particular negotiation. Template-based negotiations have been implemented by the Web Service Agreement (WSAG) framework (lately as Web Service Agreement Negotiations) [1, 20] and IBM's WSLA framework [10]. The SLA@SOI framework has also adopted template-based negotiations. Using these templates, offers and counter-offers are exchanged between the negotiating parties in a sequence determined by the negotiation protocol. In the best case, an agreement is reached and documented as a Service Level Agreement (SLA). The provider provisions the agreed upon resources and the customer starts to use the service from the time SLA comes into effect. The customer abides by the agreed usage levels and the provider maintains the agreed quality of service levels. In case of violations, penalties are enforced. An SLA may be need to be renegotiated if customers experience a change in service's demand, or the provider needs to readjust its resources.

## 2 State of the Art

Negotiation has gained a lot of interest in research. Various concepts from economics, artificial intelligence and game theory have been combined to address negotiation-related concerns through interdisciplinary approaches.

On theoretic lines, one of the first formal analyses of the negotiation process was carried out by John Nash [11] in his work on one-to-one bargaining and later on non-cooperative games. This popularised game theory, and later led to its inception in computer science, especially among distributed intelligent agents [26]. Several phenomena have been analysed when agents negotiate pursuing individual strategies. Some of these are summarised here:

- Pareto efficiency: If no agreement improving the utility of one of the negotiating parties can be found, the negotiation is considered to be Pareto efficient.
- Stability (Nash equilibrium): Two strategies are said to be in Nash equilibrium if they are the best for each of the parties involved in the negotiation. There might be multiple equilibria or none at all.
- Cooperative/non-cooperative: If the aim of a certain negotiation is to maximise the utility functions of each of the partners involved in the negotiation, the negotiation is said to be cooperative. On the other hand, when parties only take care of their own interests, the negotiation is non-cooperative.

Several frameworks and Negotiation Support Systems (NSS) have been proposed in the literature. OPELIX [16] is a European project that permits a customer and a provider to have fully automated bilateral negotiations. The OPELIX architecture implements all the fundamental phases of a business transaction: product offers and discovery, a negotiation process, payment activities, and the delivery of the product to the customer. However it does not support sophisticated negotiation protocols, rather it is restricted to bilateral negotiations.

Inspire [15], Aspire [14] and e-Agora [6] are related projects developed by Concordia University (Montreal) in conjunction with Carleton University (Ottawa). Inspire [15] supports human operators in managing bilateral negotiations, managing offers and counter-offers made by the participants. Functions guiding the decision of each participant are kept confidential.

Aspire [14] improves upon Inspire by providing negotiation support through intelligent agents that make suggestions to users regarding what operations to perform. Note that agents do not completely automate the negotiation process, but only provide support in taking decisions; they are completely aware of the status of the negotiation sessions, and implement a specific negotiation strategy defined in terms of weights on negotiation variables and objective functions.

The e-Agora [6] project provides a complex marketplace in which users interact through autonomous intelligent agents. The system provides a process model and a set of supported protocols. The process is defined as a series of activities and phases; protocols are defined by means of rules and restrictions on negotiation activities.

Kasbah [2] allows potential buyers and sellers to create their own agents, assign them some strategic directions, and send them to a centralised marketplace for negotiations. Support is limited to bilateral negotiations. The only valid action in the distributive negotiation protocol is for buying agents to offer a bid to sellers. Selling agents respond with a binding "yes" or "no". Given this protocol, Kasbah provides buyers with several negotiation strategies that determine the function for increasing bids for a product over time.

AuctionBot [21] offers a versatile online auction server. Software agents are provided that conduct auctions on the basis of particular parameters: participation (i.e., number of participants), discrete goods (bids are allowed only for integer quantities) and bidding rules that determine acceptability and improvement of offers and closing conditions.

ASAPM [18] is multi-agent system that allows automated negotiations using the FIPA Iterated Contract Net Protocol (ICNP). Agents negotiate over quality of service (QoS) terms and the ICNP accommodates this by allowing multiple rounds of negotiation.

BREin [13] provides a broker-based framework for conducting SLA negotiations. A multi-tier negotiation protocol is used that is based on the FIPA Contract Net Protocol. The protocol scope is extended to allow for negotiation interactions among different service chains.

CAAT [19] is another framework that can be used to design multi-agent systems for automatic bilateral and trilateral negotiations. The negotiation protocol allows valid sequences of interactions using messages built upon the FIPA Agent Communication Language (ACL). An ontology defining communication semantics is developed and used in messages to convey a certain action.

The approaches presented above make interesting advances towards automated negotiation, yet they are not flexible enough to design custom interaction behaviours or to easily customise negotiations for individual application domains.

To this end, SECSE [8] provides a flexible infrastructure that can be tailored in terms of multiplicity, workflow, protocol and decision model to fit a specific application domain. The architecture of the negotiation framework is composed of a marketplace that harbours multiple agents. Each agent is associated with a specific negotiating participant and a negotiator component. Negotiators interface human participants with the negotiation framework through GUIs that allow them to place offers and counter-offers. Additionally, a built-in decision model or user-defined decision model can be encapsulated to execute automatic negotiations. SECSE supports hybrid negotiations, where some participants are automated agents while others are human beings. A participant may exploit a negotiation coordinator, which is responsible for coordinating the actions taken by its various negotiators. The marketplace acts as an intermediary in all interactions between the participants, providing validity checks for the offers exchanged. These checks are based on the structure and current state of the negotiation workflow. To make the search for agreements more efficient, the marketplace provides a mediator component, which guides the generation of offers towards a convergence of the individual objectives. This, however, requires that participants share their objectives with the mediator. The negotiation framework allows designers to define their negotiation workflow as a state chart using ArgoUML, and their negotiation protocol as a set of rules in the JBoss rule syntax.

WSAG [1] is a standardising effort from the Open Grid Forum (OGF) delivers a specification for web-service-based agreements. A language is developed that can be used to specify an agreement template and standard operations for managing the life cycle of the service. In addition, it provides a negotiation protocol that allows for take-it-or-leave-it styled bilateral negotiations. More recently, work on Web Service Agreement Negotiation (WSAG-N) [20] has addressed broadening its scope to specify custom interaction behaviours and thus support a host of negotiation protocols written as per given specifications.

Analysing the architecture and design approaches proposed for the NSS, different patterns are observed: 1) broker-based architectures, where a broker component manages one-to-one negotiations on behalf of involved parties; 2) marketplace-based architectures, where the parties involved in M-to-N negotiations are managed by an intermediate marketplace (approaches 1) and 2) require negotiation participants to expose their preferences to the negotiation framework); and 3) independent agents negotiate with each other without mediation. These patterns freely compete or cooperate based on individual rationality. From the protocol description perspective, we observe rule-based approaches where business rules regulate the negotiation process, use of ontologies and schemas represent message content and semantics, and negotiation protocols have parameter-based configurations.

# 3 Protocol Engine

In SLA@SOI, agents modelled as SLA managers (see also Chapter 'GSLAM – The Anatomy of the Generic SLA Manager') conduct automated negotiations using a generic platform called the Protocol Engine. The Protocol Engine is an integral component of the Generic SLA Manager and is therefore available to all concrete implementations of GSLAM. The Protocol Engine establishes communication between negotiating parties by using a negotiation protocol. The negotiation protocol in this text does not refer to a low-level communication protocol like TCP or routing protocols like IP. In fact, it refers to a higher-level interaction mechanism that is employed by the negotiating parties under a unique context. This context is called the negotiation session and is managed by the Protocol Engine at each negotiating end. In SLA@SOI, a flexible approach to encoding negotiation protocols has been developed. The basic idea circulates around modelling interaction behaviour as a state machine. This approach is further discussed in Section 4. In addition to interaction behaviours, the negotiation protocols may consider domain-sensitive content that may affect negotiations, keeping in sight past negotiation experience and current business policy. The Protocol Engine, however, is designed to operate at a higher level of abstraction than the negotiation protocols, and is therefore able to execute them without tight coupling to the domain or universe of discourse served by its SLA manager. Domain agnosticity of the Protocol Engine, combined with domain sensitivity of the negotiation protocols, allow SLA@SOI to achieve a generic mechanism for conducting automatic negotiations among various SLA managers.

## 3.1 Design

The functionality provided by the Protocol Engine is broken up into three tiers, as shown in Figure 1.

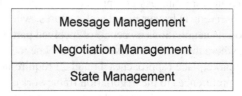

**Fig. 1** Tiers of the Protocol Engine

- Message management: This tier acts as the Protocol Engine's façade to the outside world. All negotiation requests and responses are handled here by a singleton message handler component. The message handler implements an INegotiation interface, as seen in Figure 2, which provides all operations needed to conduct negotiations. This interface is exposed as a web-service for remote access. A client program offered by the SyntaxConvertor component (as described in Chapter 'GSLAM – The Anatomy of the Generic SLA Manager') of the GSLAM is used to invoke operations of the web-service. The message handler passes incoming requests to the negotiation management tier. Additionally, it posts requests from the negotiation management tier to the negotiating parties, as in the case of the *initiateNegotiation* and *negotiate* operations.
- Negotiation management: This tier allocates a negotiation manager for each negotiation. The negotiation manager maintains the negotiation session identifiable by a unique identifier. This identifier is used by the negotiating parties in subsequent operations. The session is initialised using two artifacts: a) the negotiation protocol and b) the template(s) of the service under negotiation. The session also stores information such as the involved parties, offers received, counter-offers sent, reasons for cancellation or termination of SLAs (when applicable) and protocol parameters. This tier further collaborates with the state management tier to ensure that the protocol rules are abided by before control is handed over to the planning and optimisation (POC) component (see Chapter 'GSLAM – The Anatomy of the Generic SLA Manager').
- State management: This tier implements a state engine that maintains the states of the negotiation based on the execution of the state machine as defined in the negotiation protocol. In SLA@SOI, the protocol is encoded using rules. The state

management tier therefore acts as a wrapper over a rule engine. It implements a feedback control loop by passing events to the rule engine corresponding to the invoked operations, and receiving the processed results. Inside the state engine, protocol-specific events are converted to rule-engine-specific commands and *vice versa*.

Figure 2 shows an architectural view of the Protocol Engine.

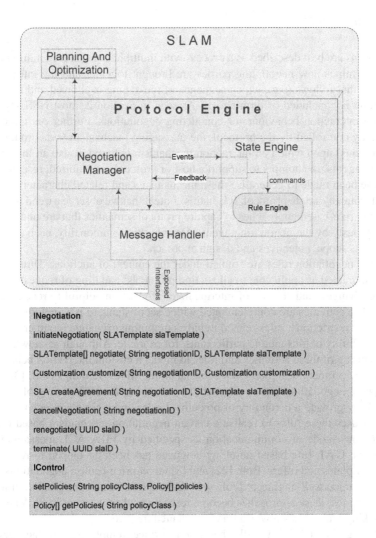

**Fig. 2** Architecture of the Protocol Engine

# 4 Protocol Description

Negotiation protocols have been widely studied in the literature. Before we present the objectives set for our work, and the resulting approach we developed, it is worthwhile to have a walk through the closely related work.

## 4.1 Related Work

Negotiations are best described as a process with multiple aspects. Negotiation protocol determines how negotiating parties are brought together and the interaction behaviour that follows (e.g., which sequence of messaging is allowed and how the negotiation is concluded or terminated). As seen in Section 2, most NSS support restricted interaction behaviour for conducting negotiations. Further on, although not directly controlled by the protocol, the messaging mechanism (synchronous or asynchronous) upon which an interaction mechanism is based is also an important factor for agents. In attempts to support a host of protocols as required, research efforts have been made to generalise these mechanisms and related characteristics to abstract from any single protocol. It is in this context that we observe a trend towards employing rule-based approaches to capture protocol semantics that are understood unambiguously by the negotiating agents. Despite this commonality, each solution differs in its scope, objectives and design approach.

In [22], negotiation rules are studied under the context of auctions. Three activities are extracted as applicable to all auction protocols: handling of requests, computing exchanges, and sharing of intermediate information helpful to reach a conclusion. The activities are complemented with a set of standard parameterised rules that impose restrictions: rules related to bids, computing exchange (counter-offers), and the visibility of bids among participants, for example. Although acknowledged, the structuring of these activities and rules to model a custom interaction behaviour is left to the protocol designer. On somewhat similar lines, Jennings et al. [3] have developed a negotiation framework that can be used to model a variety of negotiations. They provide a taxonomy of predefined rules and a simple interaction protocol that uses these rules to realise a certain negotiation mechanism based on an asynchronous mode of communication as specified by FIPA ACL messaging. In addition, an OWL-Lite-based ontology language has been developed to represent service templates and offers. Both [22] and [3] target price-centric negotiations that try to build upon well-engineered rule sets. Although befitting controlled traditional auction settings, these approaches become restrictive when it comes to SLA negotiations taking place in open world service-oriented markets.

SLA negotiations are usually based on service templates that the service providers make publicly available for negotiation. The templates contain a set of properties, with price being just one of them. Most of these properties concern the quality of service (QoS) that the customer and the provider negotiate to agree upon. Each QoS property contains a set or range of values that the customer may choose from. This is a fundamental shift from a single attribute price-centric model towards a multi-attribute model. Needless to say, a single template may also be used to conduct multi-unit negotiations, which usually require special considerations as in multi-commodity auctions. The problem is further complicated by the fact that in service-oriented markets, most agents are self-interested and would not like to share information related to their business objectives or utility-maximising functions. This introduces challenges for the above-mentioned approaches, which for instance try to deliver a standard rule for judging improvement in offers received in subsequent negotiation rounds. Among self-interested agents conducting SLA negotiations, complicated correlations among the negotiable properties are kept private.

A generic approach for conducting SLA negotiations therefore requires more flexibility and loose coupling between the domain-specific and generic aspects. An attempt to draw this fine line has been made in [25], where a set of generally applicable negotiation parameters have been identified and implemented as an XML language. A meta-negotiation phase allows the negotiating agents to fix the values of the negotiating parameters that serve as a concrete negotiation protocol. Some parameters include party roles, permissions, cardinality, admission credentials, starting and termination criteria. Rule-based restrictions can be appended to parameters in external rule languages without limiting choice. In addition to multilateral negotiations, bilateral negotiations are also given due consideration. The language inherits its service description and guarantee term constructs from WS-Agreement.

## 4.2 Design

In the SLA@SOI project, a broadly scoped meta-model called SLA* has been developed to describe a service template that includes negotiable QoS properties, provider information and more[1] . Negotiations take the service template into account. This serves to clearly differentiate the subject of negotiation (i.e., the QoS terms of the service) from the aspects that govern the negotiation process. In this section, we present our methodology in representing the negotiation process. We abstract this process as a set of phases that can be structured together as a general purpose state machine (GPSM). This representation is highly generic and is termed a generic protocol that basically serves to develop an interaction behaviour. We further employ a customisable parameter-oriented approach to transform the generic protocol into a concrete negotiation protocol that would govern negotiation behaviour. In the following section, we first describe the GPSM and how the approach is modeled, making it easy to plug protocols into our execution platform: the Protocol Engine. Although not related to the field of negotiation, we do draw some design principles from past experience in encoding and executing medical protocols intended for the personal health records domain [28].

---

[1] The model is described in full detail in Chapter 'The SLA Model'

We adopted event-driven design in liaison with modestly engineered rules to reach our technical objective: specialisation of generic negotiation protocols still able to be executed in a standard manner. The generic negotiation protocol is structured as a GPSM that abstracts upon different phases of negotiation, as shown in Figure 3. The generic protocol provides a reference interaction behaviour; however, the approach does not restrict the protocol designer to a given state set, or to any particular structure, thereby allowing the design of custom interactions. The GPSM comprises five states: initialise, customise, negotiate, decide and end. At any point in time, the negotiation process resides in a single state. Each state determines what operations are allowed or disallowed by entertaining the trigger events in a certain manner. This also determines the next state to which the machine will transit. The protocol is encoded using rules that are divided into two categories: The first category comprises *generic rules* that encode the state machine; a reference rule set is provided for GPSM. The second category comprises *domain-sensitive rules* that take into account an agent's local considerations when conducting the negotiation. Before addressing the encoding details for the rules, we briefly describe the semantics of the five GPSM states.

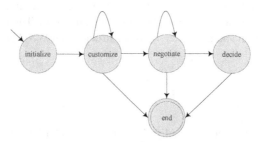

**Fig. 3** A General Purpose State Machine

- *initialise*: This state represents establishment of a negotiation session between negotiating parties. A unique identifier is assigned and used by involved participants for conducting subsequent operations. This state is mandatory and is influenced by the arrival of an initialisation event.
- *customise*: This optional—but important—state follows the initialise state and constitutes a customisation mechanism where negotiating parties attempt to customise generic protocol parameters. An output is a concrete protocol for governing subsequent behaviour. This state is influenced by the arrival of a customise event. More details on the customisation mechanism are provided in Section 5.
- *negotiate*: In this state, parties negotiate with each other by submitting offers and counter-offers to reach an agreement (SLA). Usually multiple rounds would be required to conclude this state. This state is influenced by proposal-related events.

- *decide*: This state determines if negotiation can be gracefully concluded. It is reached if an agreement creation is requested, negotiation rounds are consumed, or a timeout occurs. Several events may trigger this state.
- *end*: This state marks the end of negotiation, which could possibly result in the creation of an SLA.

A lightweight data model has been developed that provides classes for concepts like events, protocol parameters, negotiation sessions, and states. Generic categories of rules employ states to encode the state design pattern. A rule represents preconditions specified in the IF part, that when met execute the post-conditions specified in the THEN part. Rule qualification is driven by arrival or departure of events; therefore rules are coupled with events to regulate success or failure scenarios. In the case of the latter, appropriate exceptions are generated with a specialised message as provided in the rule. A taxonomy of events has been realised as a result. Following this simple rule-encoding scheme allows a loose coupling with the Protocol Engine component that is responsible for generating, passing and receiving processed events from the rule engine that executes the negotiation protocol. Keeping behavioural logic in rules inherits additive benefits of the rule-based approach: for instance, the protocol remains maintainable over time, as it is humanly readable and machine executable. Further, rules can be externally configured without requiring code recompilation or deployment. Two reference rules representing a success and failure scenario are shown in Figure 4.

Negotiation protocols are divided into two basic categories: bilateral and multilateral negotiations. For proper demarcation, these are kept under distinct negotiation interfaces and are to be provided over different ports. The interfaces provide actual operations that the client programs may use to conduct negotiations. Our protocol description approach proves beneficial when negotiation interfaces are conjoined with behaviour-regulating rules while maintaining a plethora of information in the session associated to the ongoing negotiation.

Session management is important for the seamless functioning of other components involved in performing negotiation. In this regard, the planning and optimisation component (POC) plays a special role. It acts as the local executive controller of the SLA manager. The POC implements domain- and use-case-specific strategies that drive negotiation from the back seat. A strategy implements some decision-making logic to process an incoming offer and generate counter-offer(s) by considering the current state of available resources as well as business objectives. Further on, the POC resolves service dependencies (if any) and decides when to outsource incoming requests to third parties by conducting nested negotiations. For reasons of convergence, POCs benefit from information available in the negotiation session by analysing the offers exchanged with the negotiating party and its profile (Section 5.1). This analysis provides a possibility of cooperation even among self-interested agents by understanding their partner's sphere of interest. In Section 5.2, we outline how an optional critique may be provided by the POC to encourage a negotiating partner to move future offers in a particular direction of interest, or to pull him to a middle ground.

A rule demonstrating a success scenario

```
IF
   { currentState : State(name == NEGOTIATE && status == RUNNING
     && currentRound <= ProtocolParameters.negotiationRounds) }
   AND
   { allowedEvent : Event(name == PROPOSAL_ARRIVED) }
THEN
   { currentState.incrementNegotiationRounds(1) }
   AND
   { update(currentState) }
   AND
   { allowedEvent.setProcessedSuccessfully(true) }
```

A rule demonstrating a failure scenario

```
IF
   { currentState : State(name == NEGOTIATE && currentRound >
     ProtocolParameters.negotiationRounds) }
   AND
   { disallowedEvent : Event(name == PROPOSAL_ARRIVED) }
THEN
   { retract(currentState) }
   AND
   { insert (new State(StateName.DECIDE && status = RUNNING)) }
   AND
   { disallowedEvent.setProcessedSuccessfully(false) }
   AND
   { disallowedEvent.setProcessingAfterMath(MAX_ROUNDS_VIOLATED) }
```

**Fig. 4** Reference rules

The justification for separating strategic behaviour from the negotiation protocol is made on two levels: Firstly, strategies tend to get domain-specific, and secondly, they have high computational intensity (as in case of composite services that perform QoS-aware service composition, a known NP-Hard problem [4, 5]). These are therefore best served as black box implementations clearly separated from the generic aspects of conducting negotiations. For these reasons, the protocol rules are intentionally spared from implementing strategic behaviour: a functionality delegated to the POC during negotiations (Figure 2).

## 4.3 Bilateral Negotiations

One of the most widely occurring forms of negotiation among independent agents is bilateral negotiation. As bilateral negotiation serves most of the use cases considered in the SLA@SOI project, we have early adoption results for the same. In a bilateral negotiation, a customer negotiates directly with a provider. If the provider has further dependencies, nested or sub-negotiations are possible in a similar fashion. A somewhat advanced scenario would involve a customer negotiating over a product offered by a certain enterprise: The on-line business unit of this enterprise is represented by an instance of SLAM called BSLAM. The BSLAM could depend upon external software services, offered by an agent called the Software-SLAM or SWSLAM. The SWSLAM in turn must deploy and instantiate its software services over an infrastructure capable of delivering a guaranteed QoS as required by the BSLAM. For this, the SWSLAM needs to negotiate with an infrastructure service provider, represented by its agent, called INSLAM. This scenario helps expand the negotiation scope over multiple providers and exposes a possible chain of dependencies to be resolved through negotiations. This depiction realistically sketches how SLA negotiations would be employed in service-oriented markets. Interestingly, each stage in this potentially long hierarchy of negotiations can negotiate successfully with the next agent in line in a bilateral manner, by customising the negotiation protocol with parameter values considered realistic.

Request multiplicity is taken care of by conducting multiple bilateral negotiations in parallel. The responsibility of having a unified view of currently available resources at any time considering ongoing tentative reservations is kept internal to POC. A simplified interaction is illustrated in Figure 5. Here, a customer initiates negotiation with a provider and receives a negotiation identifier. This is used in subsequent steps, first to customise the protocol, and later to negotiate offers and counter-offers. Both of these may require certain iterations. At some point, the customer requests an agreement by submitting a final offer. If accepted, the provider sends back the SLA, which is then provisioned.

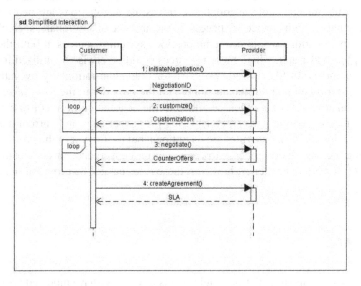

**Fig. 5** Simplified interaction

As an extension of our work, multilateral negotiations are being considered under the context of auctions.

# 5 Negotiation Rationality

Negotiation technologies have garnered a lot of interest in recent years, and are seen as a key coordination mechanism for the interaction of providers and consumers in electronic markets. Such technologies provide means to reduce the costs of efficiently managing resources in fast-changing service-oriented markets. Their importance surfaces especially in the case of multi-attribute SLA negotiations, where agents engage in sophisticated protocols to intelligently negotiate over complex services to achieve mutual gain.

Complex services are usually offered by composing or aggregating other services. Considering time and other restrictions imposed by the negotiation protocols, it becomes challenging to converge upon an agreement with the customer at one end and possibly multiple providers at the other end. The dependencies among providers require the establishment of a hierarchy of SLAs at negotiation time [27]. Therefore, a sound rationale for conducting negotiations is of fundamental importance. Optimal outcomes are obtained, as per cooperative game theory, by assuming maximum information on the objectives of the involved parties. In classical multi-attribute utility theory [23, 24], the proposed solution is the use of an independent mediator that both parties can trust to reveal their preferences. However, in the case of self-interested agents doing business in e-commerce settings, it is not possible to determine what mediators would be impartial or trustworthy for establishing the rationale.

Negotiation rationale determines the degree of feasibility of a negotiation. It also serves to rule out infeasible negotiations. Infeasible negotiations are negotiations that do not have a high chance of success. In the absence of a rationale, such blindly instigated negotiations would consume precious system resources at both the customer and provider end, where these resources could otherwise be utilised for productive outcomes. In SLA@SOI, we cater for individual rationality by gathering high-level information about the customer and the provider in the form of *profiles*. Domain-sensitive rules may then be added to the negotiation protocol to compute ranks for the negotiating partner, considering past experience and current business policy. The domain-sensitive rules are an optional but useful part of the protocol that may guide the negotiation process towards a faster convergence or conclusion. For reasons of domain dependency, however, these rules cannot be provided out of the box.

## 5.1 Profiles

Keeping business and negotiation requirements in view, we have modeled profiles to contain information about these characteristics of the negotiating actors. For reasons of brevity, only summarised features can be discussed here. The idea is to cross-profile the negotiating party: that is, service customers profile the service providers and *vice versa*. Additionally, the product or service being negotiated can also be profiled by its provider. The profiles add value to the negotiation process by providing negotiation- and business-related history that serves as an experience base. This high-level information about the customer and provider is inspired from the business perspective of negotiations. Domain-sensitive protocol rules raise the level of abstraction of this information to determine ranks that allow judging of the negotiating party upon negotiation setup time. In the following section, we expand this concept to shed light on how this high-level information forms the basis for customising the generic negotiation protocol as hinted earlier in Section 4.2.

Providers may classify customers as companies or end users who are the direct beneficiary of the negotiation. In case of former, the size of a company (characterised as a small, medium or large enterprise) along with other factors can be considered by using a rule to determine, for instance, the number of negotiation rounds one is willing to negotiate with this entity in the future. An abstract view of a customer's economic situation is also of importance for the provider. This is ascertained by assessing punctuality in payment of dues against already established SLAs, and the worth associated with the SLAs. Profiles also depict summarised penalty information that provides further insight into previously established SLAs. All these factors can be processed by a rule that assigns a rank to the customer using current business policy. Yet another rule may build upon this information to generate an acceptable value for maximum counter-offers exchangeable during negotiations, for example.

On the other side, customers are interested in conducting further negotiations with providers that have delivered a good quality of service for previously established SLAs, while avoiding providers who have not. Customers can also associate a rank with a provider, based on the worth of the SLA under negotiation, past services, and penalty satisfaction levels. Based on the ranks, strict business policies may be encoded in yet other rules that blacklist or whitelist the negotiating partner. If this criteria changes over time, only the related rules need modification, and this does not jeopardise the overall negotiation behaviour. Other elements of interest for doing business are aspects of location: These may restrict aspects of a business due to laws in the country of the negotiating partner, or disallow trade of a certain product in that country. This same information may allow higher prioritisation of another negotiating partner if, for example, the business policy is to increase clientele in a certain location for strategic reasons. Soft counter-offers may be generated by the POC after considering the ranks and other profile information at negotiation time. Hence, the profiles provide a degree of freedom for the POC to tune its algorithm such that generated offers and counter-offers are personalised for the party, but also in line with business objectives.

After considering the number of SLAs already made, providers may forecast the selling frequency of a certain product and establish business derivatives such as the minimum markup ratio/benefits (i.e., minimum sales required for the product/service to be profitable). These forecasts may also influence the degree of flexibility shown while negotiating over the said product. Additionally, profile information may serve to influence decisions regarding product retirement (i.e., terminating agreements with a partner due to bad service, defaulting on payments, or penalty situations). The latter may also be used to perform penalty-driven renegotiations.

Customer and provider profiles can also log vital negotiation history, including past attempts to negotiate, renegotiate, or terminate SLAs. The frequency of these attempts, along with their outcomes, can be used by a rule to assign a rank for the requested negotiation. As with the scenarios presented earlier, the negotiation rank also may influence the customisation of future negotiations. For example, if the rank is high, the customer can be considered faithful or promising, and the provider may suggest a greater number of negotiation rounds or maximum counter-offers.

## 5.2 Protocol Customisation Mechanism

As mentioned in Section 4.2, the customise state allows negotiating parties to mutually agree on values for any customisable protocol parameters that govern the negotiation. This is done by exchanging customisation suggestions. Domain-sensitive rules come into action and set values to these parameters by coupling profile-based ranks with business policy and customisable values suggested by negotiating partners. This forms a pre-negotiation mechanism that may span several rounds until consensus is reached. It is important that the parties share the same protocol parameters to avoid undesired anomalous behaviour in later stages, and this is achieved through the protocol customisation mechanism. If consensus is not reached, negotiation is aborted.

The customisation mechanism is an active part of ongoing work on the SLA@SOI negotiation platform. We now summarise some of these customisable protocol parameters.

- *credentials* allow parties to verify each other if such an understanding exists. This could be an individual key under Primary Key Infrastructure (PKI)-based certification environments.
- *customizationRounds* informs the negotiating partner that there will be an attempt to reach consensus on customisable parameters in a particular number of rounds, starting with two. This is a sliding value that may be extended during customisation. Nevertheless, at any point in time, each party may respect its own value and end the customisation process as dictated by its side of the customisation rules.
- *processTimeout* determines the lifetime of the negotiation process. Negotiation is considered invalid after this timeout has occurred.
- *negotiationRounds* determine the maximum allowed number of rounds for exchanging offers. If it is set to zero, negotiation will not take place.
- *maxCounterOffers* sets a cap on the number of counter-offers allowed in response to a submitted offer.
- *optionalCritiqueOnQoS* serves as a tip to the POC to optionally annotate critiques on the QoS terms of generated counter-offers. Critiques may involve keywords like INCREASE, DECREASE, CHANGE, and so on, thus helping to convey a message to the negotiator to consider submitting values for which the chances of reaching agreement is higher. In this way agents may guide or pull each other in their direction of interest.

- *isSealed* is of interest in multilateral negotiations such as auctions. For example, it would be false for an English auction but true for First-Price-Sealed-Bid or Vickrey auction.

In addition to above parameters, which are customised in a mutual manner, there are parameters that remain non-customisable, to avoid sharing vital information. These are especially applicable to auctions (e.g., minimum and maximum bidders, auctioneer's listening time to receive bids, and the start time of an auction).

## 5.3 Business Take-Up of Negotiations

Business requirements drive the negotiation process for each entity involved in the negotiation. These requirements need to be met *in addition to* fulfilling customers' QoS requirements. Profiling the negotiating parties can help in adapting negotiations to a specific manner. From a business point of view, particular aspects of the negotiation need to be controlled. As seen earlier, profiles can be used to customise negotiations to better suit business goals, while assigning each negotiator a personalised negotiation field. Negotiation profiles can be applied and mapped to different ranks, which are obtained by rules-mapping current business policy to past negotiations and business information about the product, customer and provider involved. Once ranks have been determined, negotiation commences in a personalised and rational manner. This lightweight approach helps manage and drive the negotiation, while at the same time allowing it to benefit from volatile policy logic that can be easily and rapidly updated in rules.

**Business Negotiation Flow:**
Aligned with business-level control of the negotiation, negotiations are materialised in different adoption styles. Automatic, semi-automatic and manual negotiation are the different proposed negotiation flows.

- Automatic negotiation: Agents negotiate directly with each other and exchange offers and counter-offers that are automatically processed and generated. The agents have preset decision-making capabilities and try to maximise or minimise their own utility. Depending on the agents' decision models, agents may or may not attempt to cooperate with the other in converging upon an agreement.
- Semi-automatic negotiation: Automatic negotiation can be split in two halves: the first half involves a special subset of cases in which business personnel could be given manual control of the negotiation, while the second half includes those other cases that can be managed automatically.
- Manual negotiation: In this scenario, business personnel receive customer offers in real-time and make counter-offers or reject the offers by practicing full control of the offers being exchanged.

Each of these behaviours is adopted by different use cases that use the SLA@SOI framework. The framework provides necessary hooks and programmable interfaces to intercept the various interactions involved in negotiations to implement a certain negotiation flow. Early adoption results show that controlling the negotiation flow becomes an important consideration for various businesses interested in the SLA@SOI framework.

# 6 Conclusion

In this chapter, we reviewed the state of the art available on negotiations and presented our generic negotiation platform for conducting SLA negotiations. We illustrated the flexibility of our approach, which also takes into account domain-based rationality. Early adoption results from use cases encourage us to extend our work, while also considering contemporary efforts.

Diversity in research is expected to reveal new facts regarding the process of automatic SLA creation, especially in areas such as nested dependencies, efficient and fruitful optimisation algorithms, negotiation strategies that quickly converge upon agreements, analysis of market trends, and party profiling. These areas have been established as solid research fields but have not yet been fully exhausted. As the field matures, scientific progress will be harnessed to produce tangible results that will lead towards a successful service-oriented economy.

# References

[1] Andrieux A., Czajkowski K., Dan A., Keahey K., Ludwig H., Nakata T., Pruyne J., Rofrano J., Tuecke S., Xu M.: Web Services Agreement Specification (WS-Agreement), https://forge.gridforum.org/projects/graap-wg/.posted-at2006-09-05

[2] Chavez A., Dreilinger D., Guttman R., Maes P.: A Real-Life Experiment in Creating an Agent Marketplace. In: Proceedings of the Second International Conference on the Practical Application of Intelligent Agents and Multi-Agent Technology (PAAM'97) (1997)

[3] Lomuscio A.R., Wooldridge M., Jennings N.R.: A Classification Scheme for Negotiation in Electronic Commerce. Journal of Group Decision and Negotiation (pp.31-56) **12**(1) (2003)

[4] Ardagna D., Pernici B.: Global and Local QoS Guarantee in Web Service Selection. In: Proceedings of the Third International Conference on Business Process Management (2005)

[5] Bonatti P.A., Festa P.: On Optimal Service Selection. In: Proceedings of the 14th international conference on World Wide Web (2005)

[6] Chen E., Kersten G. E., Vahidov R.: An E-marketplace for Agent-supported Commerce Negotiations. In: Proceedings of 5th World Congress on the Management of eBusiness (2004)

[7] Dubey A., Wagle D.: Delivering Software as a Service. White paper, The McKinsey Quarterly (2007)

[8] Di Nitto E., Di Penta M., Gambi A., Ripa G., Villani M.L.: Negotiation of Service Level Agreements: An Architecture and a Search-Based Approach. In: Proceedings of the 7th International Conference on Service Oriented Computing, ICSOC 2007 (2007)

[9] Elfatatry A., Layzell P.: Negotiating in Service-Oriented Environments. Communications of the ACM **47**(8), 103–108 (2004)

[10] Ludwig H., Keller A., Dan A., King R.P., Franck R.: Web Service Level Agreement (WSLA) Language Specification 1.0 (wsla-2003/01/28) (2003)

[11] Nash Jr.J.F.: The Bargaining Problem. Journal of the Econometric Society **18**(2) (1950)

[12] Bennett K., Layzell P., Budgen D., Brereton P., Macaulay L., Munro M.: Service-based Software: The Future for Flexible Software. In: Proceedings of the Seventh Asia-Pacific Software Engineering Conference (2000)

[13] Karaenke P., Kirn S.: Towards Model Checking and Simulation of a Multi-tier Negotiation Protocol for Service Chains (extended abstract). In: Proceedings of the 9th International Conference on Autonomous Agents and Multiagent Systems (AAMAS 2010) (2010)

[14] Kersten G.E., Lo G.: An Integrated Negotiation Support System and Software Agents for E-Business Negotiation. International Journal of Internet and Enterprise Management **1**(3) (2003)

[15] Kersten G.E., Noronha S.J.: WWW-based Negotiation Support: Design, Implementation and Use. Journal of Decision Support Systems **25**(2) (1999)

[16] Hauswirth M., Jazayeri M., Miklos Z., Podnar I., Di Nitto E., Wombacher A.: An Architecture for Information Commerce Systems. In: Proceedings of the Sixth International Conference on Telecommunications (ConTEL) (2001)

[17] Turner M., Budgen D., Brereton P.: Turning Software into a Service. Proceedings of the IEEE Computer Society **36**(10), 38–44 (2003)

[18] Chhetri M.B., Mueller I., Goh S.K., Kowalczyk R.: ASAPM An Agent-based Framework for Adaptive Management of Composite Service Lifecycle. In: Proceedings of the IEEE/WIC/ACM International Conferences on Web Intelligence and Intelligent Agent Technology - Workshops, 2007 (2007)

[19] Ncho A., Aimeur E.: Building a Multi-Agent System for Automatic Negotiation in Web Service Applications. In: Proceedings of the Third International Joint Conference on Autonomous Agents and Multiagent Systems (2004)

[20] Waeldrich O., Battre D., Brazier F., Clark K., Oey M., Papaspyrou A., Wieder P., Ziegler W.: WS-Agreement Version Negotiation 1.0 (2007). URL https://forge.gridforum.org/sf/go/doc15831?nav=1

[21] Wurman P.R., Wellman M.P., Walsh W.E.: The Michigan Internet AuctionBot: A Configurable Auction Server for Human and Software Agents. In: Proceedings of the Second International Conference on Autonomous agents (1998)

[22] P.R. Wurman, M.P. Wellman, and W.E. Walsh: Specifying Rules for Electronic Auctions (2002)

[23] Raiffa H.: The Art and Science of Negotiation. Harvard University Press (1982)

[24] Raiffa H.: Lectures on Negotiation Analysis. PON Books, Harvard Law School (1996)

[25] Hudert S., Eymann T., Ludwig H., Wirtz G.: A Negotiation Protocol Description Language for Automated Service Level Agreement Negotiations. In: Proceedings of the IEEE Conference on Commerce and Enterprise Computing (2009)

[26] Weiss G.: Multiagent Systems: A Modern Approach to Distributed Artificial Intelligence. The MIT Press (2000)

[27] Theilmann W., Happe J., Kotsokalis C., Edmonds A., Kearney K., Lambea J.: A Reference Architecture for Multi-Level SLA Management. Journal of Internet Engineering 4(1) (2010)

[28] Yaqub E., Barosso A.: Distributed Guidelines (DiG): A Software Framework for Extending Automated Health Decision Support to the General Population. Journal of American Health Information Management Association (AHIMA) (2010)

# Part V
# Management of the Business Layer

# Management of the Business SLAs for Services eContracting

Sergio García Gómez, Juan Lambea Rueda, and Augustín Escámez Chimeno

**Abstract** The management of Service Level Agreements is a complex task that requires to be specialized in the different domains it involves. Since SLA management can eventually be an integral part of eContracting environments, several topics have to be tackled in this layer: third parties management, Business Level Objectives, penalties, etc. This chapter explains the foundations of such specialization in relation to the business concerns. Specifically, it describes the business terms and conditions that must be taken into account and the architecture of the business layer of the project SLA@SOI. Moreover, the roots and more innovative aspects of the business layer in the project are explained.

## 1 Introduction

Service-Oriented Architectures (SOAs) and the delivery of applications and resources as services have consolidated into new methods for integrating and delivering functionality from vendors and providers. In recent years, an important effort has been made to solve many of the technical and scientific challenges associated with this approach. One of the challenges — and a main rationale of SOA— is the creation of business environments in which providers and consumers can trade services. The emergence of cloud computing technologies has fostered the need to monetise the services provided, including software as a service (SaaS), platforms as a service (PaaS), infrastructures as a service (IaaS), and so on.

Sergio García Gómez
Telefonica I+D, Boecillo, Valladolid, Spain, e-mail: `sergg@tid.es`

Juan Lambea Rueda
Telefonica I+D, Madrid, Spain e-mail: `juanlr@tid.es`

Augustín Escámez Chimeno
Telefonica I+D, Granada, Spain, e-mail: `escamez@tid.es`

Typical proposals for interaction and trading of services between providers and consumers are e-marketplaces [3], e-contracting environments and service ecosystems [1]. These frameworks usually convey different phases of the trading process. This chapter considers four such phases: information, in which the technical and commercial offer is published, shown and rated; negotiation, in which the business and technical aspects are calculated and agreed upon; contracting, in which the agreement is signed and the service provisioned; and runtime, in which the service is delivered, managed, charged, reported and terminated, etc.

Once the relationship between a provider and a consumer is based on a monetary transaction, the quality of the service provided, and the terms and conditions under which it is offered, are of vital importance. SLAs become critical in this context, and — given that elements of business are relevant to many common SLA management tasks (negotiation, agreement, management of breaches, etc.), some business guarantee terms must be natively considered in the management of services and SLAs.

This chapter covers several aspects of services e-contracting, describing existing work, including SLA management in different phases of the process, as well as explaining the functionality offered by the SLA@SOI e-contracting tools. It also describes the business layer architecture and the business model for SLAs, and highlights future work and conclusions.

# 2 Business SLA Management in Current e-Contracting Proposals

This section examines existing work in e-contracting. To the best of our knowledge, there is no comprehensive proposal that covers the full e-contracting life cycle. For that reason, this analysis is divided into the four above-mentioned phases (information, negotiation, contracting and runtime).

## 2.1 Information

The information phase of e-contracting covers all activities related to defining, publishing, browsing, searching and rating the commercial offer of a services e-marketplace. In the context of SLA management, this means integrating the business terms and conditions of an SLA model and the management of a products catalogue into a business SLA templates registry.

As described in Chapter 'The SLA Model', several initiatives have attempted to model automatically managed SLAs. However, these alternatives mostly focus on modelling technical issues-related service definitions and guarantee term specifications. For instance, [25] proposes a semantic model for integrating business-oriented service level management objectives with technical objectives that include pricing and payment terms, service installation, revisions and terminations, maintenance, support, problem escalation procedures, and so on.

The Universal Service Description Language (USDL) enables modelling of business terms in its business perspective [4], supporting availability, payment, pricing, obligations, rights, penalties, bindings, security and quality. However, this specification of services is decoupled from the specification of the SLA (WS-Agreement), an approach that makes it difficult to integrate business-related elements into the SLA management tasks.

Another important aspect of the information phase is the registration and discovery of information about the service. Usual service registries are based on UDDI (Universal Description Discovery and Integration) and more recently on LDAP (Lightweight Directory Access Protocol) [7]. In the Telco environment, service descriptions are usually registered and stored in service catalogues, which are an essential component in new Operational Support Systems environments [1].

## 2.2 Negotiation and Offer Building

Negotiation is one of the most important and frequently tackled issues in SLA management, and is covered in Chapter 'A Generic Platform for Conducting SLA Negotiations'. SLA negotiation in an e-contracting environment requires a broad approach that takes into account business terms relevant to both providers and customers, providing a more efficient environment for partner management and services trading [11].

There are several issues to be considered when negotiating and SLA from the point of view of an e-contracting framework: better matching of providers' and consumers' business goals [11], ranking of services based on price or quality, sensibility of offers and counter-offers on different issues (price, KPIs, etc.), past transactions [3], and so on.

To increase flexibility, the negotiation process usually involves three topics [16]: the negotiation protocol, or the rules that govern the interaction (participants, states, valid actions); the negotiation objects, or the issue(s) the agreement is about; and the decision-making model, or the strategy for assessing how to proceed during the negotiation. This approach is also followed in [24] and [26], to implement state machines for different negotiation protocols (fixed price, English auction, Dutch auction, bilateral and multilateral bargaining and double auction, etc.). Depending on the protocol, customers may require strategies and tactics for the negotiation of a range of SLA terms for a given price range. Equally, providers may offer discounts to a specific category of consumers based on their contextual information (customer segment, location) or business potential (economic value, length of contracts, etc.). In [27], a policy-based approach to automatically modelling these criteria in a bargaining process is proposed.

Another important issue is offer building. Service environments are usually based on the aggregation of services; thus, the individual SLAs of the atomic services must be taken into account in the final offer [3]. When complex value chains are created — in which a service consumer can be a provider of an aggregated service — composing the QoS elements of a number of aggregated services is a challenging task, since the nature of each parameter and the flow of aggregation [11] must be considered. In [5], several SLA aggregation patterns useful to automation of the aggregation process for cross-company hierarchical SLAs are explained. For example, terms like price or penalties must also be aggregated from a business perspective. Dynamic composition of an offer can include not only the bundling of services, but also the current supply and demand or historical data [10], as well as the parameters defined above. One added complexity when defining service prices is the pricing schema (per transaction, per period) and the relationship between the different QoS levels and price (absolute value, percentage value, etc) [19].

## 2.3 Contracting

Electronic contracts are used to specify the terms and conditions under which a service is provided and consumed, and they represent the basis for a business-based e-marketplace function. Even though the law-conformity of electronic SLAs is still an open issue due to its complexity, and there are still many challenges to solve, contracts are a important aspect of an e-contracting environment. A service contract is a contract associated with a specific service that involves the parties to the agreement, the service (including a description of the interfaces and expected interactions), promises about the service provision and consumption, business issues and legal procedures [13]. An important drawback of electronic contracts is information structuring and reuse, and thus many proposals for establishing e-contracts are based on contract templates: empty forms that must be filled [8].

SLAs can undoubtedly represent e-contracts, because they include, in the case of SLA@SOI model, all the information related to the service being provided, including business terms and guarantee terms. As mentioned above, there are a number of languages defined to specify electronic contracts, such as Web Service Level Agreement (WSLA) and WS-Agreement [14], and USDL [4] adds an SLA-decoupled layer to specify business terms.

Another important aspect of the contracting phase is management of the contract life cycle. Although there are already many commercial contract management tools on the market, this topic presents a number of interesting challenges that improve the efficiency when establishing a contract, help to reduce errors and risks, or improve revenue forecasts. For instance, [6] presents a flexible framework for the automation of service contracts based on standard SOA middleware and [17] shows a contract management solution for multi-tenant SaaS applications whereby contractors may customise and configure the contracted services. In [15], electronic contracting between agents is also tackled, providing interesting novelties as violation scale-up to humans, SLA versioning, SLA hierarchies, contract dependencies and termination, extension and renewal of contracts.

## 2.4 Runtime

The most important business-specific SLA management processes during the run-time phase are those related to calculating penalties derived from SLA breaches [22] and, if possible, the self-adjustment processes that allow spare resources to be used to prevent such violations and penalties before they happen. In [18], a method that accounts for economic penalties caused by SLA violations is proposed such that resources are monitored and allocated in the cloud with the aim of maximising a single Business Level Objective (BLO): the revenue of the provider.

In [23], the effect of economic penalties caused by SLA breaches on providers and customers is analysed. This study recommends giving priority to different SLOs to minimise the effect of an undesired penalty or contract cancellation. In any case, a third party — not the provider — must carry out the monitoring, SLA breach detection, and eventual penalty allocation.

Following these arguments, [21] presents a method for defining policies that modify the effects of SLA violations and penalties, depending on the cause of the violation (i.e., if it is not the fault of one of the parties), with the aim of improving long-term relationships.

## 3 An SLA-Aware e-Contracting Proposal

The business SLA management proposal of the SLA@SOI project focuses on inter-actions between service providers and customers. This framework includes a number of innovative features that are presented below.

## 3.1 Comprehesive SLA-Aware e-Contracting Suite

The SLA@SOI e-contracting layer provides a tool for the back office management of commercial offers made by service providers. This tool supports the definition and characterisation of new products and the services on which they rely. The SLAs of the atomic services that compose a customer-facing product are merged within the tool's holistic SLA framework, based on business rules that can be defined and managed by an administrator. The business SLAs can be graphically defined by the user to fit the commercial requirements of the product and the marketplace. This characterisation includes:

- The management of a catalogue of atomic services and their business SLA templates (SLATs).
- The management of a commercial products catalogue and their SLATs.
- The definition of commercial offers: prices, discounts, promotions, etc.

- The specification of policies that must be taken into account when a customer modifies some guarantee terms.
- The generation of business reports with data and graphs (SLA consumption, violations, etc.).
- The management of customer feedback.

The business SLA tool is completely integrated within the SLA@SOI architecture and information model, and interacts with two main business components: the business manager and the business SLA manager (Section 4). This framework is intended to be part of a service providers' infrastructure.

## 3.2 Customisation of Business SLA Definitions

An innovative aspect of this layer is the customisation of SLA definitions to consider the requirements and preferences of both customers and providers. In this sense, SLA@SOI aims to develop mechanisms for calculating the best business SLAs for both parties during the negotiation and establishment phases. The information required to carry out this business SLA assessment requires customer data to be gathered and customer profiles to be retrieved from the provider's Customer Relationship Management systems.

The preferences and profiles of the customer and provider are currently defined as promotions modelled with business rules associated with the offered products of the marketplace. This approach enables the business tool to define special conditions, depending on factors such as the socioeconomic situation of the customer, the country of origin, etc. These rules can define additional discounts on price, special SLAT options, and so on.

## 3.3 Business SLA Post-Sale Management

With respect to the representation and reporting of business SLA violations, the main innovation of SLA@SOI is the adoption of an architecture that separates SLA monitoring from SLA reporting and evidence representation. This separation is required since SLA guarantee terms might need to be monitored for different purposes, each with different reporting requirements. To address the diversity of reporting requirements, SLA@SOI has developed a layered architecture wherein a business SLA reporting module exists on top of the monitoring infrastructure of the SLA@SOI framework, thus managing the reporting requirements. The primary function of this component is to receive low-level monitoring information from the SLA@SOI monitoring infrastructure, and to transform this information into business SLA monitoring reports (BSLAM reports) by taking into account the requirements of the business-layer components of the SLA@SOI platform. The operation of this module is driven by business reporting policies that determine the monitored

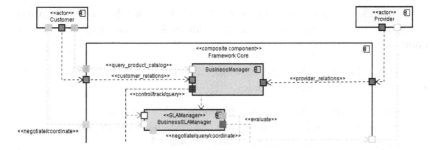

**Fig. 1** Business components and interactions.

SLA terms that should be included in a BSLAM report, the types of monitoring results that should be included in the report, and the required frequency of report generation. The specification of business reporting policies is enabled by the introduction of an XML schema for specifying reporting policies and an XML schema defining the general representation structure of business-level reports.

# 4 Business Layer Architecture

The SLA@SOI project has designed an architectural framework for SLA management across the IT stacks. The proposed architecture is defined in 'Reference Architecture for Multi-Level SLA Management' and allocates business activities to two main components: the business manager and business SLA manager. The diagram in Figure 1 has been extracted from the general framework diagram and focuses on high-level components that implement the business logic. These components expose interactions for relationships between customers and third parties, as well as interactions for communication with other components of the framework and with external parties.

## 4.1 Business Manager

The business manager (BM) is the module responsible for the overall contracting and sales process. This component is necessary because business information is needed to take proper business decisions. Part of this information is private (in some countries there are specific laws for the protection of data) and therefore must not be shared among components. The responsibilities of a business manager are:

- Make overall business decisions that affect all levels based on business information.

- Make decisions at a single point based on all available information. No other component in the architecture could link with the layers and act as a collection point.

In order to achieve this, business information is needed to indicate how decisions will be taken. This information includes:

- Global prices application, rewards, promotions and discounts.
- Service provider selection based on price and customer requirements.
- Business-addressed rules based on profits and costs.

The business manager implements `<<query_product_catalog>>` interactions that allow the final customer to search products and services. It also implements `<<customer_relations>>` interactions that permit the customer to interact with the framework and lets them register and share information with the business platform. The `<<provider_relations>>` interaction is an additional interface in the business manager that allows providers to interact with the framework. There is another interaction called `<<control/track/query>>`, which connects the business layer with the SLA managers.

## 4.2 Business SLA Manager

The business SLA manager is the component in charge of managing the negotiation process to obtain the different agreements. This component contains the registries in which SLAs and SLATs are stored and it extends the Generic SLA Manager (GSLAM). The business SLA manager is responsible for negotiating and operating SLAs with customers and third parties, overseeing the complete set of SLAs in its domain, and providing domain-wide SLA planning and optimisation. Depending on the specific context/requirements of the use case, a separate business SLA manager may be set up for complete organisations, individual departments or individual services.

This component is connected with the BM using the POC (Planning and Optimisation Component of the GSLAM) and PAC (Provisioning and Adjustment Component of the GSLAM) components (see Chapter 'Reference Architecture for Multi-Level SLA Management'). The real functionality behind those components is inside the BM.

The business SLA manager implements the `<<negotiate/coordinate>>` interaction with the end customer. This interaction enables the customer to contract a product and order the provision of SLA resources (in some cases). The business SLA manager, software and infrastructure SLA managers implement `<<control/track/query>>` interactions. These interactions allow the business manager to communicate with the SLA managers of different layers. The aim of the communication is to query the SLA and SLAT registries, to set and retrieve policies, and to receive SLA violations and monitoring information.

# 5 Modelling SLA Business Terms

SLA@SOI has defined a generic SLA model that offers several extension mechanisms that can be exploited to model domain-specific SLA information. While Chapter 'The SLA Model' explains this model in depth, this section explains how information specific to the business SLA is modelled using these extension mechanisms.

Basically, an SLA is a set of agreements between two (or more) parties. These agreements are expressed with terms, each of which denotes guarantees made by, or obligations on, the various parties. Each agreement term comprises an optional constraint expression specifying the conditions under which the agreement term holds (i.e. a precondition on the term). If no preconditions are specified, then it is assumed that the term holds for the entire effective duration of the SLA. Guarantees defined in the agreement are either guaranteed states or guaranteed actions.

## 5.1 Business Terms Integration

At the top level, the business SLA(T) model builds on the SLA(T) model and common metrics to model business-specific information. The three main mechanisms used to extend the generic model are the extension of classes of the model, annotations, and the definition of new standard terms.

To represent all the information related to the SLA business layer, this section describes how the different terms have been integrated into the model. The parameters described in this section are those identified during the project, together with the analysis of [12] and the requirements of SLA@SOI use cases (Chapter 'Introduction to the SLA@SOI Industrial Use Cases').

### 5.1.1 Guarantee Terms

Guaranteed States

A guaranteed state is a guarantee made by one of the parties to the SLA that a certain state of affairs will hold: for example, Service Level Objectives (SLOs) or KPI targets. This state of affairs is defined by a constraint expression. The following guaranteed states have been identified in the business layer:

Consumer Commitment:    The commitments that the customer agrees to in the contract in terms of service usage (for instance, maximum usage, peak times, or capacity usage).

Compliance:    The standards and recommendations that will be supported during delivery of the services, including names, versions and dates.

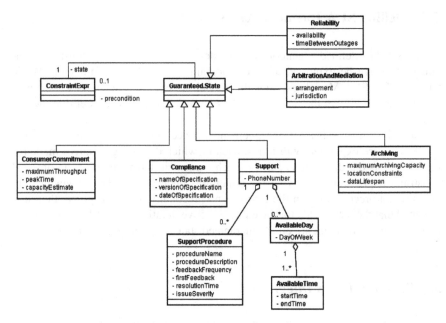

**Fig. 2** Business-level guaranteed states.

Support:    The manner in which the service will be supported; this can include the availability of contracted support, or a set of support procedures for different issues (e.g. when the first feedback has to be offered, feedback frequency, expected resolution time depending on severity).

Archiving:    The agreements regarding archiving of data related to the service (service and historical information); this specifies the maximum capacity or lifespan of the data, and restrictions in the location of such data.

ArbitrationAndMediation:    The places where legal disputes and judgments by arbitration should be arranged.

Reliability:    The maximum time of service unavailability and maximum time between consecutive failures, without causing a penalty.

Guaranteed Actions

A guaranteed action is an action that one of the parties to the SLA is obligated to perform (or may perform, or is forbidden from performing) under certain, specified circumstances. The following guaranteed actions have been defined for the business layer (Figure 3):

UpdateProcess:    When offering services, it is usual to bring down the service to update or manage it for short periods of time. This parameter specifies whether

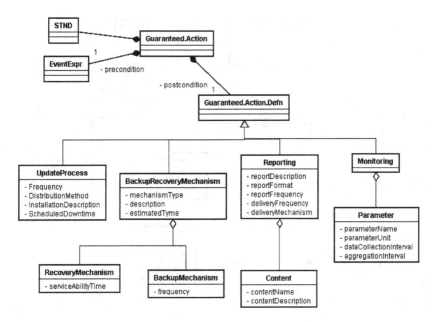

**Fig. 3** Business level guaranteed actions.

this process is periodic and its frequency, how to distribute software and install
software, if required, and scheduled downtimes.

BackupRecoveryMechanism:    The mechanisms required to backup information
essential to the service and the policies for doing so, and the agreement on the
time it should take to recover from a backup in case of service outage.

Reporting:    The commitment to send reports about service usage and SLA status
over time. It includes information about the report itself, the format and frequency, and how to deliver it to the customer.

Monitoring:    The SLA parameters that must be monitored on a continuous basis, including information on the parameters themselves, their units, and the frequency of monitoring.

The business terms related to pricing, which have been also models as guaranteed
actions, are shown in Figure 4:

Termination and TerminationClause:    The conditions under which any of the parties may terminate the SLA; every clause can include a notification method and
a fee to be paid in case of cancellation.

Penalty:    The amount of money to be paid in case of breach of another SLA term;
these penalties can also be used to trigger SLA termination clauses.

ProductOfferingPrice:    The required commitment of a user to pay an amount of
money for the product being provided, including billing frequency and the time
during which the offer is valid; the product can be divided into several compo-

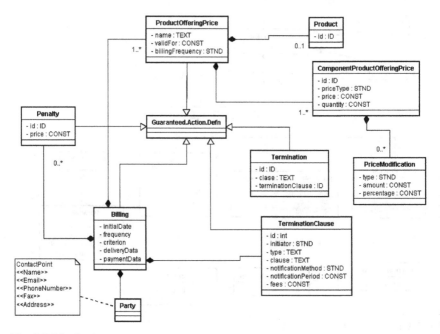

**Fig. 4** Pricing business terms.

nents, each with a price type, price and amount of components that aggregate the
service. These components can specify price modifications (such as discounts).

Billing:    The structure, content and frequency of billing sent to the customer, including information about payment or delivery information; related to the products, penalties and termination fees.

### 5.1.2 Standard Terms

The SLA@SOI standard terms are the basic vocabulary used by the expressions in
the classes described above. Further to this, the following standard business terms
have been defined:

Standard Terms for Price Types and Billing Frequencies:    Terms for specifying
different types of pricing (one time charge, flat rate, etc.) and billing frequency
(monthly, per request, etc.).

Standard Terms for Price Modification Types:    Terms that allow modification of
prices (discounts, increments) in absolute or relative figures.

Standard Terms for Business Metrics:    Terms that include a count of penalties and
violations.

# 6 Future Work

The final phase of SLA@SOI addresses two main business-related challenges: SLA negotiation and business terms aggregation.

While the SLA@SOI negotiation framework focuses on generic negotiation protocols (as described in Chapter 'A Generic Platform for Conducting SLA Negotiations'), it can be customised at the business level to tailor strategy and protocol to specific negotiation processes. For example, process and historical information (e.g. the number of negotiation rounds required in previous agreements) can be tailored to include blacklists that ban particular parties. Customers and providers can use profile information about their counterparts (such as ranks, segments, locations, business evolution, and so on.). Business objectives can be defined for particular products or providers to better align negotiation results to a particular strategy. Such objectives can cover desired sales, available resources, or risks from violations, etc. All these strategic parameters can be integrated to customise the generic negotiation mechanisms provided by the SLA@SOI framework. A complementary part of the negotiation phase will be the assessment and creation of offers and counter-offers, and consideration and implementation of new constraints, limits, conditions and relationships between guarantee terms.

Building an aggregated offer from atomic services — each of which has an independent $SLA(T)$ — involves an intelligent and automatic merge of guarantee terms of the same type. This is a challenging problem, since different terms must be aggregated in different ways; even the workflow of the aggregation process may affect the final aggregated $SLA(T)$. The focus of future work will therefore be on business terms related to price, penalties and violations, since they are the most important terms in the business layer. Some of the most-used KPIs might also be considered.

# 7 Conclusions

e-Contracting is a complex but well-known area that has been researched and developed since the start of e-commerce hype. Development in services science has renewed interest on this field, first for web-services marketplaces, and currently with cloud services and applications (app) stores. In this context, SLAs become a critical issue that must be tackled and tightly integrated within e-contracting frameworks.

However, e-contracting is a large field with many challenging facets. The business management layer of SLA@SOI covers SLA-aware management of a marketplace from a comprehensive perspective, with innovative contributions including business terms modeling and post-sales management, including penalties and violations or dynamic pricing and KPI-based negotiation.

The business-layer architecture presented in this chapter has the double function of managing business SLOs throughout SLA life cycle, and managing interactions with third parties. Thus the business components are in charge of integrating the marketplace environment with the SLA management of software/service and infrastructure layers.

The business SLA model is presented as an extension of the generic SLA@SOI model and offers a first group of terms whose management can be (to some extent) automated and performed from an e-contracting suite. The integration of some of these terms (especially those related to pricing and penalties) into some of the SLA processes (negotiation, monitoring, reporting, etc.) shows the importance of modeling this layer.

This comprehensive approach has highlighted the need to address several challenges: First, we must find a way to intelligently merge and integrate guarantee terms from different atomic services into a final service. Second, we must find a way to build offers and counter-offers in an SLA negotiation process, linking lower-level KPIs with business terms (i.e. price vs. availability). The integration of penalties management into real settlement processes is an ongoing issue.

# References

[1] GB929: Application Framework. Tech. rep., TeleManagement Forum (2011)
[2] Barros, A., Dumas, M.: The rise of web service ecosystems. IT Professional **8**(5), 31–37 (2006)
[3] Bui, T., Gachet, A., Sebastian, H.: Web services for negotiation and bargaining in electronic markets: design requirements, proof-of-concepts, and potential applications to e-procurement. Group Decision and Negotiation **15**(5), 469–490 (2006)
[4] Cardoso, J., Winkler, M., Voigt, K.: A service description language for the internet of services. In: Proceedings of the First International Symposium on Services Science (ISSS'09) (2009)
[5] Cheng, S., Chang, C., Zhang, L., Kim, T.: Towards Competitive Web Service Market. In: 11th IEEE International Workshop on Future Trends of Distributed Computing Systems, 2007. FTDCS'07, pp. 213–219 (2007)
[6] Chieu, T., Nguyen, T., Maradugu, S., Kwok, T.: An enterprise electronic contract management system based on service-oriented architecture. In: SCC 2007. IEEE International Conference on Services Computing., pp. 613–620. IEEE (2007)
[7] Davis, J.: Open source SOA. Manning (2009)
[8] Fantinato, M.: A Feature-based Approach to Web Services E-contract Establishment . Ph.D. thesis, Institute of Computing, University of Campinas, Brazil (2007)
[9] Haq, I., Schikuta, E.: Aggregation Patterns of Service Level Agreements. In: Frontiers of Information Technology (FIT2010) (2010)
[10] Hasselmeyer, P., Koller, B., Kotsiopoulos, I., Kuo, D., Parkin, M.: Negotiating SLAs with Dynamic Pricing Policies. In: Proceedings of the SOC@ Inside07 (2007)

[11] Hasselmeyer, P., Wieder, P., Koller, B., Schubert, L.: Added Value for Businesses through eContract Negotiation. In: Collaboration and the Knowledge Economy: Issues, Applications, Case Studies (Proceedings of the eChallenges Conference 2008), Cunningham, P. and Cunningham, M.(eds.), IOS Press, Amsterdam, NL, pp. 978–1 (2008)

[12] Hiles, A.: The Complete Guide To IT Service Level Agreements. Rothstein Associates Inc. (2002)

[13] Hoffner, Y., Field, S., Grefen, P., Ludwig, H.: Contract-driven creation and operation of virtual enterprises. Computer Networks 37(2), 111–136 (2001)

[14] IST-CONTRACT: State of the Art. Tech. rep., FP6-034418 (2006)

[15] Jakob, M., Pěchouček, M., Miles, S., Luck, M.: Case studies for contract-based systems. In: Proceedings of the 7th international joint conference on Autonomous agents and multiagent systems: industrial track, pp. 55–62. International Foundation for Autonomous Agents and Multiagent Systems (2008)

[16] Jennings, N., Faratin, P., Lomuscio, A., Parsons, S., Wooldridge, M., Sierra, C.: Automated negotiation: prospects, methods and challenges. Group Decision and Negotiation 10(2), 199–215 (2001)

[17] Kwok, T., Nguyen, T., Lam, L.: A software as a service with multi-tenancy support for an electronic contract management application. In: SCC'08. IEEE International Conference on Services Computing, vol. 2, pp. 179–186. IEEE (2008)

[18] Macias, M., Guitart, J.: Maximising Revenue in Cloud Computing Markets by means of Economically Enhanced SLA Management. Tech. Rep. Tech. Rep. UPC-DAC-RR-CAP-2010-22, Computer Architecture Department, Universitat Politecnica de Catalunya (2010)

[19] Marchione, F., Fantinato, M., de Toledo, M., Gimenes, I.: Price definition in the establishment of electronic contracts for web services. In: Proceedings of the 11th International Conference on Information Integration and Web-based Applications & Services, pp. 217–224. ACM (2009)

[20] Menasce, D.: Composing web services: A QoS view. IEEE Internet Computing 8(6), 88–90 (2004)

[21] Miles, S., Groth, P., Luck, M.: Handling Mitigating Circumstances for Electronic Contracts. In: AISB 2008 Symposium on Behaviour Regulation in Multi-agent Systems (2008)

[22] Padget, J.J.: A Management System for Service LevelAgreements in Grid based Systems. Ph.D. thesis, University of Leeds (2006)

[23] Rana, O., Warnier, M., Quillinan, T., Brazier, F., Cojocarasu, D.: Managing violations in service level agreements. Grid Middleware and Services pp. 349–358 (2008)

[24] Rinderle, S., Benyoucef, M.: Towards the automation of e-negotiation processes based on web services-a modeling approach. Web Information Systems Engineering–WISE 2005 pp. 443–453 (2005)

[25] Ward, C., Buco, M., Chang, R., Luan, L.: A Generic SLA Semantic Model for the Execution Management of E-business Outsourcing Contracts. In: Proceed-

ings of the Third International Conference on E-Commerce and Web Technologies, pp. 363–376. Springer-Verlag (2002)

[26] Wurman, P., Wellman, M., Walsh, W.: A parametrization of the auction design space. Games and economic behavior **35**(1-2), 304–338 (2001)

[27] Zulkernine, F., Martin, P., Craddock, C., Wilson, K.: A policy-based middleware for web services SLA negotiation. In: IEEE International Conference on Web Services, ICWS 2009., pp. 1043–1050. IEEE (2009)

# Part VI
# Management of the Software Layer

# Model-Driven Framework for Business Continuity Management

Ulrich Winkler and Wasif Gilani

## 1 Introduction

Nearly one in five businesses suffer a major disruption every year. These disruptions often affect thousands of customers and consumers. A disruption could result in financial and legal losses, as well as damage to reputation. For example, on 4 January 2010, SALES FORCE, a company offering online enterprise support services, experienced an outage for over an hour, affecting 68,000 customers [6]. Another example is PayPal, a service for processing online payments. PayPal was down for 4.5 hours worldwide on 4 August 2009; PayPal usually processes 2,000 USD per second for its customers.

The key industrial sectors—such as energy, gas, oil, pharmacy or finance—must demonstrate BC competence, as required by regulations and laws. A study to quantify the BC risks caused by information and communication technologies (ICT) at ESSENT NETWERK, a Dutch electricity and gas distributor, revealed that a four-hour outage of an IT service might result in withdrawal of ESSENT NETWERK's license to operate, eventually taking the distributor out of business [11].

IT BCM aims to:

- identify potential threats to an IT system, services and operations,
- assess the business impact of a threat, estimate probabilities and compute risk exposures,
- determine strategies and responses to these threats, and model an IT BC plan to overcome or mitigate possible business disruptions.

Ulrich Winkler

SAP Research, The Concourse, Queen's Road, Titanic Quarter, Belfast, BT3 9DT, United Kingdom, e-mail: ulrich.winkler@sap.com

Wasif Gilani

SAP Research, The Concourse, Queen's Road, Titanic Quarter, Belfast, BT3 9DT, United Kingdom, e-mail: wasif.gilani.@sap.com

IT BC managers struggle to conduct comprehensive, thorough and valid analyses. The reasons for this are manifold:

- IT landscapes are complex and it is hard to formulate a complete picture; to conduct a thorough dependency analysis, a BC manager needs to comprehend and incorporate a complete end-to-end picture of resource dependencies of the entire IT stack.
- Different methodologies are used to model and document different aspects of complex IT landscapes. For example, business processes are modelled in workflow charts, the behaviour of software artefacts is expressed in UML activity diagrams, and the IT infrastructure deployment layout is documented in topology models. BC managers find themselves lost within this variety of heterogeneous—but related—models, which results in limited vision.
- IT landscapes are adaptive systems and evolve over time; new technologies, such as virtualisation and cloud computing, can alter a landscape deployment layout within minutes.
- Current tool support and methodologies are insufficient to comprehend the impacts and consequences of failed elements of the entire landscape and dependent business processes.
- Visualisation and reporting of analysis results is not automated and does not meet the expectations of involved stakeholders.
- Lastly, and most importantly, currently available data sources—such as process knowledge, UML or topology models—are not utilised or reused for BCM.

Any of these issues may lead to inaccurate decisions being made to circumvent disruptions.

In this chapter, we present a novel framework that addresses the needs of IT BCM by:

- using model-driven engineering techniques to tap into business process knowledge and IT landscape models,
- providing a BC model to simplify work for BC managers and
- providing a two-level model refinement process that increases the quality of the resulting analysis model in terms of accuracy and precision, utilising automated model transformation chains to connect to a variety of data sources, and analysis tools utilising automated model transformation chains to feed analyses results into various reporting tools to visualise analyses results.

The remainder of this chapter is organised as follows: Section 2 provides an overview of BCM, Section 3 discusses related work, and Sections 4 and 5 introduce our framework: first motivation and challenges are discussed, followed by an architectural description. Finally, Section 6 concludes the chapter with a summary and outlook on future work.

## 2 Business Continuity Management

Business continuity management (BCM) is standardised by the British Standards Institution and is formally defined as:

> A holistic management process that identifies potential threats to an organisation and the impacts to business operations that those threats, if realised, might cause, and which provides a framework for building organisational resilience with the capability for an effective response that safeguards the interests of its key stakeholders, reputation, brand and value-creating activities [4].

BCM comprises four types of activities: understanding the organisation, determining business continuity strategies, developing and implementing a BCM response, and exercising, maintaining and reviewing BCM arrangements. All four activities are organised by a fifth activity—BCM program management—which initiates BC-related projects, assigns responsibilities, observes and manages activities, conducts training, and provides documentation.

To understand an organisation, the BC manager must understand the effects of an adverse incident on a business and the dependencies among business processes, dependent resources, and possible root-causes of an adverse incident. A BC manager uses two different but complementary analyses: dependency and risk analysis (DA), and business impact analysis (BIA). BIA aims to distinguish between mission critical processes, and non-critical processes and functions. The BC manager must consider that a disruption of processes may have a financial impact, legal consequence or effect on other business values and indicators, such as reputation or customer satisfaction. For each process and function, various different BC metrics are assigned. Return time objective (RTO) and recovery point objective (RPO) are examples of BCM metrics. RPO defines "the maximum amount of data loss an organisation can sustain during an event". RTO defines the "target time for resumption of product, service or activity delivery after an incident" [4].

A dependency analysis is conducted to identify dependent resources, involved stakeholders, assets and internal/external services dependent on a critical business process. Also identified are possible failure modes and disruption causes. A BC manager must be enabled to analyse how failures propagate through the system and layers. For example, the manager needs to understand how a broken air-conditioning unit may affect a data centre as well as servers deployed in that data centre, and eventually if and when a process will be disrupted.

Finally, a recovery plan details the steps that need to be taken to restore business operations to defined operations levels within given time-frames.

## 3 Related Work

BCM is close to reliability engineering. Fault tree analysis (FTA) is a common technique used in reliability engineering to determine combinations of failures in a system that could lead to undesired events at the system level [5]. The modelling process starts with the undesired event and is broken down into a fault tree. Each fault is analysed in more detail and, if necessary, broken down again, until a reasonable level of understanding is achieved. The logical relationship between faults is defined by logic "gates", such as AND, OR, XOR or NOT. Probabilities are assigned to basic events and the overall likelihood of an undesired event can be calculated. Although a fault tree analysis can provide a better estimation of the probability of adverse events occurring, such an analysis cannot model the dynamic behaviour of systems, since Boolean gates are not able to capture the order in which events occur, nor is it possible to model time constraints, such as deadlines. This limits the application of FTA in IT BCM to very simple analyses.

The Tropos Goal-Risk (GR) framework is used for requirement analysis and risk assessment for critical socio-technical systems, such as air-traffic management [1]. First, it provides means to model combinations of failures in a manner similar to FTA. Second, it provides semantics to model other aspects, such as time dependencies, treatments and assets, which are useful for BCM. Asnar and Giorgini demonstrated that the GR framework could be used to analyse and compare the efficacy and cost-efficiency of different treatment strategies [2]. However, the analysis does not provide means for determining business impact, nor does it provide means for determining BCM metrics, such as RTO. Moreover, Tropos lacks strong process integration and does not provide means for generating Tropos graphs from existing models, or integrating analysis techniques other than the ones provided by Tropos itself.

From the model-driven engineering point of view, performance models have been extracted from development models [3]. Most approaches focus on software development models (e.g. UML models) as input models, whereas our approach aims to take various kinds of models from different levels of the IT stack into account (e.g. business process models and IT topology models). Moreover, we aim to provide a cross-layer performance and dependency view. Below, we describe our approach of consuming available models from different levels of a technology stack, thus providing a systematic and process-centric BCM solution.

ROPE provides a risk-aware business process modelling and simulation methodology [8, 9] that provides an approach to analysis of the business impact of threats and the effect of countermeasures. ROPE uses a three-layered model approach: The first layer is the business process layer, the second layer refines process layers with resource requirements, and the third layer models threats, impacts and related recovery actions. ROPE utilises simulations to estimate the expected downtime of a business process and to evaluate recovery actions. Like our work, ROPE analyses business impact on the process activity level, provides a dependency model, and considers threats and responses in a process-centric way. However, ROPE does not provide any means for generating models for each ROPE layer from existing models, and hence is limited to manually created scenarios. Further, ROPE restricts itself to three layers, as this simplifies modelling activities. However, due to this simplification, ROPE is not able to analyse various important scenarios. For example, all recovery processes depend on resources themselves, but if a resource required by a recovery plan is not available, the recovery activity will fail. Due to the three-layered approach in ROPE's modelling methodologies, it is not possible to assign resources to recovery activities. Hence ROPE is not capable of analysing the important feasibility properties of recovery plans. Our framework is not restricted to three model layers and therefore permits more comprehensive analyses, including, for example, feasibility analysis of recovery actions. To minimise and simplify modelling activities, our approach utilises automated model transformations in combination with predefined libraries.

# 4 Model-Driven and Process-Centric BCM Framework

Business processes are the main subject or starting point of a business impact analysis and dependency analysis respectively. However, existing approaches are primarily focused on IT layers only, and do not take detailed business process knowledge into account. The processes are generally abstracted as single black boxes in the top layers of dependency graphs. An increasing number of businesses are now employing business process management (BPM) tools to model and execute their processes. Incorporating detailed process information—available via process models such as BPMN [7] and YAWL [10]—can help to identify dependencies, threats, and so on at the process step level, and this provides greater context for BCM. Further, tools used to conduct BCM analyses are not tailored according to the needs of BC managers; often BC managers use drawing tools like Visio, with no analysis support at all, to model a dependency graph. Without sufficient support from analysis tools, BC managers struggle to cope with the vast number of processes and rapidly changing IT landscapes.

Our approach relies on model-driven engineering techniques. Model-driven engineering simplifies the development of tools for domain-specific languages (DSL). This increases adoption of domain-specific models as software artefacts and permits contribution of domain experts (such as business process analysts) to system design and problem analysis. The use of models as software artefacts is not uncommon in industrial applications. For instance, process knowledge is no longer hard-coded into software, but rather exists as well-defined process model artefacts. These process models can be accessed by auxiliary software, opening up new ways to improve business management in related areas, such as BCM.

## 4.1 Requirements

We have identified two important requirements for a model-driven business-process-centric framework for BCM:

*Heterogeneous meta-models and tools*: BCM covers the whole stack of an enterprise. This stack comprises various different domains and layers, such as the business process domain, service composition and execution domain, IT infrastructure domain (software, hardware, network, etc.), and facility items and human resources. Each domain is modelled by specific domain experts: for example, a business process analyst or software architect, etc. Every domain expert potentially utilises different meta-models and tools to model and express their domain-specific needs. For example, processes are documented with BPMN or YAWL, whereas software artefacts are depicted in UML. Of course, this separation of concerns is useful and desirable, since every model covers specific aspects of its respective domain. In most cases, there exists no need for domain crossover. However, BCM needs a cross-domain viewpoint on all domains to conduct a comprehensive and thorough business impact and dependency analysis. Designing and implementing a system that can cope with heterogeneous but complementary meta-models in a multi-tool environment is a major challenge.

*Multi-paradigm model analyses, reasoning and model optimisation*: In the context of the business impact and dependency analysis, BC managers employ various analyses to quantify risks, validate recovery plans, and so on. In essence, BC managers must be able to answer the types of questions given in Table 1:

**Table 1** BCM-related questions

| Issues | Example question |
| --- | --- |
| Temporal failure propagation | What is the expected time delay until a broken air-conditioner in a data centre causes business disruptions? |
| Performance analysis | How many servers are needed to guarantee a sales order processing time of six hours even if one server breaks down for two hours? |
| Dead-lock detection | Is a recovery plan comprising repair of a broken air-conditioner, reboot of all servers and replay of database transaction logs sufficient to guarantee a business process RTO of less than four hours? |
| Worst-case / Residual risk analysis | What is the likelihood that a recovery plan fails? |
| Sensitivity analysis | Which is the single point of failure? |
| Estimated value analysis | Is the organisation willing to spend 5,000 USD per month for additional air-conditioning units to remove the 10% risk of a broken air-conditioning unit, which would cost the organisation 70,000 USD? |

A BC manager should be able to run any kind of analysis across all layers of the enterprise stack by "pushing a button". This is a challenging task, requiring the integration of knowledge captured from different levels of the enterprise stack using different domain-specific models and data sources analysed with existing multi-paradigm analyses tools (i.e. simulation engines, optimisation tools, model check-ers, etc).

*Role-based analysis results' presentations*: BC analysis results have to be pre-sented to various stakeholders, including (but not limited to) BC managers, business process analysts, line-of-business managers, IT architects and external reviewers. Every stakeholder has distinctive interests and hence has distinctive requirements in terms of how BC analysis results should be evaluated and presented. For example a business process analyst is interested in finding out how well certain business pro-cess activities perform in case of disruption, whereas the line-of-business manager is more interested in capacity for overall process resilience and the potential impact of adverse events on strategic business values. The IT architect's interests are fo-cused on IT deployment requirements and the external reviewer needs to verify that the conducted BC analysis is complete, coherent, current and covers all critical busi-ness functions. Every stakeholder has a preferred environment in which he or she wants to review analysis results. Business process analysts and IT architects may prefer to work with analysis results in their respective modelling and editing en-vironments, whereas line-of-business managers and external reviewers may prefer Office documents, such as Microsoft Excel.

## 4.2 Architecture

Below, we give a more detailed description of our architecture. First, we identify in-volved stakeholders and introduce the tooling environment our architecture targets. Then, we discuss the overall workflow, followed by a detailed description of major building blocks in our architecture.

Figure 1 gives a high-level overview of our architecture and servers as a refer-ence.

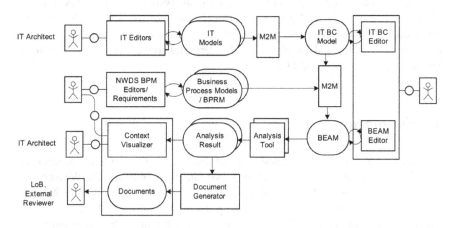

**Fig. 1** BCM framework architecture

## 4.3 Stakeholders

A BC analysis project involves various stakeholders. Every stakeholder contributes respected domain knowledge, domain business requirements, constraints, and objectives to the overall BC analysis. Our solution supports multi-stakeholder analyses by providing user interfaces and tooling, modelling, and analysis support that is suited to every stakeholder.

We anticipate five types of stakeholders will be involved in an IT BC analysis and will use our tool: the business process expert, IT architect, business continuity analyst, line-of-business manager and external reviewer.

The business process expert designs and models business processes. He/she is responsible for ensuring all process activities are executable and perform according to stated requirements.

The line-of-business manager/process owner is interested in overall business process performance. He/she defines process performance indicators, which are aligned with the overall strategy of an organisation. He/she has to be assured that a business can deliver products and services even in case of disruption.

The task of an external reviewer is to validate whether an organisation has sufficient BC competency. The external reviewer must ensure that a BC analysis is coherent, complete, current and accurate. The analysis should contain all critical and important business processes, functions, dependent resources and potential risks. The external reviewer also has to ensure that planned responses are appropriate and sufficient to circumvent or mitigate adverse effects.

The primary concern of the IT architect is the deployment layout of the IT landscape. An IT landscape is a set of hardware, software and network elements arranged in a specific configuration, which serves as a fabric to support the business operations of an organisation. The IT architect must ensure that the IT deployment layout is suitable for supporting an organisation's business and capable of meeting other requirements, such as BC requirements.

The BC analyst manages and drives the BC analysis work. He/she is responsible for determining critical processes, critical resources, risks to IT elements and processes, and appropriate risk response strategies. The BC analyst must communicate analysis results to all involved stakeholders, and convey change requests to the business process expert and IT architect.

## 4.4 Environment

SAP's solution to designing, modelling and documenting business processes is the NetWeaver Business Process Modelling Environment (NW BPM). NetWeaver BPM supports process modelling based on the Business Process Modelling Notation (BPMN) standard from OMG. NW BPM provides two editor tools: the NW BPM Process Composer (Process Composer) and the NW Business Process Scenario Editor (Scenario Editor). These tools are used by the business process expert to define process scenarios and model processes. The Process Composer tool provides graphical modelling of activity flows using BPMN. Scenario models are used to organise a collection of processes and provide an end-to-end view of these processes. Both tools operate on a set of models (NW BPMN and NW Scenario Model), which are grouped into the NW Common Process Layer model set. Figure **??** depicts the relationship between Process Composer, Scenario Editor, business process expert, and the related model artefacts.

Besides the aforementioned modelling tools, NW BPM also provides tooling support for creating other process-related artefacts, such as business rules tables. However, as stated previously, NW BPM provides no means for adding business-continuity-related information, nor does it offer any BCM-related analytics.

## 4.5 Workflow and Methodology

A BC analysis project is managed by the BC analyst and conducted in five phases: the business process requirement analysis, IT BC model derivation, BEAM derivation, business continuity analysis, and analysis result presentation.

*Business process requirement analysis*: In this first phase, the business process expert, in cooperation with the line-of-business manager, determines any process-relevant requirements. The output of this phase is the Business Process Annotation Model (BPAM).

*IT BC model derivation*: In the second phase, the BC manager determines what resources and dependent resources are needed to support a process. This phase involves the IT architect, who provides the needed domain knowledge and IT models. As stated earlier, to conduct an appropriate dependency and risk analysis it is crucial that a consolidated and coherent view of all involved business processes and IT-related resources be generated. Our approach utilises model-to-model (M2M) transformations to generate a BC model from existing models (i.e. process models and IT topology models). Thus existing models are utilised to provide the BC manager with a profound modelling base. However, these models are incomplete and often disconnected from the BCM point of view. Hence our framework provides graphical tools to refine these BC models and to connect model elements. For instance, the user can add business-continuity-related information and connect different resource dependency graphs. The result of this phase is an IT BC model.

*BEAM derivation*: In the third phase, the BC analyst connects IT BC models with process models and adds behavioural information (either manually or in an automated fashion). M2M transformation is executed to transform the IT BC model into a Behaviour and Analysis Model (BEAM). Here again the BC manager is provided with an editor, the so-called BEAM editor. This editor permits the user to further refine the BEAM model, alter the behavioural models, and add measurement models and recovery plans if needed. The BEAM is transformed into an inputtable format for the analysis tools with the help of model-to-text (M2T) transformations.

*BC analysis*: Once the BEAM is complete, the BC manager can trigger an analysis run just by pushing a button. Our solution supports various multi-paradigm analysis tools, such as analytical or simulation tools, to yield accurate and complete results. The analysis results are stored in analysis results models.

*Analysis result presentation*: We provide two modes for presentation of analysis results: document-oriented presentation and the context-sensitive presentation. The document-oriented presentation mode generates various types of Office documents for the line-of-business manager or external reviewer. The context-sensitive presentation mode is an essential additional tool that provides the IT architect or business process expert with analysis results embedded in their respective working (modelling and tooling) environments. The analyses results help stakeholders to understand how a broken resource affects depending resources, how a failure propagates through the system, and when a failure will eventually impact the process. These users are thus able to validate recovery plans as they can decide if the average response time of a recovery plan is sufficient to meet business-level KPIs, or if the residual risk is still too high and the recovery plan needs to be revised.

## 4.6 Business Process Requirements Annotation

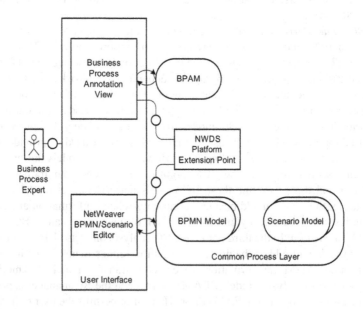

**Fig. 2** Business process requirements annotation

To capture business requirements, our solution provides a non-intrusive model-driven mechanism for annotating existing process models with supplementary information. This enables business process analysts to capture the process requirements, constraints and objectives needed to conduct a comprehensive, coherent and thorough BIA. Figure 2 depicts the major building blocks needed for this activity, which are business process annotation editor (View) and business process annotation models.

The business process annotation editor uses the NetWeaver Developer Studio platform's extension point mechanism to observe selection change events emitted from the process composer. Selection change events are emitted when the business process expert selects a process activity in the process composer. These events are carried as payload information from the process model. This means, if the business process expert selects a single process element, for example a process activity, the business process requirement annotation editor becomes aware of the selected element. The business process expert enters requirements related to this selected process element using the business process requirement editor. Business requirements and references to process elements are stored in the Business Process Annotation Model (BPAM).

A screenshot of the process annotation editor is shown in Figure 3.

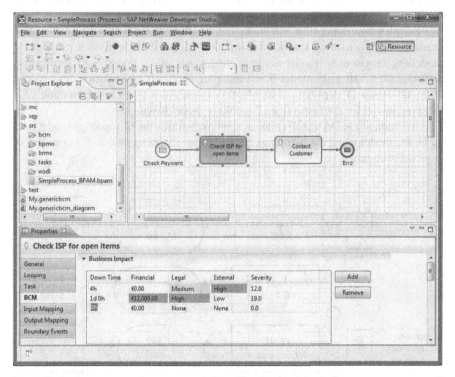

**Fig. 3** Business process requirements annotation: this screenshot shows the process composer and the process annotation view. In the process annotation view one can see various requirements (e.g. various impact values and maximum tolerable outage times).

## 4.7 IT BCM Model Derivation

*IT BC models*: These are a set of domain-specific "front-end" models in our model ecosystem. IT BC models lay the foundations for extending existing business process management tools with BC management support. IT BC models cover the resource dependency and risk modelling aspects of BC.

A BC analyst can create IT BC models in two ways: the first way is to use the IT BCM model editor to create models completely manually. This requires very detailed knowledge of IT landscape elements, configuration semantics, and deployment options, and usually a BC manager lacks this detailed knowledge. The second option is to generate IT BC models from existing IT deployment topology models. This option has several advantages: first, such automated generation releases the BC manager from manual effort, which is time consuming. Second, since human error is eliminated, the resulting IT BCM models are of better quality and complete and coherent.

To enable automated derivation of IT BC models, a mapping model is required. A mapping model maps—on meta-model level—IT topology model classes to IT BC model classes. The tool the BC manager uses for this definition is a mapping model editor.

IT deployment topologies are modelled in different modelling languages. For example, SAP uses the Common Information Model. IBM utilises a proprietary modelling language to model deployment layouts of its WebSphere application servers. Due to our meta-model-based mapping approach, our solution can process all model-based IT deployment topology designs. All it takes is the creation of a mapping model for the respective IT topology model language.

An automated M2M transformation agent transforms the IT topology model into an IT BC model using the mappings defined in the mapping model. This process is depicted in Figure 4.

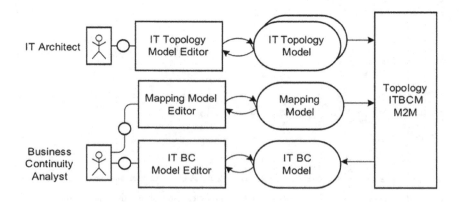

**Fig. 4** Generation of IT BC model

Once the transformation agent creates an IT BC model instance, the business continuity analyst can examine, refine and finalise this model instance by using the IT BC model editor, as shown in Figure 5.

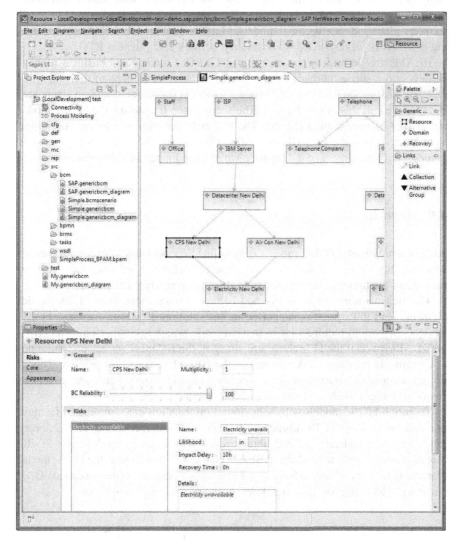

**Fig. 5** IT BC model: this screenshot shows an example IT BC model dependency graph, including facility elements.

Analysts can add supplementary information, which is not part of the IT land-scape deployment topology, to the IT BC model. Threats, failure modes, and responses to risk are examples of such complementary information.

## 4.8 BEAM Derivation

A Behaviour Analysis Model (BEAM) focuses only on behaviour, performance and analysis modelling. This meta-model refines the BC model with behavioural information on resources and dependencies. Behaviour modelling is also used to detail recovery plans and measurement models. Measurement models are meant for defining BCM KPIs for resources and business processes alike, such as RTO.

BEAMs are derived by the merging of IT BCM models and business process models into a single, unified analysis model. It takes three steps to derive a complete BEAM: in the first step, the process model is transformed into an (inchoate) BEAM. We call this Alpha BEAM. The second step transforms the IT BC model into a BEAM named Beta BEAM. The last and final step merges the Alpha and Beta BEAMs into the final BEAM, called Gamma BEAM. The whole process is orchestrated by an agent (not depicted), which coordinates all transformations.

## 4.9 Alpha BEAM

As stated previously, IT BC models only define dependencies between various resources. They do not define how these resources behave or influence each other in the case of disruption. This behavioural information needs to be added.

The BC manager can manually add behavioural information to IT BC model elements, and this option is supported in our solution. However, for large IT BC models, this would require a lot of manual work, which is cumbersome and error-prone. Moreover, if the IT architecture changes, the BC manager has no option but to discard his previous work and restart the BEAM construction process. This is not an acceptable solution in environments where IT deployments are subject to frequent changes, such as cloud-based deployments.

To enrich IT BC models with behavioural information in an automated fashion, our solution employs IT BC library models. The BC manager defines IT BC library models using a dedicated IT BC library editor. These library models map IT BC model elements types to predefined BEAM elements. For example, the IT BC model element type 'Server' would be mapped to a set of behaviour states—such as 'Off', 'Booting', 'Running' or 'ShuttingDown'—and related state transitions.

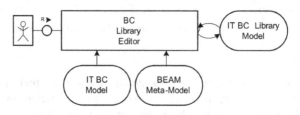

**Fig. 6** IT BC library models

Our approach minimises the manual effort involved in modelling behaviourial information in two ways: first, it requires that the BC manager models behavioural information only once for every IT BC model element type (for example, for the type *Server*). This behavioural information is then automatically applied by the Alpha BEAM M2M agent to all occurrences of the same model element type in the IT BC model. Second, the BC manager need only define IT BC library model once. Once such library models are available, the entire process can be repeated as many times as needed, with no human interaction required. This enables automated creation of Alpha BEAMs, which is necessary in a dynamically changing IT landscape.

As we aim to analyse BC on a process activity level, it is very important to identify the resources required by process activities, and to establish a link between resources and activities. This is done by the business process expert using the business process requirement annotation editor (Figure 7). The business process expert establishes references from process model elements to IT BC resources and these mappings are stored in the BPAM.

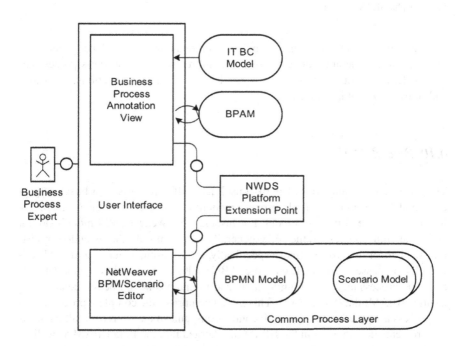

**Fig. 7** Business process requirement annotation editor

Once all required models are prepared, we can derive the Alpha BEAM. The Alpha BEAM M2M transformation agent takes as input the IT BC model, IT BC library model and BPAM, and transforms all models into an Alpha BEAM. Further, the transformation agent produces a tracing model. The need for the tracing model is explained later. The automated Alpha BEAM creation process is depicted in Figure 8.

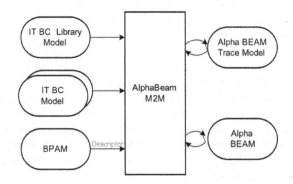

**Fig. 8** Alpha BEAM generation

This Alpha BEAM now contains information on all resources, dependencies between resources, default behaviour models, and references to business process activities. However, other important process details—such as connections, gateways, and so on—are still missing.

## *4.10 Beta BEAM*

The purpose of a Beta BEAM is to consolidate different parts of a business process model—spanning multiple process modelling and execution environments—into one end-to-end process model. For instance, NetWeaver BPM models do not cover the entire process, rather they generally represent only the extended or customised part of the process (more specifically, the front-end extension of the back-end ERP processes). To enable end-to-end BC analysis, our solution consolidates all available process models belonging to an end-to-end business process scenario into a single BEAM: the Beta BEAM. This model comprises the complete process, with all process activities, gateways, path connections, and so on. Moreover, all business requirements documented in the BPAM are merged into the Beta BEAM as well.

As depicted in Figure 9, a model-to-model transformation agent—the 'process to Beta BEAM' agent—takes the business scenario model, all related business process models, and the BPAM, and produces a single Beta BEAM. This model contains all elements of the complete end-to-end process and related business requirements.

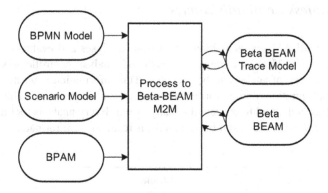

**Fig. 9** Beta BEAM generation

## 4.11 Gamma BEAM

The Gamma BEAM M2M transformation agent merges Alpha and Beta BEAMs into a combined BEAM: the Gamma BEAM. The agent also resolves missing references and sets missing default values if appropriate.

The Gamma BEAM is the final BEAM and contains all necessary elements for BC analysis, drawn from the business process modelling domain and IT landscape modelling domain. This process is shown in Figure 10.

The BC manager may want to further refine the Gamma BEAM. For example, the manager may want to detail recovery plans or modify resource behaviour. The BEAM editor is provided for this purpose.

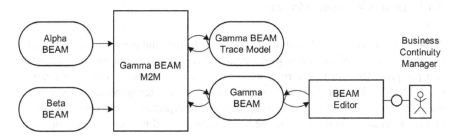

**Fig. 10** Gamma BEAM

## *4.12 Business Continuity Analysis*

The Gamma BEAM serves as input for various analyses and evaluation tools. As depicted in Figure 11, the BC manager uses the BC analysis controller to select tools based on the type of analysis to be executed. This information is written in a tool-specific configuration storage format, for example, a property file. The controller also commands the tool to execute the analysis run. Every analysis tool involved in an analysis run writes its result into an analysis result storage format.

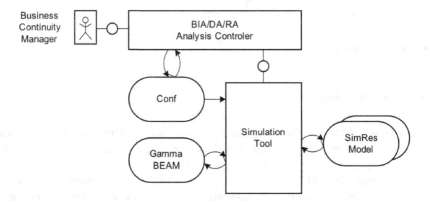

**Fig. 11** Business continuity analysis

## *4.13 Analysis Result Presentation*

Analysis results are usually not in a presentable format and generally contain irrelevant information. We therefore provide the BC reasoner. BC reasoners act as filters and pre-processors to transform analysis results into business continuity analysis result models (BCAMs). Further, some results from heterogeneous analysis tools are only meaningful if they are correlated and interpreted in one context. For example, an analytic tool can compute the worst-case and best-case execution times for a recovery plan. On the other hand, a simulation tool can predict the average execution time of the same recovery plan. To decide if the recovery plan needs to be improved, all of these execution time values are required. The task of a BC reasoner is to bring together results from heterogeneous, multi-paradigm analysis tools and compute sound and relevant BC results. These results are stored in BCAM storage as well. This post-analysis filtering and reasoning process for a simulation tool is shown in Figure 12.

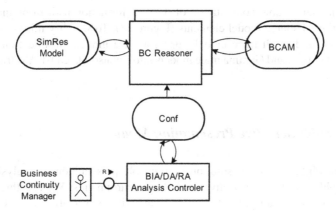

**Fig. 12** Post-analysis filtering and reasoning

Our solution provides two ways of presenting analysis results to all stakeholders: (1) an interactive and context-sensitive presentation mode, and (2) a document-oriented presentation mode.

## 4.14 Tracing

To provide context-sensitive results and to relate analysis results to source model elements (such as the business process activity model element), links are preserved via trace models across the entire transformation chain.

Every transformation agent is tracing-enabled, thus producing a tracing model. This tracing model preserves a mapping from source model elements (agent inputs) to target model elements (agent outputs).

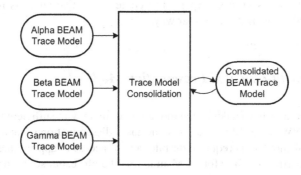

**Fig. 13** Trace models in the architecture

Trace models enable computation of the transformation path from analysis results to original source model elements (Figure 13). To simplify this computation, we first consolidate all trace models, using a trace model consolidation agent to merge Alpha, Beta and Gamma trace models into a consolidated BEAM trace model (Figure 13).

## 4.15 Context-Sensitive Presentation Mode

One major objective of our solution is to enable presentation of analysis results to stakeholders in their respective modelling environments. We call this context-sensitive analysis result presentation (or 'interactive presentation') for short). For example, the expected recovery time objective of a process activity should be displayed to business process experts if they select a process activity in their respective modelling environments. This view is provided by the context-sensitive analysis results view.

The context-sensitive analysis results view uses the same mechanism as the business process requirement editor to detect model element selection changes in the NW BPM process editor. On selection change events, the context-sensitive analysis results view displays analysis results related to the selected model element. For example, if a business process expert selects a specific business process activity, the view will only display analysis results for this process activity.

For example, Figure 14 shows the resulting view for an IT model, while Figure 15 depicts the view for a process model.

The interactive presentation mode has various advantages. First, it allows stakeholders to visualise analysis results in their modelling domain. They are able to change the models (e.g., alter a process or an IT landscape model) and get immediate feedback about how changes affect the business continuity aspects of a process or IT landscape.

Figure 16 shows architectural details of the context-sensitive analysis results view for the business process expert. The context-sensitive analysis results view for the IT architect works in a similar way.

## 4.16 Document-Oriented Presentation Mode

Not all stakeholders have a dedicated modelling domain with sufficient tooling support, such as NW BPM. Moreover, in some cases dissemination of analyses results to external stakeholders is required despite lack of access to appropriate modelling tools. This is particularly true for BCM auditors. Therefore, our solution provides an additional presentation mode: document-oriented presentation. In this mode, report generators transform analysis results into Office documents.

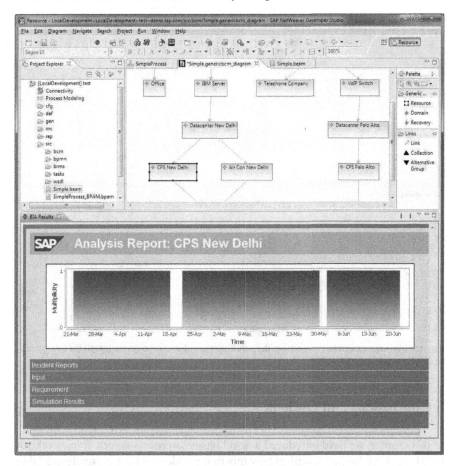

**Fig. 14** Context-sensitive presentation: the resulting view depicts two lengthy downtimes for a selected IT resource.

The report generator uses BCAM and other information sources—such as business process models—as inputs, and generates BC analysis documents in various formats (e.g. Microsoft Excel).

Our solution also supports chaining of generators. For example, the xCelsius report generator reuses reports generated by the Microsoft Excel document generator and produces SAP xCelsius dashboards.

The BC manager controls the document generation process via the BIA analysis controller. The BIA analysis controller orchestrates and configures report generators and report generator chains by means of configuration files.

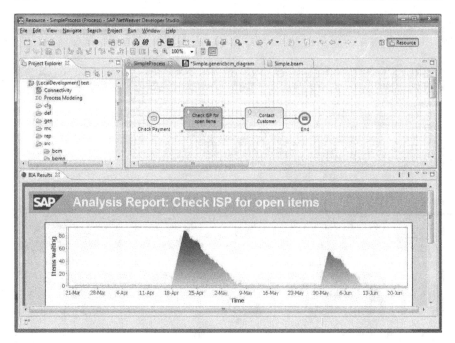

**Fig. 15** Context-sensitive presentation: the resulting view depicts the queue length for two disruptions of a single process activity.

## 5 Conclusions and Outlook

In this chapter, we have introduced a novel business-process-centric framework for BCM. We have further described how this framework consumes currently available process models and IT landscape models to automatically uncover dependencies between resources in different layers of the enterprise stack. Within the transformation chain, the business continuity manager is further provided with two editors to refine the models: the BCM editor and the BEAM editor. The availability of these editors enhances the quality of the resulting analysis model in terms of its completeness, accuracy and precision. The BC editor allows the manager to assign resource dependency graphs to process activities, and to use his/her expert knowledge to further enhance knowledge captured about the resource dependencies within the automatically generated resource dependency graphs. Once the BC model is transformed into a BEAM, the user can use the BEAM editor to further refine the BEAM, alter the behavioural models, and add measurement models and recovery plans. The proposed architecture allows connection to various types of analysis tools.

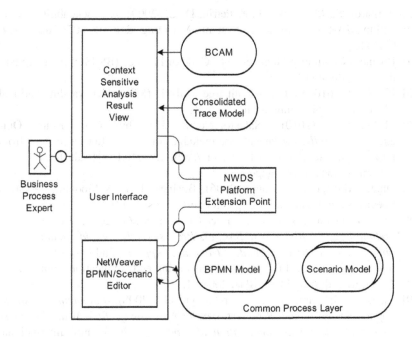

**Fig. 16** Architecture of the context-sensitive analysis result

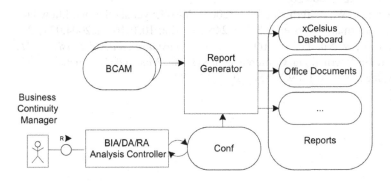

**Fig. 17** Document-oriented result presentation

# References

[1] Asnar, Y. (2009). Requirements Analysis and Risk Assessment for Critical Information Systems. PhD Thesis
[2] Asnar, Y., & Giorgini, P. (2008). Analyzing Business Continuity through a Multi-Layers Model. Proceedings of the 6th International Conference on Business Process Management.

[3]  Bernardi, S., Merseguer, J., & Petriu, D. C. (2009). A dependability profile within MARTE. Software & Systems Modeling. doi: 10.1007/s10270-009-0128-1.

[4]  Business Continuity Management : Code of Practice (BS ISO). British Standards Institution (2006).

[5]  FTTA IEC 61025 ed2.0 - Fault tree analysis (FTA). Geneva: International Electrotechnical Commission.

[6]  Miller, R. (2010). Salesforce.com Hit by One Hour Outage. http://www.datacenterknowledge.com/. Retrieved from http://www.datacenterknowledge.com/archives/2010/01/04/salesforce-com-hit-by-one-hour-outage/.

[7]  Object Management Group. (2006). Business Process Modeling Notation Specification, Final Adopted Specification, Version 1.0.

[8]  Tjoa, S., Jakoubi, S., Goluch, G., & Quirchmayr, G. (2008). *Extension of a Methodology for Risk-Aware Business Process Modeling and Simulation Enabling Process-Oriented Incident Handling Support.* 22nd International Conference on Advanced Information Networking and Applications (aina 2008), 48-55. Ieee. doi: 10.1109/AINA.2008.81.

[9]  Tjoa, S., Jakoubi, S., & Quirchmayr, G. (2008). *Enhancing Business Impact Analysis and Risk Assessment Applying a Risk-Aware Business Process Modeling and Simulation Methodology.* 2008 Third International Conference on Availability, Reliability and Security, 179-186. Ieee. doi: 10.1109/ARES.2008.206.

[10] Vanderaalst, W., & Terhofstede, a. (2005). YAWL: yet another workflow language. Information Systems, 30(4), 245-275. doi: 10.1016/j.is.2004.02.002.

[11] Wijnia, Y., & Nikolic, I. (2007). *Assessing business continuity risks in IT.* 2007 IEEE International Conference on Systems, Man and Cybernetics, 3547-3553. Ieee. doi: 10.1109/ICSMC.2007.4413845.

# Managing Composite Services

Sam Guinea, Annapaola Marconi, Natalia Rasadka, and Paolo Zampognaro

**Abstract** Highly dynamic systems, such as those built using the Service-Oriented Architectures style, are built under an open-world assumption [3], meaning the system's functionality and quality of service are determined by the set of services with which it interacts, and this set can evolve in many ways. Designers need to be sure evolutions will not lead to qualitatively inadequate behavior, or to unforeseen failures. Such systems need to be able to reconstruct themselves when the services they use change, and react to, and cope with, unforeseen runtime anomalies. Such systems are said to be self-adaptive, and they are typically augmented with control loops. In this chapter, we illustrate how the SLA@SOI project manages a complex system, keeping it aligned with its service level agreement (SLA). Each service in the system is considered a manageable entity and must provide the hooks to install appropriate sensors, to understand how the system is behaving, and effectors, so that it can be adjusted and kept on track. This chapter also details the sensors and effectors developed within the project for composed services, built using the BPEL standard.

## 1 Introduction

Highly dynamic systems, such as those built using the Service-Oriented Architectures style [15], are presenting designers with novel requirements. These systems

Sam Guinea
Politecnico di Milano, Via Golgi 42, 20148 Milano Italy, e-mail: guinea@elet.polimi.it

Annapaola Marconi, Natalia Rasadka
Fondazione Bruno Kessler, via alla Cascata 56C, 38121 Povo, Trento, Italy,
e-mail: {marconi, rasadka}@fbk.eu

Paolo Zampognaro
Engineering, Engineering Ingegneria Informatica Spa, Via Riccardo Morandi, 32, 00148 Roma,
Italy, e-mail: paolo.zampognaro@eng.it

are built under an open-world assumption [3], meaning the system's functionality and quality of service are determined by the set of services with which it interacts, and this set can evolve in many ways, for better or for worse. Designers need to be confident that evolutions will not lead to qualitatively inadequate behaviour, or to unforeseen failures. Such systems need to be able to reconstruct themselves when the services they use change, and react to, and cope with, unforeseen runtime anomalies.

A typical way of coping with uncertainties introduced by the open world is to include some sort of control loop in the system. Autonomic computing introduces the MAPE loop, which consists of four steps: monitoring, analysis, planning, and execution [10]. The monitoring and analysis steps collect runtime data and determine whether the system is providing the desired functionality and quality of service. The planning and execution steps attempt to identify and enact a strategy that can allow the system to continue to behave according to users' needs.

In the SLA@SOI project, a system is required to provide functional and non-functional qualities that have been established through a negotiated Service Level Agreement (SLA) [13]. The project provides a reference architecture for an integrated SLA management framework. Not only does the framework manage the SLA over its entire life cycle, but it also continuously realigns the system with the SLA itself.

In this chapter, we will focus on how the SL@SOI framework manages the domain-specific services that compose a complex system. The framework requires that each service become a manageable entity, and provide hooks for installing control loops. More specifically, a service must allow the installation of sensors, for collecting runtime data regarding its behaviour, and effectors, for attempting to keep the service's behaviour on track. After presenting the overall SLA@SOI approach to managing services, this chapter will present the domain-specific sensors and effectors that have been developed for services composed using the BPEL [11] standard. Sensors adopt aspect-oriented technology [12] to dynamically weave data collection code into a running process, while two different kinds of effectors are provided. The first kind of effector enables dynamic binding; the second allows for the dynamic restructuring of a process' internal logic. The overall approach, as well as the domain-specific sensors and effectors, are exemplified using the project's Health and Mobility use case.

The rest of this chapter is organised as follows: This section concludes with a brief presentation of the SLA@SOI project's Health and Mobility use case. Section 2 illustrates the SLA@SOI approach to managing domain-specific services. Section 3 presents the Dynamic Orchestration Engine (DOE), a BPEL execution environment that has been extended with sensing and adjustment capabilities, and briefly explains how AOP is used to enable sensors. Sections 4 and 5 explain and exemplify the dynamic binding and process restructuring adjustment capabilities we have implemented within the project. Section 6 discusses the most prominent existing work in the literature, and Section 7 concludes the chapter.

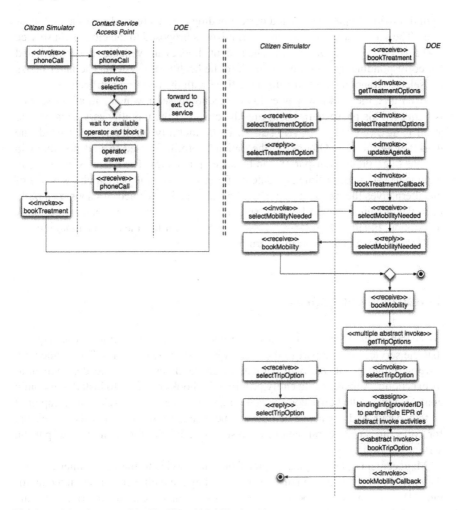

**Fig. 1** Activity diagram of the Health and Mobility booking use case.

## 1.1 The Health and Mobility Use Case

The Health and Mobility use case involves a patient, a health care service, a set of mobility services, and a call centre. Patients are interested in booking, modifying or cancelling an appointment, and in finding a mobility service that can help them reach the health care centre.

The overall workflow is shown in Figure 1. The citizen makes a call to a contact service access point. The call is assigned to a call operator that communicates with the citizen. As soon as the citizen gets a response, she invokes service bookTreatment to request a treatment booking. The requested treatment is passed to the health care system, which invokes service getTreatmentOptions to find possible appointments and corresponding options (e.g., date, time and location). The set of such appointment alternatives is proposed to the citizen via service selectTreatmentOptions. The patient chooses an available appointment and the corresponding options are sent back to the health care system. The latter books the selected appointment and calls the citizen with the booking notification.

After that, the workflow passes to the second phase, in which a mobility service is booked. This phase starts by asking the citizen if the mobility service is needed at all (checkIfMobilityNeeded). If the mobility service is not needed, the workflow terminates. Otherwise, the patient's profile is used to find possible trip options (e.g., public transport, an ambulance, a taxi, etc). The citizen's profile may include her address, or time and date preferences. Once the patient chooses one of the alternatives the selectTripOption service is executed. As soon as a reply from the citizen is received, a corresponding mobility service is contacted to book that option. Finally, bookMobilityCallback notifies the citizen about the end of the booking, and the workflow terminates.

## 2 Management Approach

To guarantee an SLA is satisfied at runtime, the SLA@SOI framework requires that the services taking part in the system be manageable entities. The framework governs a manageable entity throughout its entire life cycle, from its deployment to its execution. A manageable entity provides the hooks required to install autonomic control loops, so that erroneous behaviours, with respect to an SLA, can be captured as they occur, and corrective actions can be taken. These hooks consist of sensors for collecting behavioural data to analyse, and effectors for attempting to put the service back on track.

Management details typically vary from one service to the next, either because they pertain to different domains, or because they are built using different technologies. This is why we propose a general-purpose manageability interface that the SLA@SOI framework can use to govern a service. Moreover, we do not require that all services implement this interface, but provide an agent-based approach. Instead of interacting with the end service itself, the SLA@SOI framework interacts with a manageability agent that hides the technical and domain-specific details.

Figure 2 illustrates how the manageability agent bridges the SLA@SOI framework and a domain-specific service. The framework interacts with a service through a service manager. This manager is responsible for preparing, deploying, and governing a service instance. It does not interact with the service itself, but with the service's manageability agent, using a well-specified interface. In particular, the manageability agent allows the service manager to configure and use the sensors and effectors within the service instance.

Once a sensor is configured, it autonomously collects runtime data and sends them to the SLA@SOI publish and subscribe EventBus. SLA@SOI analysers need to be configured to subscribe to these data. The manageability agent achieves

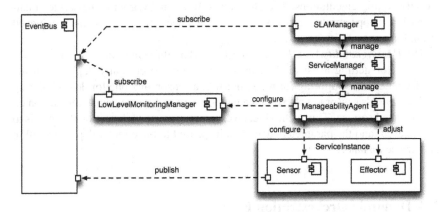

**Fig. 2** The manageability agent in the context of the SLA@SOI framework.

this configuration through the framework's `LowLevelMonitoringManager`. Not only does it tell the analysers what data they must subscribe to, but it also explains how to extract the required data from the bus' event and what analysis properties needs to be checked. When an anomalous behaviour is detected, it is communicated to the *SLAManager* through the event bus. This component contains the knowledge needed to determine what corrective actions need to be taken. These actions are achieved indirectly through the service manager, which in turn interacts with the manageability agent.

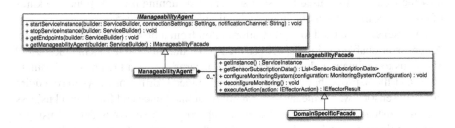

**Fig. 3** The manageability agent's generic interface.

Figure 3 illustrates the generic interface that is provided by a manageability agent. Through the *IManageabilityAgent* interface it is possible to obtain a list of services for which the agent is responsible, to start and stop these services, and to configure and activate their domain-specifc sensors and effectors.

Sensors and effectors are often domain-specific because they need to cope with the technical intricacies of the services they are attached to. This is why we propose the notion of a domain-specific manageability facade. A facade offers a generalised interface for coping with sensors and effectors, and hides the technical details tied to the service implementations. Therefore our solution is to provide the service manager with an appropriate facade for each service it needs to manage. This is achieved through manageability agents.

The *IManageabilityAgentFacade* interface offers three monitoring-related methods: one for getting a list of the sensor configurations currently deployed in the service, one for configuring (or reconfiguring) a sensor, and one for de-configuring all the service's sensors. It also offers a method for invoking an adjustment action on the managed service. This method receives both the name of the action that needs to be achieved, and the parameters that must be passed to the effector deployed within the service instance.

## 3 A Dynamic Orchestration Engine

Through the SLA@SOI framework, it is possible to manage both simple and composite services. In general, the management of composite services presents challenges, mainly due to limitations of the WS-BPEL standard [11]. Therefore, we provide a Dynamic Orchestration Engine (DOE), built as an extension of the open source ActiveBPEL engine, that allows us to install advanced sensors and different kinds of effectors. Sensors can be used to intercept an executing process and extract important runtime data for analysing the system's behaviour. Effectors can be used to change the binding between the system and its partner services, or to more deeply modify the process by altering its control and data flows.

For the DOE, we have implemented a specific manageability facade according to the IManageabilityFacade interface described in Section 2. We shall now discuss how the facade can be used to install sensors in a running process. (Our two kinds of effectors will be discussed in more detail in Sections 4 and 5.)

DOE sensors are used to extract information from a process instance at runtime. A sensor is enabled using aspect-oriented programming (AOP) techniques. AOP allows us to maintain a clear separation of concerns between the process' business logic and the sensors that we want to install. Indeed, different SLAs may require different sensors, which means they cannot be defined once and for all in a business process. Instead, we propose a rule-based approach. A sensor is defined using a sensing rule that contains sensing directives that are weaved into the execution as required. The directives instruct the engine on how to intercept the process instance, and gather the content of a BPEL variable, taking into account BPEL's visibility rules.

A rule consists of a ⟨ *condition, sensing information* ⟩ couple. The condition consists of ⟨ *position, status check* ⟩ . The position is an XPath that uniquely determines a BPEL activity within the process with respect to its XML definition, and a special keyword which can be either 'before' or 'after'. The AOP sensing capabilities are thus activated either before or after that specific BPEL activity. Once the sensing capabilities are activated, the sensor performs a status check. The status check is a list of ⟨ *variable, value* ⟩ couples. A variable is an XPath that specifies how to extract a string, number, or Boolean from a complex BPEL variable; the value tells us what we expect to find therein. If the check is evaluated successfully, the sensor extracts the data specified in the rule's sensing information, which is the name of a specific variable within the process. If the status check is empty, the sensing is considered to be always active.

For example, in the Health and Mobility scenario seen in Section 1.1, we may be interested in tracking appointment proposals that are made to the citizen. Suppose we are experiencing troubles with the mobility services, and they can only be provided in the afternoon. If the system is making appointment proposals for the morning, we may need to take action to ensure this does not continue. In this case, we want to sense the `selectTreatmentOptions` invoke activity, and in particular we want to sense the information contained within the message it sends. This information is contained in the BPEL variable `TreatmentOptionsOut`. Therefore, the sensing rule's condition consists of the XPATH that uniquely identifies the `selectTreatmentOptions` and the 'before' keyword. Its status check is left empty to keep the sensing on at all times, and the sensing information is simply the name of the BPEL variable we are interested in, i.e., `TreatedOptionsOut`.

# 4 Dynamic Binding

The first kind of adjustment we support involves the bindings a process has with its partner services. The BPEL standard does not specify when binding information should be provided. Most process execution engines interpret this in a simplistic manner, by requiring that binding information be provided during the process' deployment. This can produce a number of negative effects: For example, if BPEL engines adopt proprietary deployment descriptors and procedures, the process' portability will be negatively impacted. Deployment-time binding also limits a process' freedom to evolve. Indeed, a process that wants to change its bindings must be redeployed, which can be a very costly operation. It also makes it impossible to define specific bindings for specific categories of process instances or users. This is an important limitation if we consider the typical process development model. First, the process is defined in a development phase. Second it is customised to satisfy specific conditions (e.g., the quality levels agreed with a given partner). Finally, it is deployed to a BPEL engine.

This approach is far from optimal. A process that is conceptually identical could want to bind to different services depending on the different quality requirements. In our DOE we deploy an unbound process before the process' actual provisioning phase, for example, during an offering phase as seen in Figure 4. Then, after a negotiation phase in which we establish specific SLAs and corresponding binding information, we submit the binding information to the system. This way, if the bindings need to change no redeployment will be necessary. The process' portability is maintained since there is a clear separation of concerns between the process' business logic and its binding information.

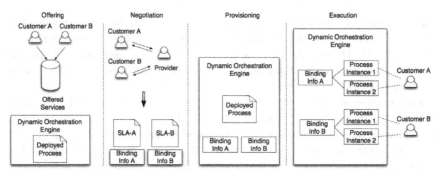

**Fig. 4** The Dynamic Orchestration Engine allows a single deployed process to exploit dynamic binding through appropriately designed binding rules.

The DOE allows us to associate binding rules with BPEL partner roles (Figure 5). A binding rule is expressed by a couple ⟨ *condition, binding information* ⟩ , where the *condition* represents the process status that triggers the adoption of a specific binding. A condition is expressed as a partner role and a set of ⟨ *variable, value* ⟩ couples. Every time the process needs to perform an invocation with a specific partner, it evaluates the binding rule and sets the binding information appropriately.

**Fig. 5** The Dynamic Orchestration Engine's binding rules management interface.

The DOE also supports the notion of an abstract process: that is, a process for which at least one BPEL invoke activity is abstract and therefore associated with a service description. During the operation phase, the service description is used to discover, select, and negotiate a specific service for that invoke activity. A service description consists of a SLA template document that, along with the SLA model, represents the requirements that need to be met in terms of functionality and quality of service. To support abstract processes, we introduced the notion of an abstract binding rule. An abstract binding rule consists of a ⟨ *condition, SLAT* ⟩ couple. Notice that the DOE also supports multiple bindings, meaning that given one SLAT, multiple services can be selected for execution. The services are all invoked, one at a time, and their return values are presented as an aggregate and single response.

We have exploited the above mechanisms in the management of the Health and Mobility process, to enable both the automatic selection of service providers and their substitutions. For instance, let us consider the fragment of business process reported in Figure 6. It consists of an *abstract process* that has been adequately configured through the manageability facade.

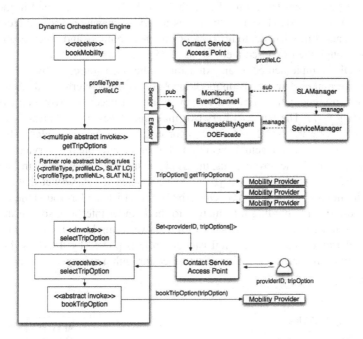

**Fig. 6** The Health and Mobility process exploits dynamic binding techniques to enable automatic selection of service providers.

The process comprises the following main activities:

- a *receive* `bookMobility` through which it acquires the citizen's preferences regarding the mobility service, such as 'low cost' (ProfileLC) or 'nearest location' (ProfileNL);
- an *abstract invoke* `getTripOptions` for obtaining the possible providers that can be presented to the citizen;
- a *invoke* `selectTripOption` that presents such options to the citizen;
- the *receive* `selectTripOption` through which it acquires the citizen's choice of option;
- the invoke `bookTripOption`, which depends on the citizen's choice and books the chosen mobility service.

We have associated two abstract binding rules to the process' abstract invoke. The DOE only executes one, depending on the condition which matches the citizen's profile. The two rules are:

- ⟨ *(profileType=profileLC), SLATLC* ⟩
- ⟨ *(profileType=profileNL), SLATNL* ⟩

When the appropriate rule is executed, a sensor in the DOE sends a *(Binding Missing Event)* to an appropriate `BindingListener`, which in the context of the SLA@SOI framework is the `SLAManager`. The SLAManager extracts, from the project's SLA registry, all the SLAs that match the template found in the rule (either SLATLC or SLATNL). It then uses a service manager, and indirectly the DOE's manageability facade, to instruct the engine to bind to, and execute, all these services through their exposed method `getTripOptions()`.

The DOE is implemented as an extension to the open source ActiveBPEL execution environment. The extension modifies ActiveBPEL's internal code to interact with a new module called the `Binder` every time it needs to invoke an external service (Figure 7). The Binder offers two main interfaces: the `IBinder` and the `IBinderInvocation`. The former is for configuring binding rules, while the latter is for requesting the actual execution of abstract and concrete services.

In the case of abstract invocations, the Binder extracts the SLAT from the abstract binding rule and asks the `BindingListener` to select a web-service that matches the requirements contained therein. Once the BindingListener has found the service, it passes the specific binding information to the IBinder interface, so that the process' execution can continue. As seen in the above example, in the context of the SLA@SOI framework, the BindingListener's role is played by the SLAManager, and the IBinderInvocation interface is accessed through a manageability agent and the DOE's specific facade.

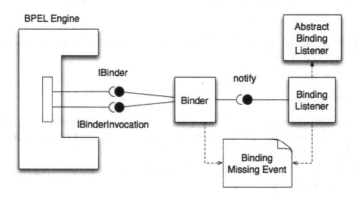

**Fig. 7** ActiveBPEL has been extended to support our dynamic binding rules.

## 5 Process Restructuring

Another kind of adjustment is related to structural modification of the process' workflow. These adjustments may be required in a range of cases, for example, when there is a need to manage time- or memory- performance with respect to the current needs of the application. Parallelisation of some workflow parts (sub-processes) can lead to a reduction in execution time[1]. On the other hand, parallel execution of sub-processes may require more memory and resources. Such trade-offs can be dynamically supported by means of continuous process restructuring.

For example, let us assume that initially the business process is structured as in Section 1.1, i.e., a health care service search is called first, and then a mobility service search is called. If we need to accelerate the queue of patients waiting to be treated, we could call both services in parallel, if they do not have data dependencies. On the other hand, if parallel services tend to exhaust a system's resources (e.g., bandwidth, computational memory, network workload, etc.), we may restructure the process so that some invocations are performed sequentially.

Of course, structural adjustment can be used to solve much more complex problems and can help optimise the process' overall execution. For example, let us once again suppose that the patient has mobility issues and that mobility services can only be guaranteed in the afternoon. A workflow like the one depicted in Section 1.1 will first search for a health care appointment, and then search for a mobility service. However, if the first step returns a health care appointment in the morning (due to a strategy that selects the earliest availability), then the second step will fail since no mobility service is available. This can be monitored by analysing the sensed information as shown in Section 3. To recover from the failure, the process might try to search for a new health care appointment. However, such redundant behavior could be avoided by simply requesting the mobility service search first, or at least in parallel with the appointment search.

Automatic detection and remediation of such structure-dependent situations is very helpful when dealing with complex workflows. Such workflows are usually difficult and error-prone to manually create, analyse and optimise since they need to account for various actors and interactions. Our approach is based on workflow composition, as in [4]. In our Health and Mobility example, we have at least three workflows for each of the high-level actors: the patient, the health care service, and the mobility service. These are composed into a single workflow for the call centre, taking into account the following requirements:

- *Control flow requirements* are used to specify a successful/unsuccessful termination of the workflow. For example, in the health care scenario, if the patient is unable to fix an appointment in any health care centre, the overall workflow terminates unsuccessfully, even if the mobility service was booked successfully. On the other hand, an unsuccessful booking for the mobility service will not impact a booked health care appointment (we consider a mobility service as an optional facility in the health care scenario).
- *Data flow requirements* are needed to specify how actors depend on each other in terms of data inputs and outputs. For example, a patient may prefer to be treated in a health care centre near his/her house, but the date of treatment may not be for a month due to queues for treatment at that particular centre. A mobility

---

[1] Unless parallel sub-processes share some common resource that can only be consumed by a single process at a time.

service booking will thus depend on this information, and will be invoked with this information in mind (i.e., in a month).

All such requirements make up the input of a planning engine [4]. The planer's output is a composed business process which is usually parallelisation-free: that is, it contains only sequential and branching components. Through *process restructuring*, we reorganise these sequential fragments into parallel ones, and *vice versa*, if possible. We developed a method for maximum parallelisation, where we parallelise as much as possible, taking into account control flow and dataflow requirements. For example, if in the original workflow, the output of the health care booking service contains a treatment date and time that must be consumed by the mobility booking service, we cannot parallelise these two bookings. However, we can parallelise the search steps, since the health care search and the mobility search are independent.

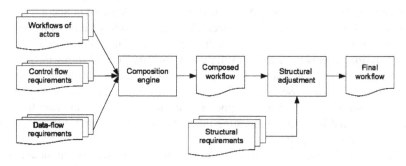

**Fig. 8** Overview of the process restructuring approach.

We restrict maximum parallelisation by means of *structural requirements* (Figure 8). These requirements keep some fragments of workflow sequential, even if they can be parallelised. In general, structural requirements are stipulated by the needs of the application, and can be introduced by workflow administrators or owners, or they can be extracted from the preferences of the workflow actors.

As an example, the parallelisation algorithm can transform the workflow from Section 6 to one depicted in Figure 9. Namely, the workflow starts in the same way as in the example: the patient makes a call and starts a conversation with the call operator. However, together with service getTreatmentOptions, a parallel branch is launched to search for a mobility service. First, the patient is asked whether she needs a mobility service (selectMobilityNeeded). If she does, the booking of both the treatment and the mobility option proceed in parallel until the former reaches activity updateAgenda. At this point, we prefer to restrict parallelisation with a structural requirement[2] and establish that the invocation of updateAgenda must be followed by bookTripOption, due to the sensitivity

---

[2] Restriction on parallelisation is implemented in BPEL via synchronisation links with source and target parameters.

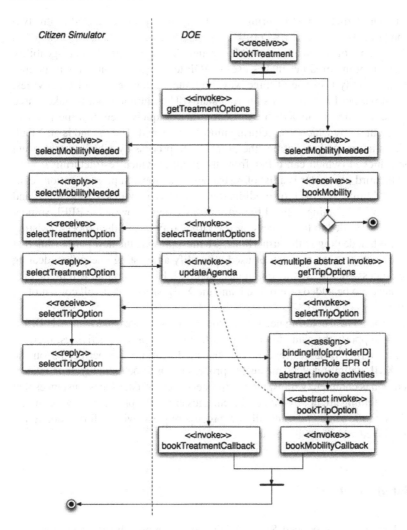

**Fig. 9** The Health and Mobility booking process after structural adjustment.

of the booking operation to failure situations. Specifically, if the health care treatment booking fails for some reason, we can easily roll back an operation without needing to roll back the mobility service booking. In Figure 9, we represent the structural restriction between the treatment booking and the mobility booking as a dotted line.

In the current example, we consider a structural adjustment of this global workflow. However, any underlying workflow of a single hospital (e.g., HSC booking service) or mobility service (e.g., extra-urban bus schedule info) can be also restructured according to the same principles.

To support process restructuring, the DOE has been extended with two main components: a `process runtime modifier`, and a `static BPEL modifier`, both of which are accessible through the DOE's specific manageability facade. The runtime modifier makes use of AOP techniques to intercept a running process and modify it in one of three ways: by intervening on its BPEL activities, on its set of partner links, or on its internal status. The runtime modifier takes three parameters. The first is an XPath expression that uniquely identifies the point in process execution by which restructuring must be activated. The second is an XPath expression that uniquely identifies the point in the process by which restructuring must be achieved (which can differ from the point at which restructuring is activated). The third parameter is a list of restructuring actions. Supported actions consist of the addition, removal, or modification of BPEL activities, partnerlinks, and data values. When dealing with BPEL activities, we must provide the BPEL snippet that needs to be added to the process, or used to modify one of the process' existing activities. When dealing with partnerlinks, we must provide the new partnerlink that needs to be added to the process, or used to modify an existing one. When dealing with the process' status, we must uniquely identify a BPEL variable within the process that needs to be added or modified, and the XML snippet that will consist of its new value.

When process restructuring needs to be more extensive, we can use a static BPEL modifier. It supports the same kinds of modifications to process activities, partnerlinks, and internal variables, except that the modifications are performed on the process' XML definition. This means the process needs to be redeployed. However, this operation is completely transparent to process users. First, process instances that are already running are not modified; the changes are only applied to new instances. Second, using the same endpoint, all new process requests will be forwarded to the newly deployed version of the process.

# 6 Related Work

In this chapter, we introduced SLA@SOI's generic approach to service management, and then focused on specific adjustment techniques for composed services. Due to lack of space, below we shall focus on some adjustment techniques that we deem of interest and comparable to our own.

Ardagna et al. [1, 2] propose the PAWS (Processes and Adaptive Web Services) framework. Their proxy-based framework optimises a BPEL process' QoS by selecting the most appropriate partner services at runtime, and by providing a set of simple recovery actions. First, designers define global and local QoS constraints. Second, these requirements are analysed and used to produce a set of candidate services, retrieved from an extended UDDI repository. Third, the system provides a series of mediations that allows it to deal with retrieved services. If a QoS requirement cannot be met, the framework can choose among a set of recovery actions: retry, substitute, and compensate. Like our approach, PAWS has paid attention to

separation of concerns. Indeed, there is no notion of monitoring, discovery, or mediation to be found in its processes, but these issues are treated externally in proxies
that are placed between the process and the partner services. Unfortunately, the extensive use of proxies brings with it a high performance overhead. Moreover, their
recovery strategies are defined statically at design-time. The way they implement
separation of concerns does not allow them to add to or modify recovery strategies
at runtime, nor does it allow them to select strategies at runtime depending on the
actual context of execution. Instead, if, for example, our negotiated SLA changes,
we can use the notion of facade to enable modification of management activities at
runtime. This also allows us to fine-tune our sensors, which do have a small impact
on process performance, and tailor them to specific needs that exist at a certain point
in the process' life cycle.

Colombo et al. [7] offer a composition language that allows designers to declare
policy (re)binding rules. Policies are defined using an extended version of the Drools
language [16] (a language for defining Event-Condition-Action rules), and can be
either global or local. This approach is proxy-based. Every time the process invokes
a service, the proxy interacts with the rule engine to see whether (re)binding is
necessary. The authors also added mediation capabilities through a special-purpose
mediation scripting language, and an interpreter that behaves as a proxy [6]. Once
again, there is a clear separation of concerns between business logic and management that is enforced by the use of proxies. However, the definition of rebinding is
given statically.

Moser et al. [14], in their VIeDAME approach, also provide a dynamic adaptation and message mediation service for partner links. Using the data collected during
the monitoring step, the system chooses the most appropriate service, while XSLT
or regular expressions are used to transform messages accordingly. An important
difference between our approach and all of the above solutions for dynamic binding
is that we make a clear distinction between concrete and abstract BPEL processes.
Moreover, our approach also supports multiple bindings, without placing new restrictions on the BPEL process' internal structure.

The first steps towards BPEL process restructuring were taken by Finkelstein et
al. [8] in their work on aspect-oriented weaving applications. They propose use of
AOP both at the engine level, to enable capabilities such as monitoring and dynamic
binding, and at the process level, to enable hot-fixes such as the addition, removal,
and substitution of BPEL activities. Their contributions were more specifically in
the realm of software engineering, since they illustrated the advantages of having
different domain-specific languages for AOP, depending on the level at which the
AOP is to be applied. Indeed, their application of this logic to BPEL engines and
processes was merely an exercise, and has not lead to the distribution of an AOP-
enriched execution environment.

Geebelen et al. [9] propose a template-based approach to the dynamic composition of BPEL processes. They start from a generic master process that models the
workflow without the specific implementation details. The concrete modules (i.e.,
the BPEL activities) are modelled as templates and stored in a registry. An executable process is obtained by choosing specific templates from the registry and

integrating them into the master process. The templates are chosen depending on the values of some domain-specific parameters defined within the master process; these values can change, and therefore, the executable process can change as well. The approach maintains a clear separation of concerns between the definition of the overall business logic and the implementation details of the templates. In the current implementation, modules simply consist of the concrete details needed to actually perform a service invocation, while the actual process structure is defined once and for all in the master process. This makes the approach more similar to a solution for dynamic binding. It is possible, however, to extend the approach to include more complex modules that impact the process' structure.

Structural modifications to workflow systems were extensively investigated in Adept Project [17]. The proposal is dedicated to *ad hoc* deviations from the defined business processes on-demand (e.g., process activities may be dynamically added, deleted or moved around the process). Corresponding patterns of structural adjustment are provided and analysed with respect to the requirements of completeness, correctness and efficiency of change operation.

In [5], process views reflecting user perspectives over business processes are obtained via operation reduction and aggregation. These transformations often cause a restructuring process graph similar to our structural adjustment, where some activities are placed in parallel while others are organised sequentially. However, such a restructuring is usually done for reasons of security and confidentiality, rather than to improve quality of service intentions.

# 7 Conclusions and Future Work

This chapter has presented the SLA@SOI approach for managing services, and for keeping them aligned with the functionality and quality of service negotiated and described in an SLA. Each service is considered a manageable entity, and must provide the hooks for installing sensors, to allow the framework to understand its runtime behaviour, and effectors, to allow it to adjust the service and keep it on track. The chapter also presented the project's Dynamic Orchestration Engine, which allows for the installation of AOP-based sensors, and for two different kinds of adjustments: dynamic binding in concrete and abstract processes, and AOP-enabled process restructuring.

In future work, we will continue to evaluate the project's manageability approach in the context of different technical domains, both at the software and infrastructure levels. In particular, we are interested in continuing to implement a manageability facade for atomic services that use Axis technology, and a manageability facade for virtualised infrastructure services. We will continue to evaluate this approach within the SLA@SOI project's industrial use cases and against their requirements, and will also continue to perform academic lab tests.

# References

[1] Danilo Ardagna, Marco Comuzzi, Enrico Mussi, Barbara Pernici, and Pierluigi Plebani. PAWS: A Framework for Executing Adaptive Web-Service Processes. *IEEE Software*, 24(6):39–46, 2007.

[2] Danilo Ardagna and Barbara Pernici. Adaptive Service Composition in Flexible Processes. *IEEE Transactions on Software Engineering*, 33(6):369–384, 2007.

[3] Luciano Baresi, Elisabetta Di Nitto, and Carlo Ghezzi. Toward Open-world Software: Issues and Challenges. *IEEE Computer*, 39(10):36–43, 2006.

[4] Piergiorgio Bertoli, Marco Pistore, and Paolo Traverso. Automated Composition of Web Services via Planning in Asynchronous Domains. *Artificial Intelligence*, 174(3-4):316–361, 2010.

[5] Ralph Bobrik, Manfred Reichert, and Thomas Bauer. View-based Process Visualization. In *BPM '07: Proceedings of the 2007 International Conference on Business Process Management*, pages 88–95, Berlin, Heidelberg, 2007. Springer-Verlag.

[6] Luca Cavallaro and Elisabetta Di Nitto. An Approach to Adapt Service Requests to Actual Service Interfaces. In *SEAMS '08: Proceedings of the 2008 International Workshop on Software Engineering for Adaptive and Self-managing Systems*, pages 129–136, New York, NY, USA, 2008. ACM.

[7] Massimiliano Colombo, Elisabetta Di Nitto, and Marco Mauri. SCENE: A Service Composition Execution Environment Supporting Dynamic Changes Disciplined Through Rules. In *ICSOC '06: Proceedings of the 2006 International Conference on Service Oriented Computing*, volume 4294 of *Lecture Notes in Computer Science*, pages 191–202. Springer, 2006.

[8] C. Courbis and A. Finkelstein. Towards Aspect Weaving Applications. In *ICSE '05: Proceedings of the 2005 International Conference on Software Engineering*, pages 69–77, 2005.

[9] Kristof Geebelen, Sam Michiels, and Wouter Joosen. Dynamic Reconfiguration using Template based Web Service Composition. In *MW4SOC '08: Proceedings of the 3rd workshop on Middleware for Service Oriented Computing*, pages 49–54, New York, NY, USA, 2008. ACM.

[10] P. Horn. Autonomic Computing: IBM's Perspective on the State of Information Technology. *IBM TJ Watson Labs.*, October 2001.

[11] Jordan, Evdemon, Alves, Arkin, Askary, Barreto, Bloch, Curbera, Ford, Goland, Guizar, Kartha, Liu, Khalaf, Konig, Marin, Mehta, Thatte, van der Rijn, and Yendluriand Yiu. Web Services Business Process Execution Language Version 2.0. BPEL4WS specification, 2007.

[12] G. Kiczales, J. Lamping, A. Mendhekar, C. Maeda, C. Videira Lopes, J.M. Loingtier, and J. Irwin. Aspect-Oriented Programming. In *ECOOP'97: Proceedings of the 1997 European Conference on Object-Oriented Programming*, volume 1241 of *Lecture Notes in Computer Science*, pages 220–242. Springer, 1997.

[13] H. Ludwig, A. Keller, A. Dan, R.P. King, and R. Franck. Web service Level Agreement (WSLA) Language Specification. *IBM Corporation*, 2003.

[14] Oliver Moser, Florian Rosenberg, and Schahram Dustdar. Non-intrusive Monitoring and Service Adaptation for WS-BPEL. In Jinpeng Huai, Robin Chen, Hsiao-Wuen Hon, Yunhao Liu, Wei-Ying Ma, Andrew Tomkins, and Xiaodong Zhang, editors, In *WWW '08: Proceedings of the 2008 Internationl World Wide Web Conference*, pages 815–824. ACM, 2008.

[15] M.P. Papazoglou. Service-oriented Computing: Concepts, Characteristics and Directions. In *ICSOC '03: Proceedings of the 2003 International Conference on Web Information Systems Engineering*, volume 10. NW Washington: IEEE Computer Society, 2003.

[16] M. Proctor, M. Neale, P. Lin, and M. Frandsen. Drools Documentation. *Available on: http://labs. jboss. com/file-access/default/members/jbossrules/freezone/docs/3.0*, 1, 2006.

[17] Manfred Reichert, Stefanie Rinderle, Ulrich Kreher, and Peter Dadam. Adaptive Process Management with Adept2. In *ICDE '05: Proceedings of the 2005 International Conference on Data Engineering*, pages 1113–1114, Washington, DC, USA, 2005. IEEE Computer Society.

# Part VII
# Management of the Infrastructure Layer

# SLA-Enabled Infrastructure Management

John Kennedy, Andrew Edmonds, Victor Bayon, Pat Cheevers, Kuan Lu, Miha Stopar, and Damjan Murn

**Abstract** This chapter documents a successful reference implementation of an SLA-enabled compute infrastructure. Limitations of current Infrastructure as a Service (IaaS) offerings are discussed, and an SLA-enabled implementation is introduced. Infrastructure SLA and services managers have been developed, as have extensions to Apache Tashi [11] and a low-level monitoring system. Efforts to develop a generic open interface to heterogenous infrastructure have helped to create the recently published Open Cloud Computing Interface (OCCI) [2].

## 1 Introduction

Service Level Agreements (SLAs) for computing infrastructures are often verbose documents, written in legalese, that even if read, are typically set aside once a contact is entered into. As there is no standard for documenting SLAs, consumers must manually explore the details of the SLA that each potential provider offers. Once provisioned, sometimes it is up to the customer to detect and indeed prove any SLA violations, and manually submit any claims for disposition.

On the service provider side, for manageability purposes, service offerings are typically offered with a very limited range of fixed SLAs. The possibility of broker-

---

John Kennedy, Andrew Edmonds, Victor Bayon, Pat Cheevers
Intel Labs Europe, Leixlip, Co. Kildare, Ireland,
e-mail: {john.m.kennedy,andrewx.edmonds,victorx.molino,patx.cheevers}@intel.com

Kuan Lu
TU Dortmund University, Service Computing Group/ITMC, August-Schmidt-Strasse 12, 44227 Dortmund, Germany, e-mail: kuan.lu@tu-dortmund.de

Miha Stopar, Damjan Murn
XLAB d.o.o., Pot za Brdom 100, 1000 Ljubljana, Slovenia,
e-mail: {miha.stopar,damjan.murn}@xlab.si

ing third-party services is frustrated by the absence of standard (and automatable) ways to interrogate, evaluate and negotiate third-party SLAs.

Thus consumers are forced to accept SLAs that are perhaps more extensive (and expensive) than they truly require. Similarly, providers cannot offer their consumers individualised SLAs, and may miss out on opportunities to consolidate their infrastructure (and reduce expenses) whilst still confident that they are satisfying their customers' SLAs. There is no standard automatable way to adopt or broker third-party services.

Providers able to offer personally customisable SLAs, which the providers can automatically negotiate, provision, monitor and optimise, gain a significant competitive advantage. They can also participate in automatically brokered and composed services exposing new business models.

Enabling compute infrastructure with machine-readable SLAs delivers significant advantages to both consumers and providers of infrastructural resources.

## 2 SLA-Aware Infrastructure Architecture

The infrastructure layer has been SLA-enabled by adopting and implementing the overall SLA@SOI architecture as described in Chapter 'Reference Architecture for Multi-Level SLA Management'.

Accordingly, the SLA@SOI model has been used to define an infrastructure SLA template. It exposes all service-level parameters and valid values that the customer may select when requesting a service. Services can contain bundles of virtual machines, each of which have parameters such as number of CPU cores, speed of CPU, memory size, image location and persistence defined. A wide range of Quality of Service (QoS) terms can be supported.

A reference infrastructure SLA manager has been implemented by developing infrastructure-specific Planning and Optimisation (IPOC) and Provisioning and Adjustment (IPAC) components and instantiating them within the Generic SLA Manager. This manager deals with all SLA-specific concerns: negotiation, planning, provisioning, adjustment and optimisation as per the agreed SLA. The IPAC and IPOC manipulate the infrastructure via the infrastructure service manager (ISM).

The ISM contains all the logic to manipulate the underlying infrastructure. In this reference implementation, the ISM interfaces with the provisioning system through the Open Cloud Computing Interface (OCCI). SLA@SOI helped to develop this open standard to create a generic, extensible way in which arbitrary virtualised infrastructure could be manipulated and managed, independent of the provisioning system.

Apache Tashi is the open-source provisioning system on which this reference implementation was built. Several new Tashi modules were developed during the course of this work, to introduce additional functionality and enhancements. The source code for these new modules was contributed back to the Tashi community to help share these improvements.

Whilst high-level SLA monitoring concerns are controlled by the monitoring manager within the Generic SLA Manager, low-level infrastructure monitoring in the implementation is managed by the low-level monitoring system. This system has the ability to configure infrastructure monitors, gather infrastructure monitoring data and escalate significant events to higher-level components via the Extensible Messaging and Presence Protocol (XMPP) [3].

An XMPP bus is used to allow components up and down the stack to communicate. In particular, monitoring alerts are passed from the LLMS to the ISLAM via the XMPP bus.

These components are now described in some detail.

# 3 Infrastructure SLA Manager

The Infrastructure SLA Manager (ISLAM) is an instantiation of the Generic SLA Manager (GSLAM) tailored to infrastructure services. The ISLAM does not try to replicate all exotic features of every possible infrastructure service, rather it focuses on the most important features typically provided by IaaS offerings.

In brief, the GSLAM includes all those features necessary for the full life cycle management of SLAs. It supports:

- Negotiation mechanics via an extensible protocol engine and interoperable syntax converters;
- Persistency for SLAs and SLA templates via the two respective registries;
- A publish/subscribe system for advertising SLA templates, thus enabling service discovery based on both functional and non-functional properties; and
- The flexible definition of per-SLA monitoring frameworks, through a generic monitoring manager.

The GSLAM also includes two components considered to be domain- or use-case-specific; the Planning/Optimisation Component (POC) and the Provisioning/Adjustment Component (PAC). These two components are expected to be implemented by interested parties, and replace the default placeholders. The ISLAM is, ultimately, a GSLAM with custom POC and PAC, targeting the least common denominator of IaaS.

Figure 1 illustrates a high-level overview of the ISLAM architecture, as an extension of a GSLAM.

As can be seen from this figure, the ISLAM interacts externally with:

- The business (SLA) manager, from which it receives policies and business-specific customisations related to negotiation, while it also provides runtime status information used to make business decisions; and
- The infrastructure service manager (as described below), which provides resource information, and controls resources in general (reservations, initialisation, runtime management).

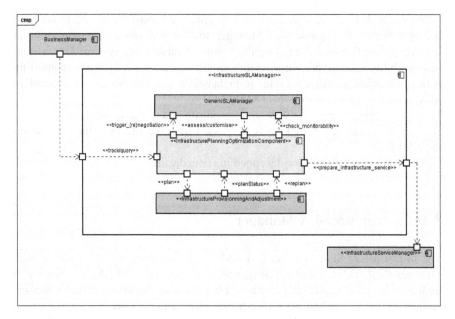

**Fig. 1** Infrastructure SLA Manager architecture

The POC is responsible for the planning and optimisation of infrastructure SLAs. Concretely, it receives requests for infrastructure, queries the infrastructure service manager for potential provisioning solutions, selects and reserves an optimal solution, and requests the PAC to provision the selected plan as appropriate. If local resources cannot satisfy the request (due to lack of resources or specification discrepancies, for example), the POC can attempt to satisfy the request by outsourcing to third-party providers. This could therefore be regarded as a business strategy by planning local resource configuration, outsourcing for infrastructure services that are subject to SLAs, and intelligently offering flexible solutions, thereby gaining customer satisfaction.

The PAC is responsible for the provisioning and adjustment of infrastructure SLAs. It directs the infrastructure service manager to provision as per the plan supplied by the POC. It also decides on any adjustments required, to avoid potential SLA violations.

# 4 Infrastructure SLA Manager Implementation

The implementation of the ISLAM can be essentially decomposed into the implementation of a POC and a PAC customised for infrastructure.

## 4.1 Infrastructure Planning and Optimisation

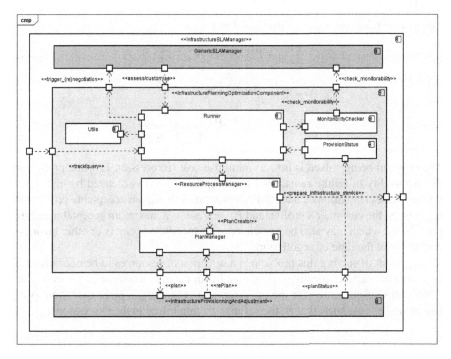

**Fig. 2** Infrastructure Planning and Optimisation Component internals

Figure 2 depicts the internal architecture of the IS-SLAM POC. The core component is the *runner*, which executes the (usually complex) tasks of evaluating SLA offers or creating new SLA offers, according to some utility measure. The *MonitorabilityChecker* communicates SLAs to the monitoring manager, so that the capability to monitor a SLA can be confirmed. The *PlanManager* submits the plans that the *ResourceProcessManager* creates to the PAC. Then, *ProvisionStatus* receives information from the PAC, so that if some provisioning is violated, other options and alternatives can be evaluated.

The algorithm implemented essentially solves the following problem:

- Minimise the cost of implementing an SLA for infrastructure resources of a specific type and quantity;
- Give a base cost that may be increased by the provider to achieve better quality (without the customer having requested it) as a means of improving Quality of Service (QoS) and therefore, in the long run, reputation;
- Take into account mass-purchase reductions, and the cost of implementing some increased QoS requested by the user;

- Ensure that the standard profit, according to implementation costs, minus extra costs (voluntarily taken up by the provider) exceeds some threshold value; and
- Keep failure probability (as predicted based on models, monitoring data and so on) lower than some threshold value.

The problem definition can be illustrated as follows:

$$\sum_i (1+\beta^i) \cdot N^i \cdot \sigma^i \cdot C_B^i + C_E^i \qquad (1)$$

$$\sum_i [g^i(C_I^i, C_E^i) - \beta^i \cdot C_I^i] \geq F^* \qquad (2)$$

$$h^i(\beta^i, T^i) \leq P_V^{i*} \qquad (3)$$

$$0 \leq \beta^i, \forall i \qquad (4)$$

The problem being solved is how to minimise cost (Expression 1) while profit and the probability of failure remain within acceptable limits as dictated by high-level business rules (Equations 2 and 3). $F^*$ represents a minimum acceptable profit, that depends on the customer's profile; and $P_V^{i*}$ represents a maximum acceptable failure probability, which may also be associated with specific customers or other business conditions at the time of negotiation.

The result of solving this problem is a selection of resources to be outsourced if they are not available locally (represented by an external implementation cost), the additional QoS measures for the provider, and eventually, a price quotation to be handed to the customer: that is, the value to be minimised in the expression 1.

## 4.2 Infrastructure Provisioning and Adjustment

The Provisioning and Adjustment Component has a generic part (Figure 3), and a non-generic part that must be customised before application to a specific use case.

In the case of the ISLAM, the *ActionExecutionTask* had to be re-implemented to properly invoke the Infrastructure Service Manager (ISM). This task must be added to an agent. On system start-up, this agent configures and instantiates itself, after which it starts the specified tasks by communicating with the ISM.

Once the system is provisioned, the PAC starts listening to the event bus to receive messages informing it about the status of the service. These messages are usually domain-specific, so the format and a parser that will translate the xml message to Java classes must be provided and added to the configuration file.

Monitoring events are fed into a drools rule engine managed by an *AnalysisTask*. For the infrastructure layer, specific rules have been written which analyse the different received events and trigger different actions: re-provisioning, restarting of a Virtual Machine (VM), or allocation of extra resources.

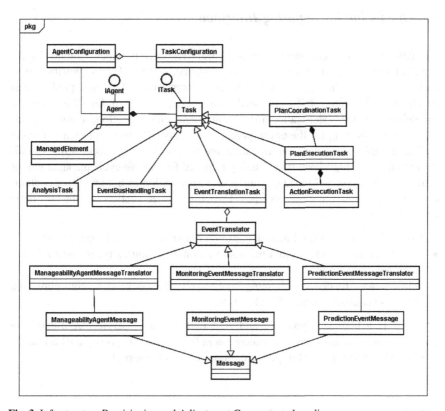

**Fig. 3** Infrastructure Provisioning and Adjustment Component class diagram

## 5 Infrastructure Service Manager

Conceptually, the infrastructure service manager (ISM) is responsible for the creation, life cycle management, internal optimisation and manipulation of infrastructure resources. The scope of infrastructural resources includes:

- Compute resources - entities that perform computation
- Network resources - entities that link two or more resources
- Storage resources - entities that allow for state to be persisted

The ISM communicates with the actual provisioning system(s) that manage such resources and is not aware of SLA concerns. The ISM exposes its functionality to clients through a generic interface and an associated data model and both abstract the low-level details of the provisioning system supported.

## 5.1 Open Cloud Computing Interface

To facilitate a consistent interface into arbitrary resource providers, the need for a standard, extensible, open interface was identified, and this led to contribution to and co-chairing of the Open Cloud Computing Interface (OCCI). Now published as an Open Grid Forum (OGF) proposed-recommended standard, OCCI is designed to "deliver an API specification for remote management of cloud computing infrastructure, allowing for the development of interoperable tools for common tasks including deployment, autonomic scaling and monitoring. The scope of the specification will be all high level functionality required for the life-cycle management of virtual machines (or workloads) running on virtualisation technologies (or containers) supporting service elasticity" [4]. The current specification is split into three complimentary documents:

- Core - defining the OCCI model, common resource types and shared attributes.
- Infrastructure - defining the infrastructure domain resource types, their relevant attributes and actions.
- HTTP header rendering - defining how the OCCI model can be communicated and thus serialised using HTTP headers.

OCCI is a boundary protocol and API that acts as a service front-end to a provider's internal infrastructure management framework. It exposes a RESTful interface [5] and a number of implementations[1] and tools support it[2].

## 6 Infrastructure Service Manager Implementation

The reference implementation of the ISM was designed for flexibility rather than for speed. It illustrates and prototypes several different layers of abstraction, rather than implement the most efficient way to manage an infrastructure service. The layers of the ISM are illustrated in Figure 4.

The ISLAM communicates with the ISM through an ISM proxy. The ISM proxy is an OSGi [6] bundle that implements the SLA@SOI ISM interface. It converts infrastructure calls to their OCCI equivalents using a JClouds [7] OCCI API developed during the implementation. The ISM core implementation itself is built on Grails [8] for flexibility, and exposes an OCCI API as defined and uses the OCCI ANTLR [9] Grammar[3]. It essentially implements an OCCI interface, controllers (computer, storage, network, query, reservation), model (the infrastructure landscape), and services (infrastructure, reservation and messaging) and implements all necessary logic to manipulate the underlying provisioning system.

---

[1] http://occi-wg.org/community/implementations/

[2] http://occi-wg.org/community/tools/

[3] https://github.com/dizz/occi-grammar

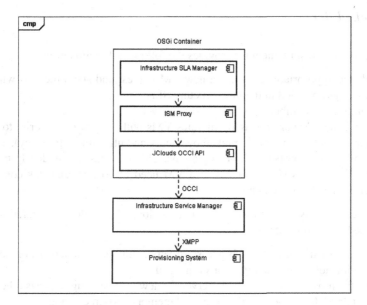

**Fig. 4** Layers of the infrastructure service manager

# 7 Provisioning System

Apache Tashi was selected as the primary provisioning system for the reference
SLA@SOI infrastructure layer implementation. Tashi can manage KVM and Xen
hypervisors that run on a clustered set of physical machines. Several enhancements
were developed and integrated into Tashi to better support an SLA-enabled infrastructure. In particular, two modules for VM management were designed, developed,
tested, contributed back into the Tashi open-source project and made available for
integration into other provisioning systems. These modules addressed scheduling
and VM re-provisioning.

The new scheduler controls allocation of virtual machines to physical machines.
The allocation takes into account infrastructure SLA specifications for virtual machines as well as data centre policies which might, for example, influence allocation based on server efficiency, energy consumption, user priorities and over-
provisioning targets for the resources.

The new VM re-provisioning extension enables dynamic resource management
of CPU, memory, network bandwidth and disk bandwidth for the virtual machines.

These modules are now described in some detail:

## 7.1 Scheduler

The SLA@SOI Tashi Scheduler provides the following functionality:

- Finds the appropriate server for a new VM request and starts the VM with parameters as specified in the infrastructure SLA;
- Minimises the number of active physical servers;
- When some VMs are released, migrates VMs with the highest priority to more efficient servers (servers are ranked by energy and utilisation efficiency); and
- Minimises the number of VM migrations. This is necessary as during the live migration process two instances of a VM need to coexist, and this consumes potentially valuable resources.

The scheduler is implemented as an endless loop. The following operations are performed in a single iteration:

- Checks if distribution of VMs across servers complies with server policies and user priorities. Triggers migrations if needed.
- Finds the most efficient available server for new provisioning requests (checking for available CPU speed, CPU cores and memory resources); and
- If no available servers are found, identifies the most appropriate server for over-provisioning based on the CPU over-provisioning policy, if any. CPU over-provisioning policies define if virtual CPU speed and cores can exceed the actual physical resources (and if so by how much) .

A search for the appropriate server for a new VM request can be essentially viewed as a constraint satisfaction problem. Let $h^i_{cores}$ denote the number of CPU cores on a physical server $h^i$, let $h^i_{cpu}$ denote the CPU speed in MHz and let $h^i_{mem}$ denote the amount of memory of $h^i$ in megabytes. The number of physical servers is denoted by $k$ and the number of VMs that are running on $h^i$ is $n^i$. A request for a new VM can be described as $v = \{v_{cores}, v_{cpu}, v_{mem}\}$, where CPU cores, CPU and memory are specified for a VM request. Running VMs are described as $v_{ij} = \{v^{ij}_{cores}, v^{ij}_{cpu}, v^{ij}_{mem}\}$, where $v_{ij}$ denotes a running VM on a server $h_i$ and $j < n_i$. Let $opr_{cores}$ denote the over-provisioning rate for CPU cores and $opr_{cpu}$ the over-provisioning rate for CPU speed. These two variables are defined by the over-provisioning policy and are part of the scheduler configuration. When over-provisioning variables are set to 1, then over-provisioning is not allowed. An example of the scheduler configuration parameters is as follows:

```
loadExpression = memUsage + coresUsage * 512 + cpuUsage
cpuCoresOverRate= 2
cpuSpeedOverRate = 1
rescheduleAfterStart = True
```

The problem of finding the most suitable server for over-provisioning can be illustrated as follows:

$$minimize(f(0, a^i_{cores}, a^i_{cpu})) \ where \ 1 \leq i \leq k \ and:$$

$$\sum_{j=1}^{n_i} v^{ij}_{cores} + v_{cores} \leq h^i_{cores} \cdot opr_{cores}$$

$$\sum_{j=1}^{n_i} v^{ij}_{cpu} + v_{cpu} \leq h^i_{cpu} \cdot opr_{cpu}$$

$$\sum_{j=1}^{n_i} v^{ij}_{mem} + v_{mem} \leq h^i_{mem}$$

$$(5)$$

The variables $a^i_{cores}$ and $a^i_{cpu}$ denote the number of already over-provisioned CPU cores and CPUs on a server $h^i$. Function $f$ is used to calculate how heavily a host is loaded or (if for a VM) what is the weight or load of the VM. This is an arbitrary formula involving three parameters and is defined in the scheduler configuration. The default load function is $memUsage + coresUsage \cdot 512 + cpuUsage$. This way the relative importance of the memory, CPU speed or CPU cores can be configured. The first parameter in the load function in the last constraint is 0, because memory over-provisioning is not allowed.

A scheduler uses a systematic search to find a solution. First the servers are sorted by the function such that servers with the smallest over-provisioning load are at the beginning of the phase of traversing the space of solutions. Memory and CPU resources are then checked. When the first appropriate server is found, the scheduler search phase is stopped and the VM is provisioned on the identified server.

## 7.2 Re-provisioning

A re-provisioning module for KVM and Xen hypervisors has been implemented to provide options should SLA violations arise or adjustments be required. Re-provisioning actions are executed when the higher-level components detect that the negotiated and provisioned resources are not satisfying the business SLA demands.

The re-provisioning module includes the functionality for runtime adaptation of VM resources, including CPU, memory, network and disk bandwidth. Virtual machines do not need to be restarted to apply changes to these assigned resources. When an SLA violation is detected by infrastructure monitoring, the ISLAM prepares the re-provisioning plan and sends it to the re-provisioning module via the ISM. Based on the new virtual machine requirements (typically including an increased amount of CPU or memory resources), the re-provisioning module executes the adjustments and spawns a live migration if required.

The re-provisioning module is implemented using Cgroups, the resource manager for Linux containers. Cgroups enables assignment of shares of CPU, memory, I/O and disk bandwidth to processes that need to be controlled. Importantly, Cgroups does not require VMs to be restarted to apply the changes in resources. Cgroups is applied directly on the VM processes. The code snippet below shows how we prepare CPU group for a new VM.

```
if not os.path.exists("/dev/cpu/tasks"):
  print "mounting Cgroups CPU module"
  subprocess.call("sudo mkdir -p /dev/cpu", shell=True)
  subprocess.call(\
    "mount -t cgroup -ocpu cpu /dev/cpu", shell=True)
if os.path.exists("/dev/cpu/tasks"):
  # create CPU Cgroup for this virtual machine:
  subprocess.call(\
    "sudo mkdir -p /dev/cpu/qemu%s" %\
    vmId, shell=True)
  print "CPU Cgroup qemu%s created" % vmId
  # specify a share for this group:
  subprocess.call(\
    "echo %s | sudo tee /dev/cpu/qemu%s/cpu.shares" %\
    (cpu_share, vmId), shell=True)
  subprocess.call(\
    "echo %s | sudo tee /dev/cpu/qemu%s/tasks" %\
    (pid, vmId), shell=True)
```

When re-provisioning is needed, adaptCpuShare is available to adjust the CPU share for a specific VM. Similar functionality is provided for memory, disk and network bandwidth.

```
def adaptCpuShare(self, vmId, share):
  status = 0
  if os.path.exists("/dev/cpu/tasks"):
    subprocess.call(\
      "echo %s | sudo tee /dev/cpu/qemu%s/cpu.shares" %\
      (share, vmId), shell=True)
    log.info("Cpu share %s given to the Cgroup qemu%s" %\
      (share, vmId))
  else:
    status = 1
    log.error("CPU Cgroup is not mounted")
  return status
```

# 8 Infrastructure Monitoring

A key part of any SLA-aware system is performance monitoring. Without it, there is no awareness of SLA violations and no knowledge of when adjustment actions need to be taken. The low-level monitoring system (LLMS) is the component in the SLA@SOI framework that is responsible for infrastructure monitoring and alerting the higher-level components about any infrastructure SLA violations. The LLMS is a key component enabling the infrastructure to cope with failure. An SLA specified at the customer-level is translated during SLA negotiation into the infrastructure SLA that defines the exact conditions under which the infrastructure services are to be delivered to meet the customer's needs. The infrastructure SLA includes a definition of the initial configuration of VMs and definition of the monitoring, logging and alerting details. The LLMS monitors the low-level infrastructure metrics, including server uptime as well as CPU, memory, storage and network utilisation, and performance, based on the settings in the infrastructure SLA.

The components of the LLMS are automatically provisioned according to the needs of the consumers of the monitoring information. Distributed monitoring components are managed intelligently, with management commands distributed from a node on one layer to all associated nodes on the layer below. This decentralised management helps ensure the solution is scalable up to very large scale infrastructure deployments. The structure of the infrastructure monitoring components is shown in Figure 5.

Infrastructure Monitoring spans all layers but focuses on the infrastructure resources. The Infrastructure SLA Manager (ISLAM) is responsible for assessing SLA offers and planning the monitoring strategies. Optimal monitoring execution is defined and sent to the LLMS via the ISM. The ISLAM also retrieves information from the LLMS historical database, analysing the repeating patterns, predicting if a problem is about to occur, and forcing adjustments to deployments totry to prevent the issue. When an Infrastructure SLA violation is detected by the LLMS, the notifying message is reported back to the ISLAM to trigger corrective actions. More details about the overall SLA@SOI monitoring architecture can be found in Chapter 'Dynamic Creation of Monitoring Infrastructures'.

Ganglia [10] is used as the LLMS base monitoring engine because of its scalability and design for high-performance computing systems. Other monitoring engines can be plugged into the LLMS or custom, arbitrary sensors can be written. Some of the monitoring interactions can be seen in Figure 6.

The LLMS exposes its monitoring features to the ISM, which sends monitoring requests back to the LLMS after synchronisation with the ISLAM. An example of a monitoring request is shown in Figure 7.

The LLMS is automatically configured on the basis of the monitoring request from the ISM, and starts monitoring the required QoS characteristics for VMs and physical servers on specified clusters. The crucial part of the monitoring request is information about SLA violation thresholds, enabling the LLMS to send notifying messages about SLA warnings and violations to higher-level components. Monitoring data is periodically stored into the historical database and can be accessed by the ISLAM to analyse the root causes of any violations.

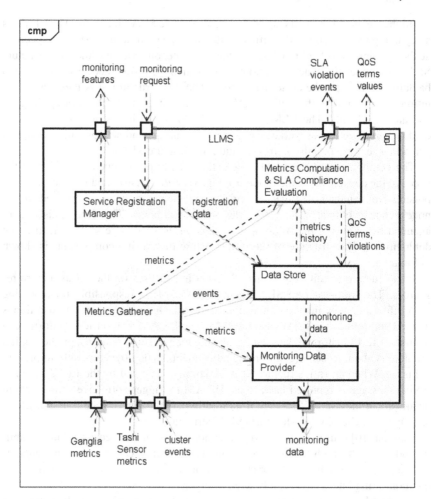

**Fig. 5** Components of the monitoring system

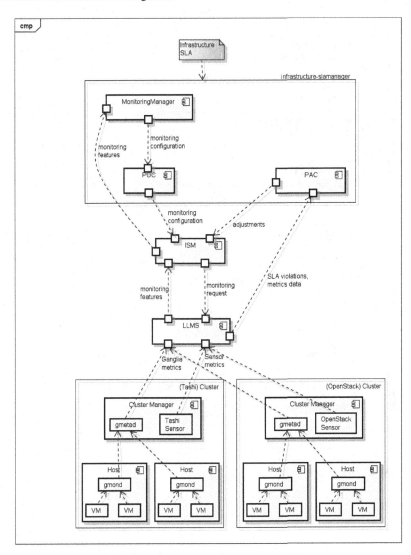

**Fig. 6** Monitoring interactions

```
{ 1
2 "serviceURL":
3       "slasoi://myManagedObject.company.com/Service/TravelService",
4 "serviceName": "TravelService",
5 "vmList": [
6   {
7     "id": "16",
8     "name": "vm1",
9     "hostName": "iricbl011.openlab.com",
10    "dnsName": "vm1.openlab.com",
11    "clusterName": "Tashi"
12  },
13  {
14    "id": "17",
15    "name": "vm2",
16    "hostName": "iricbl012.openlab.com",
17    "dnsName": "vm2.openlab.com",
18    "clusterName": "Tashi"
19  }
20 ],
21 "guaranteedQoSTerms": [
22  {
23    "qosTermUri": "http://www.slaatsoi.org/commonTerms#availability",
24    "constraintExpression": ">99.0",
25    "constraintExpressionUnit":
26    "http://www.slaatsoi.org/coremodel/units#percentage"
27  },
28  {
29    "qosTermUri": "http://www.slaatsoi.org/resources#memory",
30    "constraintExpression": ">=150",
31    "constraintExpressionUnit":
32    "http://www.slaatsoi.org/coremodel/units#MB"
33  },
34  {
35    "qosTermUri": "http://www.slaatsoi.org/resources#vm_cores",
36    "constraintExpression": ">=1",
37    "constraintExpressionUnit": ""
38  }
39 ]
40
```

**Fig. 7** Monitoring request

# 9 Conclusions

This chapter introduces the significance of SLA-enabled infrastructure management and describes the architecture and reference implementation of such a set of components. The infrastructure SLA manager, infrastructure service manager, provisioning system and low-level monitoring system are all documented. External contributions to open research initiatives including OGF's Open Cloud Computing Interface and Apache's Tashi provisioning system are also summarised, representing considerable ongoing exploitation opportunities for this work.

# References

[1] The Apache Software Foundation: Apache Tashi. URL http://incubator.apache.org/tashi/. Last retrieved 2011-06-15

[2] Open Grid Forum: Open Cloud Computing Interface. URL http://occi-wg.org/. Last retrieved 2011-06-15

[3] The XMPP Standards Foundation: The Extensible Messaging and Presence Protocol (XMPP). URL http://xmpp.org/. Last retrieved 2011-06-15

[4] OCCI Working Group: Charter of OCCI-WG. URL http://www.ogf.org/gf/group\_info/charter.php?review\&group=occi-wg. Last retrieved 2011-06-15

[5] Fielding, R: Architectural Styles and the Design of Network-based Software Architectures. URL http://www.ics.uci.edu/~fielding/pubs/dissertation/top.htm. Last retrieved 2011-06-15

[6] OSGi Alliance: Open Services Gateway initiative (OSGi). URL http://www.osgi.org. Last retrieved 2011-06-15

[7] JClouds: Multi-Cloud Library. URL http://www.jclouds.org/. Last retrieved 2011-06-15

[8] SpringSource: Grails. URL http://www.grails.org/. Last retrieved 2011-06-15

[9] ANTLR: ANother Tool for Language Recognition (ANTLR). URL http://www.antlr.org/. Last retrieved 2011-06-15

[10] Ganglia: Ganglia Monitoring System. URL http://ganglia.sourceforge.net/. Last retrieved 2011-06-15

# Part VIII
# Selected Business Use Cases

# Introduction to the SLA@SOI Industrial Use Cases

## Ensuring a Realistic Context for Evaluation and for Determining Readiness for Adoption

Joe M. Butler

## 1 Introduction

The holistic nature of SLA@SOI's SLA management framework, comprehending both the full service stack and the service life cycle, presents challenges in scope, requirements, and evaluation of technical performance and business impact. To provide practical boundaries of scope, while realistically responding to the practical and substantial real-world challenges of advancements in automatic service management, four industrial use cases have been selected to underpin SLA@SOI's technical work. The industrial use cases are complementary in nature. Individually, they focus on particular aspects of the SLA framework as they relate to the technology stack and service life cycle. Additionally, each use case is grounded in a particular usage area or application domain. Each use case is driven by an industrial partner with expertise and substantial commercial activity in their particular domain. As such, the use cases have been designed for authentic reflection of the domains they represent. Collectively, the use cases exercise the full technical scope of the SLA management framework components. They take a common approach to evaluation, ensuring the business evaluation in particular is consistent, and that evaluations from each domain can be interpreted for consideration elsewhere.

## 2 Considerations for Use Case Selection

A clear consideration when selecting the use cases was the domain representation offered by industrial partners in the project. However, the specific nature of the use cases is a result of more detailed consideration of the SLA framework and ways

Intel Ireland Limited, Collinstown Industrial Park, Leixlip, Ireland,
e-mail: `joe.m.butler@intel.com`

in which requirements and industrial assessments could be validated consistently. Examples of such considerations are detailed below.

Primary differentiation between the industrial use cases:

- Focus on software provisioning and management: SLAs will be critical for adoption of cloud/SaaS services by enterprise. Issues such as performance modelling, resource consumption, constraint management, monitoring and metering need to be comprehended in an SLA format (Chapter 'The ERP Hosting Use Case Scenario').
- Focus on infrastructure provisioning and management: It is assumed that virtualised infrastructure is consumed as a fully elastic PaaS/IaaS type service with standardised interfaces for negotiation and SLA management. It is also assumed that IaaS/PaaS service providers will require manageability stacks to comprehend internal objectives and constraints, as well as SLA-defined KPIs for new and running services (Chapter 'The Enterprise IT Use Case Scenario').
- Focus on service aggregation: Automatic negotiation and management of SLAs paves the way for a highly scalable service environment. The natural progression is the scenario of aggregation, wherein services can be dynamically composed in a multi-party environment with an SLA hierarchy managing QoS and other details (Chapter 'The Service Aggregator Use Case Scenario').
- Focus on integration of human-based services: In many domains, business processes comprise a blend of ICT-based and human-based services. This is generally driven by practicalities of the service/consumer interface or by a requirement for judgment-type decisions which cannot be automated (Chapter 'The eGovernment Use Case Scenario').


Further considerations:
- Service variation: No specific assumption is made regarding the lifetime of services. Long-lived processes and services can coexist with more dynamic, short-lived services in any of the use cases.
- Heterogeneous infrastructure landscapes: Real-world data centres are assumed, including variations in the infrastructure fleet that create specific challenges for efficient management. Also, it is assumed that different VM and VM management options will be appropriate for different services.
- Efficiency and sustainability: Efficiency is an emerging concern across industry sectors. In the context of the SLA management framework, this is most relevant to infrastructure management and is considered as an internal objective within the enterprise IT use case.
- Interoperability: It is assumed that the service marketplace for platform and infrastructure services is dynamic and that a range of offerings should be easily integrated and consumed. Open standards and interface specifications are adopted across use cases.

# 3 Use Case Key Elements

A minimal basic structure was established to enable necessary consistency across the use cases, while allowing the flexibility necessary for each to meaningfully reflect their core domain. The following elements comprise this basic structure:

- Scenario-based: To take full advantage of the domains represented, the use cases are subdivided into scenarios. Each scenario examines the contribution of the SLA framework in different ways. The scenarios, for example, can represent distinct phases of a service life cycle, or differentiate between the operation and strategic perspectives of a key stakeholder.
- Alignment to business objectives: To ensure consistency in validation and evaluation, each use case is positioned in support of objectives that are specific to its domain. These objectives are high-level and representative of typical organisations within the use case domain. Each use case has created its own mapping that allows measurable and judgment-assessed contributions from the SLA framework to be translated into positive impact in support of relevant business objectives.

The following chapters deal with the four industrial use cases individually, and describe in detail their use and evaluation of the SLA Management Framework, and its relevance to the industrial domain in question.

# The ERP Hosting Use Case Scenario
## Managing On-Demand Business Applications with Hierarchical Service Level Agreements

Wolfgang Theilmann, Jens Happe, and Ulrich Winkler

**Abstract** Business applications are increasing delivered as on-demand services and Service Level Agreements (SLAs) are a common way to specify the exact conditions under which these services should be delivered, both for business- and IT-based services. This paradigm of service-orientation is expanding into different domains, including business and IT-based services. Services are composed of other services across domains, and as such SLAs must be managed across service hierarchies. Here, we present the lessons learned from applying a generic, multi-layer SLA management framework to the context of on-demand business applications. We explain the architecture implemented and show how a hierarchy of services can be managed using SLAs. We also explain how SLAs can be established for different layers and how SLA terms are translated across the service hierarchy.

## 1 Introduction

Traditional business applications have largely been delivered as on-premise deployed solutions. However, the need for increased business agility and decreased cost of ownership has resulted in an increasing demand for business applications delivered as on-demand services (following the paradigms of cloud computing ([2]) and software as a service (SaaS)). Service customers expect increased agility and reduced effort since they can access and use business applications without having to

Wolfgang Theilmann
SAP Research Karlsruhe, Vincenz-Priessnitz-Str. 1,
e-mail: Wolfgang.Theilmann@sap.com

Jens Happe
SAP Research Karlsruhe, Vincenz-Priessnitz-Str. 1, e-mail: Jens.Happe@sap.com

Ulrich Winkler
SAP Research Belfast, The Concourse, Queen's Road, Belfast BT3 9DT, United Kingdom,
e-mail: ulrich.winkler@sap.com

manage them. Service providers consider this a model for exploiting economies of scale, but also face challenges in terms of expected quality and price sensitivity.

This chapter reports on the lessons learned from the enterprise resource planning (ERP) hosting use case, in which we applied the SLA@SOI framework to manage on-demand business applications such as ERP applications with hierarchical SLAs. We explain the architecture used for SLA management and show how SLAs can be specified at different layers of the service hierarchy. We also explain how SLA terms can be translated along the service hierarchy. The analysis demonstrates both technical feasibility and achieved business value.

The remainder of this chapter is organised as follows: Section 2 discusses the general business context and business objectives that we follow. Section 3 briefly introduces technical and organisational foundations and related work. In Section 4, we explain our use-case-specific adoption and extensions to the framework architecture. Section 5 explains the actual SLA hierarchies and SLA translations for our use case, and Section 6 summarises the business evaluation. Section 7 provides a summary and outlook.

## 2 Business Context

Within the traditional enterprise software market, enterprise customers host their own solutions, using money and resources to set up and maintain the complete environment, taking all risks upon themselves. Usually, customers buy software installations from the provider and then, with an additional contract, the provider sends regular legal updates to the customer and guarantees support.

In the past, a complementary delivery model was application service provisioning, in which service providers offered completely hosted applications or application suites. The idea was to move the burden of hosting and managing IT solutions away from customers. However, the success of these approaches — in particular for mission-critical enterprise software — was limited for two main reasons: first, application service hosting did not provide sufficient flexibility (requiring a long time to set up or change procedures) and second, it lacked transparency and dependability of actual service-level qualities.

A key trend in software markets is the shift to on-demand business based on the SaaS delivery model. Customers increasingly buy software services that suit their business needs. They demand software that can be consumed in a fast and flexible manner without concern regarding ownership of the required IT resources. In doing this, they rely on the availability and quality of these services to operate their own business. Hence, they require strong guarantees as to the quality of service provided. Dependable service levels will thus become a major differentiator in the market of on-demand software solutions and the Internet of Services.

SLAs are crucial elements for

- specifying and agreeing to the conditions under which services are delivered to customers, and

- managing a service landscape such that resources are efficiently used according to customer needs.

Looking at the current trend from service-enabled applications to SaaS and Internet of Service scenarios, we foresee an enormous competitive pressure for service providers to professionalise and automate their service offerings and management by introducing the notion of SLAs.


## 2.1 Roles

Within the environment of on-demand software services, there is a relationship between customers and providers, as well as more fine-grained roles that come into play. These are related to the different activities required in a service provider organisation, and also to the idea of applying the paradigm of service-orientation at different layers of a provider. For the ERP hosting use case, we distinguish the following main roles:

- Customer: The customer of a SaaS solution
- Sales officer: The business expert from the sales department who decides on the portfolio of offered SAP SaaS solutions.
- IT SaaS architect: The SaaS IT architect who supports portfolio planning from a technical perspective
- SaaS administrator: The administrator of software and services (SaaS)
- IT administrator: The administrator of an infrastructure SaaS provider

  Figure 1 shows use cases involving these roles.


## 2.2 Business Objectives

We distinguish three main business objectives: dynamic service provisioning, efficiency, and transparent service management.

*Dynamic service provisioning* is about delivering trusted value to customers. This value should be evident in the ease of service consumption (simplification of the processes involved in consuming a desired service), service dependability (the trustworthiness of non-functional aspects that complement the functional scope of a service), and flexibility (the ability for customers to change previous service agreements and to react quickly to a changed business context). The most relevant ways to realise this objective are to focus on automation of service provisioning activities, context-driven SLA specification, and renegotiation means for customers.

*Efficiency* relates to service providers and is about providing business value in terms of reduced total cost of ownership (TCO). This boils down to environmental efficiency (the energy efficiency of a hosted solution), technical efficiency (the

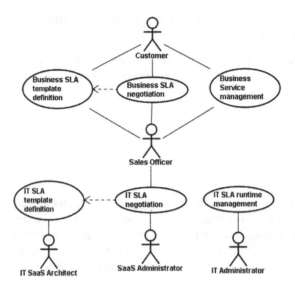

**Fig. 1** Roles and use cases.

amount of hardware and its use), and process efficiency (the ability to run day-to-day processes effectively and to complete certain management tasks and procedures on time and within budget). The most relevant ways to realise this objective are to focus on tailoring of planning and prediction capabilities, run-time adjustment possibilities, a clear governance structure that streamlines processes and fosters reuse, integrated quality management, and standardised operations.

*Transparent service management* constitutes a more qualitative value for service providers and addresses their ability to oversee the complex dependencies of advanced business solutions on various software, middleware and infrastructure artefacts. Increased transparency is a major business benefit for service providers and will eventually contribute to increased efficiency, dependability, and an ability to flexibly react to changed market conditions. The area includes indicators such as End2End manageability (the consistent and integrated management of services, SLAs and resources, including the overarching control of multiple co-running services and service offers), the ability to choose from different options (flexible use and selection from all available resources to best satisfy current needs), and the agility to change operations (the provider's ability to react quickly and adopt a running system to reflect ongoing changes in various business conditions). The most relevant way to realise this objective is to develop a predefined and clear framework with strong monitoring capabilities that allow for cross-relating events. Further, a model-driven management approach significantly contributes to agility and rapid adjustments.

# 3 Foundations

## *3.1 Service Hierarchies for Business Applications*

As a founding concept for the remainder of this chapter, we introduce a basic reference structure for business applications that sets the basis for structuring business systems in a service-oriented way. We also provide a brief sketch of aspects relevant to SLA management. Actual applications may of course differ from this structure. Our setting comes with four levels: business solution, application, middleware and infrastructure. These latter three directly match the well-known cloud hierarchy of software, platform and infrastructure as a service (SaaS, PaaS, IaaS).

*Business Solution.* At the top-most level, customers do not simply expect running software applications, but a complete solution to their business needs. These business solutions go beyond the pure provisioning of software and may include aspects such as human support (for setup and maintenance), compliance (security and archiving), or legal constraints. Any SLA at this level must be expressed in business terms: that is, it must be easily understood by business people in the customer's organisation. Lower-level technical details such as CPU specifications and such should be omitted.

*Application (SaaS).* At this level comes the actual business application: the software solution offered to the customer. SLAs covering business applications must be expressed in the language of a business analyst: that is, they must be easily understood by the person who eventually uses the software. Such SLAs cover aspects such as the number of orders that can be processed per minute.

*Middleware (PaaS).* Business applications rely on common middleware components such as application servers, messaging systems and databases. Middleware components may be shared across different applications and customers; such middleware platforms can be also considered as service offerings, where the middleware eventually hosts or is used by different client applications. Typical examples for this approach include the Google App Engine ([4]) or Amazon storage services ([1]). SLAs concerning middleware components must be expressed in the language of application (platform) developers and be independent from the actual application. They cover aspects such as application server transaction response time or throughput.

*Infrastructure (IaaS).* This lowest layer comprises infrastructure resources (both physical and virtual) that are offered as services following the infrastructure cloud ([2]) paradigm (IaaS). SLAs covering infrastructure are expressed in basic technical parameters such as the number of CPU cores, memory size, and so on.

## 3.2 Related Work

SLA management for on-demand business applications has been partially addressed from different angles. Here we consider some of the most similar known works in the areas of IT management and SLA translation. SLAs have been added as a concept to multiple IT management tools and frameworks (Governance Interoperability Framework ([5]) and CentraSite ([10]). However, these tools support SLA management at a single service layer and do not address multiple layers and their interrelations. SLA translation has been heavily researched under different contexts in multiple areas. A thorough overview of SLA translation techniques can be found in [9]. Most prominent of these techniques are Layered Queuing Network (LQN) models, which support the explicit modelling of a system of layers and subsequent performance analysis. Another prominent approach from [3] uses coloured Petri nets to capture dependencies within a chain of services.

Our work differs from these approaches in that it (1) manages SLAs across multiple layers, (2) integrates aspects of planning/prediction with actual IT management, (3) considers a larger set of SLA parameters, and (4) is applied to an existing commercial business application.

## 4 SLA Management Architecture

In the following, we describe an SLA management architecture that can be used for business applications. It relies on the general reference architecture described in Chapter 'Reference Architecture for Multi-Level SLA Management'. Following the reference structure sketched in Section 3, our SLA management solution for business applications needs to support SLAs at four layers: business, application, middleware and infrastructure.

The SLA management framework offers a range of possibilities for managing the service stack of our on-demand business applications. At one extreme, we might have a separate SLA manager and a separate service manager for each of these layers; at the other extreme, all knowledge could be brought into one SLA manager and one service manager respectively.

The solution we adopted is shown in Figure 2 and comprises three SLA managers (SLAMs) and four service managers (SMs). Arrows show general dependency relationships.

With this design, we reflect an organisation divided into three main units: the business/sales unit, the software unit and the infrastructure unit. Each unit can oversee all the SLAs it is currently operating. Further, we have four types of artefacts that contribute to the realised services. Each domain requires different administration knowledge and we have therefore encapsulated these types into four separate SMs: an SM for support services (including human resources that must be planned and managed), for application services, for middleware services, and for infrastructure services.

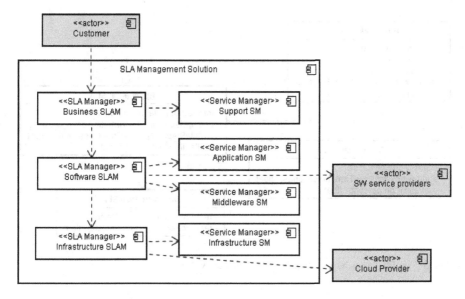

**Fig. 2** SLA management architecture for business applications.

The design also considers the two types of third party service providers: cloud providers and software service providers. Cloud providers offer infrastructure services, which can be considered at any time (to handle burst-load scenarios); software providers can be considered if the actual business application should be complemented with additional functionality.

# 5 SLA Hierarchies

This section analyses SLAs needed for dealing with the four abovementioned layers of services. In particular, we highlight the translation of SLA terms across these layers.

Figure 3 provides an overview of the SLA hierarchy and lists some main SLA terms for each layer. While in principal, cardinalities from higher- to lower-level SLAs can be one to many, our actual evaluation is based on simple one to one analysis. Business and infrastructure SLAs are managed by their respective SLA manager; application and middleware SLAs are both managed by the software SLA manager.

In the following, we discuss the management and translation of the respective terms.

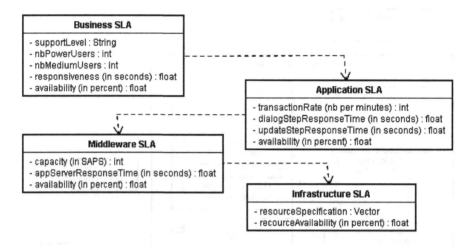

**Fig. 3** Simplified sketch of the four-layer SLA hierarchy.

## 5.1 SLA Terms and Translation

In [9], we distinguished four types of SLA translation between metric and configurables: metric-to-metric (e.g. service response time to resource utilisation), metric-to-configurable (e.g. response time to number of servers), configurable-to-metric (server specification to response time) and configurable-to-configurable (e.g. service composition to deployment options). All of these are relevant for business applications. We highlight the most important ones below:

*Solution terms* Solution terms cover conditions not directly related to the business application but describing aspects of the overall business solution. For example, the *supportLevel* term details how support around the software artefact is given (e.g. in terms of person days contributed to the setup or response time obligations for reacting to customer complaints). Solution terms can be managed by a business SLA manager in cooperation with business-level service managers. In our example, we have a support service manager, which can decide and manage the capacities of the support organisation. Other solution terms may also impact lower-level SLA managers (e.g. agreed backup schedules) and require appropriate translation.

*Workload* To plan the amount of resources needed to run a service, it is important to understand and specify the way in which customers want to use the service (e.g. does the customer only need a service occasionally or is there a complete department relying on the service in their daily work). However, it is difficult for customers to exactly predict the workload they will put on a service, and also rather unlikely that they can express this workload in technical terms. A typical approach is therefore to specify the usage profile in terms of user classes; this involves specifying the expected number of power users (working more or less constantly with a service), medium users and low users ([6]).

This specification for a business SLA now requires translation to the lower-level SLAs:

(1) The first step is to translate the user number and types into expected transaction rates, specified in the application SLA. This can be done using user type definitions for the respective application.

(2) At the next layer, transaction rates must be translated into a load characterisation of the middleware. There are many different ways to achieve this, such as benchmarking or model-based prediction. For our needs, we adopted an application-based benchmark that allows for translation of an application transaction mix into an application-independent and infrastructure-independent middleware capacity value, the so-called SAPS measure ([6]).

(3) Last, middleware workloads could be theoretically translated into infrastructure specifications (e.g. relying on micro-benchmarks). However, so far there is no generally applicable solution to this challenge. Instead, common practice is to benchmark different infrastructure setups against the respective middleware. The benchmark approach used above (step 2) can be used here to specify the capacity of a specific system setup ([6]). This allows for direct translation of the specified workload to the offered system capacity where both are expressed via the same metric (SAPS).

*Performance* The performance of a service or system is typically expressed in terms of throughput and response time. In our setup, the workload specification directly specifies the maximum throughput. If the provider guarantees a certain response time (under the condition that customer workload stays within agreed boundaries), he has also indirectly guaranteed the maximum throughput (which is exactly the maximum workload).

The specification of response time now can be done in the following way:

At the business level, the specification of responsiveness may be relatively abstract (compared to the more precise and detailed definitions for application and middleware SLAs. For example, it might simply state the general goal (that the service shall react within a certain time frame) without specifying the specific application-level operations or interactions.

At the application level, this is further refined by stating that specific classes of interactions (here dialog steps and update steps) shall be executed within a certain time-frame. The actual translation to middleware can be done using model-based or measurement-based approaches or a mixture of these. For example, in [8], we applied a specific queuing model that is calibrated by a set of benchmarking experiments.

At the middleware level, response time relates to generic elements of the middleware elements, such as application server response time on http requests or database response time on SQL operations. Response time also relates to middleware configurations such as thread pool or cache size.

At the infrastructure level, response time characteristics could be specified for aspects such as cache access time, disk seek operation, or floating point operations. In our case, such characteristics are too fine-grained and not practical for actual SLAs.

Instead, we translated response time into a configuration including parameters such as CPU speed, memory architecture, and network characteristics.

*Availability* The availability of business solutions must distinguish between planned downtimes (due, for example, to maintenance activities) and unplanned downtimes (due to actual failures at the software or hardware level). Both can and should be treated separately. Planned downtimes are typically specified via explicit time intervals within the calendar week (e.g. a maintenance window of two hours every Saturday night between 2 and 4 am). Planned downtimes can be systematically translated in a bottom-up fashion as the combination of infrastructure downtimes, middleware downtimes and application downtimes. Unplanned downtimes are specified as a percentage value via a ratio of mean time between failure and mean time to repair. Unplanned downtimes can be systematically translated in a bottom-up fashion using statistical methods ([7]).

*Energy* Energy consumption plays an increasing role in SLA specifications as customers are keen to report on their environmental compliance. Therefore, energy consumption is not just maintained as resource consumption factor at the infrastructure level, but must also be aggregated over the different SLA layers; this can be done via simple summarisaton. For simplicity reasons, energy is not in our SLAs as depicted in Figure 3.

*Cost* Costs for services at different layers can be easily aggregated as the sum of costs for lower-level services plus actual costs occurring at the actual level. At the business level, costs are typically re-labelled to a price, as here margins are added to assure the profitability of a service offer. For simplicity reasons, cost is not in our SLAs as depicted in Figure 3

## 5.2 Integrated planning

Having understood how the individual SLA terms can be translated, the next challenge is to provide support for their integrated planning. This comes with two main challenges: top-down vs. bottom-up translation, and trade-off decisions between different parameters.

*Top-down vs. bottom-up translation.* Some parameters can be translated in a top-down manner: there is a direct way to derive lower-level SLA terms from higher-level ones. For example, a workload definition for a business process can be translated to a workload of its single steps if the structure of the process is known. Other parameters must be translated in a bottom-up fashion: a higher-level term can be predicted if the values of lower-level terms are known. For example, response time and availability can be only translated bottom-up as there is a complete design space in which they must be explored (knowing the response time of a process does not determine exactly one possible response time for its individual steps).

We implemented an integrated planning algorithm that includes top-down and bottom-up translations. The algorithm works as follows: An incoming SLA request is analysed and the service manager responsible for the given service type is asked for possible service implementations, including their dependencies on lower-level services. Top-down translation is applied for selected SLA terms to narrow the search space for SLA templates for lower-level services. Once the recursive planning at the next lower level has finished, retrieved SLA templates are included in a bottom-up translation phase to predict the exact SLA guarantees that can be achieved. This algorithm is recursively executed for each SLA layer (in our case for four layers).

Figure 4 shows the flow of the integrated planing algorithm.

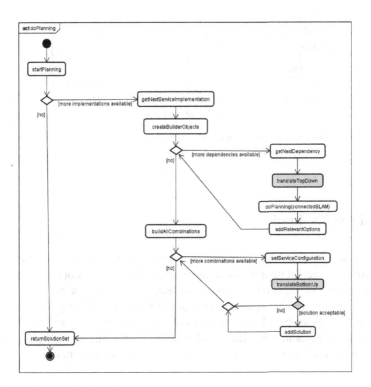

**Fig. 4** Recursive planning algorithm.

*Trade-off decisions* Conceptually, SLA planning is a multi-criteria optimisation problem where different parameters should be optimised but where optimisation of a single parameter might spoil the quality of another parameter. We addressed this issue via an evolutionary multi-objective optimisation (MOO) algorithm. This algorithm is based on a cost model (including infrastructure and energy costs) and a performance model (based on queuing networks with finite capacity regions). It computes the Pareto front of optimal trade-off solutions. Predefined business rules or humans can eventually use this Pareto front to select a solution for a specific setup. Figure 5 provides an example for such a Pareto front. It shows the trade-off between costs and performance (response time) for the TCP benchmark. Further details on this approach can be found in [8].

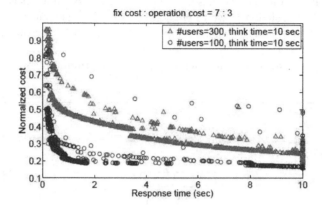

**Fig. 5** Pareto front for a cost/performance trade-off analysis.

# 6 Business Evaluation

This section evaluates the improvements achieved by applying the SLA@SOI framework. The actual improvements are described on the basis of the broader SaaS scenario, which we support by applying the framework against a comparative baseline scenario. As baseline scenario we take the traditional hosting process that realises a largely paper-based application service provisioning scenario. For confidentiality reasons, we cannot provide actual numbers in this chapter. However, we seek to provide the used metrics so that other parties can easily do comparative studies.

## 6.1 Improvements to enable dynamic service provisioning

This objective is related to two main indicators and four metrics. We assessed the indicator *Service consumption possibilities are enhanced and easy-to-use* using two metrics:

1. time to quotation, i.e. the timespan between a customer submitting a request and receiving a quote, and
2. time to provision, i.e. the timespan between a customer accepting a quote and being able to access the provisioned system.

The second indicator, *Services get dependable through SLAs*, is also assessed using two metrics:

1. number of SLA terms, i.e. the number of actual SLA terms that have been formally specified, and
2. number of SLA terms monitored, i.e. the number of actual SLA terms that are monitored and reported.

For all metrics, the evaluation resulted in an improvement by roughly a factor of ten.

## 6.2 Improvements to increase efficiency and reduce costs

This objective is related to the three indicators of environmental/energy efficiency, technical efficiency, and process efficiency, which are each assessed by one main metric, respectively:

- energy consumption per SAPS, i.e. the amount of energy required to provide a certain processing capacity
- CPU capacity per requested SAPS, i.e. the amount of CPU capacity allocated to satisfy a requested processing capacity
- the number of working hours per service request, i.e. the number of hours humans had to work to process a single customer request (including quotation and provisioning)

The evaluation resulted in improvements of between 20% and 50%.

## 6.3 Improvements to enhance transparency

This objective is related to three main indicators. The indicator *End2End manageability of a complete service hierarchy* is assessed using one metric: the number of tools/management consoles, i.e. the number of separate and not fully integrated management tools or consoles that are, or can be, used during the hosting process.

The indicator *Ability to choose from different options* is assessed using two metrics:

1. availability of an explicit product catalogue
2. customisable entries per product offer, i.e. the number of customisable SLA terms in the offered SLA templates.

The third indicator, *Agility to change*, is assessed using two metrics:

1. number of policy parameters supported
2. number of change procedures supported

The evaluation showed clear improvements in all these areas; for reasons of confidentiality we cannot provide exact details.

# 7 Conclusions

In this chapter, we have presented the lessons learned from applying a generic, multi-layer SLA management framework to the context of on-demand business applications. We described how a hierarchy of four service domains (business, application, middleware, and infrastructure) can be established. We also specified the representation of selected SLA terms at various layers and their translation across layers. Last, we sketched a method for integrated planning that combines top-down and bottom-up translation and also allows for determination of trade-offs. The business evaluation shows significant improvements in dynamic service provisioning, efficiency, and transparent service management.

Future work will focus on adjustment activities that analyse monitored SLA violations and decide on corrective actions to safeguard SLAs. Again, this is a multi-layer challenge, since both SLA violations and adjustment actions can occur at different layers and require proper synchronisation. We plan to explore complex event-processing technologies that feed monitored metrics into a reasoning engine that supports temporal logic expressions. A further long-running activity is to research advanced PaaS environments that provide both design-time and run-time environments, and to look into supporting PaaS application developers in creating SLAs in simple but dependable ways.

# References

[1] Amazon: Amazon simple storage service (2008). URL http://aws. amazon.com/de/s3/. Last retrieved 2010-09-01
[2] Armbrust, M., et al.: Above the clouds: A berkeley view of cloud computing. Report, UC Berkeley Reliable Adaptive Distributed Systems Laboratory (2009). URL http://radlab.cs.berkeley.edu/
[3] Bodenstaff, L., Wombacher, A., Reichertand, M., Jaeger, M.: Monitoring dependencies for slas: The mode4sla approach. In: Proceedings of the IEEE International Conference on Services Computing, 2008. SCC 08, pp. 21–29 (2008)
[4] Google: Google app engine (2008). URL http://code.google.com/ intl/de/appengine/. Last retrieved 2010-09-01
[5] HP: Soa governance interoperability framework (gif) (2009). URL https://h10078.www1.hp.com/cda/hpms/display/main/ hpms\_content.jsp?zn=bto\&cp=1-11-130-27\%5E2804\ _4000\_100\_\_. Last retrieved 2010-09-01
[6] Janssen, S., Marquard, U.: Sizing SAP Systems. SAP Press (2003)
[7] Kuo, W., Prasad, V.R., Tillman, F.A., Hwang, C.L.: Optimal reliability design: fundamentals and applications. Cambridge University Press (2001)

[8] Li, H., Casale, G., Ellahi, T.: Sla-driven planning and optimization of enterprise applications. In: Proceedings of the Joint WOSP/SIPEW International Conference on Performance Engineering, January 2010 (2010)

[9] Li, H., Theilmann, W., Happe, J.: Sla translation in multi-layered service oriented architectures: Status and challenges. Technical Report 2009-8, Universität Karlsruhe (TH) (2009)

[10] Software-AG: Centrasite (2008). URL http://www.centrasite.org/. Last retrieved 2010-09-01

# The Enterprise IT Use Case Scenario
## Agile and Efficient IT Systems Provisioning to Support Evolving Business Demands

Michael Nolan and Joe M. Butler

## 1 Introduction

In the following we assume a virtualisation-enabled data centre style configuration of server capacity, and a broad range of services in terms of relative priority, resource requirement and longevity.

As a support service in most enterprises, IT is expected to deliver application and data service support to other enterprise services and lines of business. This brings varied expectations in terms of availability, mean time to recovery (MTTR), quality of service (QoS), transaction throughput capacity, and so on. In response to this, a challenge for IT organisations is the delivery of a range of service levels at optimal cost levels. This challenge includes quick turnaround planning decisions, such as provisioning and placement, runtime adjustment decisions on workload migration for efficiency, and longer-term strategic issues, such as infrastructure refresh (in the case of internally managed clouds) and the selection of a hosting service provider (in the case of external clouds).

This use case is therefore based around three distinct scenarios: The first scenario, titled *Provisioning*, responds to the issue of efficient allocation of new services in an IT infrastructure, SLA negotiation, and provisioning of new services in the environment. The second scenario, *Runtime*, deals with day-to-day, point-in-time operational efficiency decisions within the environment. These decisions maximise value that can be achieved from an infrastructure investment. The final scenario, *Investment Governance* builds on the first two scenarios to demonstrate how they feed back into future business decisions. Taking a holistic cost view, it

Michael Nolan
Intel Labs Europe, Collinstown Industrial Estate, Leixlip, Ireland,
e-mail: michael.nolan@intel.com

Joe M. Butler
Intel Labs Europe, Collinstown Industrial Estate, Leixlip, Ireland,
e-mail: joe.m.butler@intel.com

provides fine-grained SLA-based data for influencing future investment decisions based on capital, security, compute power and energy efficiency.

To enable realistic and effective reasoning at provisioning and runtime, a reference is included which differentiates each of the supported enterprise services in terms of their priority and criticality. This is the Enterprise Capability Framework or ECF. From an implementation perspective, user interaction occurs via a web-based user interface, used by both IT customers and administrators.

The enterprise IT SLA template (SLAT) defines use-case-specific agreement terms that the business SLA manager has loaded to provide inputs in response to provisioning requests in the form of PaaS services. (Software services could potentially be selected by choosing a virtual machine (VM) template containing preloaded applications, but software layer implications are not considered core to this use case and are more comprehensively dealt with in the ERP hosting use case (Chapter 'The ERP Hosting Use Case Scenario').) The business SLA manager passes service provisioning requests to the infrastructure SLA manager, whose role it is to create new VMs that constitute the service along with monitoring and reporting for that service. Evaluation of the framework is carried out with reference to parameters that align with IT and business priorities. The three scenarios on which this use case is based are complementary and allow the framework to be assessed based on realistic objectives of an enterprise IT function.

# 2 Business Context

Cloud computing is changing the way the traditional IT department manages its infrastructure fleet. As a result, the adoption of multi-year enterprise cloud computing strategies has become more common: organisations are seeking to build private cloud architectures that support their business objectives by optimising the efficiency of service delivery while eliminating security concerns and waste.

SLAs support the essential attributes of clouds as defined by the US National Institute of Standards and Technology [7] by:

- specifying and agreeing on the conditions under which cloud services are delivered to internal business units,
- managing the service landscape such that capabilities are available over the network and accessed through standard mechanisms (a web-based user interface, in the enterprise IT use case) that promote use by heterogeneous client platforms,
- supporting resource pooling where the compute resources of the provider are pooled to serve multiple consumers within the enterprise, using a multi-tenant model with different physical and virtual resources dynamically assigned and reassigned according to consumer demand and ECF priorities. The customer generally has no control over the exact location of the provided resources, but can specify location at a higher level of abstraction (e.g., country, site, or data centre),
- allowing capabilities to be automatically provisioned rapidly and elastically, enabling scale-out or back as required. To the service consumer, the capabilities

available for provisioning may appear to be unlimited and can be requested in any quantity at any time.

- providing a measured service where the SLA@SOI framework enables automatic control and optimisation of resource use by leveraging a metering capability. Resource usage is monitored, controlled, and reported, providing transparency for the service provider and consumer.

## 2.1 Business Value

Service-Orientated Architectures, including cloud computing, can only realise their potential if the business model behind their implementation is well-developed and understood. To fully leverage emerging technologies, it is not sufficient for an organisation to simply implement them with little thought as to their operation or how they will produce a return on investment. The operation, performance, utilisation and ultimately the success of any computer-based system is only as valuable and useful as the business process it is based upon. A flawed business process, when migrated, will translate into a flawed computer system. The direct business value to be realised by IT as a business enabler is in the areas of agility, dependability and automated response. The derived benefits range from efficiency (via reduced cost of ownership) to governance of future investment decisions. The importance of each, in this context, is outlined below.

## 2.2 Managing IT Like a Business

The IT Capability Maturity Framework (IT-CMF) [5] is a systematic framework developed by the IVI (Innovation Value Institute TM) consortium [6]. IVI is an open innovation consortium that spans academic, industry, public sector, consulting, analyst, and professional bodies, with more than thirty member organisations around the world. The IT-CMF assists CIOs in better managing the integral complexities and trade-offs required to continuously evolve an organisation's capacity to deliver more value from its IT infrastructure. More than 200 companies around the world currently use IT-CMF. The framework consists of four interrelated strategies for improving IT capability, identifying and prioritising opportunities, reducing costs, and optimising the business value of IT investments.

The enterprise IT use case incorporates the IT-CMF philosophy into its three scenarios, as shown in Figure 1. At the lowest tier of the framework, the "IT abyss" represents those organisations whose IT departments support an unwieldy array of inflexible, complex and siloed services. In such situations, IT spend is higher than it needs to be and the services it provides are incapable of responding to business needs in an agile way. The business may well recognise the importance of IT as an enabler, but climbing out of its IT abyss requires the adoption of a strategy to drive simplicity and flexibility throughout the IT organisation.

The IT-CMF defines some basic constructs to make this process achievable: At its most fundamental level, the IT-CMF is used to assess the business based on maturity levels ranging from 1 to 5, with 5 being the most advanced. Figure 1 provides a summary of the typical advances in IT service provision for the various levels. It is important to understand what these levels represent before discussing how the enterprise IT use case scenarios align to the principles of the IT-CMF.

| Maturity Level | Capabilities |
|---|---|
| **LEVEL 1** Initial | Management of CP's at this level is ad-hoc & based on individual efforts with no systematic improvement attempts. |
| | IT may be viewed somewhat negatively as a necessary expense whose ROI is hard to measure. Budget planning is almost non-existent. |
| **LEVEL 2** Basic | Some effort has gone into understanding the IT landscape. This may be documented informally or in silo's. Some tactical-level shared-thinking is beginning to emerge but not on a joined-up, organisational or strategic basis. |
| | IT is viewed as a 'cost centre' and seen simply as a technology supplier to the business. Focus is on predictable IT service performance and TCO. |
| **LEVEL 3** Intermediate | Formal organisation-wide documented processes are in place to help understand the IT landscape. It is often possible to identify & address gaps. |
| | IT is viewed as a 'service centre' and a technology expert. There is a systematic approach to cost reduction. ROI's are easier to measure and are based clearly on individual business cases. |
| **LEVEL 4** Advanced | Well established, effective and proven processes exist, which yield a comprehensive picture of the IT landscape. Efficiency is evident; gaps are systematically identified and proactively addressed. IT is aligned to business strategies. |
| | IT is viewed as an 'investment centre'. As a strategic business partner, IT engages actively in long-term strategic budget planning to meet the needs of the organisation. |
| **LEVEL 5** Optimising | IT is enabling and influencing future business strategies. Documented IT processes are optimised for efficiency and regularly reviewed. |
| | IT is viewed as a 'value centre' and a core competency of the organisation. |

**Fig. 1** IT-CMF maturity levels

## 2.3 The Provisioning Scenario

The provisioning scenario in the enterprise IT use case is presented as a first step in a strategy that enables flexibility and agility in the hosting of internal IT services. With the introduction of virtualisation, service provisioning can be greatly simplified. Services are now cloud-based and share common underlying infrastructures. With a reduction in the physical footprint, data centre consolidation also becomes possible. Previously manual business processes can be restructured and implemented more efficiently as web-based service-provisioning request systems.

The enterprise IT use case implements a web-based user interface to provision SLA-aware services within the cloud, where a service is defined as a logical grouping of VMs. These VMs are created from predefined templates that can include pre-installed software. A digital SLA containing dozens of measurable QoS terms is instantiated and linked to the service at the time of provisioning.

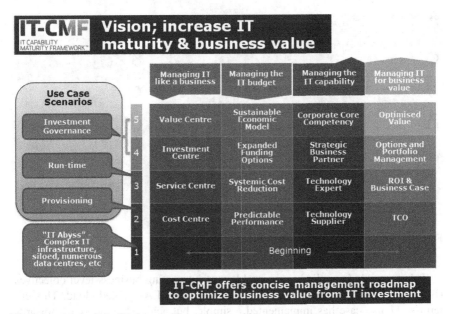

**Fig. 2** Moving from the IT abyss to IT as a value and investment centre

## 2.4 The Runtime Scenario

The runtime scenario supports an organisation's transition to the service centre tier of the IT-CMF. Optimisations are applied to runtime operations within the cloud, thus achieving systematic cost reductions. More advanced policy-based management of IT services is introduced. The ECF, shown in Figure 3, is an example of a tool that can not only help manage and guide investment decisions, but can also feed into policies that support these optimisations within the cloud. Business units are defined in the ECF and are classified as providing services that are deemed to be Base (B), Competitors (C) or Differentiators (D) of our operations in the market. The health of each unit is color-coded, helping to identify areas where investment will provide the greatest return.

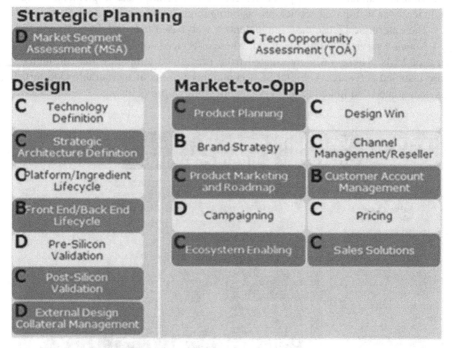

**Fig. 3** Enterprise Capability Framework (ECF)

This principle is applied to the problem of integrating business-level objectives (BLOs) in a machine-readable format for a private SLA-enabled cloud. This enterprise IT use case has implemented a simple, but achievable, approach towards demonstrating this capability, where the ECF is used to assign relative default priorities to services that belong to the various business units. The specific source of the policy—in this case, the ECF—is not important. Rather, this is a sample mechanism where default service priorities could be assigned at provisioning time. Assuming a heterogeneous infrastructure fleet, runtime decisions can be made within the cloud by the SLA@SOI framework, allowing migration of the most important services to the most efficient hardware, as defined in Figure 4. Efficiency is calculated as a ratio of compute power versus total cost of ownership (TCO), where TCO is comprised of the server purchase price, depreciation, vendor support and energy consumption costs.

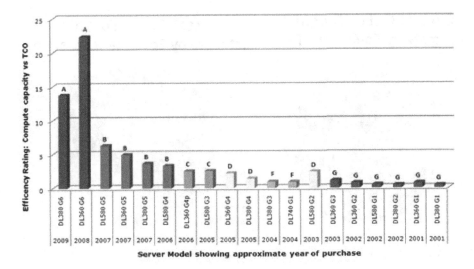

**Fig. 4** Efficiency rating of servers based on TCO [8]

The EU Code of Conduct for Data Centres [2] is an emerging standard of excellence with guidance on best practices in data centrer efficiency. Many corporate IT organisations work within those guidelines and participate in programs such as the ENERGY STAR [1] program and the Green Grid consortium [3] to understand our industry's impact on climate change.

Figure 5 shows that up to 70 percent of IT's carbon footprint is directly attributable to data centre systems, and as such, this is by far the largest contributor to the IT footprint. Expanding on the concept of varying server efficiencies within this use case, it also becomes feasible to start to address the carbon footprint challenge by dynamically powering on and off physical hardware in response to demand, thus achieving greater power consumption efficiencies.

Figure 6 is a conceptual graph which illustrates the transition of a typical 800KW data centre through the stages of pre-virtualisation (the IT abyss), to post-virtualisation (provisioning), to demand-based infrastructure allocation (runtime). Power usage effectiveness (PuE) is a commonly referenced ratio used as indicator of IT energy efficiency in a data centre. It is a ratio of IT load versus total data centre load. The ideal PuE rating is 1, which would mean that all the energy used in the data centre is directly consumed by IT systems. However, many data centres today have PuE ratings higher than 2, meaning that less than half the energy in the data centre is being consumed by IT systems. Figure 6 illustrates this concept, relating how virtualisation and a dynamic approach to service management can help to reduce energy wastage in data centres (assuming the facilities load can also scale back as IT consumption drops).

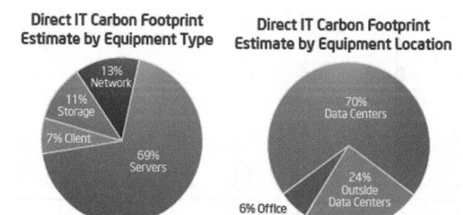

Fig. 5 IT CO2 footprint. Source: Intel IT Performance Report 2009 [4]

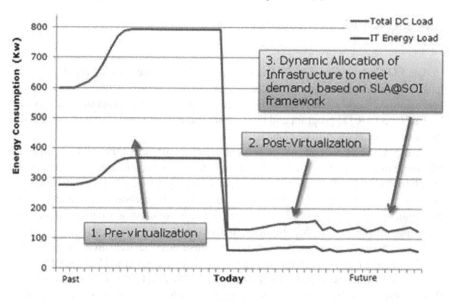

Fig. 6 Profile of energy consumption in an 800KW data centre

## 2.5 The Investment Governance Scenario

The final use case scenario, investment governance, represents the transition of IT to a true value centre. At this level in the IT-CMF, IT has become a strategic partner to the business. IT departments can remove the guesswork and define infrastructure-refresh policies based on data streaming from optimised services running in the cloud. Utilisation figures based on growing or shrinking demand can predict the point at which investment will be required to enable growth. With such a sustainable economic model in place, IT offers optimised value, where costs are predictable and IT capability is managed to meet the changing demands of the business.

## 2.6 Business Objectives

Defining business-level objectives (BLOs) provides a tool for the leadership of an organisation to break medium- to long-term ambitions and goals into tasks that its constituent parts can use to form day-to-day operational and medium-term project strategies. These objectives feed into decision-making processes, where the management at every level have guidance on how to do business, and where to spend their limited budgets and resource allocations to ensure overall prosperity and viability of the corporation. Value dials are derived from higher-level BLOs and relate characteristics that must be incorporated into service delivery if the BLO objectives are to be achieved. Figure 7 references the BLOs and corresponding value dials used in the enterprise IT use case.

| Business Objectives | Value Dials |
|---|---|
| IT Enabling the Enterprise | Agility<br>Dependability<br>Automated response |
| IT Efficiency | Agility<br>Energy Efficiency<br>Utilisation Efficiency<br>Cost Effectiveness<br>Operational costs |
| IT Investment &<br>Technology Adoption | Control of resources<br>Fine grained investment granularity<br>Optimal payback on investment |

**Fig. 7** Business objectives

## 2.7 Business Process Changes

Existing business processes for service provisioning are laborious and require a plethora of manual steps. This leads to a system that is inefficient, confusing, and even daunting to the customer: the actual provisioning of the service is often the step of shortest duration. However, such processes are easiest to automate, and in many cases, this step has already been optimised by the adoption of virtualisation. Manual intervention is needed in every other step to dispatch the request, engineer the solution, decide on a physical location and evaluate the eventual solution. These steps must take place in today's enterprise IT organisations because automated SLAs do not exist. This obvious inefficiency makes future migration to an automated SLA-driven system inevitable.

In terms of business process changes, next-generation hosting services will bring significant benefits for both customers and providers. Customers will enjoy a streamlined and clearer process, which automatically guarantees levels of service not previously possible. The provider will provide a more efficient service, which is a real enabler to the business, supplying the agility to respond to rapidly changing objectives or market-driven trends.

## 2.8 Integrating BLOs into the Digital SLA

From the initial translation of BLOs to value dials (Figure 7), it becomes possible to derive the features required to meet the business needs of the organisation. The basic process is shown in Figure 8 and a selection of the resultant use case features for our example is shown in Figure 9.

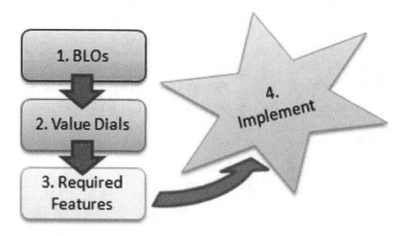

**Fig. 8** Translation of BLOs to features

| Value Dial | Supporting Use Case Feature(s) |
|------------|-------------------------------|
| Agility | Automated provisioning & negotiation. Start/Stop/Pause/Editing of services & VMs. |
| Dependability | SLA Management, including support for agreement terms. Service segregation into cloud partitions based on data classification. Monitoring and prediction. |
| Efficiency | Policy based service management. Policies based on BLOs such as ECF, server efficiency ratings, physical location of data and SLA agreement terms. |

**Fig. 9** Summary of the salient use case features

The SLA@SOI project defines a core model that operates by defining standard SLA agreement and QoS terms: for example, *qos:availability* defines availability for a service. Figure 10 illustrates the definitions of the controlled country region (CCR) and service data classification agreement terms.

Name: entit:**service ccr var:**

•*expression*: service_ccr_var( s : SERVICE): BOOLEAN
•*Definition*: Boolean value indicating if the service is allowed to be run on hardware residing in controlled countries. List of current CCR* countries is maintained in the policies DB. *A CCR is a technology Controlled Country/Region where government legislation requires that corporations operating in those jurisdictions must take additional precautions to prevent leaking technological and intellectual assets to that country. In general, these guidelines exist for political reasons based on poor government relationships, economic embargos, historical reasons or due to wars.

Name: entit:**service data classification**

•*expression*: service_data_classification( s : SERVICE): STND
•*Definition*: Data stored within the VM is classified as either "Top Secret", "Confidential" or "Public".

**Fig. 10** Two of the enterprise IT agreement terms

The translation of each term into a digital SLA is carried out as follows:

1. Each QoS term is given a unique name. A scope is defined, determining whether the term relates to a service or to individual VMs, along with the variable type,

such as Boolean, text or integer. A textual description is also included (as in Figure 10).

2. The QoS terms are translated into the SLA template (SLAT). The SLAT is a machine-readable XML representation of the QoS terms. An example is shown in Figure 11. CCR is one of the defined QoS terms and controls the physical location of the service. Physical location is one of the use case features required to support efficiency.

3. The low-level monitoring system (LLMS) component of the SLA@SOI framework can monitor adherence to this term by tracking the physical server upon which the service runs. A service that has an SLA tied to it will be restricted from running in a CCR country and will generate a violation if at any point a constituent VM is detected to be running on a physical server which resides in a CCR region.

4. Once the QoS term has been defined in the SLAT and an LLMS mechanism is in place, it is possible for an end user to create a service which has this new QoS term attached to its digital SLA.

```
- <slasoi:VariableDeclr>
    <slasoi:Text />
    <slasoi:Properties />
  - <slasoi:Customisable>
      <slasoi:Var>SERVICE_CCR_VAR</slasoi:Var>
    - <slasoi:Value>
        <slasoi:Value>false</slasoi:Value>
        <slasoi:Datatype>http://www.w3.org/2001/XMLSchema#boolean</slasoi:Datatype>
      </slasoi:Value>
    - <slasoi:Expr>
      - <slasoi:SimpleDomainExpr>
          <slasoi:ComparisonOp>http://www.slaatsoi.org/coremodel#isa</slasoi:ComparisonOp>
        - <slasoi:Value>
          - <slasoi:CONST>
              <slasoi:Value>http://www.w3.org/2001/XMLSchema#boolean</slasoi:Value>
            </slasoi:CONST>
          </slasoi:Value>
        </slasoi:SimpleDomainExpr>
      </slasoi:Expr>
    </slasoi:Customisable>
  </slasoi:VariableDeclr>
```

**Fig. 11** CCR agreement term implemented in XML

# 3 SLA Management Architecture

The following section presents the use-case-specific architecture, as illustrated in Figure 2. User interaction with the system is achieved through a web-based user interface, where both customers and administrators interface with the framework components. The enterprise IT SLAT defines QoS agreement terms that are loaded by the business SLA manager as inputs for the provisioning requests.

The business SLA manager passes service provisioning requests to the infrastructure SLA manager, whose role it is to create new VMs that constitute the service, along with monitoring and reporting for that service. This architecture runs on top of the Apache Tashi cluster manager [11], but is also extensible and capable of supporting additional heterogeneous hypervisors, such as VMWare, Xen or KVM.

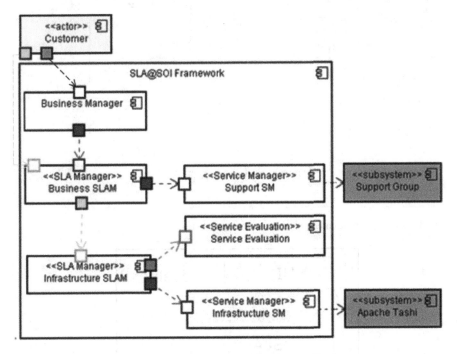

**Fig. 12** Adopted SLA management architecture for the enterprise IT use case

*Creation of an SLA-Guaranteed Service* Figure 13 outlines the steps involved in the creation of an SLA-guaranteed service. Steps 1 to 5 are controlled via customer-initiated user interface interactions with framework components. These replace the manual negotiation steps of existing engagement processes.

Steps 6 and 7 are carried out by the internal components of the SLA@SOI framework, as illustrated in Figure 14; the remaining steps are the automated process governed by the user interface. Putting these together, it is possible to create and provision a monitored, SLA-guaranteed service. Figure 14 shows the key interactions between the user interface, the SLA@SOI framework (illustrated by the dotted green lines), and Tashi, all of which occur via the XMPP messaging bus. A demonstration of the enterprise IT use case in action can be viewed on the SLA@SOI YouTube channel [10].

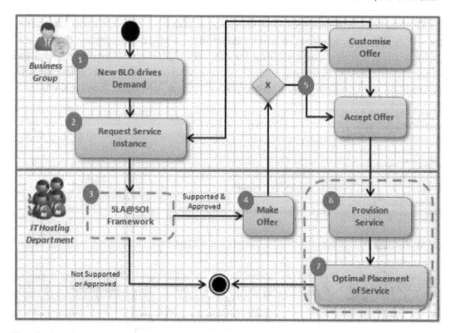

**Fig. 13** Workflow for the enterprise IT provisioning scenario

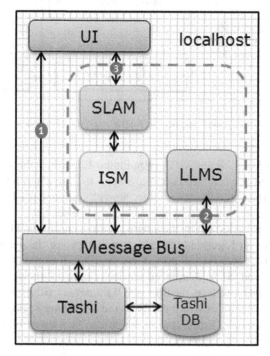

**Fig. 14** Framework component interaction

## 4 Business Evaluation

This section presents a business evaluation for the three main BLOs of the use case, as previously described in Figure 7. For baseline results, typical values from established current operations are presented. Any sources and assumptions made on either the baseline or B4 measurements are given in Appendix I of the Enterprise IT Lab Demonstrator deliverable [9]. The magnitude of some of these improvements is difficult to quantify and will require more work.

### 4.1 Improvements for IT Enabling the Enterprise

The supporting value dials for this business objective were *agility*, *dependability* and *automated response*. In these areas, the use case has seen the biggest improvements in provisioning time, scalability, automatically monitored SLA terms, and reporting.

| Value Dial | KPI | Baseline | Use Case |
|---|---|---|---|
| Agility | Time to Provision | Hours to weeks | Hours |
| | Dynamic Scalability | Difficult | Possible |
| | Scale up/Scale Out | 14 days to 3 months | Hours, assuming available capacity |
| Dependability | Number of SLA Terms | 4 | 31 |
| | Number of Automatically Monitored SLA terms | 0 | 31 |
| | Reporting <br> - Service Availability <br> - Period | No <br> Monthly, <br> Manual | Yes <br> On demand, <br> Automated |

Fig. 15 Summary evaluation for IT enabling the enterprise

### 4.2 Improvements to IT Efficiency

The supporting value dials for IT efficiency were *energy efficiency*, *control of resources* and *cost effectiveness*. The use case shows improvements in two of these categories: *energy efficiency* and *cost effectiveness*. A use case simulation has shown that this approach could achieve a 10% to 30% increase in energy efficiency [9].

Vendor support contract costs are more difficult to quantify at this point. The use case expects these to be reduced, but has not established by how much.

### 4.3 Improvements to IT Investment and Technology Adoption

The value dials for the IT investment and technology adoption objective were *control of resources*, *fine-grained investment granularity* and *optimal payback on investment*. The SLA@SOI framework makes it possible to implement policy-based management of resources using server efficiency and ECF principles. Manageability is simplified through the use of the user interface as the sole interface tool. Service location can be automatically specified through SLAT agreement terms. Service-based resource utilisation is possible in addition to infrastructure level metrics. Total cost of ownership is reduced and variable.

| Value Dial | KPI | Baseline | Use Case |
|---|---|---|---|
| Control of Resources | Automated Policy based Management | Not possible | Simple (in year 2) |
| | Number of management Tools | 6+ | 1 |
| | Location Specification | Manual negotiation | SLAT controlled |
| | Resource Utilisation over time | Infrastructure based only | Service & infrastructure based |
| Optimal payback on investment | Total Cost of Ownership | Fixed & inflexible | Reduced & variable |

**Fig. 16** Summary evaluation for IT investment and technology adoption

## 5 Conclusions

In this chapter, we presented the lessons learned from applying the SLA@SOI management framework to IT service provisioning in an enterprise context. We described the business value that SLA-guaranteed services can bring to an organisation through the modernisation of business processes and the translation of BLOs to runtime operations. We described the representation of several selected QoS terms in a digital SLA, and outlined how the digital SLA is implemented in architectural terms. The business evaluation shows significant improvements in the areas of service provisioning, efficiency, and control of resources.

Future work is focused on further quantifying these improvements, growing the capabilities of the SLA@SOI framework, additional QoS terms, and the implementation of runtime adjustments which minimise or prevent SLA violations.

# References

[1] EnergyStar: (2011). URL http://www.energystar.gov. Last retrieved 2011-01-26

[2] EU: Code of conduct for data centres (2011). URL http://re.jrc.ec.europa.eu/energyefficiency/html/standby\_initiative\_data\_centers.htm. Last retrieved 2011-01-26

[3] GGC: Green grid consortium (2011). URL http://www.thegreengrid.org. Last retrieved 2011-01-26

[4] Intel: Intel it performance report; creating business value (2009). URL http://download.intel.com/it/pdf/IntelIT\_2009APR\_English.pdf

[5] IT-CMF: It capability maturity framework (2011). URL http://ivi.nuim.ie/ITCMF. Last retrieved 2011-06-16

[6] IVI: Research and develop unifying frameworks and road-maps (2011). URL http://ivi.nuim.ie. Last retrieved 2011-01-26

[7] Mell, P., Grance, T.: The nist definition of cloud computing (2009). URL http://www.nist.gov/itl/cloud/upload/cloud-def-v15.pdf

[8] Nolan, M.: Enterprise it use case specification (2009). URL http://sla-at-soi.eu/wp-content/uploads/2009/11/D.B4a-Use-Case-Specification-Enterprise-IT-M17.pdf. Last retrieved 2011-01-27

[9] Nolan, M.: Enterprise it lab demonstrator (2010). URL http://sla-at-soi.eu/wp-content/uploads/2008/12/SLA@SOI\_EntIT\_LabDemonstrator.pdf. Last retrieved 2011-01-31

[10] SLA@SOI: Fp7 project (ist-216556). YouTube (2010). URL http://www.youtube.com/user/slaatsoi. Last retrieved 2011-01-27

[11] Tashi: Apache tashi project (2011). URL http://incubator.apache.org/tashi/. Last retrieved 2011-06-16

# The Service Aggregator Use Case Scenario
## Service Level Agreements in Service Aggregation

Juan Lambea Rueda, Sergio García Gómez, Augustín Escámez Chimeno

**Abstract** Increasingly, modern Telco operators are applying their network resources to the delivery of services based on Telco capabilities, third-party services and SLAs. Thus, Telcos must rapidly develop and adapt to new business environments based on service aggregation. In this way, they facilitate creation of marketplaces in which customers can discover products, negotiate offers, modify contracts, monitor service conditions, and be guaranteed a particular service quality. This use case shows how the SLA@SOI framework can foster this business of aggregating services, supporting an environment in which network capabilities are supported, business implications are considered, and economic consequences and negotiation responsibilities are distributed across involved partners.

## 1 Introduction

The aggregation of services into bundled offerings is an important part of emerging business opportunities for telecommunications companies, which currently face increasing competition and commoditisation alongside a decline in the profitability of their traditional markets (such as voice services).

Traditionally, the ability to model, predict, provision, monitor, and dynamically adjust resources to match the levels required for an aggregated service has been achieved in an ad-hoc manner: this is because the atomic services were provided by heterogeneous technology domains and managed in service silos. Consequently,

Juan Lambea
Telefónica Investigación y Desarrollo, Ronda de la Comunicación 1, 28050 Madrid, Spain,
e-mail: `juanlr@tid.es`

Sergio García Gómez
Telefónica Investigación y Desarrollo, Boecillo, Valladolid, e-mail: `sergg@tid.es`

Augustín Escámez Chimeno
Telefónica Investigación y Desarrollo, Granada, e-mail: `escamez@tid.es`

agreements covering these services have their origin in legal agreements whose terms were laboriously translated into business and technical domains. Today, most service offerings are at least partially realised as electronic services that run on generalised computing platforms and, in many cases, have standardised interfaces. These standardised interfaces ensure SLA@SOI's framework, model and software can work across different domains, including the aggregation of telecommunication services.

This chapter describes the challenges of electronic service aggregation in a Telco offering Internet services. The application hinges on use of a common model and framework for all SLA requirements in a Telco organisation, thus enabling electronic service aggregation from a business perspective.

The use case also seeks to demonstrate the ample technical support available for business parameters in SLA negotiation, provisioning, monitoring, violation detection, and—where possible—adjustment.

Central to this use case is modification of a service delivery platform (SDP), such that existing telecommunications capabilities are encapsulated and normalised into an electronically mediated web-services paradigm.

Although this environment is still a green field for many Telco companies, this approach could improve important business objectives, such as increased satisfaction of end users, improved agility, and increased operational efficiency.

This chapter is structured as follows:

Section 2 describes the general business context of a Telco operator. Section 3 briefly introduces technical and organisational foundations and related work. It explains how the SLA@SOI framework is adopted in this Telco-specific use case, and the components used at an architectural level (Section 4). Section 5 explains the different sorts of SLAs and the hierarchies used to construct the use case. Finally, Section 6 summarises the business evaluation and Section 7 describes the next steps and new expected outlook.

## 2 Business Context

Telefónica is one of the largest Telco operators in the world[1]. New products and services are traditionally provided based on vertical developments, in which all layers (business, software and hardware) are developed ad-hoc. Since SLAs for the resulting services are managed in the same ad-hoc manner, the quality of experience perceived by final users may increase or decrease without consequence. This approach also slows the pace at which new services can be deployed, since all vertical layers are involved in a new deployment.

---

[1] http://en.wikipedia.org/wiki/List_of_mobile_network_operators

Like many other Telco companies, Telefónica is aiming to create a new business environment in which their services can be aggregated with those of other providers based on open interfaces that expose Telefónica's Telco capabilities through a consistent and powerful Service Delivery Platform (SDP [10]). This concept is explained in detail in another great initiative called Service Delivery Framework [12]. By adopting this kind of business environment, Telefónica aim to increase their presence in new markets and thus capture the long tail of economic opportunities.

Key factors in the success of initiatives to date have been agility, efficiency and flexibility in business processes. Thus, one objective of this new business scenario is the control and monitoring of aggregated services to guarantee QoS. The reuse of network capabilities is finally supported and will provide increased revenue for the Telco operator. To this end, Telefónica supports the open source software community Morpheo[2] and has developed open APIs for accessing its own capabilities, such as messaging (SMS, MMS), localisation, identity and user profiling, Voice over IP, and billing, and will offer a number of Telco services through the aforementioned SDP. These initiatives aim to encourage programmers to develop innovative mobile services using Telefónica's offerings.

Since the end-user can also be the application developer, the catalogue of mobile services offered by Telefónica will grow quickly and can be fully adapted to users' needs. There are several initiatives within Telefónica that aim to provide developers with open APIs:

- BlueVia[3]
- OpenMovilForum[4]
- O2 UK, Litmus[5]
- MovilForum Spain[6], and
- mstore Spain[7].

As a result of the need to compete in a global market—not only with other Telcos, but also with mobile device manufacturers and platform developers such as Apple and Google—Telefónica participated in the creation of the global consortium Wholesale Applications Community (WAC), and BlueVia was launched as a global initiative for developers in all of those markets where the corporation is present. WAC aims to develop standard technologies and open tools that will drive the development of applications through multiple operators using open and unified service APIs. WAC also aims to provide the commercial enablers required to sell, pay for and share revenues from the use of these applications. In this context, the applications offered by stores can offer different SLAs and thus require translation of SLAs

---

[2] http://www.morfeo-project.org/lng/en/

[3] https://bluevia.com/en/

[4] http://open.movilforum.com/

[5] http://www.o2litmus.co.uk/

[6] http://www.movilforum.com/web/global/home

[7] https://emocion.movistar.es/mstore/

to the used services. Moreover, pricing, billing and revenue-sharing may be affected by compliance to these SLAs.

Nowadays, there is another trend among telecommunications players towards providing infrastructure for mid-sized enterprise customers. The key idea behind this is that traditional Telco services will be sold together with communications, a concept that is applicable to this use case. The same kind of service can be delivered into different available bundles of services, and all these services will have to be SLA-driven and monitored if QoS is to be guaranteed.

Interest in offering Platform as a Service (PaaS) is strengthened by Telefónica's active participation in defining new standards like TCloud[8] in the DMTF (Distributed Management Task Force[9]), and is heavily involved in other FP7 cloud research initiatives, including Reservoir and 4CaaST. Thus, Telefónica has a strong interest in cloud computing technologies and ways in which they can be sold to customers, be they SMEs, big enterprises, or end users.

Last but not least, there is a growing trend towards providing global telecommunications and IT services to multinational companies. To this end, Telefónica envisions a broad range of configurations where it makes sense for telecommunications companies to use service aggregation for wholesale SLAs.

The scenarios in the service aggregator [6] use case consider this challenging environment and aim to help the company build a business layer [8] on top of their application platform, as well as helping to guarantee QoS through automatic SLA management.

In this environment, the service aggregator aids in addressing several challenges. Specifically, it supports Telefónica's development of sales strategies for:

- third-party services through a SDP,
- software services,
- network services,
- infrastructure and cloud resources

with integrated and automatic SLA management and service monitoring, thus enabling guarantee of signed SLAs.

## 2.1 Roles

This use case focuses on the 'bundling' of services to be sold to enterprises and SMEs. For example, an SMS service from a Telco provider like Telefónica might be bundled with an Infrastructure as a Service from another provider.

We have chosen a basic example to show how SLAs could be applied in a scenario where Telco capabilities are subcontracted. The scenario aims to demonstrate the use of SLA@SOI technologies in a global operator like Telefónica, and the applicability of SLAs at different levels.

---

[8] http://www.tid.es/files/doc/apis/TCloud_API_Spec_v0.9.pdf

[9] http://www.dmtf.org/about

This use case does not set out to define possible new services, but rather to define SLA-aware Telco services that can use automatic SLAs with third-party services. As has been stated previously, a real trend in Telco operators is to sell service bundles to big companies, where the bundled services include not only traditional telecommunication services but also novel services, such as cloud services. This use case demonstrates how the adoption of formal SLAs can improve ordinary business activities, and in particular, how the SLA@SOI framework can be successfully applied to telecommunication companies.

For the service aggregator use case, we distinguish the following players:

- Bank or SME (customer): The service aggregator's customer
- IT manager (end user): The bank IT administrator who finally uses the aggregated service
- Telco provider: The telecommunication company (for example, Telefónica) supplying telecommunications capabilities (such as SMS, e-mail and VOIP) through a web-service interface (e.g. the SDP platform),
- IaaS provider: The third-party company providing the required infrastructure.

## 2.2 Business Objectives

This section outlines business objectives in different areas:

*Customer Relationship Management and Support*

- Customer satisfaction: The aggregation environments are two-sided services markets in which Telco operators must not only guarantee QoS for the services they provide, but also ensure that third-party applications provided on top of their infrastructure are of sufficient quality. This objective can be evaluated using the number of claims that customers raise, and degree of quality control provided.
- Provisioning: Use of automatic contracting improves the efficiency of this process.

*Availability*

- Dependability: Some applications will address the mass market, while others will target companies of different sizes. In the latter case, there must be some guarantee that services—and the infrastructure they use—will be available most of the time, and that in the case of failure, they can be rapidly recovered.
- End-to-end manageability: Since the services offered through an aggregation platform may be composed of multiple services provided by different partners, it is desirable that as many of these services as possible be monitored and managed.

*Operability*

- Fast decision making: In an environment with many interdependencies between services and stakeholders, it is important that operators can address issues promptly and reduce the overall penalties potentially associated with an offered service.

- Agility: Many Telco operators lack agility in managing the life cycle of new services. In the aggregation scenario, the speed with which services can be deployed, provisioned and changed is a major metric.
- Operational efficiency: A major source of economic inefficiency for Telco operators is the cost of operating their networks and services. There is a trend towards reducing operational expenditures by using innovative tools that support automation of operational processes.
- Energy efficiency: Although not a traditional business factor for Telco operators, in recent years, there has been emerging interest in minimising the energy consumption of network resources and data centres especially.

## 3 Foundations

### 3.1 Service Aggregation

This section describes how SLA management has been adopted in this use case, and how it can be applied to a Telco's network and infrastructure; however, this work is not the focus of this use case. In the context of this use case, service aggregation refers to a way of joining services from Telco providers and third-party providers, with the aim of providing a bundled product that can be delivered to customers in a service-oriented way.

In the service aggregator use case, SLA management is divided into three levels: business, software and infrastructure (Figure 1). The software layer is connected with Telco resources, like Telefónica's SDP. Telco services are based on software components that run in the software layer—on top of the infrastructure layer—and are connected with the SDP for execution and delivery.

*Business layer* At this top-most level, customers expect products that offer complete solutions. Such products comprise bundles of services that include business terms for managing business-related aspects, thus helping to ensure customer satisfaction. Business terms include: availability and hours of helpline operation, a prioritised list of maintenance requirements, backup and restore mechanisms, termination and penalty clauses, and other legal constraints. Any business SLA at this level must be expressed in business terms.

*Software layer* Telco services rely on software components, such as web or REST[10] services, which run in an application server that communicates with a messaging system; these applications probably also require database systems and the like. The software wrappers are connected with Telco infrastructure via the SDP. The SLAs in this layer are related to the availability of software wrappers, application servers, or commercial software used for software wrappers, etc.

---

[10] http://en.wikipedia.org/wiki/Representational_State_Transfer

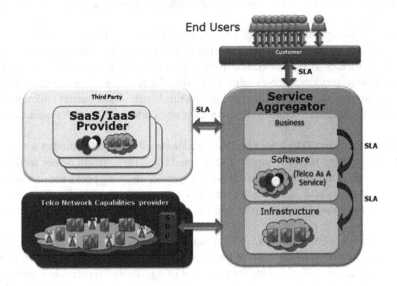

**Fig. 1** Service aggregator use case

*Infrastructure* This lowest layer contains the necessary infrastructure (both phys-ical and virtual) available for use by the software layer. SLA terms related to infras-tructure are expressed using technical parameters (e.g. number of CPUs, number of cores, size of memory, hard disk, network, etc.).

## 3.2 Related Work

Service aggregators represent a common approach to enriching the services ecosys-tem. In recent years, increased attention has been paid to composition and orches-tration of services in marketplaces [1], and service aggregation is being applied in different areas—including cloud computing (Software as a Service) and Telco environments—as a way of adding value to existing networks, IT infrastructures and services.

The development of new technologies and communications channels, along with market deregulation, has fostered a rise in service aggregation environments [7], which has allowed new companies to conduct business globally, and to reach market segments and needs previously unattainable. In the service aggregation model, there is usually an intermediary company that adds value between the service provider and customer.

In cloud computing, beyond supplying platforms and infrastructures, there is a tendency to integrate all types of service into aggregation environments in which value-added services can be provided through a marketplace (e.g. 4CaaSt FP7 project[11]).

Thus, Telco operators have been facing the challenge of the commoditisation of their network infrastructures [2]. In terms of addressing this challenge, promising directions include Next Generation Networks and SDPs that enable third parties to create new services over existing networks. There are many examples of Telcos exposing network capabilities to enable a third-party development environment: Telefonica's BlueVia, Vodafone Betavine, Orange Partner, Telenor Playground, and so on.

In both SaaS and Telco cases, the business model is a two-sided market where the platform mediates between supply and demand [4]. The platform owner facilitates an environment in which the application can operate, allowing provision of a service to end customers and subsequent extraction of revenues from them; the platform itself creates value for developers and customers, extracting revenues from both sides.

A challenge when dealing with SLA management in service aggregations is the merger of guarantee terms from atomic services to aggregated services [3]. However, determining QoS elements for a number of aggregated services is a challenging task: it must take into account both the nature of each parameter and the flow of aggregation [11]. One interesting approach, shown in [5], defines several SLA aggregation patterns useful for automating the aggregation of cross-company hierarchical SLAs.

This use case focuses on creating business SLA templates (SLATs) based on fusion of third-party SLATs and Telco SLATs. SLAs are also negotiated between banks, service aggregators and third parties. The use case integrates aspects of business, telecommunications and infrastructure, and aligns them with business management requirements.

# 4 SLA Management Architecture

The SLA management architecture used for the service aggregator relies on the general reference architecture described in Chapter 'Reference Architecture for Multi-Level SLA Management' and SLA@SOI deliverable [9].

Two framework instances were used in building this use case: the first is the core of the use case and refers to the service aggregator component. As described in Section 3, our SLA management solution for Telco service aggregation supports SLAs at three layers: business, software and infrastructure.

The service aggregator implements three layers of architecture, with the business manager at the top level, and SLA managers at the business, software and infrastructure levels.

---

[11] http://4caast.morfeo-project.org/

Inside the framework, the business manager manages relationships with third parties and customers, and—together with the business SLA manager—is responsible for the aggregated offering. The software SLA manager deals with SLAs for the complete software application. It uses the software service manager for deployment and management of software services (namely web-services for accessing Telefónica Telco capabilities (through the SDP), such as sending SMS and MMS, and requests for location information).

The infrastructure SLA manager is responsible for resources, and makes use of an infrastructure service manager for deployment of virtual machines in the Telefónica infrastructure environment.

The second framework instance is the core of the infrastructure service for the use case. Following the reference structure sketched in Section 3, our SLA management solution for IaaS service aggregation must support SLAs at two layers: business and infrastructure. In this implementation, it reuses the business manager at the top level and the SLA managers at the business and infrastructure levels. This component of the use case is oriented to be another service included in the bundle.

From the service aggregator point of view, the solution we adopted is shown in Figure 2 and comprises three SLA managers (SLAMs) and two service managers (SMs). The arrows describe general dependency relationships.

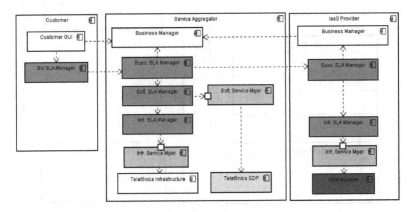

**Fig. 2** Service aggregator SLA management architecture

We encapsulated Telco service functionality between software components in the software layer and connected the software service manager to the SDP.

This scenario can also deliver a Telco's SMS service in situations where the infrastructure is a service provided by a third party. This kind of interaction is based on business needs, as can be seen in Figure 2.

## 5 SLA Hierarchies

This section outlines the SLAs adopted and implemented in the use case. It is necessary to highlight the way the final business SLA is built. In service aggregation, we create a bundle of services and include in it SLAT terms from different services and SLATs. The logic of merging different terms must take into account business requirements for the owner of the marketplace (service aggregator). These requirements are defined using business rules that allow the process of joining terms from different SLATs. For instance, a business rule can require that the *availability* term across all SLATs should be a minimum value.

Figure 3 provides an overview of the SLA hierarchy and includes some main SLA terms for each layer.

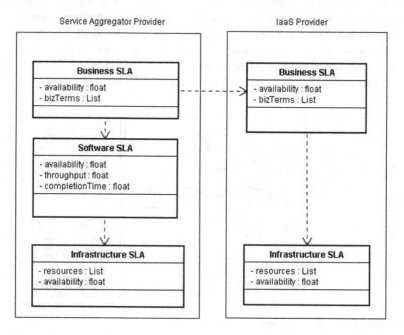

**Fig. 3** SLA hierarchy diagram

## 5.1 SLA Terms

Below we outline some terms used in SLAs involved in the service aggregator use case:

*Availability* Service availability for a Telco operator is traditionally 99.99%; however, when bundled with Internet services, this availability must decrease to ensure that the overall guaranteed terms are aligned. This metric is used in SLAs throughout the use case and thus has different values.

*Business terms* These terms relate to the business and legal conditions of the product, and include offers, prices, support, termination clauses, penalties, and so on. These terms describe the limits of the commercial offer, the kind of prices and periodic fees that will be charged, detailed conditions about delivery of service support (helpline phone number and hours, conditions under which service can be ceased), service violations that could have consequences, and so on. Business terms can be managed by a business SLA manager in coordination with third-party business SLA managers and with SLA managers from other layers. The example uses a support service manager, who decides and manages the capacities of the support organisation. Some business terms may affect SLA managers located at other levels.

*Throughput* This term expresses the number of requests per second that can be supported by the software service. To offer all capabilities of a particular Telco service, the software service wrapper and the SDP behind it must be able to support a particular throughput. In this case, the term is used in the SMS service.

*Completion time* When the service is used, some time elapses between executing the request sent by the customer and returning an answer. In this case, the term is used in the SMS service and refers to the estimated delivery time for an SMS.

*Resources* These terms relate to resources at the infrastructure level that can be reserved and used. For instance, in a computing infrastructure, resources include VMs (with specifications including number of CPUs, size of memory or hard disk, etc) and connectivity resources, such as network requirements (including bandwidth, etc.).

# 6 Business Evaluation

This section describes the benefits of adopting the SLA@SOI framework in environments such as marketplaces and service aggregators. Below, we provide a short summary of metrics that can be used to evaluate this use case:

## 6.1 Improved Customer Satisfaction

Use of the SLA@SOI platform results in a better quality of experience for end users and for third-party developers who make use of the platform. Indicators include:

- fewer unsolved or undetected SLA violations, and thus,
- fewer complaints from customers.

## 6.2 Improved Dependability

Another important indicator is improved service dependability. Service providers are better able to offer prices in accordance with actual QoS provided, since SLA breaches will eventually result in penalties. Indicators include:

- improved availability (since SLAs can be automatically adjusted, the system is more available and accessible for users), and
- reduced mean time to recover from an SLA breach (many services problems will be automatically handled by the SLA@SOI framework).

## 6.3 Improved End-To-End Manageability

The SLA@SOI platform monitors the actual QoS provided by each service or third party, as well as SLA breaches. Since each of the aggregated services are under SLA@SOI management, it is possible to identify and monitor which atomic service is responsible for an SLA breach. The SLA@SOI framework enables an increase in the number of services being monitored, indicated by:

- increased number of monitored atomic services per total number of atomic services.

## 6.4 Improved Decision-Making

Since SLA@SOI's monitoring and reporting capabilities provide information about penalties, platform managers can make more rapid decisions on commercial offers, service configurations, resource reallocations and so on. SLA@SOI's automatic adjustment and negotiation mechanisms also mean that any reconfigurations are carried out in an agile way. One indicator is:

- increased percentage of automatic penalties adjusted.

## 6.5 Improved Agility

SLA@SOI's negotiation features reduce the time required to provision new services, and to exchange one service for another service with similar SLAs. Indicators include:

- reduced average time to provision a service, and
- reduced average time to modify a service.

## 6.6 *Improved Operational and Energy Efficiency*

The efficiency of a Telco operator can be improved through increased automation and more efficient use of computing resources. Indicators include:

- reduced operational expenditure associated with platform management,
- reduced energy consumption (kWhr) per service, and
- increased energy savings (derived from improvements in this previous indicator).

This evaluation shows a clear improvement in all of the above areas.

# 7 Conclusions

This chapter outlined a use case in which SLA@SOI's multi-layer SLA management framework was adopted by a service aggregator, describing architectural layers and SLA hierarchy. It also detailed the way in which this scenario depends upon Telefónica's business and telecommunications domains, an approach influenced by the open APIs developed from existing initiatives within the corporation.

It must be noted that service aggregators, marketplaces and similar environments are new, green fields in which different research directions can be pursued. Unfortunately, this means that a detailed business evaluation cannot be undertaken, since we have insufficient feedback regarding the impact of this environment on Telefónica's various initiatives.

Future work will focus first on service aggregator enrichment, with the adoption of new features like semi-automatic negotiation and post-sale and reporting characteristics. A second focus will be on the development of a specific negotiation front-end for automatic e-contracting, which will be implemented as an extension of the service aggregator. This front-end will consider the customer's ability to negotiate the final conditions under which Telefónica's products and services will be provided, which in turn depend on QoS terms for mobile and fixed data networks. Finally, it must be noted that this new scenario will reproduce the network requirements and SLA terms of the current service aggregator use case, and will take advantage of opportunities presented by existing network resources and infrastructures.

# References

[1] Barros, A. and Dumas, M.: The rise of web service ecosystems. IT Professional **8**(5), 31–37 (2006)
[2] Chappell, C., Finnie, G.: The Agile Service Provider: A new Model For Service Delivery. Tech. rep., Cisco Systems, Inc. (2009)

[3] Cheng, S., Chang, C., Zhang, L., Kim, T.: Towards Competitive Web Service Market. In: 11th IEEE International Workshop on Future Trends of Distributed Computing Systems, 2007. FTDCS'07, pp. 213–219 (2007)

[4] Gonçalves, V., Ballon, P.: Adding Value to the Network: Mobile Operators' Experiments with Software-as-a-Service and Platform-as-a-Service Models. Telematics and Informatics (2010)

[5] Haq, I., Schikuta, E.: Aggregation Patterns of Service Level Agreements. In: Frontiers of Information Technology (FIT2010) (2010)

[6] J. Lambea, M. Evenson, et al.: Deliverable D.B5a-M17 – Service Aggregator Use Case Specification. Tech. rep., D.B5a-M17, SLA@SOI Project (2009). URL http://sla-at-soi.eu/results/deliverables/

[7] Kohlborn, T., Korthaus, A., Riedl, C., Krcmar, H.: Service aggregators in business networks. In: 13th Enterprise Distributed Object Computing Conference Workshops (EDOCW), pp. 195–202 (2009)

[8] S. Garca ,B. Fuentes, E. Yaqub, G. Spanoudakis, and J. Lambea: D.A2a – Business SLA Management (full lifecycle). Tech. rep., D.A2a, SLA@SOI project (2010). URL http://sla-at-soi.eu/results/deliverables/

[9] W. Theilmann, T. Ellahi, J. Happe, M. Vuk, B. Fuentes, and J. Lambea: D.A1a – Framework Architecture (full lifecycle). Tech. rep., D.A1a, SLA@SOI project (2010). URL http://sla-at-soi.eu/results/deliverables/

[10] Lewis, A.: Service delivery platforms and ims. two faces of the same problem. Tech. rep., TeleManagement Forum (2007)

[11] Menasce, D.: Composing web services: A QoS view. IEEE Internet Computing **8**(6), 88–90 (2004)

[12] TMF: Service delivery framework overview v2.0. technical report, TeleManagement Forum (2009)

# The eGovernment Use Case Scenario
## SLA Management Automation of Public Services

Giampaolo Armellin, Annamaria Chiasera, Ganna Frankova, Liliana Pasquale, Francesco Torelli, and Gabriele Zacco

**Abstract** The SLA@SOI framework—a solution for the automated management of services on the basis of Service Level Agreements (SLAs)—is usually applied to automated software or hardware services. The eGovernment use case aims to assess the applicability of the framework to the management of hybrid services, which involve both automated and human-based activities, as is typical in the government domain. Due the continued growth of service demand, many public organisations outsource their services to private third parties or to other public institutions. SLAs are typically adopted as a way to control the quality of provided services; however, these SLAs are typically managed manually, limiting the possible benefits. Instead, by formalising SLAs it is possible to automate a set of activities such as monitoring, negotiation, planning and adjustment. Below we describe how this can be implemented and evaluated for a specific eGovernment service.

Giampaolo Armellin
GPI, Via Ragazzi del '99, 13, Trento 38123, Italy, e-mail: achiasera@gpi.it

Annamaria Chiasera
GPI, Via Ragazzi del '99, 13, Trento 38123, Italy, e-mail: achiasera@gpi.it

Ganna Frankova
GPI, Via Ragazzi del '99, 13, Trento 38123, Italy, e-mail: gannafrankova@yahoo.com

Liliana Pasquale
Politecnico di Milano, piazza L. Da Vinci, 32, 20133 Milano, Italy,
e-mail: pasquale@elet.polimi.it

Francesco Torelli
Engineering Ingegneria Informatica Spa, Via Riccardo Morandi, 32, 00148 Roma, Italy,
e-mail: francesco.torelli@eng.it

Gabriele Zacco
Fondazione Bruno Kessler, via Santa Croce, 77, 38122 Trento, Italy, e-mail: zacco@fbk.eu

# 1 Introduction

In this chapter we present a case study for applying the SLA@SOI framework to the eGovernment domain. The case study is intended to demonstrate SLA-based management as a general concept, not limited to computational services, but applicable to any kind of service, and in particular to human-based services, which are typical in the government domain.

While most government services can not be automated, several management activities—such as negotiation, monitoring, resource planning and adjustment—can be at least partially automated thanks to the adoption of formal SLAs. To demonstrate these opportunities, we have integrated two social services currently provided to citizens by the Italian region of Trentino: medical treatment services and mobility services. We identified five related usage scenarios, each exploiting different features of the SLA@SOI framework. This chapter reports on the technical lessons learned from this exercise, including how to customise the SLA@SOI framework to cover these scenarios, and the benefits of such automation from a business perspective.

The remainder of this chapter is organised as follows: Section 2 introduces the use case, describing its general business context and business objectives. Section 3 explains the identified scenarios, Section 4 describes the architecture used for the implementation of such scenarios, and Section 5 describes the actual SLAs used for the experimentation. Section 6 summarises the business evaluation approach and finally, Section 7 provides a summary of the actual state of the work and future plans.

# 2 Business Context

From an organisational point of view, there has been a recent trend towards considering health care and social care agencies as part of the same organisation, since both provide services to citizens. For this reason, this experiment focuses on the composition of services usually offered separately from the aforementioned organisations: health and mobility services. In the following, we describe these component services, the involved actors, and the business objectives of these actors in more detail.

## 2.1 Mobility and health care services

The mobility and health care services comprise three sub-services, as shown in Figure 1.

The *medical treatment service* is provided by the local health care agency (in Trentino, the Azienda Provinciale per i Servizi Sanitari, APSS) and covers the book-

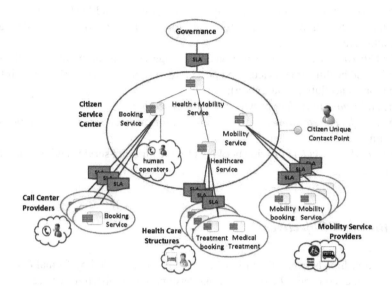

**Fig. 1** Mobility and health care service, component services, and related SLAs.

ing and provisioning of medical treatments provided by different health care structures of the health care agency according to regulations and objectives defined by the governance (Provincia Autonoma di Trento, PAT).

The *reservation* (booking) of patient treatments is provided by the local health care agency via a unique contact point, which is handled by a contact centre service (called CUP). The contact centre service may be outsourced to an external qualified call centre chosen with a request-for-tender process. The winning call centre provider adheres to the constraints and conditions imposed by the governance in a contract. In particular, the governance defines indicators to evaluate the process of the health care services and establish compliance with governance regulations.

The *mobility service* is owned by the local social care and welfare agency and provides on-demand transport services to needful people according to regulations and objectives defined by the governance. The mobility service is provided by a set of public and private companies or associations, certified by the welfare agency.

## 2.2 Roles

The set of actors involved in the mobility and health care services are:

• the *citizen* is the mobility and health care service consumer (i.e. the patient);

- the *governance* (PAT) is the customer of the mobility and health care services, defining regulations and business goals for provisioning of the mobility and health care services;
- the *Citizen Service Centre* is responsible for aggregating and monitoring the mobility and health care services, and providing the contact service (booking, information, cancellation, evaluation);
- the *call centre providers* provide the contact service;
- the *health care structures* provide bookings for medical treatments and medical treatments;
- the *mobility providers* provide bookings for the mobility service and the mobility service.

## 2.3 Business Objectives

The relationships between the aforementioned actors are ruled by formal contracts and SLAs that constrain the provisioning/consumption of different services and establish pricing and billing conditions. The management of an SLA is ruled by a life cycle that consists mainly of three steps: negotiation, provisioning, and monitoring and adjustment.

Currently, the negotiation, monitoring and enforcement of SLAs is not completely integrated and still partially paper-based. Governments and service providers must manually negotiate new SLAs and SLA evolution based on process execution is also manual. The objective of the SLA@SOI eGovernment use case is to automate such processes. Below, we summarise a way in which negotiations can be performed independently from the SLA@SOI framework:

- the SLA between governance and the call centre provider is defined in a canonical paper contract by the governance.
- governance submits the contract terms to different providers and waits for an offer.
- governance signs the contract with the provider that proposes the most convenient offer that fulfills the contract terms.

Usually the contract duration is four years. Some terms of the contract are renegotiable every six months.

In the provisioning phase, which is triggered after the contract has been signed, the contracted contact service provider (in accordance with the governance) outsources parts of the phone traffic to one or more external call centres. Management of the business relationship between the contact service provider and the external call centres is transparent to the governance and is ruled only by the resource optimisation strategy of the contact service provider. Typically the contract is renegotiated annually. More precisely, resource dimensioning deals with allocation of human operators internal to the contact service provider, and with the possibility of outsourcing some phone traffic to an external call centre provider. Currently, resource optimisation is handled manually with the assistance of some utility tools.

Between the governance and the health care structure, and between the governance and the mobility provider, there is a limited negotiation. Each provider must accept the terms specified in a governance-defined contract, which specifies the quality of business service required, while the governance must accept the price asked by the provider. The governance should monitor the SLA with the providers to identify violations, apply penalties or modify contractual terms. Currently, each service provider periodically monitors the execution of its services (with a frequency defined in the contract) and reports the results to the governance that identifies and deals with SLA violations. The contact service provider is a deputy from the governance and monitors some KPIs belonging to the health care structure (e.g. maximum waiting time to secure an appointment).

Of course, each service provider is interested in monitoring its service execution to improve allocation of internal resources. For instance, the contact service monitors its operators' work to identify any trends that may require a change in phone traffic management. This can result in optimisation (adjustment) of the use of internal operators and in resizing of phone call traffic handled by the external contact centre through a renegotiation of the contract between the contact centre and the external contact centre. Without the SLA@SOI framework, the identification of negative trends and any adjustment actions must be completed manually. Adoption of the SLA@SOI framework is intended to automate all these operations.

# 3 Use Case Scenarios

Five scenarios have been identified to describe the ways in which the enhanced SLA management features offered by the SLA@SOI framework can produce benefits for stakeholders in a typical eGovernment context. The scenarios described assume a common main storyboard in which a citizen calls the Citizen Service Centre to book a health care treatment, and possibly a related mobility service, which is offered with an attempt to match the user profile and preferences. The citizen accesses the treatment and is then asked to provide feedback about the services.

*Scenario 1: SLA-Driven Monitoring.* This scenario demonstrates how the SLA@SOI framework's SLA-based *monitoring* (Chapter 'Translation of SLAs into Monitoring Specifications') and *reporting* (Chapter 'Penalty Management in the SLA@SOI Project') can be useful for monitoring hierarchically aggregated SLAs, and for automatically producing reports and billings related to established SLAs and levels of user satisfaction. To detect sources of user dissatisfaction and SLA violations, it is not sufficient to monitor specific services in isolation, since this gives a partial and unrealistic view of the aggregate service quality. On the contrary, dependencies between services and resources in the SLA hierarchies must be taken into account; software/non-software monitoring events (e.g. web-service invocation time, percentage of busy phone calls, user feedback) must be properly recorded; and this information must be suitably aggregated to check for SLA violations. The SLA@SOI framework allows automation of these steps. Monitored properties include those related to events produced by citizens, call centre services (internal and outsourced), health care structures, and mobility providers. The collected monitoring information is then used by the framework to automatically provide periodic reports and billing information to the governance. The governance can use such reports to make decisions, review strategies and renegotiate SLAs.

*Scenario 2: SLA-Driven Service Selection.* This scenario demonstrates how the SLA-based *dynamic binding* feature of the SLA@SOI framework (Chapter 'Managing Composite Services') can be exploited within an eGovernment setting to automatically select mobility providers on the basis of their SLAs. In accordance with the mobility and health care business process offered by the Citizen Service Centre, citizens can book a mobility service to provide transport to their chosen health care structure. Thus the goal of this scenario is to automatically select a set of suitable mobility providers (e.g. shuttle, taxi, or human operator) based on the specific requirements of the service request and the user characteristics and preferences (available in their citizen profile). These selection criteria are expressed using SLA templates and are mainly based on the cost and characteristics of the provided service. Once selection is complete, the system contacts the selected providers to obtain possible appointments and then proposes different solutions so that the citizen can choose a preferred one.

*Scenario 3: Runtime SLA Negotiation and Adjustment.* In this scenario, the SLA@SOI framework's SLA-based *automatic negotiation* (Chapter 'A Generic Platform for Conducting SLA Negotiations' and Chapter 'Management of the Business SLAs for Services eContracting') and *static prediction* (Chapter 'Software Performance and Reliability Prediction') features are used to dynamically adapt to exceptional situations that lead to an overload of the Citizen Service Centre. Consider, for instance, the occurrence of a pandemic flu. Such an event can directly affect the contract terms between the governance and the Citizen Service Centre, since the governance manually triggers a request for SLA renegotiation with the Citizen Service Centre. Such a renegotiation aims to guarantee citizens more health care bookings during the pandemic flu. The negotiation—thanks to the SLA@SOI framework's capacity to model system resources, services and SLAs—is performed automatically from the side of the Citizen Service Centre. Using the *static prediction* feature, the framework (installed within the Citizen Service Centre) automatically checks whether its internal resources are sufficient to satisfy the proposed SLA, and if not, it can automatically (re-)negotiate related SLAs with third party providers (for instance, call centre providers). Eventually, negotiations between the governance and the Citizen Service Centre lead to an agreement, the Citizen Service Centre exploits the automatic adjustment feature of the SLA@SOI framework to redeploy its internal call centre infrastructure, the negotiation results are confirmed to the third parties. It is important to note that negotiations between the Citizen Service Centre and third party providers are dynamic and automatic, while negotiations between the governance and the service centre are dynamic and (a) automatic on the service centre side, but (b) manual on the governance side. The static or design-time prediction component of the framework is used by the Citizen Service Centre to select a provisioning plan that is compatible with the currently established SLA, the status of its agreement terms, and the status of the internal resources involved in the services.

*Scenario 4: Runtime Predictions and Resource Adjustment.* This scenario demonstrates how automatic *adjustment* of available resources can be triggered by the *runtime prediction* (Chapter 'Run-time Prediction') feature of the framework. In this case, a suggestion is made to the manager of the Citizen Service Centre that internal resources be adjusted, but unlike Scenario 3, this suggestion is made *after* negotiating and signing an agreement with governance and *after* service provisioning. The prediction model, used by the relevant framework component, is used alongside SLA-based service monitoring data to prevent a possible non-fulfillment of agreement terms by the service provider.

*Scenario 5: Runtime Predictions and Process Adjustment.* This scenario demonstrates how *runtime predictions* can also trigger a different kind of service adjustment that, in this case, involves software services. In fact, SLA-based monitoring of the evolution of the provisioned service—along with a model predicting the behaviour of the service itself—can determine an *automatic adjustment of the BPEL process* (Chapter 'Managing Composite Services') that embodies the service offered by the Citizen Service Centre. Modifying the structure of the BPEL process aims to improve service performance, for instance by allowing activities originally executed in sequence to run in parallel.

# 4 SLA Management Architecture

The system architecture implemented for the eGovernment use case is shown in Figure 2. We adopted a customised version of the SLA@SOI framework (Chapter 'Reference Architecture for Multi-Level SLA Management') deployed at the Citizen Service Centre (CSC). The component services of the mobility and health care service are aggregated by means of a BPEL process deployed in a modified version of the ActiveBPEL engine, called the Dynamic Orchestration Engine (DOE). The DOE offers probes to collect process variables, and adaptors to apply dynamic binding on the adopted partner services. These processes interact with call centre facilities offered by the CSC's internal call centre (ICC), and with a set of external partner services: the call centres, which allow citizens to book health care treatments and mobility services, the health care structure, which provide health care treatments, and the mobility providers, which move users to health care structures.

In general, even if the CSC has an internal call centre, it can outsource part of that service to external call centre providers if the number of virtual operators is insufficient to satisfy the contract negotiated with the governance. The adoption of an external call centre also implies that a contract must be negotiated between the

CSC and the external call centre provider. External call centre providers are not required to adopt the SLA@SOI framework, but just to expose standard interfaces for monitoring and negotiation.

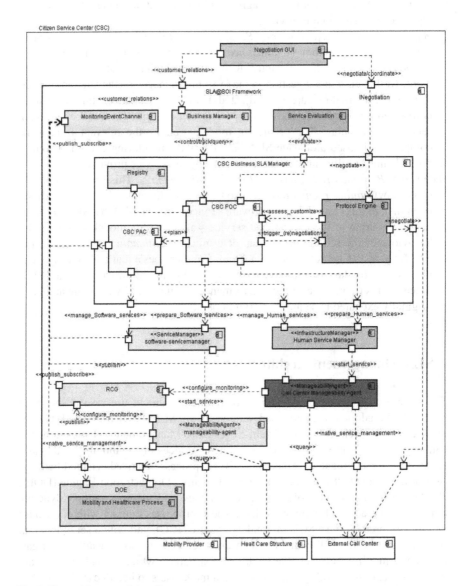

**Fig. 2** The architecture of the eGovernment use case

Each component of the SLA@SOI framework is used as-is, is configured, or is customised. Below we explain these categories:

- **As-is** Framework components are adopted without modification (see green components in Figure 2). These components include: the *monitoring event channel*, which receives monitoring data/events (e.g., information about the medical treatment, the conditions of transfer to the health care structure, or the status of a service booking). These data come from the mobility and health care process and from third party providers. The *SLA registry* and *SLA template registry* store and update negotiated contracts and templates respectively. The *RCG* controls whether warnings have been issued or violations have occurred. If violations or warnings are discovered, the RCG notifies dependent components by publishing a message on the monitoring event channel. It also uses monitoring data to dynamically predict the call centre's performance. The *service manager* coordinates the provisioning and management of resources at the software level: that is, it manages the binding and structure of the mobility and health care process. The DOE's *manageability agent* configures sensors at the DOE and in its services. It also configures a set of actuators available at the DOE to perform rebinding of partner services.
- **Configured** Some components of the SLA@SOI framework are properly configured to support the requirements of eGovernment (see purple components in Figure 2). For example, the *protocol engine* is instrumented with suitable protocols to discipline negotiations between the governance and the CSC, and between the CSC and the external call centre. Configuration does not require recompilation of the component.
- **Customised** Some components require modification or extension of the source code and recompilation. For example, the Planning and Adjustment Component (*PAC*) is customised to support the adjustment of human virtual operators at the internal call centre. Similarly, the Provisioning and Optimisation Component (*CSC POC*) is customised to generate—during the negotiation phase—suitable plans for the provisioning and monitoring of managed resources. It also plays a particular role in the negotiation phase, since it can decide to trigger negotiations between the internal call centre and an external call centre if the ICC does not have sufficient resources to complete a negotiated contract.

The architecture is also composed of domain-specific components (see pink components in Figure 2). First, a *negotiation GUI* is provided to allow the CSC and the governance access to information regarding their negotiated SLAs and fulfillment of their guarantee terms. The GUI also allows the governance to renegotiate existing SLAs. Finally, the architecture provides a *human service manager* to coordinate provisioning of the virtual operators at the ICC.

To avoid penalties, the CSC must continuously comply with SLAs it has signed with the governance. To this end, the RCG regularly performs specific prediction warning analyses to evaluate operator response time and decide whether the CSC must adjust its internal resources to allow it to fulfill the SLA. For instance, if there is a higher than acceptable probability that the daily operator response time will exceed the threshold fixed by the SLA, then an adaptation of the internal booking service will be triggered. This will result in an increase in the number of virtual operators for the next work shift. The adjustment is required to fully satisfy the contract with the governance, and also acts to minimise penalties while maximising total turnover.

Our case study also supports context-dependent binding. This is supported by the PAC, which uses established SLAs to automatically select a set of providers that suit the user's needs, then asks the DOE manageability agent to bind selected providers. When requesting a possible appointment, the process will only invoke bound providers. If the PAC cannot perform an adjustment action, it will ask the POC for an alternative plan.

Finally, the governance can renegotiate existing contracts. The renegotiation request is issued by the governance through the negotiation GUI, and is forwarded to the protocol engine. The request includes the ID of the SLA to be renegotiated and the parameters to renegotiate.

After the protocol engine receives the negotiation request, it assesses the quality of the proposal by invoking the POC. To evaluate feasibility of the request, the POC must be aware of the number of virtual operators that can be provisioned by the internal call centre. This allows the POC, using the static prediction feature, to assess whether it is possible to provide enough operators to satisfy the SLA, or whether it is necessary to outsource part of the services to an external call centre provider.

In the latter case, another negotiation must be initiated between the CSC and the external call centre provider, using a similar mechanism. The external call centre may reply with a counterproposal. The acceptance of this counterproposal is determined by the CSC, which aims to maximise the total turnover generated by handled calls (where total turnover is the difference between the generated turnover of handled calls and the cost of the external provider).

After a certain number of negotiation rounds, the external call centre will accept the SLA and this decision will be forwarded via the POC to the protocol engine, which will accept the governance SLA and notify the governance of this decision. The governance will then ask the protocol engine to sign the negotiated contract and thus create the new SLA with the CSC. The protocol engine will then trigger creation of the CSC's SLA with the third party call centre, and following reception of an acknowledgement from the call centre, the new SLAs will be stored in the SLA registry. The POC then triggers re-provisioning of the new service.

# 5 SLAs

The SLAs involved in the scenarios described in Section 3 are shown in Figure 3.

SLAs between governance and the Citizen Service Centre involve aspects such as support for citizens throughout the life cycle of service consumption (i.e. service information gathering, service booking, cancellation, and evaluation); coordinating the different infrastructures and service providers involved; and periodically reporting QoS and billing information to the governance.

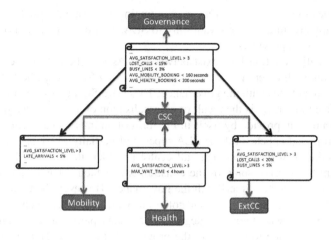

**Fig. 3** SLAs and their relationships

SLAs between mobility providers and governance deal with the booking and ex-ecution of on-demand transportation services. The SLAs rule aspects such as man-agement of the mobility service agenda and its provisioning as a web-service to the citizen contact centre; provisioning of the mobility service to citizens; and manage-ment of accounting and payment for the mobility service.

SLAs between health care structures and governance concern management of the booking system and its provisioning as a web-service to the Citizen Service Centre; the provisioning of medical treatment to citizens, and management of accounting and payment for medical treatments.

SLAs between the Citizen Service Centre and external call centres concern out-sourcing the contact service portion of the mobility and health care service to third party call centre providers, to properly address reservation and booking needs. The aspects agreed in the SLAs relate to the provisioning of a set of human operators and answering machines that can provide information on the mobility and health care service and handle related bookings, cancellations and modifications.

Figure 3 shows the relationships between the aforementioned SLAs plus details about the guaranteed states that are negotiated. The black arrows indicate that the SLAs agreed between the Citizen Service Centre and service providers (mobility providers, health care structures and external call centres) are derivatives of the SLA agreed between the governance and the Citizen Service Centre. For example, constraints on the average satisfaction level of citizens—which have been agreed between the Citizen Service Centre and the governance—are preserved within con-tracts that the Citizen Service Centre negotiates with the mobility and health care providers. However, other agreement terms—for instance, the maximum level for delays of the mobility services or the maximum time that patients should wait within a health care structure—are relevant only to SLAs that the Citizen Service Centre negotiates with its providers.

More peculiar relationships exist between SLAs that the Citizen Service Centre negotiates with external call centre providers, and SLAs that the Citizen Service Centre negotiates with the governance. These two SLA types are strongly connected, since the former is the result of externalisation of a service that the Citizen Service Centre can provide by itself in the form of an internal call centre. For this reason, terms that appear in these SLA types will partially overlap. For example, when negotiating with an external call centre provider, the Citizen Service Centre will aim to preserve some of the constraints to which it has committed in its previously negotiated contracts with the governance. However, the Citizen Service Centre also has some freedom in its negotiations with external call centre providers: depending on its own internal strategies, it can relax particular constraints in return for a minor price to be paid to the provider, for example. Hence, constraints that appear in SLAs with governance are maintained, though they may be relaxed. Scenario 3 (Runtime SLA Negotiation and Adjustment), within Section 3, demonstrates such a chain of SLAs and relevant negotiations. The renegotiation of an SLA between governance and the Citizen Service Centre, triggered by the former, results in a (re-)negotiation with external call centre providers by the latter. In this case, the SLA@SOI framework plays the role of provider for the *upward* negotiation, and the role of customer for the *downward* negotiation; it also guarantees that negotiations on the Citizen Service Centre side are automatic, while on the other side, they are manual.

# 6 Evaluation: Practice and Experience

In this section we present the evaluation process applied to the SLA@SOI features with respect to the use case scenarios of Section 3 and the SLAs of Section 5.

Evaluation is a part of a continuing management process consisting of design, implementation, and evaluation. We consider it useful to maintain this continuous cycle until the final version of the monitoring system is implemented and is shown to satisfy specified requirements and end user evaluation.

There are several stages in the evaluation process we intend to use:

- **Laboratory evaluation**: We evaluate the implemented system, taking into account the specified requirements.
- **Area evaluation**: We evaluate whether the implemented system is useful and how best to use it, trying to provide auditing notes.
- **End-user evaluation**: We work with a subset of final users to evaluate the system.

*Laboratory evaluation* or *technical evaluation* is the first of the three stages in the SLA@SOI evaluation process and is still in progress. This phase is devoted to preliminary evaluation of the system and assesses the question: "Does the system satisfy its requirements?". We answer this question by analysing the specified requirements against a first implementation of the system. By requirements, we refer to the non-functional properties that express the main benefits of the SLA@SOI framework in the eGovernment domain. A list of expected benefits can be found in [3] and includes properties such as efficient resource usage, SLA compliance, agility, and so on. Each of these properties is assigned a metric with measurable KPIs that we take into account. We have conducted the laboratory evaluation using real data—suitably anonymised—provided by the GPI call centre service provider. Indeed, the SLAs presented in Section 5 derive from real contractual terms currently used by service providers and governance. The threshold values and expected results are therefore real and derived from historical data.

In Table 1, we summarise some of the business outcomes we expect from adoption of the SLA@SOI framework. These outcomes reflect the requirements expected of the framework in terms of resource usage, SLA compliance and agility, and will be measured on the basis of the SLAs defined.

The monitoring system as a whole has been evaluated, simulating different versions of the same service (e.g. mobility providers with special prices or cancellation policies). We plan to evaluate the complete implementation of the monitoring and runtime prediction functionalities in the next stage of the evaluation process.

As summarised in Table 1, depending on the stakeholder (citizens, governance or CSC), we considered different kinds of business outcomes.

For the citizens, it is important to minimise the effort required to use health care services; thus we measure the number of phone calls required to reserve a medical treatment and mobility service, and the time required to complete that operation. In this regard, a key success factor is the ability of the framework to identify the type of service that better matches the citizen's preferences (e.g. low cost, timely, etc).

The governance value early (or advance) notice of SLA violations, enabling prompt reaction (e.g. by changing the terms of the contract). Here, we exploit the framework's ability to identify potential and real SLAs violations to enable it to raise violation warnings or notifications.

Finally, the CSC is interested in improving management of resources (e.g., operators and lines) and maintaining a timely view of their use and the state of related SLAs. In this case, the framework should help service providers by managing the busy and idle status of their resources.

*Area evaluation* is the second phase of the evaluation process and is devoted to the usability of the system. It answers the question: "Is the system useful and how can we best use it?". We plan to answer this question by gathering an entire statistical picture and accurately testing each system functionality. We also plan to provide auditing at this stage, and to suggest system improvements. During area evaluation, our heuristics, metrics and prediction capabilities will be refined using historical data produced by the service provider during operations with and without the framework. The idea is to run the framework with different configurations of the prediction feature, and to simulate various types of citizen behaviour. During this intensive sequence of simulations, we will verify the SLAs mentioned above and re-compute the business outcomes of Table 1. The results obtained will be compared to those produced by the laboratory evaluation and improvements to the framework's implementation and configuration will be suggested.

**Table 1** Business indicators and baselines.

| Business Value | Benefit | Metric |
|---|---|---|
| Citizen | User Preference Matching | $E_{call}(T) := (\sum c \in C, p \in PN_{call}(T,c,p))b/ (\sum c \in C, p \in PNservice(T,c,p))$ |
| | Integrated offer of services | $AVG(D_{bhm}(e),T) \leq AVG(D_{bh}(e),T)+ AVG(D_{bm}(e),T)$ |
| Governance | SLA compliance and performance aware-ness | $\sharp SLA_{KO}(T) :=$ SLA violations per time interval $T$ |
| Citizen Service Center | SLA compliance and performance aware-ness | $\sharp SLA_{KO}(T) :=$ SLA violations per time interval $T$ $\sharp SLA_{WARN}(T) :=$ predicted SLA violations per time interval $T$ |
| | Resource efficiency / Optimisation | $BR(T) := R_B(T)/N(T)$ % Busy resources dur-ing interval $T$ $IR(T) := R_I(T)/N(T)$ % Idle operators during interval $T$ |

*End-user evaluation* is the final stage in the SLA@SOI monitoring system evalu-ation process. We plan to conduct an evaluation using feedback from a subset of final users. As the services involved are critical and errors in their execution could impact the citizens, we plan to involve only a selected set of citizens who have agreed to use an experimental system. This agreement is also necessary because data used in the experiments could affect patient privacy. We expect that this phase of the evaluation will produce unexpected results, as evaluating levels of citizen satisfaction is a qual-itative and subjective process that depends on the personal judgment of users. We have thus based the system's evaluation not only on the quality perceived by citi-zens, but also on metrics agreed upon with service providers and governance, where these metrics are based on objective measurements of the health care and mobility services and on the behaviour of the service providers.

As described above, evaluation is part of a continuing and cyclic management process. Based on results of the evaluation process, we intend to propose revisions of system features, and of the system's monitoring and prediction capabilities in particular.

# 7 Conclusions

The introduction of the Citizen Service Centre and of the SLA@SOI framework allows a better matching of user preferences and the provisioning of integrated services with considerable advantages for citizens. Thus far, it has been up to human users to run the different services (e.g. booking health care treatments and mobility providers). The Citizen Service Centre provides a unique contact point, mediating between customers and service providers to manage service consumption, complaints about QoS, and other feedback.

Our experiments thus far demonstrate the applicability of several key features (monitoring, reporting, design time/static prediction) of the SLA@SOI framework, and we are beginning to experiment with other important features (automatic negotiation, automatic binding, runtime prediction, SLA enforcement through resource adjustment and automatic negotiation). While the current implementation does not allow a complete evaluation of its business value, expert estimates show that the adoption of the SLA@SOI framework may indeed improve the value of services to the citizen, governance and the provider of the aggregated service (the Citizen Service Centre).

# References

[1] J. Bart. SLA Savvy: Five Secrets for Making Sure you Get the Most from Your Service-Level Agreements. *Network World*, 1999.

[2] C. Molina-Jimenez, J. Pruyne, and A. van Moorsel. The Role of Agreements in IT Management Software. In *Architecting Dependable Systems III, LNCS 3549*. Springer Verlag, 2005.

[3] SLA@SOI project. Deliverable D.B1c Industrial Asessment Report. September 2011.
http://sla-at-soi.eu/wp-content/uploads/2009/07/D.
B1b-M26-Industrial_Assessment_Report.pdf

[4] SLA@SOI project. Deliverable D.B6a Lab Demonstrator eGovernment. September 2010.
http://sla-at-soi.eu/results/deliverables/
d-b6a-m12-use-case-specification-egovernment-m17/